THE EARTH DIES STREAMING

A. S. HAMRAH

THE EARTH DIES STREAMING collects the best of A. S. Hamrah's film writing for *n+1, The Baffler, Bookforum, Harper's,* and other publications. Acerbic, insightful, hilarious, and damning, Hamrah's aphoristic capsule reviews and lucid career retrospectives of filmmakers and critics have taken up the mantle of serious American film criticism—pioneered by James Agee, Robert Warshow, and Pauline Kael—and carried it into the 21st century. Taken together, these reviews and essays represent some of the best film criticism in the English language. *The Earth Dies Streaming* showcases a remarkable critical intelligence while offering a cultural history of the cinema of our times.

A. S. HAMRAH was n+1's film critic from 2008 to 2019 and was the editor of the magazine's film review supplement. He has worked as a movie theater projectionist, a semiotic brand analyst, a political pollster, a football cinematographer, a zine writer, and for the film director Raúl Ruiz. He lives in New York.

ALSO FROM n+1 BOOKS:

P.S. 1 Symposium: A Practical Avant-Garde

What We Should Have Known: Two Discussions

What Was the Hipster? A Sociological Investigation

The Trouble Is the Banks: Letters to Wall Street

No Regrets: Three Discussions

Buzz: A Play

Other Russias

Canon/Archive: Studies in Quantitative Formalism

THE EARTH DIES STREAMING

FILM WRITING, 2002–2018

A. S. HAMRAH

n+1 BOOKS

n+1 FOUNDATION NEW YORK

Published 2018 by n+1 Foundation
37 Greenpoint Avenue #316, Mailbox 18
Brooklyn, New York 11222
www.nplusonemag.com

ISBN 978-1-7322941-1-0

Printed by the Sheridan Press
Manufactured in the United States of America

Design by Rachel Ossip

Third Printing

For Rebecca

CONTENTS

REMEMBER ME ON THIS COMPUTER

INTRODUCTION

IN 2006, A NOW DEFUNCT ALTERNA-WEEKLY IN BOSTON ASKED ME TO write a short review of the movie *Little Children*, starring Kate Winslet. They told me they would pay me $100. I had been living in New York for exactly four years, and since I'd moved, newspapers in Boston had started asking me to write for them, which they hadn't done much when I lived there.

Little Children was the follow-up to its director's debut feature, a surprise hit and critical success. His new film, based on a literary novel, concerned cheating spouses in a suburban town outside Boston. Escape from that part of the world was still pretty fresh in my mind when I got to the theater. The screening was filled almost to capacity, but I spotted an empty seat in the middle of a row, next to a man I recognized. At the time he was one of the most prominent film critics in the country, with a staff position at a prestigious magazine.

I recognized him from the photo on the dust jacket of his most recent book, which I'd read the year before. The book was about how his marriage had collapsed, and how he'd become fixated on both internet pornography and making money in the stock market. In the stock market he eventually broke even.

The book was not that interesting, but it did, at least, contain forays into film criticism. He worried, for instance, that superhero movies were ruining our children's dreams—not their dreams for the future but their actual dreams at night, when they went to bed. He'd already said the same thing in the magazine he wrote for, so he must have been thinking about it a lot.

I sat down next to him and said hello. He acknowledged me without speaking and soon the film began. The then prominent film critic had a notebook in his lap, but he remained immobile until a scene revealed that Winslet's husband was an online porn addict. At that point the critic began furiously taking notes, scribbling with great force and speed. Since I had read his book, his vigorous jotting during that particular scene caught my attention. When his review came out, he called the movie, which was average and predictable, "extraordinary" and "startling."

A couple of weeks later the alterna-weekly in Boston assigned me another review. Most of the assembled critics and I were already seated in the Midtown screening room waiting for the movie to start when a movie reviewer I'd been watching on television my whole life bounded in. He looked around and detected a man he knew sitting several rows away. "I saw *Spamalot* last night," he yelled across the room to this person, referring to the Broadway musical based on the movie *Monty Python and the Holy Grail*. "It was OK. But the girls in it were not good-looking," he shouted. He then loudly asked the man he was addressing, and by extension everyone else in the room, "What ever happened to real beauties, like *Joan Crawford*?" He pronounced Crawford's name with gravity, as if here in 2006, Joan Crawford was a universally understood measure of beauty that everyone in earshot also used as a point of comparison when judging chorines.

As the movie began, I wondered who would yell that across a crowded screening room at ten in the morning. And who goes to *Spamalot* to ogle women? Who goes to *Spamalot* at all? Back in Boston I had worked as a movie theater projectionist. Sometimes in the morning I ran press screenings at the theater. The Boston critics, an unassuming bunch, did not shout insults about chorus girls to each other or write books about playing the stock market. There was one woman in Boston who silently performed calisthenics in the back of the auditorium behind the other critics while the movie was on, trying not to bother anyone. That was as boisterous as it got at press screenings in New England.

THE FIRST TIME I SAW SOMETHING I'd written in print, out in the world—I mean something that I'd written for a periodical that was not a zine—I was in the checkout line of a Whole Foods supermarket in Massachusetts. The magazine in which it was published came from the Midwest and mostly repackaged semi-leftist lifestyle content from other publications, but it also commissioned one or two new articles each issue and had a reviews section in the back.

I had recently become this magazine's film critic. Since the magazine did not publish reviews of new movies, I wrote about films that were coming out on home video, which at that time meant VHS tapes. I still don't understand why this publication had a specific policy of only reviewing movies on video; it might have been part of a larger philosophy of home consumption. Eventually they wanted me to start reviewing tantric sex instructional videotapes alongside or instead of movies.

The magazine was not the kind of publication usually sold in supermarket checkout lines. I picked it up and flipped to the page where my piece started. I had written a review of the Orson Welles film *F for Fake*, new to video that month. I was excited to see my article, and as I placed organic items on the conveyor belt I held out the magazine, open to my review, and announced to the cashier, "Hey, I wrote this! This is an article by me!"

She craned her neck toward the magazine pages, where a photograph of Orson Welles illustrated the piece. This was the corpulent Welles of the 1970s, just as he appeared in *F for Fake*, with a full gray beard and a cigar, dressed in a black fedora and a matching cape. He might have even been wearing gloves, the kind he wore when he performed magic tricks.

The cashier looked at the picture, then at me, then back to Welles in the magazine. She looked up again at my young, beardless face and my full head of black hair, which was clearly visible because I was not wearing a hat or a cape. "Is that you?" she asked, pointing at the photo.

"No!" I blurted out. "That's Orson Welles!"

"Oh," she said, scanning a can of pinto beans. I put the magazine back on the rack where I found it, gathered my grocery bags, and left through the automatic doors. Wow, I thought, that was a lesson in the artist-critic divide.

THE FIRST THING I WROTE for *n+1* I dictated over the phone to my editor, Keith Gessen, from outside a subway station on 72nd Street in Manhattan. I can't remember why I was uptown, something for my job in television brand analysis. Keith wanted a column on the Oscar nominees that year, for *n+1*'s website, because he had noticed that every year the media was becoming more obsessed with the Academy Awards. I was too busy to write it, I told him. When the economy crashed in 2008, I realized freelance work would not pay the bills, so I got a job using semiotics to analyze television programming for a brand consultancy. I stopped writing so I could have health insurance. Print was paying less and less, anyway, for smaller and smaller word counts. (Some of my earlier, pre-*n+1* pieces appear toward the end of this book.)

Keith was insistent. He wanted me to write this Oscar roundup. So he said the title of each Oscar-nominated film one at a time over the phone and wrote down exactly what I said about it, then published it without editing it. It was the easiest thing I'd ever written. After that, I wrote a long piece on movies about the war on terror and the war in Iraq, "Jessica Biel's Hand," for *n+1*'s seventh print issue.

Writing those two pieces, or speaking one and writing the other, put into perspective all the frustrations I'd had with film criticism in the 21st century. By 2008, film criticism seemed boring and repetitive, and too beholden to studio release schedules. Much of it had been obviated by the internet; its *style* was obsolete. Every review was the same, in the same format. I hated how in magazines the film column was the exact same length from issue to issue, and that I always knew which two of the week's releases would be covered and in what order. The columns always seemed too long, because they were boring. The shorter capsule reviews in lesser magazines and newspapers also seemed too long, for the same reason. They were even harder to read than the longer ones because whatever space they had was filled with extraneous material. I could not imagine that every other reader did not feel the same way I did.

By writing for *n+1* I was able to identify what I disliked most in the reviews I read and then cut it from my own work. The very first review I had ever written for the midwestern liberal digest, of a strange, disquieting movie called *Begotten*, included a bit of praise that ended up quoted on the packaging of the film's subsequent video releases. Seeing it there when I went to the video store bugged me; it made me feel like a bad writer. It continued to bother me long after the last copy of that video went up for sale on eBay. I decided I would try to never include anything in my writing that could be extracted and used for publicity.

The next thing that had to go was the endless plot description that pads most film reviews. In the 21st century, film plots are known before the movies arrive in theaters. There are few points a critic has to make that need much plot description, but critic-journalists still put everything on the record like they are preserving it for a future in which we have no way to know what happened in *Star Wars: The Last Jedi*.

The third thing I wanted to discard was having to identify actors, directors, and other artists by mentioning specific, obvious instances of their past work every time they came up, as if no one had ever heard of them before. For instance, every time a Jennifer Aniston movie came out, Aniston was described as the former star of *Friends*. This bit of non-news served no function, yet there it was, every time. It was as if the critics were writing DVD packaging copy.

These aspects of film reviewing may seem superficial, but doing away with them forged something new for me. All three represent the slow creep away from actual criticism toward thinking about movies solely on the entertainment industry's terms. Entertainment journalism teaches us to think and talk about the ever more valuable franchise-based content the industry produces in ways that infect our thinking and writing about other movies. Even when trying to dismantle them politically or read them symptomatically or just say we love them or they suck, this capitulation to the demands of the entertainment industry is ever present. When film criticism becomes one of the places where tyranny meets banality, we have to change it.

THE INTERNET DIDN'T INVENT bad criticism or gullible and complicit thinking. For that I blame *USA Today*, which began the 1980s trend of dumbing-down news into bite-size nuggets, and *Entertainment Weekly*, which institutionalized the consumer-guide approach to film criticism. *Entertainment Weekly* came out in 1990, and soon enough there were zine writers freelancing for it. I remember one of them giving a B+ to *2 or 3 Things I Know About Her* in the new-to-video section, not that I was under the illusion that anyone read *Entertainment Weekly* for the Godard coverage. Its mission was obvious: Hollywood PR. It was (and is) a trade publication with more photos and lists, with its coverage carefully tied to the studio release schedules that turn critics into publicists no matter the content of their reviews.

I was inoculated against blockbuster cinema in the years before *Entertainment Weekly* because I grew up in a small town in rural Connecticut that did not have a movie theater. The closest first-run theater was thirty miles away. The town where I lived was next to a slightly larger town, Middletown, the home of Wesleyan University. When I got my driver's license I immediately began going to all the movies they showed there at night for their film classes, screenings that were open to the public for a couple of dollars. There were two different theaters on the Wesleyan campus that ran film prints.

Before I ever saw *Raiders of the Lost Ark*, I had already seen films by Godard, Bergman, Lubitsch, Renoir, Fritz Lang, and others. When I finally got around to seeing all the Hollywood blockbusters I had missed, I wondered why *An American Werewolf in London* wasn't considered the best one.

Seeing Godard's *Masculine Feminine* at Wesleyan effected some change in me, on a cellular level. Contrary to its not being "the total film we carried inside ourselves, that film we would have liked to make, or more secretly, no doubt, the film we wanted to live," as Jean-Pierre Léaud explains in some narration Godard, I later learned, cribbed from Georges Perec's novel *Things*, my high school friends and I, watching it twenty years after it was made with older college students and the few cinephiles there were in central Connecticut, really did feel like we had discovered a secret key to life. Everything about it had an immediate and visceral effect. The sound cuts, with their audible jumps within scenes, did something to my brain that changed me. Léaud's subsequent narration in the film about his job as a pollster probably had more to do with my actual subsequent professional life than I would like to admit: "Do vacuum cleaners sell? Do you like cheese in tubes? Do you know there's a war in Iraq on?"

Jeanine Basinger, the great film historian who programmed the films at Wesleyan, used to do something I loved, something I've never seen another film studies professor do. When the movie reviewer in the local newspaper wrote a review Basinger disagreed with, she would write a sarcastic letter telling this woman why she was wrong. The *Middletown Press*, looking to fill its Letters to the Editor page, would publish these missives aimed at their hardworking film reviewer, the paper's only arts reporter. This reviewer was in her twenties back then, I later learned, but she read, to me and my friends, middle-aged and out of it compared to Basinger.

To me, their arguments were the most interesting thing in the paper, better than Siskel and Ebert on TV. Maybe those letters, which read like they took thirty seconds to write, were not Basinger's proudest moments, but they stuck with me. Today no film academic from a nearby university would bother to write to a local newspaper to comment on a syndicated four-star, fifty-word review of some superhero movie. After all, there is a cutoff point for wasting your time. Film studios and newspapers found it together.

TODAY SOME OF THE MOST AVID readers of film criticism are the fanboys who dwell in comments sections and on Twitter, eager to become enraged when film critics do not conform to their bizarre expectations about the reception of expensive blockbuster movies. Haters of the media in general, they eagerly participate in a tedious, predictable wrestling match, defending Superman and Iron Man and the franchise movies in which they appear from the people these fanboys consider the real haters, the critics. As part of their strategy, they are obsessed with manipulating Rotten Tomatoes ratings online, where en masse they think they can beat the critics at their own game while advocating for their reactionary, sexist demands. The studios are also obsessed with Rotten Tomatoes, even though the website is owned, via Fandango, the online movie ticket seller, by two of them, Universal Pictures, the producers of the *Jurassic Park*, *Fifty Shades*, and *Fast and the Furious* movies, and Warner Bros. Entertainment, the producers of the *Harry Potter*, *Batman*, and *Hobbit* movies.

The studios and the fanboys like to blame critics when movies bomb. Bad reviews for a movie that tanks are what caused it to fail, they claim. Yet bad reviews for a movie with good box office prove the critics were wrong and are therefore irrelevant and should be ignored and eliminated. The critics, we see, are both all-powerful and weak, just like the superheroes the fanboys defend, and just like the chimerical enemies Donald Trump rails against at his rallies.

It is easy to see why studios, streaming services, and ticketing apps have employed or will end up employing such trolls. On Chinese versions of Rotten Tomatoes, studios hire fanboys to write fake reviews that boost or lower scores—a “water army” of content workers flooding review-aggregator sites with bogus opinions. In the precarious gig economy, a troll can now go from outraged loony to semiprofessional phony in one easy step.

All the reviews that appear on Rotten Tomatoes have the appearance of finality—fresh or rotten—but the site often misreads the negative reviews as positive ones, and vice versa. Critics can learn from that: write so that Rotten Tomatoes cannot apprehend your work, which will allow its meaning to be deformed to the point where studios will not know what to do with it.

The blockbusters the studios make their primary business are lucrative and dominant, but they suffer from an inferiority complex. They are muscle-bound and destructive but, like their protagonists and villains, they look silly and they know it. The studios expend enormous effort endowing this kind of lightweight, childish entertainment with heft, mostly in the form of expensive, repetitive special effects, but also in the form of pseudopolitical subtext used to mask militarized, fascistic tendencies and themes. When critics and others write think pieces about whether, say, *The Last Jedi* is anti-Trump or *Avengers: Infinity War* is about immigration or something, they are playing into the con. The studios hope that writers guiding audiences to debate these productions will lend them relevance and add to their box office receipts.

The actual political content of these movies lies there, in this cynical desire to leverage ambiguous, implanted meaning. The blockbusters made by the Hollywood studios reflect a period of US-sanctioned war, in which the police have been militarized at home while death and destruction (and torture) continue overseas, with no end in sight. "It's not all war," says the title character in *Lady Bird*, a film tellingly set in 2002, the last year a character in a movie could make that claim and still be honest. Lady Bird didn't know the war her boyfriend prattled on about was never going to end.

When critics celebrate big movies in this era, it is good to remember that a large number of blockbusters and/or masterpieces of the last half decade or so were executive produced by Steven

Mnuchin, Donald Trump's secretary of the treasury. Mnuchin has had money in everything from *The Lego Batman Movie* to *Wonder Woman*, from *Inherent Vice* to *Mad Max: Fury Road*. Just this morning in the Sightings section of the *New York Post*'s Page Six website I saw a story about Mnuchin at a garden party in Southampton, Long Island, where he was enjoying the summer weather with Steven Spielberg.

ONE OF THE PRE-TRAILER ADS appearing on-screen in the big movie theater chains these days is for an app called the Fantasy Movie League. In this version of fantasy sports, players pick the movies they think will make the most money at the box office. While success for this app is a pipe dream—the real fantasy is that *it* will make money—it reflects a fandom emotionally invested in the success of men like Steve Mnuchin more than in any artist, even Spielberg. Just as in fantasy football, players in the Fantasy Movie League pretend they are owners. Concentrating on box office this way aligns players with big corporations. It's no different from publishing take after take about the politics of *Incredibles 2* in a magazine or on a website. Box office stats determine cultural importance, which in turn determines column inches and website word counts.

Identification with the system has gotten so extreme that it has replaced a functioning critical culture. When it comes to movies today, we are constantly being asked to exult in other people's successes and to gang up on their failures. Congratulating movie studios on making lots of money on films that are not very good is a real turning point in film criticism—the ultimate refinement of the consumer-guide model.

What is now being celebrated, we're told, is the system's newfound commitment to greater inclusiveness. But there is a sharp distinction to be made between celebrating the appearance of new talent in filmmaking and celebrating the continued box office success of the blockbuster form itself. For moviegoers it is not always so easy to tell the difference, but every film executive understands it.

Criticism's function is separate from that. "All that is required of the embattled critic as a test of his courage is that he never lose faith in his own judgment," the film critic Andrew Sarris wrote in 1970. That kind of critical courage has waned in the age of the blockbuster. Jonathan Rosenbaum's retirement from the *Chicago Reader* in 2008 left a vacuum in critical conscience that was filled by a strange, renewed interest in the opinions of the top critics at major media outlets, even as their opinions became more wishy-washy and noncommittal. No critic wants to get owned by Samuel L. Jackson on Twitter, like one did when the *Avengers* movie before last came out. It's easier and safer for critics to embrace the style of feeble criticism that has emerged alongside the blockbusters they would prefer to avoid. For all the anger at critics, film criticism is very gentle these days.

We can partially attribute it, I think, to how infantile Hollywood cinema has become. The American film industry is dominated by children's films—superhero movies, post–*Star Wars* franchise films, and animated family films. As the audience becomes similarly infantilized, the critics have followed suit. No one wants to be too mean to these babyish productions that audiences cart their families to again and again, or that they leave on permanent repeat in the back seats of their cars.

AFTER A BIG-BUDGET MOVIE has underperformed at the box office, all the prescheduled profiles, interviews, and behind-the-scenes stories still have to come out as planned, revealing that kind of content for what it is: empty. When this happens, as it did earlier this year with *A Wrinkle in Time*, it's a blip on the screen, so to speak, a momentary glimpse into the void of entertainment journalism. Things go back to normal a week later. The publicity becomes seamless again. Even as fanboys and studios and Samuel L. Jackson blame critics for the slightest digression from the party line, directors are never really held responsible for the failure of their movies. When something like *Batman v Superman: Dawn of Justice*, with its sophisticated lawsuit title, comes out to universal horror and disgust, its director's career is unaffected. It is guaranteed he will work again, and after a few months, some critics on Twitter will reconsider their initial reactions to find the good in this director's style and preoccupations. When a hacky Hollywood director goes down, the culprits are the perennially greedy, anxious studio executives or, in a new twist, alt-right personalities who militarize the outrage machine to make the studio heads even more nervous. Film critics have nothing to do with it.

And yet each week brings with it a new frustration with film critics. After *Ocean's 8* was met by reviewers with suggestions that it was less than perfect, Sandra Bullock, the film's star and one of its producers, stated that this mild disapproval resulted from a lack of diversity among critics. American film criticism is not as diverse as it should be, but a different critical establishment would not have made *Ocean's 8* a good movie. And what did some grousing about it matter to the film's box office? As of this writing, *Ocean's 8* has already quintupled its budget in ticket sales. What Bullock wanted was more deference from a profession already noted for its servility to movie stars.

From the 1950s through the '70s, film and television criticism was defined by a questioning stance toward mass media. But anti-idiot-box polemics began to disappear as audiences lined up for blockbusters in the late '70s. Forty years on, film and TV have begun to merge, and there is no longer any discourse that can conceive of being *against* cinema or *against* TV. There is nothing left but celebration of the greatness of American entertainment. When I saw the documentary *Generation Wealth* recently, I was shocked that the left-wing journalist Chris Hedges was allowed to point out on a movie screen that "television is a form of violence" that destroys people's inner lives and values. Soon, his observation will be streamed on TVs and other devices courtesy of Amazon, the film's distributor.

It is inconceivable today that any director would announce "I hate entertainment" to a reporter, as John Cassavetes did during the shooting of his last film, *Love Streams*, in 1984. Entertainment has won, on its own terms. "The locusts had their day / The suckers pay and pay," as Aimee Mann put it last year in a song about Hollywood success.

IN HIS 1995 BOOK, *Placing Movies*, Jonathan Rosenbaum, writing from Chicago, described the "institutional glibness" of movie reviewers, which he saw as widespread and unjustifiable. This was especially true of New York critics, he wrote, with their "star auras." Rosenbaum was also critical of academics, who he said are passive and reactive when they write about movies, meaning they are not on the front line.

When Rosenbaum was writing in 1995, a new world of cinephilia had to be created, and it waited to be ushered in via the internet. Today, serious film criticism operates in that world. Following the template established by Rosenbaum, it is fair-minded, open to films from all over the world made by all different kinds of people, and knowledgeable about classic cinema and the avant-garde. It seeks to rediscover forgotten films, it is supportive of micro-indies, and it strives to be polite and respectful. Trying to find the good in everything in this best of all possible subcultures, however, does little to improve an art form dominated by blockbusters and streaming television, especially when writing about those things dominates arts pages. At the same time, social media discourse around film fluctuates between too nice and too mean. The dearth of jobs in journalism, which has gotten worse year after year over the past two decades, had led to more and more film criticism being written for free on the web. Increasingly it is boiled down to tweeting, a form in which there is truly no upside but which commands the time and attention of many writers.

I have seen this described, glibly, as "film criticism's transition out of print," as if film criticism were being uploaded and stored to the cloud, the way we're told our memories will be after we die. Besides the fact that that is not happening, this description ignores the way software and content production are taking over the American economy. As those become the dominant industries in the US, there will be more and more film critics, most of them underemployed, many of them working for free in the hope their tweets will attract employers. At least in the days of *Entertainment Weekly*, writers got paid to be conformists. They had the potential to end up with full-time jobs in journalism. Now they go to grad school and do it for the likes.

Dedication to the cinephile world Rosenbaum brought into being will have to steadily decline for writers to keep up with the new ant-like production of the movie-TV-streaming industry. How are we to face this world? By writing about the new *Avengers* movie as a group, each person with a take just as good as everybody else's? Each take will crumble into digital dust like the evaporating superheroes at the end of that movie. The new generation of post-Rosenbaum cinephiles will end up performing much of the same labor as recappers, and to survive, recappers and reviewers will have to merge into one being, a new breed of plot describers who add commentary and serve the studios more than their employers or themselves. Seeing the good in everything will have helped.

A few excellent critics may emerge from the recapping subgenre, but staying up all night to produce writing that describes TV shows is proof of the industry's hold over its transcribers. In a system that properly compensated writers instead of endlessly auditioning them, such writing would not exist. The *New York Times* used to do the same thing, with the same amount of wit, in one sentence in its weekly TV listings. "The American critic is well paid," François Truffaut wrote in 1975 to explain the difference between film criticism in the US and in France. "Even if he doesn't publish books, or have a second trade, he can manage, and he doesn't feel as if he belongs to a different social class from those in the film industry. . . . Having a certain peace of mind, he is able to simply relate what he sees." The phrase *relate what he sees* has surely taken on a different meaning in the age of the recapper and the immiseration of critical life.

I HAVE READ OLDER CRITICS on social media happily announcing that, because of the internet, we now live in a world where more movies are available than ever before. They are delighted that they can view Roberto Rossellini films at home and never have to enter a movie theater unless they decide to go to an overseas film festival. Middle-aged film fans take refuge in streaming services, glad they don't have to pay for a babysitter or parking. Young cinephiles short on funds sit at home and catch up on canon by watching *All That Heaven Allows* on the screens of their computers or phones, sitting at their kitchen tables or lying in bed. We are all becoming like the underground miners on Mars in a Philip K. Dick novel, watching Perky Pat and pretending we are living full lives back on Earth.

Mostly it's Netflix that people watch. Netflix began by making thousands of films available on DVD before they switched to streaming and became content producers themselves. Now the company offers only a handful of movies made during each decade before the 21st century, sometimes just one or two. "We are not in the old-movie business," one of their executives once told me. At the same time, the new, non-blockbuster movies and straight-to-streaming films they offer are difficult to find, almost like they are hiding them. They disappear into a void, buried in a virtual content mound.

When I used to rent movies through the mail from Netflix, there was, on their website, a sign-in screen with a box you could check. Next to this little box, there was some text that said, "Remember me on this computer." That already seemed post-cinema and melancholic. It reminded me of the Christina Rossetti poem that appears in Robert Aldrich's movie *Kiss Me Deadly*: "Remember me when I am gone away, / Gone far away into the silent land"—the silent land of life not lived online.

Since Netflix started making their own television shows and movies, I have become skeptical of any company that offers films that are not new. Successful multinational companies are gentrifiers: they move in on old content before they start to make their own content and become television networks. As a result, the old content has to move to a cheaper area. Some of it just disappears. *Remember those people who lived next door? No? They moved away. We never saw them again.*

With the ability to stream content over the internet, any company can now do what Netflix did. Netflix leveraged cinephilia to their own acquisitive and cynical ends, morphing into the website that ate TV. MoviePass, which started as a way to see any movie—new or old—playing in any theater, looks like the same shell game. It has turned into a content provider that limits what users can see. It will try to take over the motion-picture-exhibition industry the way Netflix usurped TV, unless its ongoing cash shortages and service outages sink it too fast. I've used MoviePass to see everything from *Phantom Thread* to *The Other Side of Hope*, but it is easy to hear a MoviePass executive saying, "We are not in the quality movie business." Like Netflix and Amazon, they want to go mass.

In February 2017, Greenpeace issued a report on the ways smartphones are ruining the environment. The report was only about phones, but its findings extend to tablets, laptops, and everything else that ends up as e-waste. Manufacturing and getting rid of our devices to replace them with new ones leaches copper, lead, lithium, cadmium, mercury, zinc, and arsenic into groundwater, contaminating soil. Cleaning it up will take decades, if anyone bothers, and if it can be cleaned up at all. Streaming also has a disastrous environmental footprint. Hyperscale data centers are using up most of our electricity. Every time you stream something on Netflix, the kilowatt hours at a data center in Utah or Virginia tick up and another barrel of oil sells in Jeddah.

The other day I was on the subway at eight in the morning, sitting next to a man watching the first *Star Wars* movie on his iPhone. It was a weekday and rush hour, so the train was crowded, but he looked happy. He was in his own world, blotting out the rest of us with his headphones. Hollywood has gone carbon neutral and now on movie sets they print screenplays on both sides of the page, but soon this placated commuter was going to throw his phone away and replace it with an all-glass, no-bezel True Tone display model on which he could watch *Return of the Jedi* while jabbing people with his elbows on the way to work.

PART OF WHAT MADE THIS VICTORY of perpetual blockbuster reanimation possible was the abandonment by most baby boomers of the film-critical cultural sphere, a flight that culminated in the publication of Susan Sontag's 1996 essay "The Decay of Cinema" in the *New York Times.* Sontag claimed that both cinephilia and cinema were dead, an argument that now resembles the early 1990s "end of history" posited by Francis Fukuyama. At the beginning of the 21st century, however, as internet cinephilia began to rise, world cinema gave us, to name only a dozen, *Mulholland Drive, In the Mood for Love, The Werckmeister Harmonies, In Vanda's Room, Trouble Every Day, Khrustalyov, My Car!, Platform, The Piano Teacher, Kandahar, The Circle, Batang West Side,* and *Millennium Mambo.* A serious, vital cinema of great originality, emotional depth, and beauty—the kind beloved by Sontag—was not in decline at all.

If the directors who made those films are not household names like Fellini and Bergman, their relative obscurity reflects a lack of interest in their work from newspapers and magazines that had covered serious cinema from Italian neorealism through New German Cinema and then, abruptly, stopped. While it is racist to ignore films by Abbas Kiarostami and Hou Hsiao-hsien by dismissing them as too difficult, the truth is that by the time those directors made their greatest films, the US media had already lost interest.

As critics of a certain age ceded cultural ground and declared the fight over, their fellow baby boomers were busy running entertainment conglomerates. They, at least, showed no sign of giving up. They did not desert the movies, where, unlike in journalism, there were still big bucks to be made. Newspapers and magazines played into their hands so thoroughly that by the end of the 1990s, average readers in the US could be forgiven if they didn't know movies were made anywhere but Hollywood.

Today, right now, there are probably more good movies, from the entire history of filmmaking, showing in theaters in New York than there were in Paris in the 1950s, the heyday of canonical cinephilia, or in Sontag's 1960s New York. As new movie theaters like the Metrograph and the Quad (to name just two) open in New York, and as places like Film Forum expand, the cinema has found a way to work around streaming services.

This should be a model for the rest of the country. The cineplexes of the blockbuster era have made people go to them. In many parts of post-collapse America they now sit abandoned next to or inside dead malls. New movie theaters will have to go where the people are.

THE ESSAYS AND COLUMNS in this book cover about a decade and a half of writing and thinking about movies. More than half of them were originally published in *n+1*, where I have been the film critic for more than ten years, with a new column in each issue since 2015. In pieces for other publications I've mostly written about canonical directors and films—or those that should be canonical—and about the critics who have shaped the profession. My *n+1* columns almost always focus on new releases, but include forays into other areas. There are things I missed because so much of what I wrote during this period I wrote while working a full-time job, so I often wrote in haste. I've amended things in cases where my haste was too obvious.

There were a lot of movies I wanted to see but couldn't get to. Even so, there were three films from this period I kept going back to when I could. *The Turin Horse, Hard to Be a God,* and *Melancholia*—one by a retired filmmaker, one by a dead filmmaker, and one by a filmmaker a lot of people wish would retire or die—exist as art-house films that are still in some kind of proximity to the mass market they repudiate; they played in first-run movie theaters. Though contemporary, two of them are in black and white. They depict, respectively, the promise of centuries of barbarity without change, the lights going out on civilization forever, and the end of the world.

I focus on these difficult, depressing films, which give themselves over to what the film critic Manny Farber called "long stretches of aggressive, complicated nothingness," without resort to any compensating knee-jerk poptimism. I don't feel compelled to tell you that I also love Edgar Wright movies to show that sometimes I luxuriate in mediocrity. I don't love movies like that, I don't do that, and it doesn't matter.

When I think about those three films by Béla Tarr, Aleksei German, and Lars von Trier existing in the same world as the endlessly optimistic franchise films that keep coming out, the constant replacement of one thing by another that is just the same, the repetitive cycle of festivals that critics somehow manage to jet to every year on the fairy dust of other people's money, the Tarr-German-von Trier pessimism keeps me going. They are the antidote that restores life by nullifying entertainment.

At the New York Film Festival in 2016 I saw a movie that really worked that kind of movie non-magic on me, a feeling that is better and longer lasting than whatever it is the entertainment industry is trying to sell. The film was called *The Human Surge*. It's the first feature by an Argentine filmmaker named Eduardo Williams. I didn't get *The Human Surge* at first, but I have been thinking about it for a long time since I saw it. An experimental documentary, the film moves between an actual anthill and the anthill of the internet, ending up in a factory where a robot voice intones over and over again the same message to a worker in a sterile lab: "OK, OK, OK." Williams shot the film in Buenos Aires, in Mozambique, and in the Philippines, using digital video and 16mm film, some of it rephotographed from a computer screen.

The Human Surge provided a dreamlike, underexplained look into contemporary life akin to what is found in Apichatpong Weerasethakul's films, but more chilling, more linked to global disasters and smartphone realism. Weerasethakul might have made the best films of anyone in the period this book covers. I wish I had written more about them, but only *Cemetery of Splendor* came out near any deadline I had or assignment I got. I did shout out *Syndromes and a Century* in that first Oscar roundup, and at least when I was editing the *N1FR*, the *n+1* film review, I assigned a piece on his work when *Uncle Boonmee Who Can Recall His Past Lives* came out. Now the

Thai government seems to have cracked down on filmmakers, and Weerasethakul plans to make his next film in Colombia. In the first decades of this new century, his ghostly reanimations and animal transformations, so flat and matter-of-fact, pointed the way for a cinema without bombast or special effects.

There are two filmmakers who have come to the fore in recent years in ways I did not expect. Both are gone, but the stark confrontational truculence of each makes them of the moment to me, or at least of a moment I sense existing simultaneously behind the present. One is Chantal Akerman, the other is Stanley Kubrick. Their films are so unlike anything being made today, yet cinephile audiences seem to hunger for what they were doing. Each got rid of so much of the baggage of cinema, in completely opposite ways. Their hardness, their intelligence, and their recalcitrance has made them difficult to follow, in more ways than one. The urge to give in to entertainment is strong in most filmmakers, and the ones who ignore it are too self-conscious. Akerman and Kubrick avoided that by making demands on producers and on the audience and not giving in. Akerman I responded to from the first film of hers I saw when I was a teenager, but Kubrick was a filmmaker who for a long time I just didn't get. Some filmmakers, I have come to understand, reveal to me over time how slow I am to grasp things.

It is nothing to mention Akerman and Kubrick at this point, and it seems odd to link them. But the ways they subverted acting, backstory, cheap psychology, framing—all the feints of cinema—points somewhere new, the opposite direction of everything else.

August 2018

CORRUPTIONS AND DUPLICATES OF FORM

A Quiet Place

This portrait of the American family under attack from alien invaders comes in the form of a horror movie for MAGA-ites. Here, it is the aliens who snatch children, not ICE. Defeating these aliens requires dry-erase conspiracy charts, a trip-wired perimeter, homeschooling. It's a paranoid fantasy for dads who want to move upstate. The family is Pinteresty and wholesome in a *Kinfolk* magazine way: sustainable-farm craftspeople who the director-stars John Krasinski and Emily Blunt have observed from their Brooklyn town house on the way to Court Street Grocers. So averse to talking about their postapocalyptic nightmare situation is this last family in a world without liberals that, for them, complaining equals death.

Krasinski now exists at the midpoint between Ben Affleck and Mel Gibson. *A Quiet Place* has a Shyamalanian quality but is less personal and clunky, more generic and crowd-pleasing. He gives Blunt a farmhouse scene in which she delivers her own baby in a dirty bathtub without making a sound—a fascinating preview of a post–*Roe v. Wade* world. Krasinski was once comfortable in the worlds of Dave Eggers and David Foster Wallace (*Away We Go, Brief Interviews with Hideous Men*) but has apparently switched his focus to militarized action (*13 Hours, Detroit*). *A Quiet Place* may be reactionary, but it only wants to be entertainment, the same way Affleck and Gibson movies do. The goal in this one is effective horror. Just keep telling yourself, “It's only a movie, there's no such thing as society, it's only a movie, there's no such thing as society . . . ”

Annihilation

Monsters with long, sharp teeth have been the ultimate representation of our worst fears in American cinema since *Alien* in 1979. As in *A Quiet Place*, so in *Annihilation*. Here, a fairy-tale monster in the form of a sightless, mutated bear threatens women scientists with what big teeth it has.

Natalie Portman and her team at least escape the mommy-ism of *Gravity* and *Arrival*, in which sci-fi heroines had to fret over their children. What they don't escape is the rampant backstory-mongering of genre movies starring women. Where men are allowed to be existential and blank in genre cinema, preunderstood as representative, women must announce their past trauma to justify their actions, resulting in the kind of bad screenwriting that puts what should be actors' preparation on the screen.

Jennifer Jason Leigh sidelines bad dialogue with her usual twitchy brilliance. Her presence as the head scientist also telegraphs doom. No mission could end well where Leigh is in charge. Mutations in the Zone-like Shimmer are “corruptions of form, duplicates of form” in this B movie of overexplanation that copies *2001: A Space Odyssey*, *Stalker*, and *Solaris*, all filtered through the yarn-bombed landscape of *Fraggle Rock*. Director-screenwriter Alex Garland's next-step-in-evolution thematics are the same as in his *Ex Machina*, making the film another warning to Elon Musk and Peter Thiel instead of to humanity at large. To appeal to such a subset, *Annihilation*'s scenes with Portman alone in the Shimmer, where she is transformed into something beyond run-of-the-mill humanity, resemble prog-rock album covers from the 1970s. CGI has finally made it to the level of Yes and Rush.

Unsane

Once routinely compared to Howard Hawks, Steven Soderbergh was seen in the late 1990s and early 2000s as a director who could do anything. By the early 2010s, he seemed more like a director who *would* do anything. Constant activity, the avoidance of big movies after his *Ocean's* films, and an ability to employ any actor he wants have rooted Soderbergh in a space all his own. From there, he concentrates on marginal Americana: strippers, kickboxers, doctors who kill, heisters, and NASCAR fans. His latest, *Unsane,* which he shot on an iPhone 7 Plus, fits right in. Its quickness and cheapness, and its posture as a basic genre film, elevate it. By acknowledging *Unsane* as an experiment and as cinematic filler, by keeping it fleet and under a hundred minutes, Soderbergh found a way to enhance how low-key and professional he is. Even the end credits go by fast.

The film is a modern *giallo* with an everywoman (Claire Foy) gaslit into a sketchy mental-health treatment center. This facility, an insurance scam, employs her stalker (Joshua Leonard), who has followed her across the country after she moved to escape him. The film's most outré and exploitative elements kick in when the stalker has her at his mercy in a rubber room. Foy's uncertain American accent, which moves across the country with her, from Boston to Chicago, works in this context of personality breakdown, as does her character's bizarre name, Sawyer Valentini, which sounds like an alias. And Matt Damon's surprise appearance as a home-security professional would increase anyone's paranoia and cause them to change their address. It's one of the surprises that propels *Unsane* forward, right up to its final, unresolved scene, which takes place in the kind of nothing restaurant that is everywhere in the US but that is never shown in movies.

Thoroughbreds

The thoroughbreds in question are two overprivileged prep school girls in whitest, wealthiest Connecticut, whose affluenza takes the form of disaffected homicide. Equally lifeless and murderous, the teens swan through the foyer and breakfast nook of a lonely mansion on their way to the TV room, where they conspire against a world that has given them too much. They scheme and meet their sad end while watching classic movies that happen to be in the public domain, and were therefore cheap to include in this movie about the rich. Finally someone said no to them, and it was Turner Classic Movies.

Screenwriter-director Cory Finley has created a *Heathers* or a *Jawbreaker* for the contemporary wealth gap, but in doing so he has replaced the busy, unpredictable action and wit of those films with an arty minimalism that is Bressonian or at least Hal Hartleyan. One of the girls says to the other that her inability to feel empathy "just means I have to work a little harder than everybody else to be good." The same thing is true of the film. It just lies there, but crisply, neatly, like an Instagram photo or gallery art. It refuses to work the way more middle-class movies starring homegrown proponents of American madness like Winona Ryder and Rose McGowan did, so it becomes the story of two English girls playing American (Olivia Cooke and Anya Taylor-Joy), a record of their faces and voices, their super-professional acting in a void. *Thoroughbreds* criticizes a society these idle teens manipulate out of boredom and alienation, while their youth, talent, and beauty make the system that benefits them seem natural.

Ready Player One

This post-Wonka kids' movie about future video-game competition in dystopian cyberspace contains every pop 1980s reference imaginable, including "Blue Monday," and stuffs them by the handful into a recycling bag like cans worth five cents each. The movie is cynical and manipulative because the '80s it exploits means nothing to Spielberg. He uses items from that decade because he noticed that's what kids are into, even though the movie takes place three decades from now. To Spielberg, the digitized fodder of *Ready Player One* is not truly *classic*, and can therefore be further trivialized for any reason. If money can be squeezed out of it from an undiscerning audience of nerds, so it should be and must be. Here, Spielberg has truly become Disney.

Listing the sources of the fodder in *Ready Player One* is a mug's game. The movie could be called *Google That*. Only Spielberg's use of *The Shining* is really noteworthy, because it includes lots of actual footage from the film, over which Spielberg has pasted his Scooby-Doo action. Spielberg loves Kubrick so much he has done him the favor of defacing his work in public, something the director of *Lolita*, being dead, could not agree to or prevent.

His ultimate special effect is Mark Rylance. Rylance's weird West Coast accent goofs on the all-American awkward man-child who never grew up, who ruined society, and who works out his psychological problems and moral failures from beyond the grave as he continues to extract time and money from those who must live in the dystopia he created and monetized. The port-wine stain on Olivia Cooke's face supposedly reveals why she has an avatar in the cyberworld of Rylance's game. But both her avatar and her birthmark hide who she really is: Princess Leia. At the end, *Ready Player One* recapitulates *Star Wars*, an ultimate irony as Spielberg absorbs Lucas by turning *Ready Player One*'s lead teens into crypto-versions of Luke and Leia, sidekick Lena Waithe into a combination Han-Chewbacca, and two Asian boys into human C-3PO and R2-D2. Part of our dystopian future, Spielberg suggests, is that the hierarchy created in a truly classic movie from the 1970s will pertain forever.

Black Panther

The present-day need for new myths is laid bare in *Black Panther.* Not the myth of the individual superhero, like Superman, in which one exceptional figure survives the death of his planet, but a collective African American myth about a people and their kingdom here on earth. The battle for Wakanda's soul presents ideology as pure entertainment. Director Ryan Coogler steers it between James Bond–style raids in other lands and inner-city tragedies in Oakland, an epic battle on a Homeric plain and a journey on snowy cliffs. In the end, opening the riches of Wakanda to the outside world proves to be the right thing to do, because if they closed the borders, there wouldn't be a sequel and Black Panther (Chadwick Boseman) couldn't continue to hang out with the Avengers and elevate their box office with his presence.

Cartoonish-archetypal performances swirl around Boseman and Lupita Nyong'o, each one more interesting than the two leads are allowed to be. Boseman and Nyong'o are king and queen, everybody else a knave or knight. Similarly, the brutal-seeming civil war that divides Wakanda is interrupted by a cute rhinoceros that licks your face. Michael B. Jordan, the tragic villain who emerges as a true threat to Wakanda, hits his conflict hard, hams it up but not Loki-style, and emerges as the first bad guy in movies who is handsome hunk and matinee idol at the same time. On the border of Wakanda there appeared to be some kind of subsidized farming going on, with peasants pretending to till and plow so no one would know Wakanda was really a technology hub and a gated community, just like in California.

Deadpool 2

The hyperreferentiality in *Deadpool 2* is more pointed, brazen, and violent than in *Ready Player One* because this film wants to demonstrate above all else that it has nothing to be ashamed of. Teaching its intended audience that it's smart and fun to be a jerk, a clown, and a nuisance is its goal. More blatantly than in other superhero movies, its consumer-friendly method of pop-culture mania underscores how obsessed we are with our own brainwashing.

The conundrum of *Deadpool* is that Ryan Reynolds in the title role is better than any other male lead in superhero movies. In this context nihilism is liberating. Reynolds also voices a second character here, Juggernaut, a super-strong behemoth and lout who only wants to rip people in half. His amoral violence and daffy voice expose the heart and soul of the whole pulpy enterprise. In the end, Deadpool doesn't resemble other superheroes that much. He's more like the Noid from the old Domino's TV commercials. They even dress the same. The pitchman for a genre, Deadpool's smart-ass frenzy exists to make the other superheroes look legitimate in their boringness, just as the Noid made crap pizza look like a logical alternative to leaving your house to get food or making it yourself. I took a lesson from that. Only able to stand being hectored for so long, I left the theater when the fat kid set fire to the orphanage, because I realized I had something better to do.

The Death of Stalin

It is to Armando Iannucci's credit that he lets his cast speak in their own accents, like in a Lubitsch film, whether they are from England, Brooklyn, California, or Ukraine. Allowed to act instead of doing voices, the cast brings the startling viciousness of Iannucci and Co.'s dialogue to life in this comedy of Soviet bad manners. Iannucci's touch, however, is not exactly cinematic or subtle. *The Death of Stalin* is a mean-spirited movie about corrupt grotesques jockeying for power after a tyrant dies. The film looks ugly, all brown and red, and what makes it unlike *Veep*, Iannucci's TV show, is that it looks worse and more decrepit than anything that would be allowed on HBO.

The subquality aspects of the way it portrays totalitarianism save it from being TV instead of a movie.

Given the current situation in the US, the film's endless stream of vulgar one-liners and its brutal ending serve the dual purpose of satirical exposé and wish fulfillment. This queasy-funny mixture of alarm and panic with bleakness and horror underscores our desire for something nasty to happen in the halls of power. It lessens us to watch it, even if, as is usual with Iannucci, funny is its own excuse. Turning the most terrible events following the Doctor's Plot and Stalin's death in 1953 into Ealing-esque farce is a strange idea in the first place, as is ending the film with the execution of Beria, the homicidal letch and secret policeman who is played with calm fury by the heavyset Simon Russell Beale, a brilliant actor I have never seen in a movie before. Beale's late-middle-aged advent on the screen in *The Death of Stalin* is comparable to but more intimidating than Sydney Greenstreet's in *The Maltese Falcon.*

Aleksei German's black-and-white *Khrustalyov, My Car!*, a terrifying Russian film from 1999, is not a comedy. It covers the events in *The Death of Stalin* in a very different, much more shocking way. German's film remains a definitive statement on the horrors of the 20th century, even without Jeffrey Tambor in it.

Sorry to Bother You

Oakland plays itself in *Sorry to Bother You*, unlike in *Black Panther*, but its message extends to the whole country. A damning portrait of things as they are in the US, this movie's accurate and wild version of the present moment is Brechtian—alienated, sardonic, and disreputable. Boots Riley's vision, which combines *Repo Man* and *Idiocracy* yet remains wholly his own, encompasses shit jobs, union organizing, and horrible tech billionaires who turn people into lifelong slaves and captive half humans desperate for rebellion.

Riley breaks the frame in the first scene, an intimate one between Cassius "Cash" Green (Lakeith Stanfield) and Detroit, his performance-artist girlfriend (Tessa Thompson). A garage door and Detroit's text-based earrings give way to scenes in which Cash, working as a telemarketer, collapses from his basement cubicle into the kitchens and bedrooms of the unsuspecting people his calls interrupt in their domestic nonbliss. Cash's ability to sound white on the phone elevates him to an upstairs job and then into the lair of the company's CEO (Armie Hammer). This ascension has a kinetic energy that bursts into viral embarrassment and reality-TV debasement before it returns Cash to the Oakland streets.

Riley's cinematic examination of racism is unique in its focus on voices. Detroit's British accent during her self-abusive performance piece is another fourth-wall-breaking device, a comment on contemporary movie acting. Riley even fits in a corporate promotional video made in the style of Michel Gondry (whom it mocks). The video's cute-rotten Claymation happily presents a new breed of exploited labor, but leaves out the combination lavatory-abattoir where the workforce is imprisoned. The film is brilliant, although an unexpected strain of millennial niceness dilutes it a little, a mixture that I guess makes sense from the man who put out the album *Genocide & Juice* in 1994.

You Were Never Really Here

Scorsese's *Taxi Driver* (1976) dwells in a cinematic twilight zone where it is both overdetermined and not quite classic in the Criterion Collection sense. It retains its aura of wrongness and it is still very popular with oddballs and weirdos, some of whom are probably dangerous. The memory that it inspired John Hinckley Jr. to shoot President Reagan has not faded. The film's sick combo of underage prostitution and graphic violence captured New York City in a downward spiral and looked fascistic and reactionary to serious critics when it came out. So it makes sense that now Paul Schrader, *Taxi Driver*'s screenwriter, has returned to it as a source of inspiration in writing and directing *First Reformed*, and that Lynne Ramsay, a filmmaker interested in the most violent aspects of the human condition, has recast it in a contemporary New York of sour exploitation and political disgust.

In *You Were Never Really Here*, Ramsay has melded politics with pimping and made killing the day job of her protagonist (Joaquin Phoenix). In the age of Uber, Joe does not have to drive a hack. With ball-peen hammer in hand, he roams a wider range than just the Manhattan of Scorsese's film. Phoenix plays him as a dangerous bum mumbling into his beard. He looks near-homeless at times, a street creature in a movie where pizza rat meets Pizzagate.

The city and its discontents have outgrown Times Square and Midtown since the 1990s. During the same period, the rescue narrative of saving young women from evildoers has become the main story for Gen-X men, in the movies anyway, where Bickles have grown like fungi. Some have shown up in real life, like the Pizzagate shooter, who drove to Washington DC from North Carolina. He didn't look all that different from Phoenix in this film, just younger. We should beware of images of such dudes rescuing "little blond girls," as Jeff Sharlet pointed out in a recent breakdown of the Blue Lives Matter movement. The "ominous sentimentalism" of their narratives flatters and repels.

Ramsay locates political corruption alongside pedophilia in brownstone Brooklyn. The violence in *You Were Never Really Here* is abstracted from '90s indie films so that it is the aftereffects of sudden bursts of mayhem that concern her, along with PTSD and loss, the other great Gen-X themes. Judith Roberts, the sexy neighbor from *Eraserhead*, plays Joe's dying mother in an inspired '90s-style casting move, and such moves extend to Ramsay's use of music. The film includes a détourned interlude with Charlene's "I've Never Been to Me," an early '80s Motown number considered one of the worst hits of all time. I've always liked it, and haven't heard it since

The Adventures of Priscilla, Queen of the Desert in 1994. The song's mix of saccharine obviousness and despair is a form of truth telling. The film's last scene, with Phoenix and a little blond girl (Ekaterina Samsonov), takes place in a restaurant similar to the one at the end of *Unsane*. This one, however, is a more Lynchian kind of establishment, where Ramsay ups the shock factor, lest we forget for a second the omnipresent anguish that lurks in banality.

First Reformed

Ramsay shot *You Were Never Really Here* in anamorphic widescreen but keeps the camera close on Phoenix. She sought to reconnect emotional pain with physical suffering in this area of genre filmmaking that is now mostly a repository of crass postmodern lying. Schrader's *First Reformed*, shot in the classic square aspect ratio, doesn't get as physically close to its characters but aims higher than *You Were Never Really Here*, seeking to reestablish and dramatize the deep connections between environmental collapse, capitalism, and despair. As a self-avowed proponent of "transcendental style in film" (the name of a book he wrote in 1972), Schrader goes about his mission in stark fashion, barely moving the camera and focusing on one minister's story in a small community in upstate New York. It is a hardboiled, wintry film that explodes into desperation.

Schrader contrasts the film's simple meetinghouse, built in plain style, with the megachurch that owns it. The big church funds the smaller one, keeping it intact for historical purposes that appeal to tourists more than parishioners. Ethan Hawke's tortured minister runs it for an expansive, welcoming pastor played with warmth and understanding by Cedric (the Entertainer) Kyles. Do they serve the same God? Hawke, it might be said, represents serious cinema—art. Kyles is Hollywood—box office. The secular religion of the movies reflects what has happened to American religion. Both blockbuster Hollywood and megachurch fundamentalism reflect the corporatization of everything into inhuman systems of exploitation posing as spectacular entertainment. Many films on religion are murky about what they believe. *First Reformed* is clear: it is too late to fix things. People can only be comforted and soothed into ignoring how the planet is doomed.

After Reverend Toller (Hawke) meets a radical environmentalist (Philip Ettinger) and his more levelheaded blond wife (Amanda Seyfried), the film moves into Travis Bickle territory, with Toller recording his spiritual failings in a journal by night as he drinks whiskey and forgets to eat. As in *Taxi Driver*, Schrader combines the spiritual alienation of Bresson's *Diary of a Country Priest* with psychopathology, only here more literally and directly. *First Reformed* is a de facto remake of the Bresson film, an update with a suicide bomb attached. The film is a risky proposition in which Schrader sets the bar for artistic and ethical success very high. He succeeds beyond what any of us could have hoped from him at this stage in his career: *First Reformed* is his best film. Perhaps he had the last paragraph of his book in mind, where he writes that to expect or settle for any less than art and mystery from movies underestimates and demeans them.

To that end, *First Reformed* is daring and unrelenting—it searches for and pinpoints real harm. Ten people walked out of the theater where I saw it, most of them Schrader's age. I think they left because the film's intensity was too much in a world where they had the option of seeing *Book Club* at a theater down the street.

Most people at the screening were younger, and they stayed put for an ending that includes a glass of Drano and a barbed-wire vest. As I've tried to convey, the film is bleak. But contrary to what we're told, I don't think audiences want upbeat films in bad times. Hollywood takes advantage of bad times by telling people that's what they want, because that's what they were going to make anyway.

In his portrayal of a man of God in a constant self-imposed Gethsemane, Hawke, with his tight haircut, planed head, lined face, and cowboy eyes, resembles the actor Randolph Scott, star of the 1950s Budd Boetticher westerns that Schrader also claims as examples of transcendental style, and which made Peter Wollen ask, "How then can there be any meaningful individual action during life?" It is time to admit that Ethan Hawke is the great survivor of his generation of male leads, and a great actor. In a world of generational embarrassments like Johnny Depp and Robert Downey Jr., Hawke has survived with his strength of character and his convictions as an artist intact, and he has improved with age.

He has avoided the pitfalls of blockbuster franchises and kiddie movies, instead choosing to work with worthwhile directors, including Richard Linklater, the auteur he is most identified with. Once seen as a proto–James Franco because of his novel-writing sideline and the post–*Dead Poet's Society* arty-pretty roles that culminated in *Reality Bites*, Hawke has proved himself capable of decency and honesty on-screen, and he didn't even have to go to six grad schools to do it. He may play too nice sometimes, a trait that Schrader uses against his persona, but he never showboats. *First Reformed* would not have worked without him.

Let the Sunshine In

In her new film, Claire Denis puts Juliette Binoche through a series of frustrating encounters with men, each one illustrating the perils of middle-aged dating. Binoche, as an artist who looks like she has not updated her wardrobe since *Live Through This* came out, wears a series of deep V-neck T-shirts, a little leather jacket, and stiletto-heeled boots as she navigates the maze of an underpopulated Paris at night. It leads her to a provincial city and a working-class man (Paul Blain). They dance together to Etta James's "At Last," which French people don't know is the Obama song.

No relationship works out for Binoche in this film. The brilliant last scene, which deftly and strangely includes the end credits, surprises us with Gérard Depardieu, still half man, half wildebeest. He plays a thoughtful astrologer Binoche goes to for advice. Like all the men she meets, he has intentions on her he can't quite articulate.

There is a slight upward trajectory in *Let the Sunshine In*, from the obnoxious banker (Xavier Beauvois) Binoche is dating at the beginning to a manic drunken actor (Nicolas Duvauchelle) to the quieter men at the end, including Depardieu and Alex Descas as a gallery owner. The film imperceptibly slides toward maturity and becomes more profound but less eventful, as Binoche settles into calmness without giving up her quest for love. In the early scenes of the film, Denis seemed to parody the work of macho French directors or French cinema in general, with the rude banker demanding "gluten-free olives" at a bar and giving the bartender and Binoche detailed instructions about everything else. The banker also mentions "the dictatorship of the proletariat" and alienation, a parody of French socialists who sold out to finance and got so rich they had time to worry about the invisible enemy, gluten, in foodstuffs that are free of it.

Zama

In 1790, the year *Zama* begins, George Washington was in the first year of his presidency and the United States Supreme Court had just been established in Manhattan. The city of Asunción, however, was already 250 years old and the center of the Provincia Gigante de Indias, a colony of Spain, whose colonial glory days were behind it. Buenos Aires was where the action was, 640 miles to the south and the capital of Spain's Viceroyalty of the Río de la Plata. That's where Don Diego de Zama (Daniel Giménez Cacho) longs to go—there or to Spain.

An official of the Spanish crown in Asunción, he lives apart from his wife as an underpaid administrator in a declining city in the middle of nowhere. He is European but was born in South America, so despite his title and achievements he is not accepted as a true Spaniard. He can never rise to the top of the provincial government.

Zama is a colonizer without a homeland or a future. "Here I was, in the midst of a vast continent that was invisible to me though I felt it all around, a desolate paradise," Zama explains in Antonio Di Benedetto's excellent, existential 1956 novel, the basis of Lucrecia Martel's new film. "America existed for no one if not for me, but it existed only in my needs, my desires, and my fears."

Zama is the third in an inadvertent series of major but under-appreciated art films made in the 2010s about colonizers lost in the wilderness of empire. All three are based on novels, including Chantal Akerman's *Almayer's Folly* (2012), from Joseph Conrad's first novel, and *Hard to Be a God* (2013), by Alexei German, based on a sci-fi novel by the Strugatsky brothers. *Zama* is elliptical, violent, and lush, like the other two, with the same mournful, deadpan approach to dismantling the pretensions and fantasies of its European protagonists. Like Zama, each of these men is mired in failure and prone to lashing out.

Zama is a ghostlike presence in his own story, a man cut off from all that is dear to him and equally detached from the landscape and the natives around him, some of whom he spies on when they bathe. Others he sells into slavery when he thinks he has to. Years pass and Zama's position doesn't change. He longs to do something to prove himself, so he makes the mistake of undertaking a mission to chase a notorious outlaw, Vicuña Porto (Matheus Nachtergaele), into the jungle and arrest him. The film becomes like Herzog's *Aguirre, the Wrath of God* or like *Annihilation*, as Zama and his men enter a landscape where they are disoriented and unwanted. Martel films it in jewellike greens, in long shots that retain an essential mystery and alien beauty. By that point in the film, it is too late for Zama to turn back. Even if he did, he'd have nowhere left to go.

Hotel Artemis

I love the new Quad Cinema in Manhattan. The rep programming there is great. As I write this, they are doing an Elizabeth Taylor retrospective—*The Sandpiper* and *Boom!* are in it; people shouldn't miss those. They just finished a major retrospective of British horror films made by Hammer Films in the 1950s and '60s with thirty-two films, two dozen of which were shown on 35mm film, including *Frankenstein Created Woman*. But whenever I go to see something there that I plan to write about, something weird happens.

This time it was my own fault. I went to see Jean Cocteau's 1948 film *Les parents terribles*, which has not been officially released in the US until now, but I forgot my MoviePass card. I wasn't going to not use MoviePass to see it, so I didn't go in. The next night, there was a preview screening going on for a new movie called *Hotel Artemis*, a Hollywood "dystopian neo-noir crime" movie starring Jodie Foster, directed by the guy who cowrote *Mission: Impossible—Rogue Nation*. The lobby of the Quad was filling up with paparazzi and the theater staff had been thrown into confusion by their arrival. I ran into a writer I know who was going to see *Les parents terribles*, too, and we got in the line we were instructed to get into so we would not disrupt the *Hotel Artemis* crowd. "This is the line for *Les parents blahblahblegh*," the staff member yelled, speaking French like Pee-wee Herman in *Pee-wee's Big Adventure*.

The paparazzi elbowed people out of the way and called to each other through us and over our heads, like shoppers hailing each other in Walmart or IKEA. Publicists ran around nervously and came in three types. Types One and Two were well-dressed middle-aged men who looked like either Tim Gunn or Roger Stone. Type Three was impossibly skinny chicks in their early twenties dressed in very tight midlength skirts who worked for the Gunn-Stone men.

A fourth group was there to keep the peace, rent-a-cops in dark gray blazers with logo patches on the front pockets. They were from PSI, which "provides world-class security for special events and all aspects of the entertainment industry including major motion picture studios, iconic landmarks, and celebrities." Is that in order of importance? After the manager announced that the Cocteau film would be starting half an hour late because of this excitement, some people on line groaned. One of the security guys from PSI came over to reassure us. “Don’t worry folks, we’re gonna load you in soon,” he said, making an open-palmed pushing gesture with his hands at waist level.

When we were finally seated to watch the movie we had come to see, the Quad staff passed out free popcorn, which was nice. I will never see *Hotel Artemis*, but thanks for that.

Les parents terribles

“Cinema is an event seen through a keyhole,” wrote Jean Cocteau, which André Bazin points out in an essay from 1951 called “Theater and Cinema.” The *Hotel Artemis* Quad lobby situation was an event that gave my friend and me a keyhole view into the world of Hollywood film publicity in New York, but that was not what Cocteau had in mind. *Les parents terribles* was an important film to Bazin because for him it proved that filming a play did not have to be uncinematic. This was a theoretical argument in postwar France, where directors like Bresson asserted that the theater and the cinema were distinct media that should have nothing to do with each other. By directing his own play for the screen just as he had staged it, and with the same actors, Cocteau, Bazin claimed, had shown that filmed drama did not have to be stagey, even if the action was restricted to a couple of sets.

I already agreed with Bazin, so I wish I could say that I found more in *Les parents terribles* than an illustration of Bazin’s article. Among the films Cocteau directed, this seems to me the least interesting, despite the freedom of its mise-en-scène within the confines of the drama. Jean Marais, Cocteau’s boyfriend, plays the part of a young man, Michel, who lives at home and wants to marry a slightly older woman, Madeleine (Josette Day), whom his parents have not met. Marais and Day had starred in Cocteau’s *Beauty and the Beast* in 1946. By 1948, Marais was too old for his part in *Les parents terribles*, which he plays as a giddy mama's boy. His performance makes the film seem like it's about a man who wants to move in with another man, then shocks his parents by telling them so, causing his mother to faint. Yvonne de Bray plays his mother as a theatrical grotesque, disproving Bazin. Complicating everything is that Michel's father (Marcel André) had been Madeleine's lover or sugar daddy at some point. The family is wacky like in a Capra movie, which blunts the criticism of the family implicit in the play. While the material is in some ways not dissimilar to something Fassbinder might have done in the 1970s, it struck me as piffling. Going to see it was a strange night out.

NOW

The best movie in New York is playing on five screens in one room. Chantal Akerman's *NOW*, an installation that is the director of *Jeanne Dielman*'s last completed work, is the sole occupant of a black-walled gallery on a high floor at the Jewish Museum. For an artist known for making use of one screen on which oftentimes very little happens, this horizontal series of forty-two-minute loops on five screens, each positioned at the same level in a receding V formation, goes by pretty fast. Speeds vary, but each loop was shot from a car moving between about twenty and fifty miles an hour.

The loops Akerman includes in *NOW* show deserts in border regions, but where exactly each was shot is not stated. We seem to be on the borders of Israel, Palestine, Syria, the US, and Mexico. People do not appear, but they are heard on the soundvtrack, which increases in volume and density without ever getting really loud. It's made up of gunshots, chanting, microphone crackling, other cars whooshing by, sirens, snatches of pop music on the radio, bells ringing, a muezzin, birds that sound like loons, whistling, bombing or a bulldozer, applause, someone reading a list of Spanish names.

These are middle-distance vistas, not epic like in a biblical movie. Beige and brown dominate under a light blue sky, with white clouds overhead that give way to a grayer, overcast sky and loop back. We don't seem to be *in* the car; this is not a VR environment, it's a movie theater setup. But the longer I sat there watching and listening to *NOW* by myself, the more overwhelming it became, until it got immersive and then threatening. The installation is anxiety provoking, repetitive, and sad. Who wants to be in these places? Driving through them seems enough, not stopping except to view the footage after the fact in this installation. Yet it was not boring. I could have watched it more.

NOW is a striking repudiation and condemnation of today's world conflicts and politics made before the fact by someone who has left the scene. "The images are bad for us," Donald Trump said the other day about pictures of children crying for their parents in his self-created border crisis. Akerman's loops refuse to contribute to the glut of televisual images sickening people all over the planet. They take the opposite approach of TV news, showing no one.

Akerman has visited such areas before, filming them in similar ways. *From the Other Side* (2002), a documentary about Mexican migrants crossing into Arizona, came out fifteen years ago but was largely ignored. I remember people booing at the end when I saw it at Anthology Film Archives. It was obviously ahead of its time, given the situation now. The technique Akerman uses in this installation is a ramped-up version of the long tracking shots in *From the East* (1993), one of her great films, in which she filmed long lines of people waiting in Eastern Europe right after the end of the Soviet era. Those shots moved more slowly than the ones in *NOW* and had people in them. Only traces of people remain in the sounds she recorded for *NOW*. In this last work, the people are gone.

August 2018

SANCTUARIES OF TRUST AND CARING

Darkest Hour

This masterpiece of cinema bombast introduces Winston Churchill like he's in a Murnau film. Waking up in bed, he strikes a match to light his first cigar of the day, his face revealed by the flame.

Gary Oldman's performance comes from the Emil Jannings school of German Expressionist acting, heavy on the makeup, with a fat suit to get this thin, stylish actor up to Churchill's disheveled bulk. Oldman's grumbling and mumbling, which explodes in heavy speeches ("the dark and lamentable catalog of human crime," and so on), could come from Fritz Lang's *M*. Kristin Scott Thomas, as Churchill's wife, is made up to resemble Marlene Dietrich, the Dietrich of the 1950s who retained and refined her Weimar-Hollywood look until the end.

It's unclear whether Joe Wright, the film's director, is trying to fight fire with fire in *Darkest Hour* by using a filmic style associated with the rise of Hitler to tell the story of an outmatched England preparing to fight the Nazis. As a product of Brexit Britain, the film must be seen as anti-Europe in the contemporary sense even as it declares itself antifascist. When Oldman's Churchill lumbers into a tube station to speak with the common man, we descend with him into the realm of Capraesque populism, where the will of the people is mined so it can be turned into speeches and wars.

Dunkirk

Dunkirk arrived on movie screens five months before *Darkest Hour*. We see Churchill deliver his speech in the second film, after having watched Britons hear it in *Dunkirk*, a reverse echo as we move backward in time.

Christopher Nolan's event-movie drowns out Churchill's speech, replacing it with action, total destruction, a sea on fire. If *Darkest Hour* was bombastic, it still rambled with Churchill in his drunkenness, lurching from crisis to crisis, cutting through a mob of upper-class twits and senile fraidy-cats not unlike the right-wing weirdos who run Britain today. *Dunkirk* wants to be postpolitics, its common men out of the tube and flooding across the Channel in boats.

The action, however, was not memorable to me. It was too seamless. I lost interest in the perfection of the film's technical achievement, which I never doubted for a minute would be anything but complete and astonishing. I longed for just one moment where something wasn't perfect, to remind me that humans had made this study of improvised naval success. Mostly I remember the image of Spitfire pilot Tom Hardy's face in a CPAP mask left over from whichever of Nolan's Batman movies he was in. When soldier Harry Styles survived it all, it was as though "the enemy" had been vanquished so that the real Styles could leave the set, fly to Los Angeles, hop in a car, and drive between palm trees singing the song from *Titanic* on "Carpool Karaoke."

Mudbound

Dee Rees's *Mudbound* completes this trilogy of 2017 World War II movies, focusing on the damaging effects of war's aftermath when soldiers return home. Since home is the Mississippi of the Jim Crow South, it is not the generic Everytown, USA, that greets the servicemen in *The Best Years of Our Lives* (1946). Life in rural Marietta, Mississippi, we learn, is worse than the war in Europe, which was at least honorable and only slightly gorier.

The webs of family and class relations in rural Marietta are so racist and stifling that they can only break down into lynching, patricide, and cheap burials. *Mudbound* would make a good double feature with 2016's *Hacksaw Ridge* as a liberal version of the same story. It equals and undercuts Mel Gibson's conservative vision in its portrayal of Southern religion, persecution, and masculinity. Significantly, *Mudbound* is the first American war movie directed by a black woman and the only war movie directed in the US by a woman not named Kathryn Bigelow or Angelina Jolie.

Since Netflix produced *Mudbound*, many viewers will watch it on laptops, which is unfortunate because Rachel Morrison's cinematography is so carefully burnished. Or maybe that's not such a bad thing, since *Mudbound* really brings out what life without indoor plumbing was like. When the townspeople inevitably don their Ku Klux Klan hoods the film kicks into high melodrama, but so many terrible things had already happened by then that I, like a farm implement, was worn down. *Mudbound* has the most forlorn semi-happy ending I can recall in any war movie. The protagonist (Jason Mitchell), a sharecropper's son who fought as a tank commander in a segregated army unit, survives a lynching, then returns to Germany, where a better home awaits him amid the rubble left behind by Allied air attacks.

The Post

When National Public Radio warns you about one of their upcoming pledge drives, they play a spot asking "if you believe democracy requires a free press." Probably everyone listening believes that, but you never know. Steven Spielberg's *The Post* is the perfect movie for those listeners, and for potential viewers who haven't heard that newspapers, like NPR, need money to run.

The real story in this movie is how Daniel Ellsberg (Matthew Rhys) got the Pentagon Papers to *Washington Post* reporter Ben Bagdikian (Bob Odenkirk) so the *Post* could publish them along with the *New York Times* and help bring the Vietnam War to an end. Spielberg for some reason decided that part of the movie lacked drama, and made it a subplot. *The Post* concentrates instead on bosses. We are asked to worry about the conscience of *Post* editor Ben Bradlee (Tom Hanks) and the finances of publisher Katharine Graham (Meryl Streep) as her newspaper launches an IPO while she fiddles with her glasses.

Around all that is good documentary-style footage of linotype machines in operation, terrible documentary-style footage of antiwar protests that the audience laughs at, and telephoto shots of Nixon on the phone with his back to the camera, seen through the windows of the White House. Those looked cheap on purpose, I guess, and reminded me of something from *The Private Files of J. Edgar Hoover* (1977). Democracy dies in darkness, sure, but if Spielberg really wanted to make a movie about the fate of journalism in America, he should have made one about the founding of *USA Today* in 1982.

All the Money in the World

Mark Wahlberg speaks Arabic in this movie. Other than that, he does nothing but pussyfoot around in 1970s suits that look like they were tailored for an actor who doesn't even lift. Though Wahlberg is supposed to be a billionaire's fix-it man helping Michelle Williams get her kidnapped son back, Williams struggles by herself as Wahlberg looks on. In addition to being ignored by her son's grandfather, J. Paul Getty (Christopher Plummer), who's too busy skeet shooting or clutching a painting like he's about to utter "Rosebud," and by her ex-husband, JPG Jr. (Andrew Buchan), a drug fiend who hangs out in Morocco with the Rolling Stones, she's also abandoned by a director (Ridley Scott) who works too fast to care.

But, I think, not fast enough. It took Scott only nine days to reshoot the scenes in which Christopher Plummer replaced the tainted Kevin Spacey as the elder Getty, which makes me think Scott could have shot the whole film in a month. Since the film's virtues are its shoddy, knock-off quality and its Seventies phoniness, shooting faster might have brought that out even more. In the future, I urge Scott to work as fast as he can—to make speed the defining characteristic of his late style more than it already is.

Molly's Game

Aaron Sorkin tries too hard. He's the opposite of Ridley Scott. Buried within *Molly's Game* is what may be the best Hollywood movie on poker, better than *Rounders* (1998), but Sorkin overstuffed it with backstory. Molly Bloom's (Jessica Chastain's) pre-poker career as an Olympic skier, her overachieving family, the lengthy trial after her arrest, her problems with the IRS—none of that was interesting. Nor is Sorkin's exhaustive look at a blade of grass on a ski slope, something he sees as the film's key image. I came to this movie to play cards, not to learn how to ski. The poker games Bloom runs in Los Angeles and New York, however—*those* are interesting. Attended by a hellish gallery of wealthy dilettantes, gambling addicts, finance guys, and mobsters, the games are psychodramas Bloom presides over in tight, low-cut outfits. A cool observer of obsessive male behavior in this high-stakes, rules-bound microcosm, Chastain looks on with louche disdain while she indulges the players' addictions and confusions and takes large amounts of cash off them. Away from the poker table, Kevin Costner, as Molly's father, sinks the film by park-bench psychologizing Molly's daddy issues, a scene Sorkin should have kept to himself.

I, Tonya

The ice skating in *I, Tonya* left me wanting more winter sports, not less. The CGI-enhanced explanations of the historic triple axel Tonya Harding executed in 1991 confused me, maybe because I was preoccupied with the way they got Margot Robbie's head on the body of the skater performing it. Whatever digital photo chamber they had to put Robbie in to get that effect, it worked. People used to watch movies and think, *That could be my face up there on the screen.* Now it really could be.

This antitriumph sports movie puts a morally compromised athlete through the ringer, like Scorsese did in *Raging Bull*, going so far as to take advantage of Harding's brief post-skating career as a pro boxer to pound her some more. The film is trashy in a way movies are not usually allowed to be these days, the excuse being that its trashiness is a side effect of the story itself. The main cast is either too boring to pay attention to (the husband) or too beautiful for the part (Robbie really has to Lon Chaney it like Oldman did in *Darkest Hour*). The fat bodyguard is tiresome in his grossness, but Allison Janney goes beyond the grotesque. Her performance, equipped with shoulder parrot and emphysema hose, exhales malice in an anti–*Lady Bird* evocation of resentful working-class motherhood that scars Tonya's life and skews her moral compass.

The Disaster Artist

One can no longer argue about the success of Tommy Wiseau's ridiculous movie, *The Room*. Unlike, for instance, all of Edward D. Wood Jr.'s movies, to which it has been compared, *The Room* was a rich man's vanity project. Wiseau made it to get famous, and he has succeeded only slightly below the level of his wildest dreams. So it is fitting that now the Crown Prince of Vanity Projects, James Franco, has made a making-of movie about Wiseau and his antimasterpiece.

Like everything James Franco directs, *The Disaster Artist* is a work of appropriation art. The postcredits sequence, in which scenes from *The Room* are displayed side by side with scenes from this movie, admits as much. By now, Franco has done his Richard Prince act on Kenneth Anger, William Faulkner, the movie *Cruising*, John Steinbeck, River Phoenix, and Cormac McCarthy. Franco does show range in his tastes within the circumscribed genre of the classic masculine outré, but his films are where appropriation art has gone to die.

Call Me by Your Name

Early scenes in Fritz Lang's *Metropolis* (1927) show the adult children of the rich at play in a high-rise nature park referred to as "the Eternal Gardens." The gardens sit next to a pre-Riefenstahlian Olympic stadium called "the Club of the Sons," a monumental fitness center. In the gardens, scions and scionesses scamper about in futuristic deco haute couture inspired by prerevolutionary French fashion, while pursuing hookups and vague artistic endeavors. Social reality does not generally intrude on them. If such people were around today and got together to make a film, it would be *Call Me by Your Name*, and the garden where it takes place would be called "the Ageless Ambiguities."

Call Me by Your Name's strength is that it really does seem like the character played by Timothée Chalamet made the film himself. Who else but an actual actor-director would end his film by staring tearfully into a fireplace in winter because he's realized he will always be separate from other human beings, even though he spent his summer having sex in Lombardy with two kind and very attractive people (Armie Hammer and Esther Garrel)? The first Sufjan Stevens song that interrupts the movie so we can concentrate on nature for a few minutes also indicates the hand of Chalamet's Elio at work, as he remembers how beautiful it was and how nothing hurt, before he found out on that last trip that Hammer's Oliver was going to start dancing in public to "Love My Way" again.

Lady Bird

Greta Gerwig's *Lady Bird* is populated by actors who, like Gerwig herself, can do no wrong. That enhances the film's goody-goody quality, which falls over the movie like a warm blanket. This goodness and warmth emanate from Lady Bird (Saoirse Ronan) herself, who we know from the beginning is going to be OK even after she throws herself from a moving car during an argument with her mother (Laurie Metcalf). After that great scene, the movie settles into itself and becomes pleasant and forgiving, allowing Lady Bird to get away with a series of dick moves that are necessary to help her achieve her goal of getting out of Sacramento, California, and into a college in New York, Connecticut, or New Hampshire. Her short bursts of insensitivity also help her grow as a person, realize who her real friends are, and love her mom.

She and the film are nice to the nuns and priests who are her teachers but who are people too, with real lives and problems of their own. One of them (Lois Smith) sees right through Lady Bird. "You clearly love Sacramento," Sister Sarah Joan tells her, in a line I had trouble imagining a real person saying. I didn't mind the amount of self-identification the film courted in its audience, even though it was probably higher than in the audience who couldn't wait to see Liam Neeson in *The Commuter.* But having to hear Dave Matthews twice, as clever as that was in context, made me long for, I don't know, Napalm Death.

Logan

A little girl (Dafne Keen) shoplifts Pringles and what looks like a can of Four Loko Frost from a gas-station convenience store in *Logan*, which takes place in the year 2029. Movies have told us our future was dystopian, but it never occurred to me that things would get so bad that Four Loko would still be around a decade from now. Wolverine, by 2029, has deteriorated, too. His claws don't retract as quickly. Working as a limo driver in a black suit and tie, he's slower to recover from his wounds. Hugh Jackman, who also has to play a younger re-cloned Wolverine double, plays the original Logan as a Humphrey Bogart character, world-weary and disinclined to get involved.

James Mangold directs this superhero action movie as part western, part noir. An eerie scene of horses loose on the highway foreshadows the film's dreamlike turn to cynical, gratuitous, and crazed bloodshed. When the little girl jumps on villains' backs and stabs them repeatedly in the head with her Wolverine claws, her frenzy reflects the Logan-like trauma of her past and predicts her violent future. The paradox of Wolverine is that he heals physically but not psychologically. He has always been the best counter to the trauma other action heroes brush off, especially human ones.

In *High Sierra* (1941), Bogart's aging gangster, Roy "Mad Dog" Earle, pays for an operation to fix a young woman's clubfoot before he goes up a mountain for his showdown with death. Here, Wolverine has to care for Laura, the girl, and save a busload of other children, future mutant heroes, before he confronts the same fate as Bogart. The movie is tough and unyielding before overexposure to these kids sets in. The warning in *Logan*'s trailer should have mentioned that it's not mayhem you have to worry about. Saccharin will get you in the end.

Roman J. Israel, Esq.

Stuck in the 1970s, in a jacket and trousers tailored by Laurel and Hardy, Roman Israel (Denzel Washington), a lawyer newly out of work, doesn't fit in anywhere. It doesn't matter if the firms he goes to are sharky or woke. Young black lawyers scoff at his afro and dated phraseology (one scoffer is Esperanza Spalding), and middle-aged white lawyers (primarily Colin Farrell) abuse and pity him even after they've realized they can exploit his knowledge and experience. At night, he walks home (in LA!) carrying his heavy briefcase to an apartment building situated among new condo construction, like Jacques Tati's apartment in *Mon Oncle*. There, surrounded by framed photos of Angela Davis and Bayard Rustin, he makes his lonely dinner (peanut butter sandwiches) while listening to Gil Scott-Heron and Pharoah Sanders LPs on his hi-fi.

The Los Angeles of this film is murky—even the ocean water looks muddy—but writer-director Dan Gilroy makes it clear that Roman is a man out of time. Hitting that characterization hard is the film's main strategy. Washington, with his usual excellence, succeeds in making Roman intriguing and admirable rather than pathetic. He plays him as a scholar or monk with a variety of subtle sub-Žižekian tics. When Roman gives up his quest for social justice and sells out, he buys new clothes, goes on a date, and spends a weekend in Santa Monica, a series of normal indulgences he is immediately punished for. The film, at that point, goes from potential comedy to gangster movie, and Roman suffers the same fate as Logan and Bogart. It's an unhappy ending, the wrong unhappy ending for this film. Earlier, the scene of *Goodfellas*-esque paranoia scored to the Chambers Brothers' "Time Has Come Today," a song that is longer than I remembered, signaled that things were not working out in this movie.

The Boss Baby

I'm not interested in animated feature films even though I fully understand that Miyazaki is a great artist and I have been told more than once that it is in things like *WALL-E* and *Toy Story 3* that we will locate the zeitgeist. As a child of the terrifying *Watership Down* era, I am surprised anew each time a *Lego Batman Movie* or a *Coco* captures the imagination of anyone I know over 12. Once, a while ago, I was walking to a two-screen movie theater down the street from me to see a French movie called *Strayed.* As I got closer I noticed an unexpectedly long line of adult couples waiting to buy tickets. *Wow,* I thought to myself, *there sure are a lot of André Téchiné fans in this neighborhood.* When I got to the theater I saw that *Finding Nemo* was playing on the other screen.

Last summer I was on an airplane to California that only had two movies showing. I watched the first one, *Paris Can Wait,* which starred Diane Lane as an American held captive in a car by a Frenchman, who drives her around against her will to show her architecture and make her eat snails. Lulled by the Provençal scenery, I decided to watch the second movie, which was *The Boss Baby.* Alec Baldwin played Lane's mostly absent husband in the first film, and now here he was again as the voice of the title cartoon baby. The animation in this movie was kind of 1960s-style, which seemed low-budget and delightful compared with the oppressive anthropomorphism of the animation I have witnessed in trailers for things like *Zootopia.* The principals here were human beings rather than talking yaks and sloths. So I watched it.

The plot began with the surprising revelation that babies are produced in factories and are, at heart, tiny fascistic CEOs concerned only with maximizing profit, which is the love they receive. They work to control every moment of everybody's lives by commandeering their attention so they ignore everything else. Everyone in the family works for the executive baby as his employee. That seemed right to me. And it's exactly the same way animated movies work in our culture today.

Combined with the film's witty conflation of labor as both giving birth and working for a corporation, *The Boss Baby* began with a lot of promise, like most babies. As usual, though, time passed and the baby got annoying. Baldwin's obnoxious CEO voicings, a gloss on his *Glengarry Glen Ross* and *30 Rock* performances, got tiresome as the movie became more frenetic. Chase scenes involved Elvis impersonators, which have not only been done to death but also depend on a real person doing them. The joke is the talent gap between the impersonator's ability to play Elvis and the glory that was Elvis himself, and I wasn't interested in contemplating a cartoon of a cartoon of a cartoon. I made it all the way through *The Boss Baby*, however, newly strong in my conviction that I don't need to see another animated feature for a long, long time. It was like getting a vaccination.

Three Billboards Outside Ebbing, Missouri

If people are comparing your hit movie to *Crash* (not the Cronenberg one), you have a problem. If half the people who see your movie find it racist, you might want to address that in print somewhere, maybe in a publication with a little more heft than *Entertainment Weekly* or *Deadline Hollywood*. If giving interviews to places like that also serves as awards-season self-promotion, you're starting to make the situation worse. Martin McDonagh is an eminent playwright as well as a screenwriter and film director. He probably could have found a place to write about his movie if he had wanted to.

For now, we only have what's on the screen. McDonagh's subjects are violence, sin, and redemption. The overlooked priest scene in *Three Billboards* is a key to the film. When Mildred (Frances McDormand) is insulting the priest (Nick Searcy) for being a useless part of a corrupt organization, she is expressing the film's theme: *My God, my God, why have you forsaken me?*

What McDonagh believes in is storytelling. Storytelling, like Catholicism, can be plunked down anywhere, and through sheer force it will conquer. So it doesn't matter to McDonagh if he finds himself in Belgium, Joshua Tree National Park, or Missouri: he will tell his story with forceful dialogue and dramatic violence, and he will get his point across—*Repent, sinners!*

At the end of *Three Billboards*, Mildred and Dixon (Sam Rockwell) find themselves in the coy limbo of possible redemption, the same place McDonagh has resided since he's been called to account. If he had not let the sin of pride interfere and had, for instance, cut the pious, godlike speech Sheriff Willoughby (Woody Harrelson) delivers to the racist Dixon in voiceover from beyond the grave, he would not have come off as so manipulative and clueless. A little humility goes a long way, as Saint Darryl F. Zanuck, who is depicted holding a red pencil, once wrote in a memo.

The Shape of Water

One thing Guillermo del Toro's *The Shape of Water* has not been accused of is racism. This reimagining of *Creature from the Black Lagoon* (1954) as a cold war love story goes out of its way to be inclusive. In addition to the species-fluid fish-man (Doug Jones), it features a mute lead character (Sally Hawkins) who can't talk because she is the victim of abuse; a gay character who loves movie musicals (Richard Jenkins); a black cleaning lady (Octavia Spencer) who is sick of her husband; a dissident Soviet scientist (Michael Stuhlbarg); and the entire civil rights movement, which is asked to leave a lunch counter. The white men in the film represent The Man in no uncertain terms. Michael Shannon is an abusive torturer who has bad sex with his wife and loves his big Cadillac more than her. The assorted military men and spies around him, both Americans and Russians, concern themselves only with winning and killing.

Despite all the positive representation of marginalized people and the explicit condemnation of men who work for the government, the film takes a gleeful delight in torture and pain. Often morose, it livens up when Shannon is tasering the fish-man or engaged in bloodletting and beatings. It is a kind of horror movie, it's true, but those scenes overpower the film's invocation of desperate forbidden love. When Shannon tortures Stuhlbarg, del Toro revels in the pain the film's villain inflicts on a weak, dying man. In this world of pain, escape into fantasy is the only recourse. The film ends by illustrating the reason W. C. Fields gave for not drinking water: fish fuck in it.

The Big Sick

What differentiates this lightweight rom-com from others is that in this one the girlfriend is in a coma and it's based on a true story. Screenwriter and star Kumail Nanjiani did sit with his real-life future spouse, Emily V. Gordon, who cowrote the screenplay and is here played by Zoe Kazan, while she was unconscious in the hospital. I was surprised there were not more scenes of Nanjiani at Emily's bedside delivering comedy monologues to her unconscious form, which would have been the ultimate in post–*When Harry Met Sally* romance. But it takes the daring of an Albert Brooks for that. It's not something producer Judd Apatow would condone. In the same way, the Smiths song was kept as far away from *The Big Sick* as possible.

Phantom Thread

Back in the 1990s, I predicted—maybe it was after I saw *Happiness* —that sound design would soon get so extreme that there would be a movie in which we heard not just the sound of salt leaving a saltshaker, but also the sound of it *hitting the food*. With *Phantom Thread*, that day has come. From the shaving scene at the beginning with its *scrape* across the cheekbones of Reynolds Woodcock (Daniel Day-Lewis), it was clear this was going to be a film in which sound was prominent. We learn that Reynolds is alert to noises and easily distracted by them. The movie is full of typically memorable Paul Thomas Anderson dialogue that demonstrates how easily disturbed Woodcock is. Toast buttered too loudly at breakfast, for instance, is "like you rode a horse across the room."

Since I have a touch of Roderick Usher in me, I am sympathetic to Woodcock's bristling. As sound design has become more intrusive in movies, my relationship with it has deteriorated. While in real life I do not notice audible eating and drinking, in the movies every moment of intimate conversation over a drink has become a symphony of slurp I can't ignore. People attracted to working in sound design no doubt have sensitive ears. But directors have got to dial this down. Either that or ban breakfast cereal from their movies. In *Logan*, the noise of Dafne Keen eating cornflakes sounded like a recording of John Goodman on a gravel road in work boots. I think she ate one of her teeth. The literalism of this kind of sound design, in which every action depicted on-screen must have an accompanying sound, even if you would never notice that sound in real life, is as distracting as an unasked-for pot of tea shuffled into the room when you are working.

In *Phantom Thread*, Anderson makes the film about that. Woodcock must get over his neurotic sensitivities so he can get on with life and enjoy being fed poison mushrooms by the woman he loves. Sounds become a joke played on this demanding soft-spoken man who is overly conscious of his talent. Romance in *Phantom Thread* swings between gothic horror and comedy. In the end it is hard to figure out what exactly has saved the House of Woodcock from the fate of the House of Usher. Whatever it is, Anderson's sense of macabre humor won't allow Alma (Vicky Krieps) to kill Reynolds. It's weirder to watch him squirm.

The Square

Lately the acting in TV commercials has gotten really good. The other night I saw an ad for some company that helps people get rid of timeshares they don't want anymore and I thought, *Man, that was great, really affecting.* That could have been an episode of *Togetherness* on HBO, if that was still on. Car commercials are particularly satisfying these days. Thirty-second-long one-acts with movie-level production design and cinematography, each one is a humanist masterpiece featuring quality acting that fits right in with streaming drama. In one, a wedding party gets caught in the rain and they can't walk to the outdoor altar so they have to jump in their mini-SUV to get there. You really get a feel for the relationships between these four people in that thirty seconds. Car manufacturers know our little victories are hard-won. Automakers just get us. In other ads, the family drama of auto insurance plays out just as insightfully.

Film criticism has become really humanist, too. The moral arguments against movies including *Good Time* and *The Square* from some of our most prominent movie reviewers really touched me last year. I didn't agree with them at all, but I was moved by the way these critics shooed away potential viewers from such unpleasant fare. I could feel their internal debate as they worried over the existence of such ethically compromised, mean-spirited films. Our top critics, in recent years, have pioneered a new form of panning movies, a soft pan in which they gently wring their hands and conclude that it's just too bad certain things exist in this world. Some of these critics mentioned how a film's formal qualities, its careful framing, the coldness of its photography or its acting revealed a lack of soul. Movies like that do not offer solutions to our present predicament. They just excoriate the bourgeoisie for no reason. After dismissing such films, these critics then turn back to the business of writing weekly roundups of the 1,001 Things Streaming on Netflix This Week You Have to See Before You Die.

Ruben Östlund's *The Square* is harsh, sarcastic, unsparing, threatening, unfair, and messed up. While it is formally rather controlled, it is also a cauldron of bad feelings and bad faith. It illustrates, with great patience and wit, something I once read that the artist Kurt Schwitters wrote: "Banality is bourgeois style." The quotation fits this movie, which takes place in a museum of contemporary art. Östlund depicts audience reactions of various kinds, in a shock-series of unforgettable scenes that rankled some critics. These scenes replicate the conditions under which art is viewed in the West, and the way artists are interviewed and feted, and appear in the movie in contrast to the way successful administrators in this administered world curate the poverty and crime they experience outside their galleries.

The square in the film is an outdoor art installation that is described, repeatedly, as "a sanctuary of trust and caring." At the end of the movie, a group of young Swedish cheerleaders performs their routine at a cheerleading competition in a white square against a black background. The squares in the movie double the movie screen. Östlund's was the only movie I saw this year that gave the lie to all the safe spaces most movies design to lure audiences and get them to shout, "Go team!" These spaces within fictional spaces, car interiors in car commercials, get safer and safer. Critics guide readers to the safe ones, steering them away from danger.

April 2018

YOU SAY YOU WANT AN EVOLUTION

2001: A SPACE ODYSSEY

STANLEY KUBRICK'S *2001: A SPACE ODYSSEY* WAS NOT A FLOP WHEN IT CAME out. It was a big hit and ended up the highest-grossing film of 1968. It was especially popular with acidheads and pot smokers, science geeks, budding filmmakers, and people under forty in general. The critics in New York, however, all hated it (except for Penelope Gilliatt in the *New Yorker*), and it had not done well in preview screenings with studio execs and celebrities, who found it boring and confusing. Those preview screenings and early reviews have become part of the film's legend. People love to remember how the snobs got it wrong.

At one studio screening, attended by, among others, a woman who had worked for D. W. Griffith in 1915, only a teenager in the projection booth had anything nice to say about *2001*. "It was the most amazing thing I've ever seen," he told Kubrick's assistant editor. Kubrick got nervous anyway and ordered nineteen minutes of cuts to the film, which movie theater projectionists had to make by hand to the 70mm prints that had already been shipped. Maybe the cuts made the difference between the reception the film got from insiders and the one it received from paying audiences. After all, as the director Don Siegel put it, "If you shake a movie, ten minutes will fall out."

Nineteen sixty-eight was a tough year for Hollywood, which was turning out overlong star-vehicle musicals (one was called *Star!*) and stodgy big-budget costume dramas. At the end of the year, the industry couldn't decide whether to give a Best Actress Oscar to Barbra Streisand or Katharine Hepburn, so it gave the award to both, one for her performance in a mummified musical (*Funny Girl*), the other for a hammy turn in a period snooze-fest (*The Lion in Winter*).

These movies were not flops at the box office, but nor were they vital, new, or engaging to the kind of younger audiences the movies depend on. Color extravaganzas seemed dated even as color TV became the norm, so paradoxically it was black-and-white movies that stood out in 1968. An unholy trinity of crucial movies made in the US that year were not in color: *Faces*, John Cassavetes's brutal takedown of middle-class values; *In the Year of the Pig*, Emile de Antonio's Vietnam War exposé; and *Night of the Living Dead*, George A. Romero's gory portrait of a cannibalistic America. None had much to do with the Hollywood film industry. Each broke ground and changed cinematic forms, each investigated the present moment, and each had more to say about contemporary America than costume pictures set in Plantagenet England or New York at the time of the Ziegfeld Follies.

In other parts of the movie world, the filmmakers of the Nouvelle Vague shut down the Cannes film festival after the French minister of culture fired Henri Langlois, the founder of the Cinémathèque Française, and shuttered his venue in response to protests. In Tokyo, Japanese cinephiles also protested. They nearly rioted when their favorite director, Seijun Suzuki, was unceremoniously dismissed by his studio, Nikkatsu, which had dumped his poorly reviewed masterpiece *Branded to Kill* and would not allow nontheatrical screenings. In New York, the black-and-white newsreels made during the protests at Columbia University showed that young people wanted to engage with cinema on their own terms. But what, exactly, did they want? The answer, it turned out, was a science-fiction movie that traced the progress of mankind from cave dweller to astronaut to "Star Child," by way of a deadly computer, a trippy acid freak-out, and an intergalactic hotel room.

THE MACHINERY OF KUBRICK'S *2001* was set in motion a few years earlier, shortly after the debut of his black comedy of nuclear annihilation, *Dr. Strangelove, or: How I Learned to Stop Worrying and Love the Bomb.* Kubrick's people telegraphed Arthur C. Clarke, the British science-fiction novelist, in Ceylon, where he lived, saying that the director was interested in collaborating with him. Kubrick wanted to hire Clarke to cowrite what he called "the proverbial 'really good' science fiction movie," something Kubrick thought Hollywood had yakked about but never managed.

Clarke responded right away: "Frightfully interested in working with enfant terrible." On the spring night in 1964 that Clarke and Kubrick finalized their deal to work together, they looked toward the Manhattan skyline from Kubrick's Upper East Side penthouse apartment and saw a UFO. They could not have asked for a better omen, but this one was too good to be true. The object, it turned out, was likely the Echo 2 satellite, a NASA communications spacecraft that had not been listed in the *New York Times* Visible Satellites table that day. (They checked.)

Clarke spent most of the year talking with the director and laboring on the as-yet-untitled script. Leaving the Chelsea Hotel each morning, he would breakfast at the Automat on Seventh Avenue and then travel to the 35-year-old enfant terrible's apartment. In Kubrick's study or on his patio overlooking Manhattan, the two men spent their days considering the nature of the universe, man's place in the cosmos, and why aliens always look so dumb in movies. At night, Clarke would return to his room on the tenth floor of the Chelsea, often eating a dinner of liver paté on crackers with an Irish sailor who lived down the hall ("a questionable new interest of his"), then typing out the pre-novelization of Kubrick's movie, slated to be published solely under Clarke's name just after the film's release. Sometimes he would sit in the hotel's bar and have a drink with other residents of the

Chelsea, among them William S. Burroughs and Allen Ginsberg. On Christmas Eve, Clarke handed Kubrick the first draft of the treatment for what would become *2001: A Space Odyssey.* Kubrick read it while Clarke waited, then pronounced his Merry Christmas to the author. They'd done it, he said. "We've extended the range of science fiction."

BURROUGHS AND GINSBERG, a kind of mirror version of Clarke and Kubrick, make but a brief appearance in *Space Odyssey: Stanley Kubrick, Arthur C. Clarke, and the Making of a Masterpiece,* Michael Benson's expansive and thorough book on the production of *2001.* They, like the Irish seaman, are part of a large, unexpected cast. The players here are not just actors, studio bigwigs, and crew. Jazz clarinetist Artie Shaw hips Kubrick to Clarke's novels. Scientist Carl Sagan, a pedant whom Kubrick does not take to at all ("Get rid of him. . . . Make any excuse. . . . I don't want to see him again"), keeps turning up to annoy the director (Clarke announces that "for every expert there is an equal and opposite expert"). Jane Birkin's brother, Andrew, works diligently for Kubrick even after he forces him to uproot and steal kokerboom trees from the Namib Desert for the "Dawn of Man" scenes. Kubrick told him to blame it on 20th Century Fox, not MGM, if he got caught.

Dan Richter, an American junkie and mime in London whom Kubrick hires to learn how to portray *Australopithecus africanus* on-screen, gets plenty of well-deserved attention and provides the book's key image. It could be a key image of the late 1960s. One day at MGM's studios in Borehamwood, England, where *2001* was mostly filmed, the budding special-effects genius Douglas Trumbull, a Californian, was jumping on a trampoline in a cowboy hat. At the pinnacle of each *boing* he could spy Richter in a grassy field teaching a teen dance troupe from a local TV show how to move like prehistoric hominids, a formation of British lads and lasses jumping, scratching, and *ook-ook*ing together like apes.

Three and a half years and $12 million later, Kubrick was still working on the film. His schedule for making *2001* was however long it took, his budget was however much it cost, and the film's delivery date was when he decided it was done. His only worry was that NASA would get to the moon before the film came out, which is maybe one of the reasons the fable persists that Kubrick shot the first moon landing on a soundstage, faking it for the US government.

Kubrick's approach put Clarke in a tough spot. He wouldn't be paid until the film and the novel appeared, and he had his own set of out-of-control expenses worrying him. Back in Ceylon (it wasn't called Sri Lanka until 1972), Clarke was producing a film himself, a low-budget Sinhalese version of a James Bond movie. The film's director, Mike Wilson, although married to a Scottish Sinhalese actress, was also Clarke's lover. As Benson puts it, Clarke "had one foot planted in an escapist, derivative Third World popcorn feature and the other in the most sophisticated evocation of human origin and destiny Hollywood had ever attempted, with the latter funding the former." Kubrick loaned him money to keep going as Clarke sent him script revisions for *2001.* The Clarke-produced "Jamis Bandu" movie emerged, before *2001,* under the title *Sorungeth Soru.*

An entire book, or at least a *Vanity Fair* article, could be written about Wilson. A photographer, a scuba diver, and a near charlatan, he had interested, by the 1970s, both Satyajit Ray and a couple of Hollywood studios in making India's first science-fiction epic. This doomed project, in retrospect, seems like the last move in an Oedipal struggle with Clarke. Later, Wilson renounced motion pictures and became a swami.

TAPIRS ARE NOT NATIVE to the deserts of southwest Africa, where the first section of *2001: A Space Odyssey* takes place, nor have they ever been. Even so, Kubrick decided the strange-snouted, pig-like mammals had an ancient look that would make them good prey. Kubrick himself filmed the bone tossed into the air after mankind makes its first kill. A straight cut, the least sophisticated thing in filmmaking, turns the bone into a spaceship orbiting the moon four million years later.

This production history of *2001* is alive with a strain of visceral weirdness. The murdered tapir is one that died in a stampede off the edge of the soundstage. Kubrick had it frozen for later use. For the "Star Child" sequence at the end of the film, Kubrick contacted the General Biological Supply House in Chicago to inquire about human embryos for sale. The firm wrote back that none was available, and that none would be. Instead, Kubrick hired the sculptor Liz Moore to make a fetus from scratch. While the camera crew was filming an eight-hour exposure of the sculpture, its eyes began to drip tears because the lights were so hot its head was melting. Douglas Rain, who voiced the HAL 9000 computer, recorded his dialogue sitting with his bare feet on a pillow.

The monolith, the film's central image, was made to appear not crafted by humans but also not machined. Kubrick wanted it to leave "that open void that we feel when we try to imagine that which is unimaginable." This object, which has become so ubiquitous in our culture that it still turns up in jokes on TV shows, was made from a massive chunk of black hardwood overpainted in coats of black paint until it gleamed with an impenetrable luster. It had to be handled with gloves so it wouldn't collect fingerprints the camera would see.

The first monolith the art department made was a two-ton piece of clear plastic, two feet thick, the largest and most expensive piece of Plexiglas ever produced in England. Kubrick rejected it because it was too visible, looked too manufactured, and had a greenish industrial hue. The mysterious black monolith that replaced it, according to Benson, became "the most powerfully opaque object in film history" (at least until Keanu Reeves). The monolith's spatially incongruous, optic-nerve-warping, two-dimensional-looking flatness, especially in the "Jupiter" and "Beyond the Infinite" hotel-room scenes, would probably not be allowed in the overly rounded sci-fi movies of today, which strive for 3D. It is too simple and unique, and does not refer to anything else.

In funding *2001*, MGM did not know it was paying for a think tank of artists who would spend over three years solving the problems of how to depict prehistory and space travel in non-risible ways. Stanley Kubrick, Benson reminds us, "didn't do risible." While trying to determine what aliens should look like, Kubrick finally decided not to show any. He and Clarke invented their artifact, the monolith, to cut extraterrestrials from the film because all their other solutions looked comic, unbelievable, or nebulous. "We don't want to watch a veil of gas," Kubrick said. Benson has to make up a filmic category, "analog reality," to explain the special effects in *2001*, a movie in which everything was done in front of the camera, and which proved twenty-five years before the fact that computer-generated imagery did not need to exist.

The trippy "Star Gate" scenes were made using a 65mm optical printer, shots of landscapes filmed from helicopters, and drips of paint in a tank filled with paint thinner. The *Discovery* spaceship was a fifty-five-foot miniature and HAL was a camera lens with a red light behind it. Kubrick's pursuit of techniques to make sci-fi look new and non-phony paradoxically extended to watching every Toho Studios monster movie made in Japan, which is how he figured out how to use front projection, a technique Toho had pioneered, for the "Dawn of Man" scenes. He was impressed, according to Benson, by *Matango*, a movie about an island of mushroom people.

BENSON'S BOOK IS FASCINATING, every page startles, and it's a much needed and comprehensive history of the making of *2001*. Its last chapter, however, falls into the "making of" trap, in which an object under scrutiny has status conferred on it by a bunch of goofy rich men who came afterward. I don't doubt that James Cameron, George Lucas, and Steven Spielberg like *2001* or that it opened their eyes to the possibilities of narrative cinema. Their work, in turn, is tech-heavy and childish and, taken in the aggregate, boring—the things *2001* was accused of by its original critics, but more so and louder.

Clarke famously wrote that "any sufficiently advanced technology is indistinguishable from magic." If that is true, then the subsequent influence of these *2001* acolytes on the movies has made magic look obvious and cheap—exactly what Kubrick and his collaborators worked so hard to avoid. Maybe that is a function of cinema's place in a world where clean, cynical modernism and hallucinogenic psychedelia have been replaced by corporate spectacle and consumer manipulation. If so, those men helped push it in that direction. One scene in *2001* seems particularly alien and futuristic today: a flight attendant switches off a seat-back television in front of a passenger who has fallen asleep. Kubrick may have predicted the tablet computer and its glow, but he did not picture a world where the screens were never shut off.

Spielberg's comments after Kubrick's funeral are an example of this kind of eyes-wide-shut banality. "You know, this is extraordinary," he explains to a film critic who attended the memorial at Kubrick's estate. "In Beverly Hills, there would have been cops and bodyguards and velvet ropes and VIP enclosures. And here we are, eating supper in an English kitchen." God knows whose Beverly Hills funeral Spielberg was imagining—his own?—but I wish I had never read that. The sentiment reminds us why, as Benson points out, no one has traveled outside Earth's orbit since the last Apollo mission in 1972. Clarke mentioned to Kubrick that he thought *2001* would be "the last big space film that won't be made on location." As computer-generated neoliberal fantasy movies about escaping the planet continue to appear, I'm praying to the aliens for a better world, and a bigger cosmos.

May 2018

CUT THE KINK

mother!

Darren Aronofsky's *mother!* is like a Pinter or an Ionesco play from the 1960s. The film is a Grove Press paperback with movie stars and lots of CGI. The whole thing could have been done on one stage set. Instead, Aronofsky opens up this allegorical drama to the plumbing behind walls, the beating of a heart in a chest cavity, the geologic forces that turn coal into diamonds, and eventually to the cosmos, where planets die and new ones are born. Aronofsky is interested in some kind of mythological physics that only he understands, which has something to do with artistic creation of the highest order. At the same time, there's a palpable feeling he's directing for the lulz. The end result, as usual for him, is the proud emergence into the world of another item of kitsch horror.

mother! opens itself to many interpretations, but the one inescapable fact of its plot is that Jennifer Lawrence's character, the film's unnamed wife and mother, gets shafted, tossed on a fire at the bottom of a well. The film is not exactly what you'd call feminist. It's designed to be a slap in the face, or maybe a wake-up call, but a slap to whose face and a wake-up call to do what is unclear. The film is murky from attic to basement. If it has a saving grace, it's that it's funny sometimes, like an absurdist play, and equally prone to violence and collapse. The loud-quiet aggression and pretentiousness of the lowercase *m* and the exclamation point in the title prepare viewers for this kind of seesawing abuse.

The film borrows its plot from *Rosemary's Baby* but moves the action to the countryside, as in the 1960s sitcom *Green Acres*, which was on TV when *Rosemary's Baby* came out. A man escapes the city and moves to a dilapidated country house with his reluctant wife, who tries to make it nice for him. The house, plopped down in the middle of a field with no driveway, might as well be in Hooterville or Stankwell Falls. When a host of kooky characters begins to intrude on Lawrence and her husband (Javier Bardem), this parade of creeps is menacing, sure, but less satanic than obnoxious. There's even a pair of sons who show up a-feudin' over their inheritance like hillbillies. It would have been interesting if one of them had been played by a woman, like the Monroe brothers on *Green Acres*. But they are played by real-life brothers, who serve Aronofsky's godlike vision for maximum Cain-and-Abel myth-remaking, before shuffling off so another biblical act can take their place.

Woodshock

Kate and Laura Mulleavy, the Rodarte sisters, designed the ballet costumes for Aronofsky's *Black Swan*. Now they have written and directed their own film. *Woodshock* stars Kirsten Dunst as a marijuana-dispensary clerk in Northern California, the Mulleavys' home turf. The film has the same dark aspirations toward the eternal feminine and its relation to Mother Earth as Aronofsky's, but goes at it with more of a Lars von Trier touch. Dunst plays a woman whose moods resemble her character's in *Melancholia*, mirroring that film's grief and depression in a fizzled-out, bleary, high-as-fuck way. The men in the film, dressed as sullen NorCal woodsmen, convey a von Trierian sense of Danes-Finns-Latvians-Scots-Manxmen playing American.

As a homegrown European art film, *Woodshock* is not afraid to be boring, or to seem pointless, repetitive, and overlong. There is little dialogue; the film could play as gallery art. The cinematography and the music score carry the audience and glide Dunst out of her house and into the woods. Semicomatose, she levitates in nature, working through her sadness as she floats among the giant redwoods and lens flares. At the dispensary and in her depopulated town's one bar, neon lighting and music from the late 1970s and early 1980s predominate. I've been to bars in that part of the country and have never once heard the Feelies, Suicide, Television, Wire, or Gary Numan, not even "Cars." In Mulleavyville, you never have to hear anything that isn't hip, and you never have to look crapped out in rural poverty. Even high and suicidal on the bathroom floor, dappled forest sunlight casts a glow. The film is a fantasy of the Trump era, in which being stoned all the time alleviates despondency. *Woodshock* would make a good double feature with another Danish-American film, *The Neon Demon*, which also went unappreciated, in which fashion models towered over the angst and gore instead of tall trees—scenes from the hard lives of the blondes.

Good Time

Robert Pattinson dyes his hair blond midway through *Good Time* and things just get worse for him. An amoral thief, Pattinson's Connie inhabits a low-down New York City where everybody exists to be used and ripped off by everybody else, including the people they love the most. His developmentally disabled brother, Nick, played without sentiment by codirector Benny Safdie as a confused, angry lug, is the only other person Connie cares about. His love for Nick comes in the form of anger at a world in which the safety net has been pulled out from under them both. Connie seems to figure that's OK if you're wise like he is, but when it comes to Nick, life's unfairness excuses any crime.

The film covers a lot of ground, yet all the interiors, even at an amusement park, look like they were shot with different-colored lights in a store in the subway stairs. Josh and Benny Safdie, along with screenwriter-editor Ronald Bronstein and cinematographer Sean Price Williams, have created a masterpiece in *Good Time,* a film of nerve, audacity, and ugliness that recaptures the cheap and broken energy of color 1970s New York crime movies. It does so without being a period piece, or based on a novel or a true story, or an imitation of *Dog Day Afternoon* that just refers to things without embodying them, pushing them. *Good Time* runs right up to a certain line and crosses it. It's the only movie I've seen this year that lays out the time in which we're living in such an immediate way, with all its desperation, violence, and inequality exposed. It's a movie about how everything sucks for everyone, whether they know it or not.

I don't know how or where the Safdies find their actors. Even the unbandaged people in the movie look like they've been punched a hundred times. The Safdies' genius is that they can fit Robert Pattinson, Jennifer Jason Leigh, and Barkhad Abdi into a cast that does not include actors I've seen before. Taliah Webster as a teenage girl who helps Connie for no good reason, maybe just to get him out of her house or because she's bored; Peter Verby as a calm, strange psychiatrist; Buddy Duress as Ray, a just-out-of-jail rat fink who makes a series of idiotic moment-to-moment decisions the Safdies present with a demented, drugged logic—none of them is expected, and all are great.

Connie's priorities shift throughout the film from helping his brother, to robbing a bank, to raising bail money by selling stolen liquid LSD in a Sprite bottle. Even in its ticking-clock pursuit of money, the film's relentless gear switching, aided by an electronic Oneohtrix Point Never score, has nothing in common with an empty film like *Run Lola Run,* which I kept sensing the audience wanted it to be. Like the best bank-robbery films, the Safdies' journey to the end of the night lacks a happy or a meta-ending—it is the opposite of an action-adventure blockbuster where the biggest crime is that the actor playing the hero took home $20 million. By the end, Pattinson disappears from the film like Robert Mitchum in *Out of the Past,* leaving his messed-up brother to figure things out alone, in the saddest possible place in New York City.

The Florida Project

For the past month I've had to watch the trailer for *Goodbye Christopher Robin* before almost every movie I've seen in theaters. It features a sad little boy with a bowl haircut moping because he's being interviewed on the radio all the time. Since he's the inspiration for the Winnie the Pooh books, journalists want to ask him if Hitler is dangerous or something. It's too much pressure for this upper-class tyke, being robbed of his childhood by the nascent mass media, which used children for its own purposes without any regard for their psychological well-being—unlike the movie industry today, where I'm sure the actor playing this kid was given plenty of time-outs, was properly instructed so he wouldn't fall behind in school, and was never exposed to anything untoward from producers or agents. Yes, I understand that kids resent it when they are turned into valuable literary properties. I saw *Gone Girl.* By the time the *Goodbye Christopher Robin* trailer played again before I saw *The Florida Project,* a movie that features mouthy children on the loose at a motel in Orlando, I had already run out of sympathy. The trailer for a Winnie the Pooh biopic had ruined childhood for me.

The Florida Project, a welcome antidote to the world of British costume drama, snapped me back to life and restored my faith in children and movies. Right now in Orlando, someone is pacing around Disney World in a Winnie the Pooh costume, sweating in the humidity to entertain tourists and their children. That's showbiz. Nearby, off Seven Dwarfs Lane at a motel called the Magic Castle, where *The Florida Project* takes place, children live with their mothers in cramped rooms paid for by the week. In the slums of the Magic

Kingdom, kids spend their days doing modern American kid stuff: swearing, begging strangers for ice-cream money, spitting off ledges, giving the finger, setting fire to abandoned condos.

The film depicts childhood against a contemporary landscape of access roads and the purple, orange, and green buildings that dot them, garish structures built to house businesses that siphon cash from Disney. The area is a non-neighborhood with the poor as permanent residents. Helicopters take off and land next to Walmarts and gift shops, sometimes blotting out the kids' swearing. When she talks, the main kid, a 6-year-old girl named Moonee (Brooklynn Prince), sounds like Ruth Gordon from *Harold and Maude*, wacky, cute, and old before her time.

She and her mother, Halley (Bria Vinaite), haul bags of knockoff perfume through parking lots, trying to sell to tourists. When they get kicked out by security guards and can't make the rent, Halley turns tricks via Craigslist. Her neighbor at the motel, Ashley (Mela Murder), a diner waitress who gives Halley and Moonee free breakfasts, finds out when she sees Halley's ad, a "swimsuit selfie" cropped at the neck she had Moonee take in their motel bathroom. Halley denies it's her. "Those are your tats, bitch," Ashley points out. "Are you fucking kidding me?"

Halley's pastel mint hair and her flower tattoos stand out against the film's acid-magenta color scheme. Shot on 35mm, *The Florida Project* brings to life a sticker world of rainbows and unicorns underneath a store sign that reads MACHINE GUN AMERICA. A sad-eyed Willem Dafoe, the motel's manager, presides over the lives of its "guests," chasing off creeps and dragging broken ice machines into the two-floor elevator. Church groups feed Moonee and her pals out of vans, while an angry Halley orders plain pizzas for her daughter and explains the facts of life: "Pepperoni costs money." Like *Good Time*, the film is vibrant and alive, and it ends the same way, with the principals separated by institutions whose attention they draw when it's already too late. It joins *Moonlight* in a new pantheon of Florida-based cinema defined by harsh reality and beautiful sunsets.

Blade Runner 2049

The academic institution of *Blade Runner* Studies takes a hit in this dull, belated sequel to the 1982 Philip K. Dick adaptation. *Blade Runner 2049* succeeds for a while as a mood piece, like *Woodshock*, then does little to justify its existence. *Good Time* and *The Florida Project*, movies set in the present, are more about the future than this is. Ryan Gosling is good, underplaying as a replicant hit man named Joe K. after the Kafka character he isn't much like. His holographic girlfriend, played by Ana de Armas as a manga Audrey Hepburn, is abandoned by the film after a three-way with Gosling and another replicant, so the film blows her up to skyscraper proportions, removing her clothes to taunt him and the film's audience of fanboys and tenured professors. Her nebulous existence is not made more tragic by turning her into a giant translucent ghost.

The movie's potential is also undercut by its familiar color scheme, circus-peanut orange and jazz-cup teal, just like in *X-Men Origins: Wolverine* and any other big Hollywood action movie. No space seems real in this movie. By the time Jared Leto appeared to manipulate floating stones reiki-style in an orange chamber, I had lost any interest in suspending my disbelief. Leto was an arty choice, but is anybody ever happy to see Jared Leto? Here he plays yet another sinister Hollywood role better suited for Jim Carrey.

Gen X was the original audience for *Blade Runner*, but this film is an insult to it, or maybe just an unnecessary recapitulation of how things are for that generation. Here, in a reversal of *The Force Awakens*, Harrison Ford survives and Gosling, his surrogate son, dies. The last shot of the film shows baby-boomer Ford creepily watching his daughter, a maker of memory implants, through a glass partition. Somehow, this generic version of the female has become the creator and repository of false memories, a scrapbooker of all the unnecessary backstories that have been weighing down screenplays since the original *Blade Runner* came out. At one point we meet some official Hollywood-movie Tribal Scavengers, followed later by some official Hollywood-movie Meaningless Revolutionaries. Since at least the Matrix movies, such figures have heralded a revolution that never comes, though President Donald Sutherland did get trampled to death by rebels in *The Hunger Games: Mockingjay, Part 2.*

It

The happy ending in *It* is that a group of kids beats a clown to death. Today that qualifies as wishful thinking. The clown wanted to divide the kids by their fears, so it makes sense that this 1980s-set film awaits a sequel set in the present, with the kids grown up and returning to their Spielbergian hometown to beat the clown some more. As an evocation of '80s childhood, *It* depends on the existence of prior Stephen King adaptations like *Stand by Me* and the earlier *It* TV miniseries, as well as *The Goonies* and recent nostalgia items like *Stranger Things*. Period-specific music from the Cure, XTC, and New Kids on the Block bolsters the tone, but with all the talk in the movie about how everything floats down here, it's disappointing that the music supervisor missed Hüsker Dü's "She Floated Away." Maybe a check from Warner Bros. would have kept Grant Hart alive a little longer. One difference between this movie and its predecessors is that here all the adults are monsters. There are no nice families, a welcome admission from Hollywood that in the 1980s they were fudging American family life to keep the 1950s on artificial respiration.

Happy Death Day

The sole teen girl in *It* (Sophia Lillis) decorates her bedroom with Replacements and Young Fresh Fellows posters, for that throwback '80s feel (plus she's edgy). In *Happy Death Day,* which is set in the present, the protagonist (Jessica Rothe) wakes up every morning in a dorm room decorated with posters for the 1980s cult movies *Repo Man* and *They Live.* If the film is aiming for the semi-underground insidiousness of those films, it falls short, which is predictable in a movie that's a self-confessed horror remake of *Groundhog Day.* The scariest and most mysterious thing about it is that midway through we find out the film takes place in Louisiana. That's what you call a random reveal.

Before its premise is undercut by its lame ending, *Happy Death Day* manages to encapsulate three key aspects of the Trump era. (1) We wake up every day from a recurring nightmare in which we are threatened by a homicidal man-baby; (2) a preemptive strike is necessary in dealing with the outside world, where it's kill or be killed; and (3) we all long to see an amoral bully magically turn into a good person. Rothe is Rachel McAdams's character from *Mean Girls* who, through repetitive learning, transforms herself into Glinda, the good witch of her sorority house. In the end, after dispensing with the red herring of a generic serial killer, the film's villain turns out to be a woman of color (Ruby Modine), who is also the only student in the film with a job. Revealed to be a phony and a cheater after seeming merely obsequious and pathetic, she is done away with so Rothe and her heroic new nerdy boyfriend (Israel Broussard, from *The Bling Ring*) can sit in a classic diner, where he instructs her on how great Bill Murray was in *Ghostbusters* during the fade-out.

The Meyerowitz Stories

Noah Baumbach's new film, with its multiple chapters, feels something like a TV series, too, and is also filled with '80s references: Danceteria, Cindy Sherman, a clip from *Legal Eagles* on VHS. The film is a mild Gen X revenge fantasy, in which Baumbach once again ponders the failings of his father, here personified by Dustin Hoffman as a clueless, self-centered artist named Harold. Adam Sandler and Ben Stiller give thoughtful performances as his divorced sons, who argue over their inheritance and come to blows. Sandler is a homebody and house dad who never made it as a musician, Stiller a successful Hollywood financial manager who has moved as far away from Harold as possible. Their sister, Jean, a mousy woman who fades into the background, is nonetheless brought to life by Elizabeth Marvel with the same skill and nuance Sandler and Stiller bring to their characters. After Harold has a stroke, Stiller is able to work things out with Maureen (Emma Thompson), Harold's fourth wife, an aging hippie who takes trips to Easter Island and Cuba. There's a happy ending for everybody.

Baumbach's ability as both a screenwriter and a director of actors has never been more in evidence. Everyone is so perfectly cast and operates at such a high level in *The Meyerowitz Stories*, including Judd Hirsch as a successful artist and family friend, that I wanted the movie to go on longer. When it went on longer than I expected, I began to feel about the film the same way I felt about Harold's life: End it. Baumbach's refusal to kill Harold off reflects his continuing acceptance of generational damage. Now that the next generation, represented by Sandler's daughter, Eliza (Grace Van Patten), is reaching college age and thriving, Baumbach's more placid. Or maybe just contented, like the ending of the film. But if the videos Eliza makes at Bard are any indication, the generation after hers may have some issues of its own.

Marshall

In the past four years, Chadwick Boseman has played Jackie Robinson and James Brown, and now he's playing Thurgood Marshall. That is a lot of historical and cultural significance for any one actor to bear in less than half a decade. Even in the 1940s, Gary Cooper did not follow Sergeant York and Lou Gehrig with Bix Beiderbecke. Boseman is also starring as the Black Panther in a Marvel superhero movie, so maybe it's time Hollywood got the message that it has too few black leading men.

Reginald Hudlin's *Marshall*, in any case, is kind of a superhero movie. We meet Thurgood Marshall in 1941, twenty-six years away from being appointed the Supreme Court's first African-American justice. He cuts a dashing figure as a lawyer for the NAACP, traveling the country defending black men accused of crimes they did not commit, winning case after case. Betweentimes, he drinks at Minton's Playhouse in Harlem, where bebop was invented, and hangs out with his lady love (Keesha Sharp) and his pal from school, Langston Hughes (Jussie Smollett). It's the kind of movie where, when another woman walks into the bar, Boseman stands up Errol Flynn–ishly and shouts "Zora!" across the room. Then we meet Zora Neale Hurston, played by Chilli from TLC.

The film covers a trial in which Marshall was dispatched to territory he had never worked before—*Connecticut!*—where a white society woman (Kate Hudson) has accused her black chauffeur (Sterling K. Brown) of rape. This time Marshall has to prove a man innocent with his hands tied: a crusty WASP judge (James Cromwell) won't let Marshall speak in court, so he enlists a local Jewish lawyer (Josh Gad) to appear with him for the defense and to follow his written instructions during the trial. For all its old-school movie élan, the film hews closely to a true story (maybe not the bar fight), and Marshall and Sam Friedman predictably win their case. *Marshall* should usher in a series called *Two-Fisted Tales of the Supreme Court Justices*, in which we learn about the early, rambling years of Felix Frankfurter, Oliver Wendell Holmes, and Ruth Bader Ginsburg, as they go from town to town, duking it out for the Constitution.

Professor Marston and the Wonder Women

"What is normal?" asks Dr. William Moulton Marston (Luke Evans) in this biopic about the Holy Trinity–style birth of the comic book *Wonder Woman*. Marston, a professor and the author of a tome called *Emotions of Normal People*, lives with his wife, Elizabeth (Rebecca

Hall), who is also a psychologist, but who isn't allowed to practice because Harvard won't issue her a degree. Both are having an affair with one of William's students. She is Olive Byrne (Bella Heathcote), the niece of Margaret Sanger who, with Olive's mother, Ethel Byrne, opened America's first birth-control clinic, in Brooklyn in 1916.

Marston's theory of human behavior, which he calls DISC theory, holds that people can only be happy when submitting to some kind of discipline, which they must learn to accept and love in a mature, responsible way. Angela Robinson, who wrote and directed the film, follows Marston's line of thinking as he and Elizabeth observe a humdrum spanking party at Olive's sorority and struggle to invent the first functional lie detector, which finally works when they strap Olive to it and ask her which of them she loves. (Both of them.)

After the Marstons are dismissed from Harvard for their sexual nonconformism, William studies a bunch of Tijuana bibles he picks up in a Manhattan sex shop that also sells bondage gear. The idea for *Wonder Woman* hits him in a eureka moment, at least in the movie. Then Elizabeth modifies it and Olive models the costume. In 1941, the same year Thurgood Marshall was defending that innocent chauffeur in Connecticut, the publisher of *Superman* and *Batman* began printing copies of *Wonder Woman* in New York. Starting then, the Marstons hope, the masses will come to lead healthy lives by reading cleaned-up smutty comics featuring a female superhero who comes from a Sapphic island, wears a skimpy star-spangled outfit, and is frequently depicted tied up when she's not using a lasso to get the truth out of men.

Instead, Marston's heroine is accused of promoting "violence, torture, and sadomasochism," three things, along with patriotism, that become more prominent during wartime. The film, to its detriment, plays such things down. In the early 1950s, Marston's publisher orders him to tame his Wonder Woman stories and "cut the kink," the same way the film already has. *Professor Marston and the Wonder Women* makes an argument for the emancipatory effects of polyamory, but the whole thing comes off as quaint, with the hulking Evans a John Wayne in Wayne's tweed suit from *The Quiet Man*, Hall a desexualized intellectual Olive Oyl mixed with 1930s character actress Edna May Oliver, and Heathcote as much Kewpie doll as proto-superhero.

Harry Dean Stanton

The reopened Quad Cinema in Manhattan is still so new that the ticket seller asks if you want a senior discount even if you're only middle-aged and have gray hair. Take it from someone who once had your job, kid: even if Warren Buffett shows up to see something in your Greta Gerwig Selects series, he'll be all too happy to ask for the senior discount himself.

Harry Dean Stanton, existential journeyman of marginal movies, died in September at age 91, old by any standard. The youthful Quad had already programmed a retrospective of this singular actor's films in anticipation of *Lucky*, a new one starring Stanton, which the theater premiered in New York. I went to see *Death Watch*, a 1980 French-British coproduction directed by Bertrand Tavernier. Tavernier casts Stanton against type as a TV executive who hires Harvey Keitel to film Romy Schneider's last days. She's dying from a fatal illness, a rarity in this futuristic setting. Stanton's exec thinks her decline would make good television, in this movie made two decades before the onset of reality TV. After the film, my date and I went to the Quad bar for a drink, where David Bowie's *Blackstar* was playing on the sound system.

In *Lucky*, Stanton plays the resident of a desert town in Arizona who follows a rigorous schedule of exercising in his underwear, smoking cigarettes, drinking coffee in a diner while doing the newspaper crossword puzzle, buying more cigarettes, then watching game shows at home before going to a bar, where he isn't allowed to smoke but tries to anyway. As a valedictory for Stanton's life and career, the film is minor and low-key, a less fussy Jarmusch film in which Stanton's Lucky muses on his past as a child in Kentucky and as a Navy man during World War II. He faces his future by proclaiming there is no soul and that nothing matters after you're dead.

As a character actor in the 1970s, Stanton already looked death-haunted, his gaunt face a signal to leading men that he had seen things they hadn't. When he got his chance as a lead himself, in 1984 in Alex Cox's *Repo Man* and Wim Wenders's *Paris, Texas*, he did not change. He ramped up his character actor's severity, a kind of sliding (or burrowing) into scenes, and came off more worse for the wear than ever, more fatalistic, his drawl more deadpan and serious, more intense—a word his character associates with his life and his profession in *Repo Man*.

His battered soul, or whatever it was, and his haggard face found their equivalent in the long silences in Wenders's film, but more so, I think, in the cracked speeches Cox wrote for him. "Not many people got a code to live by anymore," he told Emilio Estevez in *Repo Man*, becoming a father figure for the deadbeat-dad generation as he conned Estevez's Otto into helping him repossess a car. The car, he tells Otto, using the most fake-sincere voice he can muster, is in "a bad area." Stanton plays against Cox's sarcasm throughout the movie, becoming parental when Otto irks him. "Not happy in your job?" he asks him in mock concern, unlit cigarette in hand. "I feel like we're not *communicating* anymore." Unceremoniously shot by cops after violating his code, Stanton asks for a cigarette as he's dying. Earlier in the film, driving around at night, looking out on the LA freeway, he summed up the milieu he was in but not of: "All these people, man. They all have one person in each car. The city wants us to carpool. Nobody gives a shit."

December 2017

HEADS WITHOUT BODIES

TRUMPANCHOLIA AND *TWIN PEAKS*

IT RAINED IN BROOKLYN THE DAY AFTER DONALD TRUMP WAS ELECTED. Overnight it had become a damp, drizzly November. The ceiling in the room where I'm writing this developed a leak that morning. Rust-colored water stained the white paint around the light fixture, spreading outward until a steady drip fell off the light bulb into the square glass shade, filling the translucent pan with brown water.

I noticed the leak when the water began to trickle off the corner of the shade nearest my desk. I got a bucket and a stepladder, tipped the shade into the bucket to pour off the dingy water, then unscrewed the shade and removed it. I put the bucket on the floor, looked up, and saw a hole in the ceiling, open to the rain. Here it is, I thought, the first day of the Trump era. I stopped writing, went to the store, bought some cigarettes, and started smoking again.

Late that summer a friend had called from Canada to predict that Trump would win the election, and to invite me, should that happen, to come up and check out the democracy. I lit a cigarette and phoned her. I wanted to be out of the US for Trump's inauguration in January. Could I come up then? I mentioned there was a hole in my ceiling. When we got off the phone I bought a plane ticket to Toronto. It was not expensive. Most people do not travel to Ontario in January if they can help it.

THE CITY OF HAMILTON, where my friend lives, is about forty-five miles southwest of Toronto on Lake Ontario, which, as I found it, was covered in dense fog. Despite the sunlessness, the lake was only part frozen. Hamilton was chilly and gray, a steel town in winter dotted with thrift stores, coffee places huge by New York standards, and record shops selling thrash and grindcore LPs.

My friend does not have television, so we looked for a bar where we could watch the inauguration live on a big flatscreen. I was glad not to be in the US, but I wasn't going to miss the moment a reality-TV con man was sworn in as President of the United States. For some reason I figured Hamilton would have a lot of bars with TVs in them open by 11:30 on a Friday morning. That was not the case. Some bars were open by 11:30 for lunch but had gone gastropub and didn't have televisions anymore.

Our search turned up a place called Fisher's two blocks from the lake, a spot with a long bar, booths, plenty of TVs, and menus in Lucite frames on the tables advertising fishbowls, giant drinks made to share, served in clear globes. Three dozen or so local businessmen, who probably would have gone there to eat anyway, had also gathered to watch the inauguration. Some regulars at the bar cheered when Trump appeared on-screen. The people at the tables looked concerned as Trump was sworn in and surprised when he let go with his "carnage" outburst. The waitress, realizing I was an American, told me she was sorry.

On TV, the Missouri State University Chorale, dressed in black overcoats and burgundy berets, sang "Now We Belong." They sounded as joyless and funereal as they looked in their black coats. It was overcast in Washington DC and the student chorus sang in the rain, which Donald Trump later claimed let up for his address even though it had not.

Behind the new President, Barack Obama looked like he had a migraine. Paul Ryan grinned his new grin, a crazy-looking rictus he had worn since the Republican National Convention. The new Vice President, Mike Pence, appeared serious to the point of menace, as if he had bitten the head off a bald eagle to prove a point and would do it again. George W. Bush, goofy in the kind of transparent rain poncho sold in vending machines in bus stations, showed the world he was a man who had left care behind now that he would not go down as the worst President in American history. Much of the rest of the crowd was made up of *Dick Tracy* villains, rubber masks from a forgotten part of the 20th century, and blondes in the Fox News style. On TV, the helicopter that took away Barack and Michelle Obama rose in silence and slow motion.

After the inauguration, the network cut to a group in the crowd called Bikers for Trump, there from New Jersey. One of them, a man wearing a cap that said Sick Boy on it, complained about the protesters in Washington that day. "I don't have time to protest because I have a job!" he yelled at the camera, even though he was there and not working. Trump declared his inauguration a "national day of patriotic devotion," but it was not a federal holiday. Even as he bellowed about "tombstones across the landscape of our nation" in his crap-weird speech in the rain, postal workers delivered mail in the US and life went on. We ordered another pint as lunch hour ended and the businessmen of Hamilton went back out into the fog.

The next day we went to the Hamilton Women's March, which, with Canadian concern for inclusiveness and safety, had been changed to a Women's Rally because of "accessibility issues." It was held in front of Hamilton's impressive modernist City Hall, a two-tiered, eight-story mini-UN next to the Canadian Football Hall of Fame. Outside, a statue of a receiver reached prayer-like for a football in the sky while a tackler wrapped him around the waist. The two silver athletes looked like toy spacemen from a 1960s version of the future. My Canadian friend pointed out that the tackler also looked like he was giving the receiver a blow job. We stood among the pink-knitted pussy hats dotting the gray weather in the nonmarching crowd and listened to Canadian speeches about what had happened in the US. Nearby, a teenage girl stood on a concrete planter holding a large sign she had drawn in neat serif caps, the first line in mint green, the next in pink, the last in cornflower blue. It read

NO ♀NE
IS AN
ISLAND

The night before the inauguration, we saw a movie at a place where bands play. Doors Pub features an outsize portrait of the heavy-metal singer King Diamond's face in close-up next to the bar, and hosts a 16mm-movie night called Trash Palace. That Thursday, the film was *The Thing with Two Heads*, a cheap American B-grade movie from 1972. It stars Ray Milland as a white surgeon and Rosey Grier as a black convict on death row for killing a cop. Grier is the football player who was standing next to Robert Kennedy when he was assassinated in 1968. The Welsh Milland won an Oscar in 1946 for *The Lost Weekend*, in which he played an alcoholic. By 1972 he was choosing his roles with less care, more daring.

The film's tagline was "They share the same body . . . but hate each other's guts!" I was told that the timing was a coincidence, but even before the film began it was clear that this was a movie about America under Donald Trump. I wasn't prepared, however, for how much Milland would resemble our new President, especially after his head is cut off and grafted onto Grier's left shoulder. Trump and the Ray Milland of 1972 have the same hairstyle and hair color and the same bellicose, insulting demeanor. Their look-alike hair is especially obvious in shots where Milland's head is fake, a mannequin wig-holder for when his decapitated head is carried around independently of its body, or in long-shot chase scenes in which Grier rides a motorcycle with the bewigged paste head attached to him.

Milland's character is terminally ill but has a plan for survival. "I want to transplant my head on a healthy body," he explains. "There is no other way for me to live." The catch is that for a month the two men must share Grier's body while it gets used to the new head.

Then Grier's head will be cut off and the body will be Milland's alone. Grier volunteers for this because he believes he can prove himself innocent while the two men share his body. Milland, already established in the film as a racist who won't work with black doctors, is not told who the only volunteer is.

After the operation, Grier wakes up and sees Milland's Trump-esque head on the operating table next to his own. "Where's the rest of you?" Grier shouts in this new, extra head's face, a reversal of Ronald Reagan's "Where's the rest of me?" from 1942's *Kings Row.* Appalled that he is now attached to a black man, Milland has Grier chloroformed. "The black bastard," he says. "How am I ever going to control him? He could kill me."

The Thing with Two Heads devolves into chase scenes and jokes about racism, but not before making it clear that men like Milland's wealthy surgeon believe experimenting on and killing black men is fine if it allows white men to live, if it gets them closer to living forever. The film is resonant because we know this happened in this country in real life. The story of the Tuskegee syphilis experiment broke in the *New York Times* the same week *The Thing with Two Heads* premiered at drive-ins and in grind houses around the country.

Forty-five years later, little has changed. Jordan Peele's *Get Out,* which premiered a month after the inauguration, updates *The Thing with Two Heads* by eliminating the severed head and making the "coagula" a mind-meld requiring just a touch of brain surgery. In Peele's film, the white man, seeking to extend his life, completely inhabits and controls a younger black man's body, head and all. The body cannot reject the mind that now occupies it, can't argue with it or punch it in the face. The two are fused, and black consciousness stares out from within the film's "sunken place," immobilized and silent. *Get Out,* unlike *The Thing with Two Heads,* decouples *The Defiant Ones* from *The Brain That Wouldn't Die.*

Grier's character in *The Thing with Two Heads,* sitting on death row, was already expendable and doomed. This campy sociopolitical horror film from the Watergate years literalized the conflicts of the civil rights struggle in a grotesque way, asking viewers to take it seriously while inviting them to mock it at the same time. Since then, the film has existed below the level of serious commentary. Yet all of a sudden it speaks to us, because of Trump's head.

Earlier in his career, in 1989, when he was merely a rich gasbag and an annoyance, Trump bought a big ad in the *New York Times* so he could publicly call for the executions of the Central Park Five, young black men accused and convicted of assault and rape. The men were exonerated by DNA evidence in 2002 and released from prison. They sued the City of New York and settled for $41 million. Trump went out of his way last year to let voters know he still believed they were guilty. This is how he thrives. Now he has grafted his head onto our collective body, with his horror-movie hairdo always in our face. Trump's head is struggling to control our actions and responses the same way Milland's head struggled to control Grier's body in this cheap movie. The devil finds work where he can. *The Thing with Two Heads* was too dumb to be noticed by James Baldwin in his book-length essay on race and the movies, and I had to go to Canada to run into it. Now it's the kind of stupid we live with every day.

IN MAY, THE COMEDIAN Kathy Griffin posted a photo on Twitter and Instagram in which she's holding a model of Donald Trump's severed head by the hair, blood dripping from its neck and eyes. The caption she provided referenced Trump's sexist comments about Megyn Kelly, the former Fox News host who moderated a Republican debate during the campaign. "There was blood coming out of his eyes, blood coming out of his . . . wherever," it read, gender-switching Trump's remark about Kelly.

The photo's resemblance to various paintings of Judith holding the severed head of Holofernes, the Assyrian general bent on destroying Judith's city, was noted by some, casting Griffin's stunt as feminist and political beyond the way she had intended. Judith's story, which appears in the Apocrypha, has been a subject for artists since the Renaissance. Caravaggio and Lucas Cranach the Elder painted Judith with Holofernes's head, as has, more recently, Kehinde Wiley. Komar and Melamid depicted Holofernes as the stone head of a statue of Stalin held aloft in a little girl's palm. Women artists have been understandably drawn to Judith as a subject. Artemisia Gentileschi painted Judith's beheading of Holofernes in the 17th century; Tina Blondell in 1999. Judith has appeared in movies, too. The year before he made *The Birth of a Nation*, D. W. Griffith made a film called *Judith of Bethulia*.

The image of Trump's decapitated head created an uproar. Griffin was condemned by pretty much everybody, including Trump himself, who claimed the image upset his youngest son. Everyone agreed Griffin had crossed a line, and that she was even lamer and more useless than before, now truly abject. Griffin is not a painter or a film director. She is a reality-TV star, like Donald Trump, former host of *The Apprentice,* and, like him, an avid Twitter user. Griffin's photo was judged to be a stupid, ill-conceived publicity grab, reflecting on her desperation as a self-conscious D-list celebrity—*My Life on the D-List* was the name of her Bravo reality show. Her social-media stunt delivered both politics and art history as trash, little more.

Griffin casts her opposition to Trump in a War of the Reality Stars, using an image of Trump's head, the "big head" of TV close-ups, disconnected from the rest of its body. More artfully, the German magazine *Der Spiegel* depicted Trump's head as a flaming planet hurtling toward Earth, like the planet gone out of its orbit in Lars von Trier's *Melancholia*. Griffin's apology for her photo, her botched non–press conference, and her public crying jag all point to Trumpancholia, a psychological condition now afflicting much of the planet's population, who have traded the things they used to enjoy for the constant monitoring of Trump's reality-TV spectacle, which is broadcast twenty-four hours a day and consumed worldwide. In claiming he wants to make America great again, Trump promised to bring the country back to the Reagan era, to "morning in America." Instead, we have entered a period of mourning in America, with Trump not as Ronald Reagan but as another 1980s character, Max Headroom, a demented TV pitchman, all face and head: an irreal, televised presence in a rubber mask who can pop up anytime because he doesn't sleep.

IN THE AGE OF STREAMING prestige drama, it looked like reality TV was on the wane. But since the Trump retrenchment, the dinosaur broadcast networks have brought back *American Idol* and *Big Brother*. While networks are desperate to get viewers to watch live television in prime time, they have less of a problem in the off-hours. The inauguration, White House press conferences, the Comey hearing—these are examples of reality television unfettered from prime-time scheduling and its half-hour or hour-long formats. As streaming drama can leech onto viewers' lives in the form of binge watching, so can the constant stream of Trumpian reality TV consume viewers' lives in the form of browser-based live bingeing, a back-and-forth between news sources with a heavy thumb on the refresh button. The scheduling of this kind of reality TV is unpredictable, spontaneous, and extends out from live television into social media. It starts and stops according to Donald Trump's whims, while viewers wait for it. It can assemble itself quickly and appear suddenly, going from buffering to full-on catastrophe in a second, with twenty-four-hour news networks trailing behind. Its goals are to monopolize our time and waste our lives as we feed it and keep it alive.

As with competition reality shows in prime time, there are no real winners here besides the producer-host. Any season's winners are discarded and forgotten, and fast. At the time they appear, competitors are main characters, future celebrities, potential stars. In the end, they are all the USA Freedom Kids, those tween girls who performed a Trumpified version of the World War I song "Over There" in patriotic cheerleader costumes at a Florida Trump rally early in the race. Unpaid, the Freedom Kids had to sue the Trump campaign for the money they lost when they were not allowed to sell CDs at their performance.

Where are they today? Nowhere, neither here nor over there. They existed to be televised, briefly. Such acts show up to manipulate our emotions, then disappear. We are appalled by their awkward brainwashed patriotism, or we love it, or both. Like the contestants on *America's Got Talent*—a deaf girl with a beautiful singing voice, or a little blond girl who projects her equally beautiful singing voice without moving her lips, through the puppet mouth of a cartoon rabbit ventriloquist's dummy—they create a momentary disjunction that tugs on the heartstrings, a kitsch mini-catharsis. "America's Got . . . *what is going on*?" becomes our reaction to these convulsive post–Susan Boyle performances, in which ordinary people overcome their disadvantages through televised displays of short-form virtuosity, just to give us one more minute of hope. Humankind cannot bear very much reality, but it can bear a lot of reality TV.

IN CHARLES CHAPLIN'S 1952 movie *Limelight*, a dancer tells Calvero, the character Chaplin plays, that an upcoming benefit might be "the greatest event in theatrical history." "I'm not interested in events," he responds. As Trump news has shoved everything else out of the way this year, the same way Trump pushed aside the prime minister of Montenegro in Brussels, I have begun to feel like Calvero. I'm not interested in events. Or I wish I wasn't.

It has been hard to concentrate on reading books and seeing movies since the election, let alone the kind of blockbusters that begin to appear in early summer, the kind for which critical reception is a selling point. Mild controversy is built into these event movies, a kind of bait for critics, superfans, and trolls. This year, in any case, that has backfired on the studios, who blame the domestic failures of *Alien: Covenant*, *Pirates of the Caribbean: Dead Men Tell No Tales*, and *The Mummy* on the aggregated critical response at Rotten Tomatoes. When most critics love a movie, as was the case with *Wonder Woman*, the system is working fine. When they don't, critics are destroying the film industry. The studios have the same relationship to the press as Donald Trump. It's love or nothing, and anything less is treason. The studios love an embargo as much as Trump hates leakers, and they depend on China to finance and sell their toxic, low-grade products to an audience they consider even less discerning than the one in the US.

I made it to one failed blockbuster this year, *Baywatch*. It was playing at the Alamo Drafthouse in Brooklyn at the same time as the restored version of Tarkovsky's *Stalker*, "one of the most immersive and rarefied experiences in the history of cinema," as the Drafthouse put it. I could not picture myself sitting in the theater, contemplating ordering an alcoholic milkshake named for a *Big Lebowski* character while rewatching a film the Soviets tried to shut down, a film shot in an irradiated landscape that poisoned people who worked on it. My mistake.

If the people who worked on *Baywatch* were not sickened, they should have been. Ostensibly an opportunity to ogle girls in bathing suits, *Baywatch* is instead wall-to-wall dick jokes and father-figure longing, featuring a corpse-defilement scene in a morgue that is also a dick joke. Who is the audience for watching Zac Efron fondle a dead man's penis? Paramount thinks everyone is. The film ends with Dwayne "The Rock" Johnson, pumped into rage on natural steroids, killing a woman with a bottle rocket. That she is one of the most beautiful women in the world makes it sexy.

Baywatch, like the Trump Administration, was made for the fans, not the critics. As a soft-power exercise in indulging Dwayne Johnson's presidential dreams, the movie works as preview of his future cabinet. His lifeguard character is presented as a natural leader whose battle with drug lords is impeded by a stickler cop. Johnson, a nice-guy strongman, surrounds himself with bimbos played by actresses who went to the Dalton School and Greenwich Academy. The men on his team are Efron, a former Disney star who could someday introduce the candidate at a nominating convention, and an overweight, lovelorn tech nerd, the movie's clumsy fixer and audience stand-in. This mismatched cast made *Baywatch* the only movie I've ever seen that should have come with a chart showing how tall everyone is.

PAMELA ANDERSON'S CAMEO in *Baywatch*, reprising her role from the original TV series, comes at the end of the film. The living Anderson of the present day is pasted into her scene using digital effects, making her appearance seem posthumous. A ghostly presence returned from the 1990s, she is like Laura Palmer in the new *Twin Peaks*. She is dead, yet she lives.

Twin Peaks, a revival from the 1990s like *Baywatch*, is also an event. But *Twin Peaks: The Return* is an event that is an antidote to these other events. It begins with the boredom of staring at a glass box, then demands that we slow down, experience it, think. The sense of dread that the show creates settles in after each episode is over, and the credits roll over some indie band playing a slow song (please bring back Julee Cruise or even Chris Isaak). These interludes provide a contemplative break in this enigmatic anti-cliffhanger's narrative of violence. If it is an exercise in nostalgia and franchise-building, *Twin Peaks* is not an empty spectacle like *Baywatch*, in which a trivial item from the past is resurrected solely for financial reasons, underscoring the growing gap between artistic worth and presumed box-office value. (The show is seven parts in as I write this.)

FBI special agent Dale Cooper resembles James Comey now that Kyle MacLachlan has gotten older. Trapped in the Red Room, seated in a chair in his black suit and dyed black hair, his aging Boy Scout's confusion in the first episode was a preview of the Comey hearing in the Senate. Maybe this is what it was like to be alone with Donald Trump, when Trump nonasked Comey to drop the Flynn investigation. I can hear Trump saying it backward-forward: "I *hhhhope* you can let this *ggoe. Hhheee's* a *ggood gguy.*" Picture Comey at the White House, our new Black Lodge and Trash Palace, reluctantly moving away from the curtain and toward Trump with that awkward smile on his face, waiting to receive the handshake. It's a scene from a David Lynch film, the nice guy pulled toward Frank Booth in *Blue Velvet* or Mr. Eddy in *Lost Highway*. We are pulled in the direction of madness.

And possible decapitation. The severed head has been an image in Lynch's films since *Eraserhead*. Right away, in a bed in an apartment in South Dakota, the new *Twin Peaks* exposes us to a woman's decapitated head placed on top of a dead man's headless body. This confusion of heads and bodies points to forces the characters in *Twin Peaks* can't see, which can nevertheless inhabit them and control their lives. *Twin Peaks* foregrounds a kind of American emptiness of the soul that is filled by violence. The show, hopscotching between its original locations and South Dakota, New York, Las Vegas, and Philadelphia, places this evil in the whole country now, not just in a single town.

Dale Cooper slowly wakes up to this new world after twenty-five years in the suspended animation of the long post-Reagan era. The original Gen-X viewers of *Twin Peaks* were presented with two possible futures that mirror the lives of the now-fragmented Dale Coopers. One future was to become an amoral criminal; the other, a doddering office worker and domesticated nobody. The "real" Dale Cooper, who confronted esoteric mysteries and searched for answers while flirting with Audrey Horne, has been held in place by evil beyond his control, frozen in the nonspace of the Red Room all this time.

Laura Dern's Diane, Agent Cooper's natural match in Lynch's mystical FBI, has escaped those choices, but is now embittered by the loss of Cooper to a parallel universe. Looking at the evil Cooper through the glass of an interrogation room, she can tell something is wrong but only knows for sure that at some point her world broke with no explanation. Diane is not a murder victim like Laura Palmer, or a housewife like Laura's mother, but she lives bereft, in alcoholism, in alienated rage, and in a helmet wig covering her ears.

"Cheers to the FBI!" Diane snarls as she downs a vodka nip, her belief in the bureau destroyed by years of neglect. We wonder what Cooper and Diane will find when they come back to consciousness amid the random violence and pervasive corruption that has spread from Twin Peaks to the darkest corners of the American nightmare. Longing for resolution, we wait for another head to roll.

September 2017

LET'S GO TO PARIS

ON SOFIA COPPOLA

IN SOFIA COPPOLA'S 2013 FILM *THE BLING RING*, A TEENAGE THIEF IN LOS Angeles sends a text to another of the home-invading adolescent burglars in her gang. "Let's go to Paris," it reads.

The Paris in this text message does not refer to the one in France. Here, Paris is code, meaning both Paris Hilton, the blond It-girl heiress of the George W. Bush era, and Paris Hilton's house, in the Hollywood Hills. It is an oblique reference to all the glamour and riches of the French capital, the fashion and jewels that it represents to these teenagers in Southern California who live on the periphery of undeserved wealth and dubious fame in America's celebrity capital.

These upper-middle-class teen burglars can drive through that world in their parents' cars, but they are not really part of it. Tourists in their own hometown, they surveil this other world online via stars' Facebook pages and the websites of gossip magazines. Like their absent parents, they know France is only a plane ride away, but Paris is right next door.

The *bande à part* in *The Bling Ring* is more of a hard-partying after-school club than an organized mob. Bored and usually alone, they have internalized the values of the media they consume. When they get together, it's to display their knowledge of this other world, to show how they conform to its codes of behavior and display.

They are not immigrants trying to establish themselves in America by building a dynasty of crime, like in Coppola's father's *Godfather* films. These are the natives. All they want is a taste of what they see online and in nightclubs. They glimpse Paris Hilton in a club one night, doing nothing but wearing a dress, holding a drink, clutching a handbag, faking a smile. Unlike the Mystery Man in David Lynch's *Lost Highway,* another dissection of life in Los Angeles, Paris cannot be in two places at once. If she's out of town, hosting a party at a Las Vegas casino or somewhere, that means her house is empty, except for her pet monkey and her jewelry, her clothes, her shoes, and the stray piles of cash and drugs she leaves around. Drawn to her house, the teens find out Paris leaves her door unlocked when she's out of town, or leaves a key under the doormat. When they begin to rob her, and then come back for more, Paris doesn't notice. Soon they are doing the same at the houses of other absent celebrities. This, by the way, is a true story.

So is *Marie Antoinette.* Coppola's 2006 biopic of the Austrian princess's rise to the French throne, and her eventual dispossession by a revolutionary mob, annoyed some viewers and critics when it was released. They saw it as the work of an overprivileged Hollywood princess, granted access to shoot in Versailles because of who she was. The film, with 1980s new wave and post-punk music accompanying Kirsten Dunst's all-American Marie through gilded hallways and endless lawns, arrived at the height of Paris Hilton's trash-media reign. If the film's displays of 18th-century excess grated, they were only as annoying as the present. A decade later, with the current American First Family as a new Bourbon monarchy based on inherited wealth and filled with a bizarre sense of divine right, Coppola's film appears more contemporary than it did in 2006.

Ivanka Trump is a modern Marie Antoinette, leaning in as she accompanies her father to international summit meetings, addressing crowds as a corporate pseudo-feminist wholly in line with King Trump's destructive policies. When we meet Rip Torn's Louis XV in *Marie Antoinette,* it's in a Trumpesque moment. "How is her bosom?"

he enquires about his soon-to-be daughter-in-law. Jason Schwartzman's dauphin, Marie's husband, is a quiet and mild-mannered rich kid with a position beyond his brainpower, an 18th-century Jared Kushner. To cap it off, there is Melania, Donald Trump's Comtesse du Barry. In Melania's defense, she is icier and more remote than Asia Argento's du Barry in the Coppola film. Argento plays the courtesan as alternately fawning and louche, with lots of public displays of affection toward her king, and evil glances for everyone else.

The Comtesse du Barry has a pet monkey. When Louis XVI and Marie become king and queen after Louis XV dies, Coppola shows us the comtesse cast out from Versailles, monkey in tow. Perhaps the monkey moved from the palace that it formerly inhabited in France to Hollywood, where it took up residence in Paris Hilton's house in *The Bling Ring.* The human emptiness of the houses that the teen thieves rob, which is the inverse of *Marie Antoinette*, the other side of its coin, are like Versailles in miniature, piled with jewels, clothes, shoes, et cetera—exquisite finery of all types, they overwhelm the film. Like Versailles, these Hollywood palaces are barely guarded. To get in, all it takes is a mob that reads the news and has had enough.

This mob's ultimate heroine is Lindsay Lohan, the actress and tabloid mega-sensation who is also a convicted jewel thief herself. Robbing Lohan to become Lohan, by wearing her clothes and carrying her handbag, is the cannibalistic intention of *The Bling Ring*'s main burglar (Katie Chang). Such rituals call to mind high-class new cannibal movies like *The Neon Demon* and *Raw*, but also this quotation from Jean-Paul Marat, firebrand journalist of the French Revolution: "Man has the right to deal with his oppressors by devouring their palpitating hearts." The characters in *The Bling Ring* don't go so far as that. They are more like an Archie Comics version of the thieves in Louis Feuillade's 1915 serial *Les vampires*, who don the clothes of the wealthy in order to rob them at their balls and parties. But who is to say they would not eat their hearts if they had the chance?

Or vice versa. The masked ball in *Marie Antoinette*, part of the film's centerpiece section, presents a tableau of intrigue ripe for robbery. In Coppola's film, the masked bandit is Marie, stealing the heart of a Swedish count played by Jamie Dornan, S&M capitalist of the *Fifty Shades* movies. "We should all go to Paris for the masked ball," one of Marie's courtiers announces during the clothes-shoes-wigs-cakes-Champagne montage that precedes the ball scene, a line that is echoed in the *Bling Ring* text message. Kirsten Dunst as the masked Marie has become the film's enduring image. It is an image that says *partying is robbery.* The recent debacle of the Fyre Festival, a con job in which Instagram models lured the wealthy to a music festival that turned out to be more of a FEMA camp, could be the next Sofia Coppola movie.

Or maybe after Trump the world is too tawdry for her. The photos from the Fyre Festival of limp wheat bread, petroleum cheese slices, wilted lettuce, and supermarket tomatoes in a styrofoam takeout container have a Juergen Teller quality, but as a report on a party, they lack a certain something. The delicacy of parties in Coppola films is a break from the ordinary and the real, nothing like the bacchanal described in the secret dossier on Trump in Moscow. While the masked ball scene has become a reference point for the parties of the 1 percent, partying today is more of a Harmony Korine movie, with all the damaged underclass gaucherie his name calls to mind. Watching Donald Trump visiting Emmanuel Macron in Paris proved this. A marching band playing Daft Punk songs to our oblivious American head of state is not exactly Bow Wow Wow at the masked ball in *Marie Antoinette*, but it's what things have come to.

Late in *Marie Antoinette* we learn that "life is getting harder for the people of France." "Tell the court jeweller to stop sending diamonds," Marie responds. I rewatched the film the same day that Steven Mnuchin, Trump's secretary of the treasury, married the actress Louise Linton, an event Vice President Mike Pence officiated and the Trumps attended. Before the wedding, Linton enumerated for the magazine *Town & Country* all the diamonds she was going to wear to her wedding. "Where do they go from here?" she asked of her jewels. "What did they signify to the women who wore them before me?"

Maybe somebody bought them at Tiffany & Co. on Fifth Avenue. The party scene in *Breakfast at Tiffany's* (1961) is regarded by some as the best party scene in cinema. The last time that I watched it, I no longer wondered why Audrey Hepburn's Holly sics the police on her own party. What I wondered was, why does the novelist, played by George Peppard, go to such great lengths to help a jet-setting Brazilian millionaire (José Luis de Vilallonga) escape before the cops show up? Let them arrest this slick playboy, I thought. Who cares if he's thrown in the clink for a night? At one time we were all supposed to understand that it would be bad for his image. Now it's the least he deserves.

In Coppola's films, deserters from this equation are punished in atmospheric scenes of morbid or lonely beauty and alluring mood. Her latest, *The Beguiled*, is fully in line with this movement toward societal breakdown. The Southern women in *The Beguiled*, trapped in their finishing school by the Civil War, are products of a regime of exploitation that they can't (or won't) name or describe. They continue with their tea parties and candlelit dinners as their world collapses around them, in their own little decaying Versailles, the sound of cannons in the distance and smoke in the sky.

As usual, Coppola's new film was greeted harshly. Critics took her to task for not grappling with slavery in the South, of therefore eliding historical injustice in favor of studying the manners of an isolated group of upper-class women under pressure. Coppola dispensed with slavery in one line in the film—"the slaves left," including, presumably, the slave character played by Mae Mercer in the original 1971 film version of Thomas P. Cullinan's novel. Instead, Colin Farrell's Union soldier becomes the women's slave, in a psychosexual relationship in which nothing is explicitly stated, a more passive version of Clint Eastwood's portrayal in the Don Siegel version.

Coppola's restraint, her lack of concern for character development or backstory or psychology—her good qualities as a film director—frustrate critics. Winning Best Director at Cannes for *The Beguiled* somehow only added to her image as a dilettante. As something of a Hollywood deserter, with each new film she makes Coppola finds out that there really isn't any refuge from the things she has left behind. The rich will always be with her, only slightly less of a problem for her than they are for everybody else. It is to her credit that she understands them, even as her elegance restrains her. If she elides the harsh truths that underpin the fading lives of her glamorous characters, her oblique approach does not save them from moral rot. Their eventual destruction is off-screen, indicated by shots of the ransacked interiors where they once celebrated their privilege.

September 2017

GERMANIC EPISODES

ON WERNER HERZOG

"THIS ANIMAL SLEEPS ITS WHOLE LIFE AWAY. IT'S NEVER REALLY AWAKE." The Spanish conquistador and mutineer Aguirre (Klaus Kinski) thus describes a sloth in the 1972 West German anti-epic *Aguirre, the Wrath of God*. The same lethargy cannot be ascribed to the film's director. Werner Herzog's unceasing activity as filmmaker, author, lecturer, world traveler, actor in other people's movies, and rescuer of strangers on the highway makes the paltry accomplishments of other human beings look inadequate and lazy by comparison. He gives the impression of a tirelessness that does not allow for rest, of any kind.

As Herzog catalogues man's inhumanity to man and nature, he seems to peer nonstop into the abyss—*Into the Abyss*, in fact, is the title of one of his recent documentaries. The last scene of *Aguirre*—with Kinski adrift on a raft in the Amazon, a conqueror of nothing—is the quintessential Herzog synthesis, combining vainglory, cruelty, and madness. Those are the coordinates at which Herzog geolocates humanity. In the end, he seems to say, we will alienate everyone with our mania and our crimes, and then drift into a sea of nothingness, beset by spider monkeys.

Yet Herzog's films somehow buoy us. Their coming-into-being, the fact that he made them at all, is a challenge to the entropy they describe. If Herzog's persona has eclipsed his filmmaking accomplishments, it is largely because we now inhabit a world in which the actual achievement of grand, worthwhile ambition seems impossible. To gently and lovingly mock him cuts him down to size. Les Blank's 1982 documentary *Burden of Dreams*, in which Blank interviewed Herzog on location in Peru while Herzog was making *Fitzcarraldo*, is the standard-bearer for making-of docs, but it gave audiences the definitive dour, gloomy Herzog, a German in a rugby shirt, khakis, and white Adidas sneakers pronouncing on risk, death, and the indifference of the universe.

"Nature here is vile and base," Herzog tells Blank. "I would see fornication, and asphyxiation, and choking, and fighting for survival, and growing, and just rotting away. Of course there's a lot of misery, but it is the same misery that is all around us. The trees here are in misery, and the birds are in misery. I don't think they sing. They just screech in pain." If Herzog overstates, his intensity is effective. "We, in comparison to the articulate vileness and baseness and obscenity of all this jungle," he continues in *Burden of Dreams*, "we only sound and look like badly pronounced and half-finished sentences out of a stupid suburban novel." To drive home this experience of insignificance in the Amazon, Herzog eventually published his diary of the making of *Fitzcarraldo*, which he called *Conquest of the Useless*.

Herzog, of course, did manage to drag a three-hundred-ton steamship over a mountain for *Fitzcarraldo*, proving that his worldview was effective as more than just rhetoric. That film came out after other ambitious films had helped end a period of serious, self-consciously heroic auteur cinema. Michael Cimino's *Heaven's Gate* (1980) and Francis Ford Coppola's *Apocalypse Now* (1979) are notorious examples (Coppola's film was influenced by *Aguirre*).

Maybe Herzog replaced Wagner's *Die Walküre* with Bellini's *I puritani* in *Fitzcarraldo* because *Apocalypse Now* had beaten him to the punch. In any case, it was a wise choice given the film's theme of one man's work ethic conquering nature before he loses what he's gained in favor of art. In the 1980s, producers turned away from grand projects like these in favor of studio-controlled blockbusters, keeping the scale without the vision. Herzog's films resisted the meddling of producers by the way they were made. In the '70s and early '80s, before the digital age, producers couldn't send notes into the jungle.

Nor could they have controlled Klaus Kinski, Herzog's on-screen alter ego, a raving maniac on set and in his personal life. Kinski's existence (he died in 1991) as an actor and as what is now called a "public figure" made Herzog look sane and reliable. Herzog's documentary about Kinski, *My Best Fiend* (1999), memorializes their collaboration over five films, during which the two men were often at each other's throats. Kinski called Herzog "the llama killer" for the unsafe conditions on his remote film sets, but it was Kinski whom the native bit players and extras wanted to kill.

The new book *Scenarios* collects the treatments (these are short narratives, not screenplays) for *Aguirre* and *Fitzcarraldo* along with those for *Land of Silence and Darkness* (1971) and *Every Man for Himself and God Against All* (1974), which was originally released in American theaters as *The Mystery of Kaspar Hauser* and then on home video as *The Enigma of Kaspar Hauser.* That film reminds us that the nonactor Bruno S. was as much Herzog's alter ego as Kinski. In *Every Man for Himself and God Against All,* Bruno S. plays an adult foundling in 19th-century Germany, a young man who has been kept in a cell his entire life. When he is released, he is a total blank slate, a man who knows nothing, has had no experiences, and to whom all human activity is strange and alienating. Bruno S., possibly autistic and definitely a victim of childhood trauma, was a street musician Herzog sought out after seeing him in a short documentary. "Why is everything so hard for me?" asks Bruno S. as Kaspar Hauser ("his mind completely engrossed in realms of twilight," says the director). Kaspar is Herzog in the raw, a character who could easily ask, as Herzog does in *Conquest of the Useless,* "Has anyone heard rocks sigh?" It is this Herzog we should remember whenever he signs the back of a check from AT&T or American Express to fund another film, just as Kaspar Hauser was forced to learn to sign his name by the "Unknown Man" who held him captive in *Every Man for Himself and God Against All.*

When Herzog takes a stroll down Main Street, USA, he ends up making something like *Stroszek* (1977), also with Bruno S., the film Ian Curtis watched before he hanged himself. In *Stroszek*, which Herzog shot in Wisconsin and North Carolina, he reduced life to the repetitive circular movements of automata—chickens on display in arcades dance and play miniature pianos, a truck without a driver goes around in circles until it catches on fire. With its insistent look at lower-class degradation within the American landscape, *Stroszek* seems to recapitulate and combine, and then pulverize, the recurrent obsessions of Herzog's New German Cinema rivals, Rainer Werner Fassbinder and Wim Wenders. In *Stroszek*, Herzog reduced his themes and the themes of his contemporaries to a zero of triviality, pitting his obsessions against American banality.

Despite Herzog's self-awareness, cutting his pretensions down to size is an American pastime dating to the release of *Fitzcarraldo*. In 1983, the novelist Cathleen Schine wrote a parody of Herzog's *Fitzcarraldo* diary for the *Boston Phoenix*. In her version, Herzog makes a film about a man obsessed with bringing professional hockey to Westport, Connecticut. To fund his dream, he will drag a commuter train fifteen miles between two towns. "There is no hockey in this place," writes Schine's Herzog. "If there were hockey here, it would be wanton, monstrous hockey. . . . There are no butterflies in this place, only moths. There are no flowers, only pollen. No joy, only death and chaotic sneezing." Such swipes at Herzog continue. The Twitter account @WernerTwertzog adopts Herzog's persona to deliver reflections such as this: "Jello is made of pulverized animal bones. Shots made from it are memento mori."

One of Herzog's most recent documentaries, last year's *Lo and Behold: Reveries of the Connected World*, was produced by NetScout, a software developer. The star-driven feature films he makes these days with Nicole Kidman and James Franco are barely released in the US. Nonetheless, the indefatigable Bavarian auteur soldiers on, a

Thomas Bernhard who has made peace with a shrinking world. He lives in Los Angeles now, but he once walked from Munich to Paris because he thought doing so would save the life of Lotte Eisner, the German film historian and critic, who was ill at the time. Herzog completed that journey, Eisner lived another nine years, and Herzog published a diary of his cross-continent trek, called *Of Walking in Ice*. When he'd passed through the town of Sontheim, Germany, Herzog wrote, "Spending the night is going to be difficult, the area is bad. Industry, smells of sewage, silo fodder, and cow dung." A German Romantic but also a realist to the core, Herzog knows that epic journeys stink. He makes them because, as he told Les Blank in *Burden of Dreams*, "We have to articulate ourselves, otherwise we would be cows in the field." The sentiment calls to mind the sights and smells of his earlier trip more than what he found in the Amazon. In his films, as in his life, Herzog has crisscrossed vast distances to avoid bovine complacency and its associated stench.

At fourteen pages, the transcriptions from the documentary *Land of Silence and Darkness* barely qualify as a scenario. Made the year before *Aguirre*, this disturbing, heart-wrenching film is one of the prime examples, with *Fata Morgana*, of the kind of unconventional documentaries Herzog was making at the time. This film about people who are both blind and deaf does without the murky grandiosity of Herzog's Amazonian films. The deaf-blind in *Land of Silence and Darkness* can't see the plants and animals around them. At a petting zoo or a botanical garden, they can touch the spines of a cactus and feel the hair of a goat or a deer, but their relationship to other forms of life is tender, not exploitative, as it often is in other Herzog films.

The phrase *out of touch* reclaims its original meaning in *Land of Silence and Darkness*. Isolated by their condition, even when sitting right next to someone else, the deaf-blind might as well be thousands of miles away from any other person. Out of disgust with sentimentality, Herzog gave many of his other films from this period a harsh and unflinching quality. In *Land of Silence and Darkness*, Herzog found subjects who allowed him to be poignant. The trade-off was that they also had to allow him to present the human condition as opaque and impenetrable. He says of the deaf-blind, “What they understand as ambition, hope, or happiness will always be a mystery to us.”

September 2017

ONE WORD: AUTHENTICITY!

HOLLYWOOD IS A MESS. THE DEBACLE AT THE OSCAR CEREMONY IN February was clumsy and revealing. At the end of a long, dull evening, Warren Beatty and Faye Dunaway announced *La La Land* the winner for Best Picture instead of the actual winner, *Moonlight*. Neither Beatty nor Dunaway had bothered to read the front of the envelope they were holding. When it became obvious to Beatty that something was wrong, he didn't reverse course. Instead, the great ladies' man gave Dunaway the card to read. Confused by Beatty's jokey demeanor, Dunaway read it even though it reannounced the Best Actress award, which had been handed out minutes before.

The mistake made all actors look bad, like automatons who read whatever's put in front of them. The show must go on, even if the script doesn't make sense, and professionalism means never having to admit you're an idiot. The revelation of Beatty as a doddering, self-impressed, and unfunny old man was at least a contrast to his sister Shirley MacLaine's fortitude, earlier in the evening, when she received a tribute from Charlize Theron as an alleged inspiration to the younger woman's career. This makes sense in Hollywood, because Theron is the contemporary actress most unlike MacLaine. This dual celebration of Beatty and MacLaine portends at least thirty more years of fawning over the Affleck brothers.

Jimmy Kimmel, the evening's host and an official representative of ABC, the Oscar network and broadcaster of his late-night show, did all he could to pre-dumb the proceedings, apologizing for his inadequacy throughout. As he struggled with the syllables *Isabelle Huppert*, he joked that no one watches foreign films. Later he asked, "What does a production designer do, anyway?" He belabored his phony TV rivalry with Matt Damon, but at least his segment mocking the Damon-starring clunker *We Bought a Zoo* was funny. It was funny because it was mean.

When Kimmel brought a bunch of regular people off the street and allowed them to kiss the hands of the celebrity actors seated in the front row, especially royal Meryl Streep, I heard tumbrels in the distance. Parading these goggle-eyed tourists across the stage probably wasn't what the Academy intended when it decided to be more inclusive. During the confusion at the end of the show, a dazzled white man onstage leaned into the microphone and brought up his "blue-eyed wife." That didn't help either.

Almost pushed to the side, Barry Jenkins, the director of *Moonlight*, remained composed as things disintegrated around him. When he finally got to give his speech for his Best Picture Oscar, he extended love to everybody, but not before he said, "to hell with dreams"—a strange but fitting end to the dream factory's annual celebration of itself.

La La Land

Damien Chazelle's resuscitation of the movie musical sets out to demonstrate a basic tenet of cinema: love fades, but lives on in music. Ryan Gosling's struggling jazz pianist Sebastian, therefore, is privileged over Emma Stone's Mia, who just wants to be a movie star. The scene in which Sebastian jazzsplains music to Mia is inadvertently the most realistic in the movie. Llewyn Davis got his ass kicked for that kind of behavior, but in *La La Land* only hearts get broken.

Chazelle makes sure we can see Gosling and Stone in full when they dance, right away proving he's a better director of musicals than Baz Luhrmann or Rob Marshall. But when Sebastian complains about the dumbness of a tapas restaurant that's also a samba club, Chazelle sets up a problem for his film that lesser directors spare themselves. He raises the question of why people love crap, then answers it by making the kind of crap people love.

Never does the film allow that maybe people can like both a-ha and Thelonious Monk, or that there's a time and a place for everything. That is a hard-won sentiment, but it's in great supply in American musicals of the 1950s, where frivolity and maturity play on a soundstage more level than this one. Here, the director is happy, but his characters are not. The post-classic French musicals that do away with singers and dancers (*A Woman Is a Woman*) or emphasize melancholy and failed romance against a backdrop of societal drabness (*The Umbrellas of Cherbourg*) serve as models for *La La Land*. Their use here seems academic, befitting a director running for Student Council President of the Movies.

Florence Foster Jenkins

Several of the films nominated for Oscars in 2017 are already earnest relics of the Obama era. Not *Florence Foster Jenkins*, which takes on unexpected resonance now that Donald Trump is President. Florence (Meryl Streep) is a talentless rich lady and syphilitic weirdo who wants to be an opera diva. The obvious truth of her condition must be ignored by her various courtiers, whose careers depend on her largesse. Her fans, a curious mix of soldiers and snobs, embrace her because her terrible singing provides lulz, while establishment luminaries, like the conductor Arturo Toscanini, humor her while lining up for checks. How does she keep this act going? "One word: authenticity!"

Or, as her cheating husband (Hugh Grant) explains to a reporter he tries to bribe, "Isn't it the truth that a lot of hurt people are having some fun?" It is unclear if the film's director, Stephen Frears, saw *Florence Foster Jenkins*'s aristocratic farce as a lighter, uptown version of *A Face in the Crowd*'s native fascism, or why anyone thought that was needed. After her exposure in the press, Florence's angelic deathbed redemption furthers her self-deception into the cardboard heaven she sought in reality. Her dementia ends in the music of the spheres, hurting no one. It's a cheesy, gentle apotheosis with no repercussions outside her little world.

Arrival

The alien-invasion tale in *Arrival* is a calming parable of breakthrough to opaque beings we can befriend so they won't destroy us—an allegory for dealing with men. It's a reverie dreamed by a wake-and-bake mommy-blogger as she contemplates the rings made by her coffee cup on the morning paper and thinks about the spider sculptures of Louise Bourgeois. Fantasies about her husband leaving her and her child dying bubble to the surface as the day slips by, visions of freedom and solitude.

As in several films made last year, the protagonist is a woman who works as a translator: Amy Adams, named Louise, maybe after the sculptor whose *Maman* resembles the movie's aliens. As a sci-fi drama about international cooperation and defusing violence, *Arrival* values thinking over ray guns, renegotiating the terms of battle between sensitive eggheads and macho soldiers typical of alien-invasion films. Adams's super-translator shouts in Mandarin to convince the Chinese military she can see through time now that the aliens have revealed its secrets to her, an outburst and a plot twist that make sense if you're high and caffeinated.

Lion

Google Earth has finally made a movie, which seems surprising only at first, because while it's hard to believe this story actually happened, it's easy to believe this film was made. Helicopter shots and god's-eye views define this true story of a boy in India who gets lost in a train station, is adopted by Nicole Kidman, and grows up to be Dev Patel. Watching him search Google Earth for his hometown is boring, but it posits the West as a place where people look into computers all day, while in the developing world people carry rocks for a living. This stark distinction would not pass muster in a film made by UNICEF. The contrast is introduced when little Saroo meets his new Australian mother in his new home. Kidman, playing someone in the 1980s, looks like a porcelain doll and waves her non-rock-carrying fingers at a television set in the living room. "Television . . . pictures," she explains to Saroo, enticing him into the world of screens that will one day allow his story to be told in a movie. A final scene could have shown pirated DVDs of *Lion* for sale in the streets of his long-lost village.

Loving

Richard and Mildred Loving were the couple in the 1967 Supreme Court case *Loving v. Virginia*, which finally overturned state laws against interracial marriage. They are portrayed in this film with kindness and dignity by Joel Edgerton and Ruth Negga, who continue the recent trend of imported actors portraying Southerners in American films. Jeff Nichols, who wrote and directed *Loving*, saturates the film with longing for a rural America where a couple can build their own house and don't need a phone, where the state won't nose around and interfere, and where there is no racism and no politics—where the only law is natural. In this pastoral idyll, Richard and Mildred are Adam and Eve, until they are expelled from their garden by racist sheriffs and county judges.

The couple's last name plays into the film's metaphoric significance as a story about genuine commitment beset by injustice. Exiled to Washington DC after they are asked to choose between the State of Virginia or divorce, Richard and Mildred long to return to their rural paradise. Under Nichols's direction, the film achieves the simplicity and perfection of certain silent films that pitted city life against country life as lovers were separated and reunited.

Edgerton's Richard barely speaks under his blond crew cut, changing expression as little as possible. Negga, who has eyes that convey so much thought and meaning, gazes with the intensity of Lillian Gish. As this couple seem to reinhabit a cinema that doesn't need dialogue, one in which the racism of Griffith is vanquished by love, so does Nichols's film seem to reinhabit the rural America of the late 1950s and '60s, an analog America the movies inhabit like a shell.

Hidden Figures

Hidden Figures has a sexy title that the film downplays in favor of pure math and basic domesticity, so maybe it's fitting to point out that the IBM 7090 was first turned on by a black woman. The progression from analog to digital provides an important subtext in *Hidden Figures*, also set in Virginia in the same period as *Loving.* As Octavia Spencer's Dorothy Vaughan teaches herself Fortran in the back of the bus, she has to confront automation and figure out how to make it work for her and the other women on her staff of math geniuses, the "colored computers" who do calculations for NASA as it gears up to put John Glenn into space.

Theodore Melfi's film takes the opposite tack from Nichols's. This is an all-star feel-good movie about American ingenuity, in love with the future, stocked with hit music on the soundtrack and titles on-screen that tell us where we are. The film makes room for everyone in its cast. Taraji P. Henson, Mahershala Ali, Jim Parsons, Kirsten Dunst, and Janelle Monáe each get plenty to do, whether they are pure and good or shifty professionalized racists. Old pro Kevin Costner chips in, desegregating the restrooms at NASA, a smaller triumph than John Glenn's space flight but one that sped the US in the race to the moon.

Hidden Figures lacks the self-seriousness and concern with special effects of recent space arias like *Gravity* and *The Martian*, proving that history and human society are more entertaining than the lives of lonely astronauts divorced from social context, who talk to themselves on another planet or float alone in space. The future in *Hidden Figures* is in our past, but it unrolls a blueprint to get back there.

Hacksaw Ridge

A third movie set in Virginia (and Okinawa), Mel Gibson's *Hacksaw Ridge* concerns itself with justice only to show how ideals and beliefs can be used to transform people into killing machines. In Gibson's worldview, that combination is the pinnacle of human achievement. Andrew Garfield plays Desmond Doss, a real hero, a conscientious objector who enlists in World War II and finds himself in a rifle unit. Doss signed up to be a medic, refusing to carry a gun, and after enduring several rounds of bullying by Vince Vaughn (his sergeant) and a court-martial trial, which he wins, he's shipped to Japan with his brigade. There he rescues dozens of his wounded comrades, hefting them one at a time across gory terrain and lowering them down a cliffside by rope, under fire by the Japanese infantry the whole time.

Gibson bathes this spectacular battle in viscera, concentrating on literal blood and soil, with a lot of literal guts strewn everywhere. Rats chew dead bodies in tunnels, a human eye looks out from the mud, half of another corpse shields a soldier from enemy fire as he charges. The actors are plastic army men come to life, here to mouth the clichés of 1940s World War II movies—this is Gibson's *La La Land*. Vaughn, while climbing the cliff at Okinawa as blood rains down on his men, points out to them that "we're not in Kansas anymore, Dorothy," a phrase I somehow doubt drill sergeants shouted in battle in 1945. After Garfield's Jesus figure spends half the movie telling the higher-ups he's not crazy and that he really does believe killing is wrong, he announces, "I never claimed to be sane." That must be how Mel Gibson gets things done, too.

Hell or High Water

This bank-robbery movie opens with signs dotting the West Texas landscape that say things like 3 TOURS IN IRAQ BUT NO BAILOUT FOR PEOPLE LIKE US, establishing *Hell or High Water* as the only Oscar-nominated film that grappled with Trump's America as the train wreck approached. Right up to the unsatisfying, to-be-continued ending, the film's lugubrious quality marks *Hell or High Water* as an example of grievance cinema, art-directed for a new era of violent self-pity, economic decline, and racial appropriation.

The film indulges its white characters on both sides of the law in fantasies that their pain is the same as that of the minor characters who are Native American. One of the bank-robber brothers (Ben Foster) confronts a Comanche gambler (Gregory Cruz) at an Indian casino, getting in his face to inform him they are the same, and Jeff Bridges's Texas Ranger confronts a sunrise wrapped in a blanket, the film's big chief. When Foster kills Bridges's Native American deputy (Gil Birmingham), it's up to viewers to decide whether the film means to indict this kind of posturing or not. The bank robbers and Bridges face different kinds of disenfranchisement, but the film's analysis of American history favors deadly confrontation as the best way to save the farm, or buy it.

Fences

Denzel Washington directs and stars in this film adaptation of August Wilson's play, opening it up to real locations in Pittsburgh without marring its essential qualities as a stage drama. His performance and direction are generous and sensitive, allowing plenty of room for the actors in smaller parts (Mykelti Williamson, Russell Hornsby) to dig into their characters. Washington's portrayal of Troy does not shy away from the character's bitterness or his unfairness to his son and wife (Jovan Adepo and Viola Davis), and he doesn't make himself look bad in a false, movie-star way. He looks bad because he has embraced Troy's decline. The film unfolds in the limited spaces of the Maxsons' backyard and house, crowding Troy, who is lonely and death-haunted despite the love of his family and his best friend, Bono (Stephen Henderson).

Wilson's evocation of the limitations imposed on the black working class offers a remedy to too much *La La Land*. If Washington holds his thumb down on the scale, it's to emphasize the downer aspects of serious American theater against the relentless optimism of fake unhappy endings.

Captain Fantastic

Viggo Mortensen, in all his indie glory but also somehow bordering on Jeff Daniels, plays a survivalist family man and amateur Maoist in *Captain Fantastic*. Living off the grid in an Oregon forest with his many children, he has taught his kids to hunt with bows and arrows and knives, to revere science and Nabokov, and to speak proper English. If they break into Esperanto to talk behind his back, he scolds them for it. He wants them to "contribute to making a better world" away from the horror of malls, McMansions, and video games, but after their mother commits suicide, this modern Swiss Family Robinson has to reenter modern life in all its bland stupidity.

Here is a film not afraid to point out that many of the people you encounter after leaving the woods are fat.

Mortensen's wife (Trin Miller), who has been away from the family, hospitalized for bipolar disorder, is seen only in dreams, flashbacks, and photos. It's enjoyable the way Matthew Ross's screenplay and direction try to denaturalize ordinary American life as it's lived in the suburbs, but nothing everyone hasn't thought a million times before. To provide mainstream balance, Ross tempers Mortensen's nobility by presenting him as a danger to his family, a radical who hasn't really thought things through.

What becomes the most interesting thing about *Captain Fantastic* by the end is the absence of Mrs. Fantastic, his wife and the mother of all these kids. She gets two funerals in the film, one traditional, at the insistence of her wealthy parents, and one presided over by Mortensen after he and the kids dig her up and cremate her. They flush her ashes down a toilet (her idea), then hold an oceanside ceremony at which they group-sing her favorite song, "Sweet Child O' Mine," a music choice that constitutes a shock ending if ever there was one. In the film's coda, a newly responsible Mortensen has become both mother and father to his brood, emancipated into domesticity on a chicken farm.

Nocturnal Animals

The first truly Trumpist film of its era, this disgusting and absurd neo-noir, by the fashion designer Tom Ford, flaunts its malice and misogyny, presenting them as criticisms of the art world and its hangers-on. Ford cribs from the films of David Lynch, Stanley Kubrick, and Sam Peckinpah as if no one has ever seen them before and he's doing the audience a favor. A notorious recovering Botox addict, he inserts a meaningless close-up of a society lady's surgically altered face into a conversation, just to drive home how much better he is than the people who have made him rich. The obese nude women presented as Jenny Saville–style art objects in the film's opening gallery scenes are used as props and dismissed, a bunch of performers duped into freak-show self-empowerment.

Since most of the film is concerned with brutal rape and murder, Ford's animosity to Amy Adams's character in *Nocturnal Animals* is all the more repellent when the film flirts with exposing her as a rape victim in the story within the story. Instead, we learn she just broke Jake Gyllenhaal's heart when she aborted their child while having an affair with another man. The tables have turned, however, and now Adams's new husband is cheating on her. This handsome, empty-souled dimwit (Armie Hammer) gets off the hook pretty easy here compared with everyone else. Gyllenhaal, a sad-sack novelist, needles Adams by sending her galleys of his new book, a spiteful tome Ford seems to think redeems him as an artist and a man. "Who are the real animals?" Ford asks, which is a stupid question that probably occurred to him at a dinner party like the one in the film. The lengthy sub-Antonioni ending makes Adams pathetic and unattractive despite the rich trappings of her wardrobe and makeup (more irony), while Aaron Taylor-Johnson, as the main hillbilly rapist, has a perfect haircut throughout the film. The difference exposes Ford's sympathies, if you can call them that.

April 2017

RED BADGE OF COURAGE

HIGH NOON

AMONG THE ICONIC HOLLYWOOD WESTERNS OF THE 1950S, *HIGH NOON*, with Gary Cooper as Marshal Will Kane, remains a classic movie in the most basic sense. More people know what it is than have seen it. *High Noon* has, in many ways, been reduced to one black-and-white image: Gary Cooper walking down an empty western street, wearing his badge, ready to draw his gun and face his enemies alone. In 1989 this image was used, with an added red splash, as the campaign poster for Poland's Solidarity movement, Cooper-as-icon standing in for the trade-unionist Lech Wałęsa in his quest to become the country's first postcommunist president.

In the US, however, John Wayne long ago overshadowed Cooper as America's heroic ideal of the West. Wayne did great, enduring work in the films of John Ford, lived eighteen years longer than Cooper (who died in 1961), and appeared in nearly thirty movies during that time. But Wayne replaced Cooper as an icon for other, better-known reasons, too, not least because he was so politically contentious, so quick on the draw as a right-winger. In the competition for mythic identity and meaning, the anti-communist, Red-baiting, hippie-hating John Wayne won, leaving Gary Cooper in the dust.

Wayne, in fact, actively participated in this semi-erasure. He disparaged *High Noon* for years after Cooper's death, even though, in 1953, at Cooper's request, he had gone onstage to accept Cooper's Best Actor Oscar for the film while Cooper was working on location. Wayne's speech at the Oscars praised Cooper, and he said he wished he had played the lead in *High Noon* himself, but even then, in private and in later interviews, Wayne said the movie offended him. With its stark portrait of a lawman abandoned by his townspeople, the movie raised issues of loyalty and authority during the time of the Red Scare. Wayne considered it the work of communist traitors. Desperation, cowardice, asking for help to defeat a common enemy—these themes troubled Wayne as an American. He saw *High Noon*'s exploration of them as evidence of weakness and subversion. In 1959, seven years after *High Noon* came out but more than a year before the blacklist ended, Wayne and director Howard Hawks issued a response to it in the form of another movie. In *Rio Bravo*, Hawks's ideological undoing of *High Noon*, Wayne played a counter-Kane, a sheriff who does not ask for help in his standoff against bad hombres. Almost against his will, he draws the most stalwart people in town to help him do what's right. Even the useless town drunk is redeemed, transformed from *High Noon*'s shabby Jack Elam into *Rio Bravo*'s appealing Dean Martin.

Rio Bravo is a celebration of camaraderie in the face of danger, like Hawks's films in general. It rejects bitterness and disappointment, feelings Hawks kept at arm's length throughout his career. Hawks was a more skillful director, and a greater artist, than Fred Zinnemann, the director of *High Noon*. The film critic Andrew Sarris accused Zinnemann of making "antimovies for antimoviegoers," of being unable to "risk the ridiculous" to get to the sublime. The popular success of *Rio Bravo* and another, lesser Wayne vehicle, *North to Alaska*, in 1960, had the side effect of turning many subsequent Hollywood westerns into corny romps: overlit, all-star celebrations of rowdiness in which chairs splinter over heads with little pain or consequence. *Rio Bravo*'s lighter touch may have added to its artistry for cinephiles, but in the Hollywood westerns that followed it, the ridiculous routed the sublime. While Ford's *The Man Who Shot Liberty Valance* (1962), also with Wayne, is a notable exception, it took Italian westerns, which drew specifically on *High Noon*, to keep the genre from triviality. When Sam Peckinpah emerged with *The Wild Bunch* in 1969 and revised Hollywood westerns for the Vietnam era, the genre returned to its dark core. Such films might have been made in America sooner if not for the blacklist.

Glenn Frankel, a Pulitzer Prize–winning journalist who has written books on Israel, South Africa, and another iconic dark 1950s western, John Ford's *The Searchers* (which also starred John Wayne), has now given us a production history of *High Noon* that is not far removed from a James Ellroy novel. The 1950s film industry portrayed in *High Noon: The Hollywood Blacklist and the Making of an American Classic* is, like Ellroy's Los Angeles, stocked with hard-core commies, idealistic fellow travelers, paranoid Red-baiters, union busters, corrupt congressmen, power-hungry gossip columnists, secretive FBI agents and their snitches, philandering actors and eager starlets. But far from being a *Hollywood Babylon* of the Red Scare, Frankel's book is a detailed investigation of the way anti-communist persecution poisoned the atmosphere around one film, which succeeded nonetheless, and damaged the lives of the people who made it.

The book's twin heroes are *High Noon*'s screenwriter, Carl Foreman, and Gary Cooper. Foreman, named as a communist by a jealous screenwriter before the House Un-American Activities Committee (HUAC) on live TV, saw his friends and colleagues desert him during the production of *High Noon*, with the exception of one person. Cooper—fading movie star in ill health, wealthy socialite and celebrity, staunch Republican, cheating husband, lead actor in the infamous screen adaptation of Ayn Rand's novel *The Fountainhead*—stood up for a man who was his polar opposite because he thought he was talented and getting a raw deal. In the paranoid context of Hollywood at the time, Cooper's behavior was unexpected. Maybe he was too big to care at that point, but he did it pretty much like he was acting in one of his Frank Capra movies.

The connection between Cooper in the movie and in real life is apparent, so Frankel does not have to overplay it. It's obvious that Cooper's and Foreman's personal lives somehow doubled the film's story after Cooper was cast in the lead. Foreman stood up to HUAC and Stanley Kramer (*High Noon*'s producer), then exiled himself to London so he could continue working. Just as Will Kane hesitantly confronted the outlaw gang in the movie, Cooper reluctantly backed Foreman at great potential risk to his career, which Frankel suggests he had stopped believing in anyway.

Cooper went so far as to start a production company with Foreman after he was called by HUAC. (The company failed to get off the ground before Foreman had to leave the US.) When Cooper's marshal in *High Noon* tosses his tin star to the ground and leaves town at the end of the film, the scene and gesture seem to encapsulate both men's careers in Hollywood. In truth, Cooper was no hero. "Darkness and doubt / Just followed him about," as the Mekons sang about John Wayne. Frankel relates how Cooper beat up Patricia Neal, his *Fountainhead* costar and mistress, after he found her in a clinch with Kirk Douglas. And Cooper came and went in various right-wing organizations, not just the Motion Picture Alliance. One, an armed "paramilitary polo club" called the Hollywood Hussars, drilled under the supervision of ex-army officers and active-duty cops.

A pox lies dormant in American politics, like shingles, and it has broken out again. The Trump Administration, even before taking power, began to request lists of government employees who might disagree with its policies on climate change, gender equality, and anti-terrorism; a right-wing website is compiling a watch list of professors it accuses of liberal bias. Frankel's book makes clear how volatile and destructive such lists can become, and the kind of people they empower. Here we meet men like the New Jersey congressman J. Parnell Thomas, an anti–New Dealer and Red-baiter who was chairman of HUAC but was arrested for common fraud and ended up in the same prison as some of the Hollywood screenwriters he hounded out of work. Then there is Richard Arens, staff director of HUAC, a "paid consultant for a shadowy and racist pro-eugenics group known as the Pioneer Fund" who warned that the fight against communism was "a total war, a political war . . . a diplomatic war, a global war . . . a war that they and not us are winning internationally and domestically at an alarming rate."

As such men return to government now, it is interesting to remember what the blacklisted writer-director Abraham Polonsky said about his fellow communists in the film industry: "The Communist Party was for years the best social club in Hollywood. You'd meet a lot of interesting people, there were parties, and it created a nice social atmosphere." Despite their bonhomie, they were outmaneuvered by the stupid and venal men who made up HUAC and by the press that supported it—the *Chicago Tribune* ran stories with headlines like "Politically Infantile Film Folk Were Easy Marks for Reds," and the *New York Herald Tribune*'s "Red Underground" column outed fellow travelers once a week.

As Frankel points out when he invokes Thom Andersen and Noël Burch's 1996 documentary, *Red Hollywood*, it is a myth that the work of the blacklistees was inconsequential, despite what viewers may have gleaned last year from *Hail, Caesar!*, the Coen brothers' comedy of 1950s Hollywood. Foreman survived the blacklist, cowriting *The Bridge on the River Kwai* for David Lean while in exile in London. He got no on-screen credit, which instead went to Pierre Boulle, who wrote the novel, had nothing to do with writing the script, and did not speak English. When the screenplay won the Oscar in 1958, Boulle, according to legend, collected it onstage, delivering the shortest speech in Academy history: "*Merci.*"

Frankel includes another odd scene in his book, in which Hedda Hopper, the vicious anti-communist gossip columnist, meets with Foreman in a London hotel in the mid-1950s after working so hard to destroy his career. She was in her sixties, he in his forties, but they found themselves attracted to each other. They polished off a bottle of Jack Daniel's and stopped just short of making out. Politics makes strange bedfellows, people rise to some occasions and fail in others.

As our new era unfolds, with the explicit promise, or threat, to make America as great as those 1950s again, we will soon find out if the bizarre tales in Frankel's book will be repeated with a new cast of actors and writers.

February 2017

ALL THAT COUNTS IS GETTING TO A NORMAL WORLD

NEW YORK FILM FESTIVAL 2016

IN HIS 1987 FILM *SOIGNE TA DROITE*, JEAN-LUC GODARD EXPLAINED THAT the hardest thing about the movie business was carrying around film cans. In the digital age, that problem has been solved, for better or worse: films are now portable media packages. It's the audience, not filmmakers, who face cinema's big challenge: figuring out where to see movies. If you are lucky or foolish enough to live in New York City, you can turn to ScreenSlate.com and always find a movie worth leaving the house for. If you live anywhere else in the US, it's not as easy. This is where film festivals come in. The big film festivals in North America, unlike those in Europe and Asia, bring masses of people to places most of them would not otherwise visit: Telluride, Colorado; Columbia, Missouri; Toronto. Film festivals, as much as music festivals, have led the way in the professionalization of experience into creative-class gatherings and industry conferences. Before there were TED Talks and South by Southwest, before there was Coachella, there was Sundance.

The New York Film Festival has always been a little different. Since 1963 it has been the premier yearly showcase in the US for serious cinema of all kinds. Held at Lincoln Center over two and a half weeks in late September and early October, the festival concentrates on a smaller slate than other festivals but is nonetheless huge. It is divided into somewhat blurry categories: twenty-five Main Slate features, fifteen documentary features (although some Main Slate features are docs), eleven additional Explorations and Special Event features, about twenty revivals of older films, thirty shorts, more than forty Projections films representing the nonnarrative avant-garde, and a section of virtual-reality items called Convergence. There are also, of course, parties, Q&As with filmmakers and actors, and "An Evening with . . ." events. This year's were with actors: Kristen Stewart, who appears in three films in the festival, and Adam Driver, star of Jim Jarmusch's new film, *Paterson*.

Many of the films have already shown in festivals around the world, and some go into general release soon after they screen. The New York Film Festival serves as their official introduction to the US, in which the tony setting of Lincoln Center confers on them the status of worthy and serious works. The Main Slate films represent a set of features not just for cinephiles but for any cultured person keeping up with the movies—anyone who is interested in film as an art form that will survive the big-studio superhero infestation and the burden of quality TV.

Before and during the festival, about fifty films are screened during the day for the press. I saw forty of them. I missed one because of a therapy appointment. (Even though I am a film critic, I hope to be able to have normal relationships someday.) I missed another because I had a hangover and couldn't face the hour-long trip to Lincoln Center from my apartment in Brooklyn. Two I paid to see, and went on Sunday afternoons after buying tickets using the festival's complicated and anxiety-inducing website, with its countdown clock.

THE PRESS SCREENINGS BEGAN as President Obama arrived in town for his last visit to the UN General Assembly the Monday after a bomb went off near Chelsea. It was mid-September and New York was a humid mess, with extra police presence, traffic jams, spottier-than-usual subway service, and the lurking shadow of a possible

Trump presidency making everybody nervous. None of that stopped film critics from arriving at Lincoln Center an hour before showtimes to make sure they got good seats in the Walter Reade Theater.

Standing in line at Lincoln Center with other journalists at 9 AM brings into stark relief the difference between artists and critics. Because Juilliard is at Lincoln Center, each morning dozens of young drama students pass by the festival press line on their way to class. An inordinate number of film critics are men, and young men are especially overrepresented. The drama students, among whom young women seem to be equally overrepresented, pass by in a parade of youthful vigor, unaware they are strolling by their future judges. This daily nonmeeting of the two groups made me want to donate money to a feminist film critics' organization.

Sitting in the auditorium, I learned that some of the young critics were Airbnb'ing from out of town to attend these screenings, while others were commuting daily from other states. Seated in front of them, a line of elderly Lincoln Center patrons occupied the extra-legroom row, dressed like they had just arrived from Martha's Vineyard to see the new Almodóvar or Lonergan. (Their wardrobes improved as summer turned to fall.) Among them was Howard Stern, wearing enviably fashionable sneakers. Whether he was there as a member of the press or as a patron I never knew, but I was surprised to learn he was a fan of contemporary art-house cinema. Maybe next time he has Donald Trump on his radio show, they'll discuss Paul Verhoeven's *Elle*.

THIS YEAR'S FESTIVAL OPENED with a documentary, Ava DuVernay's *13th*, about the racist legacy of the clause in the Thirteenth Amendment allowing involuntary servitude as punishment for crime. *13th* was made for Netflix, where it debuted a week later. Not only was this the first time in its history that the New York Film Festival opened with a documentary, it was the first time it opened with a movie that was essentially made for TV. When Quentin Tarantino said, without having seen it, that DuVernay's *Selma* was more like a TV movie that would have been made in the 1970s than an actual work of cinema, he could not have predicted how DuVernay would turn the opportunity to make a movie for Netflix into an act of defiance.

DuVernay cites Griffith's *The Birth of a Nation* (1915) as the original sin in American filmmaking, contrasting its violent racism with the power digital media has to expose police brutality and other state crimes directed at people of color. Smartphone video cameras and streaming media, in *13th*, are explicitly positioned against the cinema, which, starting with Griffith's white-supremacist epic, encouraged the racism that continues to echo in Hollywood a hundred years after his film. The radicalism of opening a film festival with this message (while also ceding the streaming future by handing Netflix this honor) was acknowledged by DuVernay, if no one else. In her press conference following the screening, she was frank about it. If digital media can keep the police from killing innocent people, it can also make Hollywood rethink the entrenched racism of the film industry, which has made money for decades by depicting people of color as less worthy than white people.

Catalan filmmaker Albert Serra's *The Death of Louis XIV* exemplified a different kind of cinema. Serra's film was designed as a performance piece for a museum. The French monarch is bedridden, almost immobile, occasionally wheeled about—a near mummy. Jean-Pierre Léaud, adolescent face of the French New Wave, now 72 years old, plays the king. (Coincidentally, seventy-two years is how long Louis XIV reigned as king of France.) Noble, sick, pampered, and weird, Louis, as played by Léaud, becomes a stand-in (more of a sit-in) for the European art cinema of the second half of the 20th century. The film's majesty and stateliness are undercut at all times by illness—deathbed scenes turn a museum into a hospice.

Serra self-consciously removes his film from the assaultive world of media. Its slow pace and dark, lush setting require attention but also a forgetting or abandonment of the world outside. Incompetent doctors minister to the king, watching over the decline of this body politic, offering many theories and no solutions. In their desperation to keep Louis alive, they resort to quack remedies sold to them by charlatans. Léaud's presence brings with it our collective memory of his former glory. We watch with these doctors as it fades out of existence.

Léaud, who is not known for his warmth or for setting foot in the US, appeared in person with Serra after the screening. His presence was a thrill—something I realized I had been waiting for since I was a teenager and saw Léaud in Godard and Truffaut films at the university near where I grew up. During the Q&A, he quoted Cocteau, one of his early mentors at the time of *The 400 Blows* and the birth of the French New Wave: The cinema is the only medium that shows death at work. Léaud gave the impression of understanding that quite well. The guy sitting next to me, not so much. He checked sports scores on his phone while Léaud and Serra talked, staving off death one ballgame result at a time.

Like Serra, Eugène Green is a foreigner working in French cinema, an American who added a grave accent to his name and makes films more French than the French do. *Son of Joseph*, about an abandoned son (Victor Ezenfis) planning an elaborate revenge on his father (Mathieu Amalric), takes place in a literary milieu and in churches that hark back to Christianity's formative years. Vincent's father, Oscar, is editor in chief at a publishing house and a mean-spirited philanderer. His office is in an underfurnished 19th-century hotel suite, where, when he is not editing manuscripts or trying to find France's next top novelist, he can be found on a couch with his executive assistant, a leggy bondage enthusiast. If it weren't so cartoonish, this setup could be the envy of cube-bound male book editors everywhere. The literary setting points to a recurring theme of the festival, one that competes with smartphoning-it-in and museumification as a trend in the postdigital cinema: the merging of movies with literary fiction.

PEDRO ALMODÓVAR'S *JULIETA* is based on three interrelated Alice Munro stories, which the screenwriter-director moves from Canada to Spain. The film takes place over three periods in the life of its protagonist, a classicist and translator (Adriana Ugarte as young Julieta, Emma Suárez when she's older). The moody plot traces her guilt and depression through her relationship with her lover, Xoan, his death at sea, and her estrangement from their daughter.

The first part of the film, with Ugarte as a 1980s New Wave Julieta during her grad-student days, is mysterious, colorful, and exciting. The Suárez sections, while typically stylish, are at odds with the usual Almodóvarian melodrama and drain the film of emotion until it abruptly ends before the moment of reconciliation. The ending, though Hitchcockian in its unexpected cutoff and mountain-road setting, still belongs more to literature than the movies. Almodóvar plants a foot on each side of the gap between the two, which is fine, but the film, like Julieta herself, seems lost on the road.

Kelly Reichardt's *Certain Women*, as its title's pun suggests, does not have that problem. This adaptation of three loosely related stories by Maile Meloy surefootedly treads its Montana landscape even when it seems to be meandering or concentrating on emptiness. Its sparse dialogue and observational style erase its literary origins the same way Antonioni erased Cortázar's in *Blow-Up*. The film takes place indoors as much as out, even in the middle of nowhere. Laura Dern's lawyer character deals with childish men in offices, in a motel room, across conference tables, and in prison, while Kristen Stewart and Lily Gladstone meet in a classroom at night or across a table in a diner. Gladstone's young ranch hand, the Native American in this western, pitchforks hay in a barn before dawn and drives her truck to town at the same hour of morning, with little landscape visible through the windows.

The ground here is frozen and hard. Stewart and Gladstone's brief semi-encounter takes place in public but away from men, while Dern has to deal in private with an uncommunicative married lover, an "authentic" type (James Le Gros). As one of Dern's clients, Jared Harris commits to a disturbing performance of confusion and longing that underscores the film's cold rage and loneliness. He's a woodworker with brain trauma who takes a hostage in an office building, an act he can barely commit to before running away. Everything in *Certain Women* is carefully constructed and potentially deadly, but Reichardt rejects the spectacle of violence associated with the American West, replacing it with silence and dark pity.

CYNTHIA NIXON, AS Emily Dickinson in Terence Davies's biopic, *A Quiet Passion*, is paradoxically louder and more insistent than Dern, Michelle Williams, Stewart, and Gladstone in *Certain Women*. Davies creates a full society around Dickinson, in great detail, making her housebound nonconformism hard to understand. One by one, her friends and family drop away, through marriage and death, leaving Dickinson nothing but her visions and her poetry. It is tragic but not romantic. Dickinson stiff-arms everybody, and Davies refuses to sentimentalize her as the Belle of Amherst, making her off-putting every chance he gets.

Nixon's performance is a self-conscious tour de force of buried fury. Dickinson's essential attitude, as Nixon and Davies take pains to point out, is bitterness ("not despair"), and at the end of her life, as she lies on her deathbed aware of her obscurity and her sacrifice, she asks why the world has become so ugly. The only cinematic comparison is another masterpiece, Mikio Naruse's 1962 film *A Wanderer's Notebook*, about the life and struggle of Fumiko Hayashi, a Japanese writer who, like Dickinson, died in middle-age.

Naruse's film is considered minor among his works, but it looms over Jarmusch's *Paterson*, too. All three films present poetry as text over images. *Paterson*, the least of them, is *A Quiet Passion* in reverse: the happy story of an obscure young man, a bus driver played by Adam Driver, who is named Paterson and lives in Paterson, New Jersey. This double cuteness is spread all over the film, like the frosting patterns Paterson's girlfriend, Laura (Golshifteh Farahani), carefully applies to the cupcakes she sells at the farmers' market the film unfortunately never visits. It would be good to see a Jarmuschian farmers' market, or maybe a flea market—then Jarmusch could catalog all the knickknacks he loves without the encumbrance of a plot. It's a saccharine film, sometimes relieved during Paterson's walks through town on the way to the bar he visits every night while walking his cute dog.

Like the shrine to writers and hepcats in *Only Lovers Left Alive*, the tribute nook to Patersonians behind the bar reveals Jarmusch as a talent obsessed with explaining what's cool. This has marred his work. He sneaks in Iggy Pop, a non-Patersonian, via faded newspaper clipping, a digression that's a shill for *Gimme Danger*, Jarmusch's documentary about the Stooges singer that also played in the festival. That film, too, descends into a treatise on cool. We learn that the proof of cool—and its endpoint—is Sonic Youth covering a Stooges song. Jarmusch doesn't mention cool's decay, its half-life: Iggy's "Search and Destroy" is now heard in a commercial for Audi on TV.

Pablo Larraín, the Chilean director, had two films in the festival. I saw them in the order they were made. *Neruda* transforms four years in the life of the Nobel Laureate and communist into detective fiction. Luis Gnecco, the star of the Chilean version of the TV show *The Office*, portrays Neruda as a friend of the workers, an enemy of the police, and a habitué of an urban demimonde where his poetry stirs lost souls, prostitutes, and drag queens. A police detective (Gael García Bernal) and his squad spy on Neruda, then track him through snowy mountains as he makes his escape into Argentina. Bernal, swallowed by his fedora and his 1940s suit, becomes a character written by Neruda in this magical-realist fable reminiscent of the weirder, less accommodating films of Raúl Ruiz. Sometimes *Neruda* beautifies fascism in a nostalgic glow of tertiary color the way *The Conformist* did, sometimes it uglifies it along the lines of Cronenberg's version of *Naked Lunch*. It brings to the cinema the kind of literary biography that traces only a short period in its subject's life.

Larraín's *Jackie* does the same, but concentrates on four days, not four years. Larraín follows Jacqueline Kennedy (Natalie Portman) from her husband's assassination in Dallas through his funeral and a subsequent interview with a reporter (Billy Crudup) on Cape Cod. Portman's performance and Larraín's flowing camera overcome a screenplay that too often seems like a one-act play. Larraín and Portman do more than just move a play outdoors. They explode it into lush, grand visions of American history and chaos. Portman, in Jackie's blood-spattered pink Chanel suit, glides through a pinpoint re-creation of the 1963 White House interior, right down to the George Catlin paintings of buffalo on the walls. Drinking vodka, taking pills, listening to the soundtrack album from *Camelot*, she considers or ignores instructions from Robert Kennedy (Peter Sarsgaard), her secretary (Greta Gerwig), a priest (John Hurt), Jack Valenti (Max Casella), the Johnsons (John Carroll Lynch and Beth Grant), each whisked through by Larraín so Jackie can cool them with icy disdain and quiet lisping. Portman's performance is one for the ages because, in its fabulous poise, it is camp. She surpasses Faye Dunaway as Joan Crawford and Glenn Close as Sunny von Bülow because the woman she plays is sympathetic. Jackie is nicer than Crawford and more iconic, and, unlike von Bülow, not in a coma.

Jackie was not on the festival press-screening schedule, but I managed to see it one night at the Fox building on Sixth Avenue. As I left, passing giant posters of Bill O'Reilly and Brit Hume in the halls, the last presidential debate was about to start, the one in which Donald Trump called Hillary Clinton, a former first lady like Jackie, a "nasty woman." No doubt he will see that moment re-created in a film someday. Midtown was quiet as the screens in the Fox windows and the ticker on the building showed pre-debate Trump news, delivering his crude messages onto empty sidewalks. Larraín's film wants us to believe that maybe there really was an American Camelot once upon a time. The blue and red glow from the Fox News building made *Jackie*'s conclusion mournful, and in comparison not tacky at all.

ALISON MACLEAN'S *THE REHEARSAL*, based on the novel Eleanor Catton wrote before *The Luminaries*, is, like *Certain Women*, an unliterary

literary adaptation. It offers serious counterpoint to college musical dramas and pop spectacle like *Pitch Perfect*. In Maclean's film, a group of acting students at "the Institute," a drama school in New Zealand, secretly put on a play based on a teacher-student sex scandal in the local news. A movie of negotiated betrayal among millennials and their Gen X mentors (like Noah Baumbach's *Mistress America*), *The Rehearsal* relies on squirm, eventually letting its characters off the hook by forcing them to solve their problems on their own. Reflecting on the suicide of one of their fellow students, a wealthy member of their acting class who couldn't hack it, they realize his internet obsession can be applied to the theater and their audience.

The film is defined by odd, unexpected touches. The tennis instructor looks like an evil cowboy and too closely resembles the teenage girl he's had the affair with. Kerry Fox, as the Institute's director and main instructor, is harsh and preoccupied, but not a *Whiplash* monster. Maclean and Fox present her as a realistic intellectual who leads her own life away from her charges. Ella Edward's performance as the sister of the girl in the scandal is maybe the oddest thing in the film. Not quite the star in this ensemble cast, her out-of-it, distracted manner shows star quality and places her above the older students, who all want to be actors and are therefore very present. They flit through *The Rehearsal* like the Juilliard students at Lincoln Center, their eyes on something outside their immediate surroundings.

•

THE TITLE OF ALAIN GUIRAUDIE'S new film, *Staying Vertical*, is a pun that might work in French but in English translates as "audience indifference." That's too bad, because this wild, original film deserves to be seen. A gay screenwriter, Léo (Damien Bonnard), blocked in his writing, travels the Pyrenees, where he meets a farm girl and a country hustler who live with an elderly Pink Floyd fan, a ranter Léo assists in his suicide by fucking him on his deathbed. Scandal, woodland homeopathy, and homelessness follow, until Léo reemerges as a hermit. Employed by his baby mama's brutal gay-farmer dad, who looks like John C. Reilly in a nightmare, the two face down wolves in the mountains, united by their mutual obsession with these predators who kill their sheep and to whom they offer Léo's baby as bait. Some people will do anything to avoid writing.

Nearby, but in a different movie, a hunky scientist (Paul Hamy) studies black storks through binoculars from his kayak. Later in João Pedro Rodrigues's *The Ornithologist*, this title character turns into a different person *Lost Highway*–style, played by Rodrigues himself. The film obscurely recasts the life of St. Anthony of Padua for modern times.

After rapids wash his kayak away, a pair of Chinese girls, Christian tourist-pilgrims lost in the woods on their way to the Camino de Santiago de Compostela, kidnap the ornithologist and tie him up in his underwear. Like the pixie-fairies from *Mothra*, they are delightful yet sinister and portend worse to come. The ornithologist escapes them, then has sex with a mute gay shepherd whom he kills for stealing his hoodie, and for possibly belonging to a sect of pagan vandals in red costumes who speak an obscure language and seem to be hunting him. By the time a gang led by a topless blond huntress appears, the film has begun to exhaust itself and the audience. These women on horseback bring it back to life as the ornithologist lies dying.

This same fallen world and potential homotopia exist in Dane Komljen's *All the Cities of the North*, a Serbian film set in the woods at an abandoned vacation resort. This postcommunist landscape, with its Brutalist concrete architecture giving way to nature, is populated by male lovers and homeless men who rearrange bed mats, wash themselves with buckets of water, and slice apples with large heavy scissors. We see the film's crew at work once in a while, and passages from Simone Weil's *Gravity and Grace* and Godard's screenplay for *Passion* are read on the sound track. I hoped for a scene in which one of the normcore vagrants placed a chip on another's shoulder while a third, offscreen, read from Thomas Piketty's *Capital in the Twenty-First Century*.

The film's slowness seems rote at this late point in the history of slow cinema. *All the Cities of the North* solidified for me, after Guiraudie's and Rodrigues's movies, that these films are part of a genre, and some genre directors are better than others. The self-conscious, desultory feel of this one underscored the power of the other two.

WILLFUL BOREDOM SMOTHERS Natalia Almada's *Everything Else*, the story of Doña Flor (Adriana Barraza), a Mexican bureaucrat nearing retirement who spends her days nitpicking paperwork handed to her by a random assortment of Mexico City residents. Her repetitive job, nightly routine, and hapless attempts to work up the courage to dive into a swimming pool compose the bulk of this film, a *Jeanne Dielman* in miniature. The severe vision of lower-class anomie in Akerman's film is leavened in *Everything Else* by a touch of connection from an obese woman in a gym shower room, another invisible woman in a teeming city. Almada spares Doña Flor a tragic end in a moment of potential violence, involving a fire-eating con man who pours lighter fluid on his victims.

After Doña Flor's cat dies, she leaves it wrapped in a towel on her bed all day while she goes to work in her office. When she gets home, she dumps it in a trash can. This cat is one link between *Everything Else* and *Things to Come*, Mia Hansen-Løve's film about a philosophy professor (Isabelle Huppert) who loses everything in middle age, including the antisocial cat her batty mother left behind after her death.

Huppert's Nathalie leads a decent life with her husband, Heinz, also a philosophy professor. They have two kids and a seaside vacation house; he reads Karl Kraus while she reads *Minima Moralia*. Arguments with her publisher about book-cover design reflect the changing world of the late '00s, in which marketing, it seems, came to dominate German-philosophy-textbook publishing in France. Nathalie's favorite student, a bearded Marxist radical named Fabien who wears ripped jeans and wants to live in the woods, ingratiates himself into her life to get published. A *normalien* in Paris at the time of Occupy Wall Street, he's supposed to be likable, committed, searching. After Heinz leaves Nathalie and she starts hanging out with Fabien and his adjunct pals in the French equivalent of upstate New York, I began to worry. Was Isabelle Huppert really going to sleep with this jive turkey? But it's the film's strategy to deny her comfort. When she goes to a movie theater to see *Certified Copy*, she's chased into the street by a lecher.

Kleber Mendonça Filho's *Aquarius*, from Brazil, is less eventful than *Things to Come*. Sonia Braga plays a woman not unlike Huppert's philosophy professor, a serious, slightly older music critic past retirement age. Clara is the last resident of her apartment building on the beach in Recife, and developers, eager to turn it into condos, have begun the nasty process of making life too unpleasant for her to stay. *Aquarius* is forty-five minutes longer than *Things to Come*, partly because it stops to show how annoying it is when the sound of construction makes thinking impossible. This rare flattering portrait of a critic as an aging, still-glamorous woman does not settle for the reheated comfort of nuclear family like *Things to Come* does. Clara turns the people around her into activists instead of hanging out with the already radicalized. The film's revelation of termite infestation, a metaphor for the crumbling infrastructure of capitalist development everywhere, is more direct and obvious than anything in *Things to Come*, more Zavattinian than the Rossellinian vision of a woman alone in Hansen-Løve's character study.

Matías Piñeiro's *Hermia & Helena* presents a potential future-Clara or future-Nathalie in Camila (Agustina Muñoz), a young Argentinian translator on a fellowship in Manhattan. She's working on a translation of *A Midsummer Night's Dream* for a theater company in Buenos Aires—we see the play's lines as text on the screen—but she also has a secret mission the film waits most of its short running time to reveal. Traveling upstate through bright snow under blue skies, she meets an older man played by the New York filmmaker Dan Sallitt, who is reserved but appealing in this role.

He's an agreeable version of the patriarchy, a millennial girl's dream of a lost good dad—the opposite of the demanding, threatening father in Shakespeare's play.

Representatives of the patriarchy are more manipulative and aggressive in Hong Sang-soo's quiet, equally short *Yourself and Yours*, which makes for a wittier, stranger, more hard-assed film. Min-jung (Lee You-young), the object of desire here, may be two women. Clueless, drunken men argue over the "good" Min-jung and castigate the "bad" one in her absence and to her face. The good one is a faithful girlfriend who has promised to cut back on her drinking. The bad one gets plastered in public and makes out with strange men in bars.

Set, like *Hermia & Helena*, in a sealed urban world of young artists and writers who only talk to one another (and, here, bartenders), *Yourself and Yours* depicts rising female fury as it confronts passive, confused men. An older filmmaker, a stand-in for Hong, proves himself to be as boozy and dopey as Min-jung's younger boyfriends. The film's signature line of dialogue could also be the tagline on its poster: "Drink up, you pathetic men!"

A BOLDER CAT THAN the one she inherited in *Things to Come* looks on placidly in Paul Verhoeven's *Elle* as Isabelle Huppert is raped on her dining-room floor—a scene the film replays more than once. Michèle's nonreaction to this attack is as dissociated as the cat's. She looks at herself from outside, a spectator to her violation like the audience watching the film, the actress observing her role as she plays it. She cleans up this crime scene and goes to her office, where she runs a video-game company specializing in perverted fantasy and violence. At a fast-food restaurant, a woman dumps her tray on Michèle on purpose. Strange, since Michèle's father, a mass murderer who dragged her to his homicides, killed people for being rude.

Elle is startling and precise, an arrow to the skull. Mordant wit and twisted joy come with Verhoeven's level of control. In a Parisian gun shop decorated with American flags, Huppert picks up an ax and eyes it coolly before rejecting it in favor of a plain-old handgun.

Verhoeven has been hackish in the past. Not this time. So much slow cinema in one festival starts to seem conservative, making a film with a killer screenplay like David Birke's, where everything is in place, look as backward-glancing and futuristic as *Total Recall.*

The festival's other insane crowd-pleaser was Maren Ade's *Toni Erdmann,* which also deals with a daughter (Sandra Hüller) and the resentment she feels for her father (Peter Simonischek). When we first meet him, it's clear Winfried is a tad sinister, a prankster-retiree who likes to greet the UPS guy with fake teeth in his mouth while wearing a wig. But he's a sad clown, and soon enough his dog dies. While Ade makes Winfried pathetic, she really stacks the deck against Ines, a self-involved lean-in-type who wears gray suits, speaks in business English, and works as a consultant downsizing industrial labor. She and the other middle-management Germans she works with are unhappy in Bucharest, hoping for appointments in other, better cities. "I like countries with a middle class," one says. Bucharest, we learn, features "Europe's largest mall and no one with money to buy anything."

Winfried shows up in Bucharest for a visit with his daughter, interfering with Ines's work schedule and ruining her weekend. Then he tries to make things right by giving her a cheese grater, that most anxiety-inducing of kitchen tools. At this point in the film, or maybe the next morning, right after Ines accidently slices open her toe before a big meeting (not with the cheese grater), something about *Toni Erdmann* became clear: no scene could be predicted from the one that came before it.

Toni Erdmann, the title character, is not a real person. He is a persona Winfried adopts to nudge Ines toward becoming what he wants her to be: nice, caring, human. Donning a lame disguise that makes him look like the son of Neil Young and Austin Powers, Winfried shows up at Ines's work events and pretends to be a leadership consultant, embarrassing his daughter into silence about his true identity as she squirms and pretends she doesn't know him. His idea that she just needs a little Merry Prankster in her soul crumbles as the pair tour an industrial excavation site in the Romanian steppe, a second-world wasteland of global capital.

The film is resolutely new and unexpected, yet somehow classical, echoing *Dr. Jekyll and Mr. Hyde*, Jerry Lewis's *The Nutty Professor*, Renoir's Boudu and Dr. Cordelier, and any movie in which someone dons a gorilla suit. The gorilla suit here—a folkloric Hungarian tree-creature getup—contrasts with the thin robe concealing Ines's nudity as she chases Winfried's final alter ego out of a naked work party she's hosting in her apartment. Winfried is a beast who hides, Ines a beauty who learns to bare her soul. The film's moment of apotheosis, a scene in which Ines is forced to belt out the Whitney Houston song "The Greatest Love of All" as Winfried/Toni plinks out the tune on a Casio, is a slow-boil demonstration of comedy's limit.

JEAN-PIERRE AND LUC DARDENNE'S *The Unknown Girl* takes place in the same despondent Belgium as their other films. More than those, it has a murky New Romanian Cinema feel. Often the Dardennes shoot the film's protagonist, a young doctor (Adèle Haenel), so we can't see her face. They shoot the townspeople the same way, hiding them in murk. This is a town populated by people who don't want to be seen or to look at others. Dr. Davin takes a technocratic view of her patients' plight in this dreary place where people live in shadows and no one gets excited about anything, ever: "If a patient's suffering moves you, you make a bad diagnosis."

One night she fails to answer the doorbell in her clinic, refusing to admit a young woman pleading outside. When the woman, an African immigrant, turns up dead, the doctor realizes she could have saved her. Far from being a lesser Dardenne effort, this dour semi-genre film about obdurate, callous people with something to hide is one of their best. The film's genre trappings as dead-girl mystery have led the Dardennes to bore deeper into their milieu. Dr. Davin does not appear to have friends or family. People in the film isolate themselves in phone booths in a cybercafé. Nobody likes to talk, and when they do, it's to make threats.

Haenel's self-effacing performance in *The Unknown Girl* is the opposite of Kristen Stewart's star turn in *Personal Shopper*, even though Stewart's Maureen is supposed to be an introvert more attuned to the spirit world than to this one. Also a semigenre film, albeit a far more glamorous one, Olivier Assayas's deconstructed Parisian *giallo* fails to make sense, as *gialli* often do. Hounded by the most unwitty barrage of sexts in the short history of texting, Maureen moves through a disconnected contemporary world in which communication is ghostly, identity slippery, and S&M meets SMS. Every moment of the film's plot is predictable. As Stewart browses racks of clothes to try on in her employer's apartment, the film's big mystery becomes: how long before she masturbates?

In his press conference with Stewart after the screening, Assayas mentioned that he is interested in radical collage. "Of course *Personal Shopper* is not a genre movie," he explained. Furthermore, things have changed in the world of image-making, he said, since he made *Demonlover* in the early 2000s. Back then he still had opinions about digital technology and the future. Now he's just a haunted man trying to survive in a world inundated with constant disposable images. *Personal Shopper* is interesting in that it gives so much screen time to Stewart, letting her sit in cafés and flip through art books on Hilma af Klint. She makes the movie work for her. All the other Americans in it seem like extras on *Silicon Valley*, and the Europeans merely members of the international creative class, stylish people with enough time on their hands to have affairs, but not enough to do their own shopping or chase their own ghosts.

COVERING A FILM FESTIVAL is like watching movies on an airplane. You start in one place and end up in another. It wears you down, seeing forty films in three weeks: sitting day after day in the dark, exposed to all that emotion and all those troubled souls. Everyone has their breaking point. Mine came during Mike Mills's *20th Century Women*, with Annette Bening.

The film begins in 1979, that fateful last year before Ronald Reagan ganked Gen X. Dorothea (Bening) is a single mom raising a son (Lucas Jade Zumann) in Santa Barbara, California, in a house she owns and shares with Jamie and two boarders, a New Wave wannabe artist named Abbie (Greta Gerwig) and an ex-hippie carpenter-mechanic who's drifting through life (Billy Crudup). The film opens with songs by Talking Heads and the Clash, and by the time Abbie and Jamie attempt to explain the appeal of the Raincoats' "Fairytale in the Supermarket" to Dorothea—in some pleasing, clunky dialogue that replicates how people really did talk about new music then—I felt like I'd been mugged. I felt embarrassed, as victims of muggings sometimes do, that I wasn't better prepared. I'd let down my guard. I told myself it wasn't my fault; there was no way I could have known Mills and I had the same adolescence and the same mother.

Here are some facts about my mother, which also describe Dorothea in this film. My mother was an ex–graphic designer who divorced my father when I was very young. She owned a Volkswagen Beetle. She smoked two packs of cigarettes a day, and they killed her in her sixties. She would listen to my records when I wasn't around, trying to figure out what I liked about them. She preferred Talking Heads to Black Flag. She was lonely, never meeting any interesting men in our small town, and she was always reading a book from the library. Interested in progress and concerned about the future, she tried to teach me to be decent and kind while the Dead Kennedys and Joy Division were teaching me to be insolent and moody. I, in turn, spent time at a nearby university meeting hip older girls, like Gerwig's Abbie, who worshipped David Bowie, and sneaking out to music shows in bars where they'd let in teenagers with IDs so fake they wouldn't have fooled a blind man.

Like that paragraph, the movie ends up being more about the son than the mother. The easy generational politics of music and T-shirt choice in *20th Century Women* define life in Southern California at the end of the '70s as much as they did present-day California in *The Kids Are All Right* (also with Bening). Mills holds down the keys on these signifiers to sound deep notes of melancholy. His film, in its second half, opens up cultural influence to feminist literature, using passages from *Sisterhood Is Powerful* and other Second Wave writing on the sound track and on-screen. The film's built-in sentimentality put me in the same position as the masses of women who embraced *Beaches* in 1988 or *Stepmom* in 1998. Cinematic melodrama is no longer as mass, and to be taken seriously it has become artier. As melodrama for men, *20th Century Women* reminds the middle-aged that they once evolved, and introduces younger men to feminism at mom's knee. "Forsake not the way of salvation, my boy," sang the Carter Family, "that you learned from your mother at home."

BY NOW, DOZENS OF ARTICLES praising Barry Jenkins's *Moonlight* will have appeared, conferring on it the definite status of New American Classic. Groundbreaking in subject matter and an obvious artistic achievement, *Moonlight* tracks the early years of a man's life over three decades, from childhood, as Little, to adolescence under his real name, Chiron, to young adulthood, in which he's known as Black. Played in turn by Alex Hibbert, Ashton Sanders, and Trevante Rhodes, he goes from Charlie Brown–ish to gawky but tough, finally emerging as musclebound and stoic, a closeted gay drug dealer who has survived teenage beat-downs and juvenile detention.

The film is contemplative and rejects tragedy. A film about a shy person set in a milieu usually defined by ego and confrontation, *Moonlight* exposes violent male competition as sublimated, psychologically wounding, and pointless but survivable. The film's great strength is the way it confronts reality head-on, with cinematic beauty but no mythmaking. Palpably indebted to films by Hou Hsiao-hsien and Terrence Malick, Jenkins and his cinematographer, James Laxton, nonetheless invent a Miami photography all their own, dark blue, yellow, and pink—then orange and brown when the film moves to Atlanta.

Chiron, like Jamie in *20th Century Women*, is raised by a single mother (Naomie Harris), here addicted to crack instead of menthols.

Jamie had no male role model; Chiron at least has Juan (Mahershala Ali), a crack dealer with a poetic soul who has learned to hide that side of himself the same way Chiron learns to hide his sexuality. Ali's performance in the "Little" section of the film seems effortless, yet it's so commanding it almost overwhelms the movie. When Juan disappears, something important goes with him.

The immediate, massive, and overwhelming adulation that greeted *Moonlight,* praising it just for existing, left me a little skeptical. Then I spoke with the Oscarologist. I was sitting with a publicist during the festival, chatting about the movie, when he broke in from the other end of the bench. An obese older white man with a cane, he told us he was gay and worked for a website that tracks Oscar predictions. "I'm an Oscarologist," he announced, and then he informed us that *Moonlight* was not going to win any Academy awards. "It's bad for gays, it's bad for blacks, it perpetuates stereotypes with negative role models." The publicist, a young woman, and I countered that Oscars were no measure of a film's quality. "In my business they are! In the film industry they are!" he shouted, adding that *Moonlight* "would not be influential." Right then the film leaped in my estimation. If *Moonlight* was that upsetting to this guy, it had to be a masterpiece.

Up the coast from Miami, in Kenneth Lonergan's *Manchester by the Sea,* Casey Affleck plays Lee, "a janitor in Quincy," calm and patient on the outside, who drinks too much, then gets into bar fights in places with names like Fibber McGee's. After his older brother dies, Lee reluctantly becomes his teenage nephew's official guardian. Lonergan's new film raises Masshole tragedy above the level of *fuckin' tragedy* at which it usually gets stuck. Despite the film's elaborate flashback structure, it does not get bogged down in plot. It reveals each character in his or her own time, meandering into scenes a conventional writer-director would cut. Lee and his nephew, Patrick (Lucas Hedges), spend what seems like twenty wasted minutes (theirs, not ours) looking for Lee's car after they leave a funeral home and can't remember where they parked.

The frozen landscape of *Manchester by the Sea* contrasts with the deadly fire in the scenes of Lee's days with his wife (Michelle Williams) and children. Lonergan gives him Freud's "Father, don't you see I'm burning?" dream before allowing Lee to understand he has to get it together enough to be a substitute father to his nephew. The film is deeply melancholy, broken, and painful, as disarming as *20th Century Women* but with fewer gimmicks. Like *Moonlight*, it's a New American Classic, a film bringing movie drama to a high level that quality TV will never reach.

ONE DAY DURING THE FESTIVAL I was sitting in Union Square eating my lunch and reading an email announcement on my phone about a lecture the film theorist Laurence Rickels was giving in New York. There was a photo of Rickels in the email, and when I looked up from my phone I saw a man go by who looked exactly like Rickels: bald, modish eyeglass frames, stocky, well dressed. I got up and stopped him to ask if he was Rickels. "No," he answered. "I am Gianfranco Rosi, the Italian filmmaker."

Rosi's documentary *Fire at Sea* takes place on Lampedusa, an eight-square-mile island in the Mediterranean Sea between Sicily and Tunisia that, according to the explanatory opening title, four hundred thousand migrants have passed through over the past twenty years in order to get to Europe. Fifteen thousand have died on their way, through dehydration and starvation, drowned or lost at sea.

The sea is as important as the island in this elemental film. The fishermen on Lampedusa, fishers of men, rescue migrants from inhumane conditions on crammed boats. Many of the migrants are burned from the diesel fuel that mixes with seawater in the leaky holds. The rescuers wear white hazmat suits, white face masks, and white latex gloves while they work, covering the migrants in gold metallic marathon blankets that glow in the night.

Rosi explains nothing except through images. Half the film is made up of scenes from the life of a boy on the island, Samuele, a native Lampedusan we meet as the platonic ideal of a boy, making slingshots with a friend to hunt birds. As the film progresses, Samuele weakens. He is diagnosed with a lazy eye and has to learn to see all over again and how to row a boat with his eye patch on. He begins to have anxiety attacks. Rosi does not draw a direct line between Samuele and the migrant crisis. The film ends with Samuele alone, making gun-shooting motions with his hands and mouthing bang-bang noises on a dock at twilight.

A crap *Koyaanisqatsi* befitting our time, Eduardo Williams's *The Human Surge*, an experimental documentary from Argentina that takes place there, in Mozambique, and in the Philippines, follows disparate young workers, singly and in groups, in their downtime or engaged in the casual labor of sex work on the Internet, in supermarket checkout lines or stocking warehouses. As with *Fire at Sea*, there is no narration in *The Human Surge*, no voice-over, no explanatory titles. Filmed, I think, with an iPhone, in floating-eyeball style, it follows ordinary people on long treks down flooded streets, into bedrooms, through cane fields, and swimming in quarries. The film all of a sudden looks better when it gets to the Philippines, as if Williams upgraded to a newer iPhone at the Manila airport.

I could not discern a reason *The Human Surge* ended one sequence and began another, but I'm confident there is one. As two men trekked through a field in Mozambique, I left the theater for a minute and came back to close-ups of ants on the screen, a sequence that went on and on and could have been even longer. The film ends in a computer factory, where workers obey the command of a robot voice repeating "OK . . . OK . . . OK" as they complete their tasks. This is post-Costa cinema, slow but chopped to average feature length, puzzling, engrossing, and alienating.

SIERANEVADA BEGINS WITH an argument about a Disney princess costume. A neurologist named Lary (Mimi Brănescu) and his wife (Cătălina Moga) snipe at each other while looking for a parking space. Cristi Puiu, the film's director, uses this discussion of blockbuster entertainment to move the film into a single apartment in Bucharest, where *Sieranevada*, despite its mountain-vista title, will spend the better part of three hours. Lary's family gathers for a memorial service for his father, awaiting a priest as they argue about 9/11 conspiracy theories, life under the communists in the old days, and the adulterous behavior of various relatives. As each new quarrel swirls around another, a growing sense of disorder and patriarchal breakdown overtakes the ritual they are there to perform. Lary's niece brings a drunk friend to the service, who spends the rest of the film puking and half-conscious while the family argues about whether she's a prostitute and drug addict or just a drug addict. When Lary needs fresh air, he and his wife escape back into the street, where more arguing about parking ensues, the New Romanian Cinema's version of breaking the tension.

Romanian cinema has the special power of finding the murkiest, most desultory way to film petty squabbles and bureaucratic nightmares, to find the worst angles for actors without distorting them and making them inhuman. All the doctor (Adrian Titieni) in Cristian Mungiu's *Graduation* wants to do is make sure his daughter passes her exams so she can accept a scholarship to college in London. After she's attacked in the street, she struggles to concentrate on her schoolwork, so the doctor pulls some strings to make sure she'll pass. His one corrupt act sets in motion a downward spiral in his life. "All that counts," Romeo tells his daughter, "is getting to a normal world." *Graduation* shambles through the same European night as the Dardennes' *Unknown Girl*, shoved along to the sound of barking dogs, breaking glass, and the classical music Romeo listens to in his car. When characters in European films listen to classical music while driving, it's always a bad sign.

The first movie screened for the press before the festival began was *I, Daniel Blake*, Ken Loach's nonmurky exposé of bureaucracy in England. Daniel (Dave Johns), a widowed carpenter recovering from a heart attack in Newcastle, negotiates health-care and unemployment systems while trying to help a jobless new neighbor (Hayley Squires) and her two children, relocated to his town by social services. The film is didactic and focused, placing its most harrowing scene, at a food bank, within a larger context of destructive policies designed by the British government to make life impossible for the poor by robbing them of their dignity one step at a time. There is something thrilling about Loach's dedication to exposing the horror and mind-numbing pointlessness of bureaucracy with as little drama as possible. Audiences are supposedly always looking for something relatable. Loach has identified the last universal subject: filling out forms online. The anger the film generates shuts off delight in entertainment, an exemplary side effect of the film's agenda.

THE EXPECTATION THAT the cinema will delight us with grand adventure while retaining a touch of the metaphysical hobbled *The Lost City of Z*, an epic of Amazonian exploration James Gray adapted from David Grann's book. Gray's admirable sensitivity to the exploitative aspects of colonialist enterprise has produced the first Amazonian epic of British imperialism in which cannibals and piranhas are too respected to be terrifying. A loss of belief defines this film, and in the end, this journey to a destination that probably doesn't exist becomes all plot. The film jumps from one place to the next and one thing happens after another, necessitating supertitles reading "The Atlantic Ocean" so we know where we are.

Gray is also admirably committed to classical storytelling, and *The Lost City of Z* feels out of place among all the festival movies that go out of their way to subvert plot. Charlie Hunnam's Colonel Fawcett is hard to remember after the film, a ghost man as lost in the jungle as he is at home in England. Robert Pattinson's movie-star-erasure of a performance as his sidekick is more interesting, and called to mind Arthur Hunnicutt's performance in Hawks's *The Big Sky* (1952), a better movie about river exploration than this one, made in a less enlightened time.

The Lost City of Z closed the festival and was the last film screened for critics. The press conference after the screening, with Gray and much of his cast, was entertaining. Gray, a supremely witty man, narrated the difficulties a Jewish guy from Brooklyn faces shooting on location in the Amazon. As he put it, he was genetically designed to be an accountant in a Polish shtetl in winter, not somebody yelling "Action!" in a humid South American jungle during crocodile season. I wish some of his verve had been present in his film. Going into the jungle to find truth and beauty is harder than doing it at an uptown film festival, but in both cases you've got to capture that elusive joie de vivre and bring it back alive.

December 2016

KIAROSTAMI AND *THE PURGE*

ON INDEPENDENCE DAY MY GIRLFRIEND AND I FELT LIKE DOING SOMETHING patriotic, so we went to see an afternoon show of *The Purge: Election Year* at the cineplex-ziggurat in downtown Brooklyn. We got there early, and while we were talking and trying to ignore the promotional videos about TV shows, I gave in to the impulse to check Twitter. The first thing I saw was that Abbas Kiarostami, the great Iranian filmmaker, had died in Paris.

I didn't know Kiarostami was fighting cancer. The unexpected feeling of loss that seized me was worsened by a jolt of self-disgust at being in that movie theater at all, for sitting there waiting for *The Purge: Election Year* to start, for presuming that somehow we would be entertained by it. There could not be a film further removed from a Kiarostami film, and all of a sudden *The Purge: Election Year* became a stand-in for America's violent, cynical, stupid cinema—the exact opposite of everything Kiarostami stood for and everything he achieved over four and a half decades of filmmaking in Iran and elsewhere.

There is a peculiar sense of dread one feels before a horror movie starts, a feeling that you are about to see something you shouldn't. The paradox of horror movies is that this feeling of dread is also a form of hope. The movie might, even against your will, expose you to something you have never seen before, something that could shake you up so much it changes you in a fundamental way. But after seeing the news of Kiarostami's death, I was seized with a different kind of dread.

All of a sudden I became aware, or I remembered, that there is a better world somewhere else, that being in this one, where we were waiting for *The Purge: Election Year* to shock us, was a waste of the time allotted to me in this life and that, if I were going to see a movie, what time I have would be better spent with a form of cinema that acknowledges something other than the bloodshed and mayhem into which the world has fallen. The image of Homayoun Ershadi as the suicidal man in Kiarostami's *Taste of Cherry* came to me. It shook me awake. I didn't know what I was doing there. I wanted out. I wanted to live.

The lights went down and trailers unspooled for a bunch of other movies, each one as dumb as the next, and then *The Purge: Election Year* began, and we sat there and watched it. Part of the time, at least, I saw it through the lens of Kiarostami, as if I were wearing glasses that made the film uglier. The rest of the time I just gave myself over to the movie's sardonic portrayal of an out-of-control America led by murderous right-wing kooks, where foreign tourists put on Abraham Lincoln masks and kill the poor for fun.

KIAROSTAMI DID NOT LEAVE Iran after the revolution in 1979. He stayed and continued to work under Khomeini and the mullahs, which meant accepting conditions more restrictive than those that had been imposed by the shah. Unlike in the US, where filmmakers are free to show pretty much anything—a freedom on which *The Purge: Election Year* makes bank—Iranian filmmakers could not and cannot depict many of the things that Hollywood cinema depends on. These include not just "some nudity" and the more generalized objectification of women that the MPAA does not warn us about, and not just the violence and destruction of the *Purge* films or superhero blockbusters. The open-to-interpretation, implanted-subtext criticism of our political system that even basic superhero films coyly trade in now, which is there to give people something to talk (and write) about besides all the cute pop-culture references, is not allowed in Iranian films at all.

The outpouring of grief in Iran after Kiarostami's death and his funeral there solidified his status as an official Iranian artist, though we should not overlook the fact that Kiarostami's protégé, Jafar Panahi, was arrested and jailed in 2010 for trying to make a film critical of the government, then sentenced to six years in prison. Panahi has been able to make films surreptitiously and by proxy and his sentence has been lightened to house arrest, but he is still banned from working. Around the time Panahi was arrested, Kiarostami himself abandoned filmmaking in Iran, choosing instead to make films in Italy and Japan. Before that, he had gone into self-imposed periods of filmmaking inactivity when he concentrated on photography and poetry. His success in the 1990s at film festivals around the world had brought him to international prominence, and he had already begun to travel outside Iran to work. Kiarostami made *ABC Africa* in Uganda in 2001, four years before the conservative Mahmoud Ahmadinejad came into office, eight years before the Green Revolution and the presidential election Ahmadinejad manipulated to win reelection.

Staying in Iran after the revolution and making films nowhere else for over two decades, however, meant Kiarostami was able to continue the work he had started in the 1970s, which concentrated on children, classroom life, families, domestic spaces, and the aftermath of natural disasters, all the things Iranian cinema was allowed to show. Kiarostami forged a unique style of contemporary neorealism and wed it to a new kind of consciousness of the cinema as medium. Thinking about his films while watching an American film leads to a sobering realization: all the things that Kiarostami could not show in his films became the only things Hollywood filmmakers chose to show in theirs. What he showed in his films were the things abandoned by Hollywood: conversation, friendship, understanding, compassion, and empathy.

When watching Kiarostami films, one also has a great sense of another kind of freedom not found in Hollywood movies, nor in most European art films: freedom from the creeping realization that a film we are watching was made by a cynical shit or a self-deluded megalomaniac. Kiarostami's films were not responding to the formulaic considerations Hollywood labors under in pursuit of big opening weekends, and their maker was not seeking fame or awards by making them. His loose stories, contemplative style, and the absence of certain plot points and backstory free us from this sense of manipulation even as we are patiently led to endings that are quite often emotionally shattering.

THE ENDING OF *TASTE OF CHERRY* (1997) is one of these, and what's startling about it has little to do with the film's plot. It is, rather, a memento mori that wrenches the viewer out of the film, back into life. I hesitate to ruin the ending for anyone who has never seen it; even mentioning it will do that to some extent. Kiarostami doesn't end the film in any conventional sense but does something wholly unexpected, something that in addition to leaving the protagonist's fate unresolved pulls back the curtain on cinema itself, by closing it. After the cinema there is something else, just like for the film's protagonist there can be something else after despair.

Kiarostami's last film, *Like Someone in Love* (2012), which he made in Japan, also has a shocking ending that forces one of the main characters, and the viewer, back into reality. He does this using the barest of means, in this case off-screen sound. *Like Someone in Love* came out in the US at the same time as Harmony Korine's *Spring Breakers*, and I saw them back-to-back. Kiarostami's film ends with an act of violence, but in his film, unlike Korine's, the effect is unexpected and jarring, an alarm clock going off instead of an ironic audience-pleasing celebration of its characters' emancipation through violence. *Like Someone in Love* forefronts a young woman's struggle with male domination. As with the starlets in *Spring Breakers*, the young woman here (Rin Takanashi) is involved with a pimp, but Kiarostami does not exploit her situation for cheap thrills. He strands her, along with an elderly professor (Tadashi Okuno) who stands in for a generation that thought itself safe from the violence of contemporary life.

Kiarostami's films of the 2000s moved away from male protagonists and began to concentrate of the plight of women. *Ten* (2002) began this period. In that film, Kiarostami gave up a certain amount of directorial control by setting up a camera in a car and focusing on the woman driving it (Mania Akbari). In *Shirin* (2008), we watch the faces of 114 actresses in a darkened theater, one at a time, as they watch a film we do not see. The film they're watching is a mythic melodrama of female sacrifice that ends in murder and suicide, which we only hear off-screen, the last death over the film's credits. *Shirin* inevitably calls to mind Anna Karina in Godard's *Vivre sa vie* (1962) crying as she watches *The Passion of Joan of Arc* by herself in a movie theater. But Godard includes what she is seeing—Renée Falconetti as Joan in Dreyer's film—while Kiarostami only provides us the sound track. (Godard chose a silent film.)

Watching a movie in a movie theater is an act of collective loneliness. *Shirin* makes that loneliness cathartic, but by not showing the film within the film, Kiarostami avoids transforming it into entertainment. The power of our individual response to entertainment is itself the film's subject. The film is unfinished and in a sense does not really exist without people to experience it. The audience makes the film with the filmmaker, a central tenet of Kiarostami's filmmaking, which he often alluded to in interviews.

Hossain Sabzian, the man in *Close-Up* (1990) who wanted to be Mohsen Makhmalbaf, who wanted to be director of someone else's movies, to claim and therefore complete them for himself, stands in for all of us as moviegoers. Kiarostami said he was seized by the need to make *Close-Up* the moment he read about Sabzian in the newspaper. Sabzian's story could be the stuff of American reality television, where the shame and humiliation of real people is exploited for as long as it takes to make a half hour of cheap TV. Sabzian's plight seems all the more pathetic because he chose to impersonate a film director rather than an actor. Kiarostami made him into the star of his own film, and Sabzian's moment of reconciliation with Makhmalbaf and their motorcycle ride together as the film ends are devastating in the way they momentarily erase the difference between the two men, the way they forgive and accept Sabzian as someone who wanted a better life. It is poignant because we understand that Sabzian, as soon as the ride ends, will go back to the life he wanted to escape.

SHAME AND HUMILIATION lead to violence in *Crimson Gold* (2002), which Kiarostami wrote for Panahi to direct. Sabzian could have ended up like the hapless, exploited pizza-delivery man in this film, and it is significant that Kiarostami did not direct it himself. His work avoided depicting violence even within the confines of what was allowed in Iranian cinema at that time. Hollywood filmmakers do not shy away from depicting violence on our screens. This violence has become a series of self-fulfilling prophecies that are immediate and clearly understood, in the way that *The Purge: Election Year* instantly predicted the Republican National Convention.

There's an interview with Kiarostami on YouTube in which he talks about Quentin Tarantino, whom he met in 1995 when both directors were on a film festival jury. Kiarostami says that while Tarantino's films are not for him, he likes Tarantino as a person and as a cinephile. He thinks for a second and then comes up with a reason why Tarantino's films are valuable. "Since violence will never leave the American film," he says, "an important thing Tarantino has done is to find a way to at least make fun of violence, and that brings down the tension in violence."

It's interesting that while both filmmakers came to prominence in the US around the same time, there was a great deal of critical resistance to Kiarostami here, while *Reservoir Dogs* and *Pulp Fiction* were almost universally celebrated. During this period of collective awe, Kiarostami's films were derided as slow, pointless, and incomprehensible. A film critic for a New York weekly was fired for writing too much about Kiarostami (and Hou Hsiao-hsien), and a kind of philistinism crept into American movie reviewing that was only alleviated as the internet began to supplant print publications as a source for writing about films.

Jonathan Rosenbaum fought against this as it was happening, and wrote about how Miramax, under Harvey Weinstein, bought Kiarostami's *Through the Olive Trees* (1994), then refused to release it in theaters or on home video. Lack of box office potential goes hand in hand with critical disregard. The 1990s were a period when filmmakers like Kiarostami and Hou, who were already regarded as important artists, were ignored or marginalized while, at the same time, intellectuals began to write about the death of cinema. In the 1960s, Hollywood cinema was much less vibrant than it was in the 1990s, but instead of declaring cinema dead, American critics celebrated filmmakers as "difficult" as Antonioni and Bergman. Looking back, willfully ignoring filmmakers from Iran and Taiwan should be called what it is: racism masquerading as populism.

The Italian filmmaker (and movie theater owner) Nanni Moretti made a short film in 1996 called *Opening Day of "Close-Up"* in which he plays himself fretting over the box office receipts for Kiarostami's film as it competes in Rome against *The Lion King* and *The Nightmare Before Christmas*. The regime of the animated American blockbuster had already begun, marginalizing Kiarostami and others without the critical support Fellini and Godard had had in the early 1960s.

MANY OF KIAROSTAMI'S FILMS are hard to find now, especially the early ones from the 1970s and '80s. Where are they? On YouTube, some of them, some without subtitles in English. This future (and present) of watching films on YouTube delivers hard-to-find films in an instant, but it is also lonely and isolating. *Shirin* depends for its effect on taking place in a movie theater, and today's Anna Karinas most often cry alone at home. Still, Kiarostami is said to be influential. (Every filmmaker who made films before 2010 is now described as influential.) More than ever films of all types position themselves between documentary and fiction, like his. Iranian filmmakers including Panahi continue to make films under adverse conditions, but Kiarostami seems like a marker in filmmaking, poised between cinema and video, central to a place that will know him no more.

Chris Fujiwara, writing in the late '90s, described *Through the Olive Trees* as "at once so basic in its technique and its view of the world and so sophisticated in what it does—as if one found out that the inventor of the alphabet wrote Plato's dialogues." In 1994, Harvey Weinstein said no to that, and now Kiarostami's films threaten to become as remote as Plato, shadows of their former selves on computer screens at home. *Where Is the Friend's Home?* and *The Wind Will Carry Us* are basic Kiarostami titles that describe his films in general, and human experience in general, and more specifically the experiences of the 1990s generation who discovered his films in theaters.

Kiarostami had a quality of immortality, even divorced from Iran. Peter Hutton and Michael Cimino also died in July, two other "difficult" filmmakers who, like Kiarostami, started out as painters. Along with all the violence in the US, unique, necessary artists keep dying these days—nobody lives forever. Alan Vega of the band Suicide died the other day, too. He also started out as a painter. "I always said I was never gonna be an entertainer," he explained about his career. "Suicide was never supposed to be entertainment." As these artists disappear, we are left with nothing but entertainment. More and more we consume it by ourselves at home. The day after Kiarostami died I heard Mohsen Makhmalbaf talking about him on the BBC. "He could show you how friendship could take you out of loneliness," he said.

August 2016

THIS QUIET PLACE TODAY

Love & Friendship

Whit Stillman's movies are like porn films with the sex scenes cut out. In *Love & Friendship*, adapted from an early Jane Austen novel not published in her lifetime, he brings his habitual fawning over the upper classes to Georgian England, where he finds the same talky couplings and uncouplings he located among privileged East Coasters in his earlier films. As in a silent movie, text in the form of letters, poems, and introductions to the dramatis personae clutters the screen in a roller-coaster ride of exposition. The film glides by in under an hour and a half not counting the credits, an ideal length for movies.

The film is meticulous and quiet, giving each actor a moment to play against the shining perfection of Kate Beckinsale's scheming Lady Susan, the title character of Austen's novel. Beckinsale's performance is as great as any lead's in any period piece ever made, worthy of Bette Davis in a 1930s Warner Bros. costume drama, but sexier and more subtle. The final arrangement she maneuvers, meant to show her savvy and independence, feels as unsatisfying as the social constraints of the era, and mirrors the unique contemporary restraint Stillman brings to what he shows and doesn't show in his films. The overall effect is a tease, ultra-tasteful, promising something we never get to see because it's resolved offscreen. Bargains like Lady Susan's aren't unheard of today, and Stillman's facility in coming to terms with them is rare in the movies, if nowhere else.

Everybody Wants Some!!

A Devo album in a crate full of records in the backseat of a car announces that we are in the past in Richard Linklater's follow-up to *Boyhood* (2014). *Everybody Wants Some!!* starts exactly where *Boyhood* ended, with a young man (Blake Jenner) on his way to college in Texas. The difference is that now it's 1980 instead of the present, and the young man is an athlete instead of sensitive. He's plunged into a house inhabited by his college baseball team, and we meet the boisterous occupants one by one before they head out to a roller disco. The film briefly calls to mind *Roll Bounce* (2005), which was set around the same time, like it's going to be a multiracial coming-of-age story about meeting girls. Then it settles into all-male camaraderie, 99 percent white, in which Jake and his teammates indulge in bouts of drinking, competitive and painful but meaningless games, and mild locker-room hazing—a list from an MPAA ratings warning.

Everybody Wants Some!! explores a buffet of lifestyle options—country music, punk, pot-haze philosophizing—until Jake meets Beverly (Zoey Deutch), a cute theater student who further expands his world. Like Stillman, an auteur who emerged around the same time he did, Linklater is deft with actors and keeps things light. Their two films could exchange titles, and both are about people to whom nothing bad happens or ever will happen. Set on green fields in rules-based milieus, these are idylls of the past in which coupledom is the goal. Both have a slight feel that the world is fragile and about to change: the American Revolution and Ronald Reagan loom, but ever so lightly, somewhere out of sight.

Green Room

Jeremy Saulnier's *Green Room* is set in a present that could just as well be 1980. It's hard to tell whether the film is nostalgic for the original hardcore punk moment or just eager to get rid of cell phones so the nonsupernatural horror-thriller can get under way. Here, another bunch of white kids pursue life in a band instead of college, fatally taking a gig at a venue in the Oregon woods that turns out to be a haven for Nazi punks and white supremacists. Alia Shawkat, bassist in the Ain't Rights, wears a Dead Kennedys T-shirt throughout, and her band plays the Dead Kennedys' "Nazi Punks Fuck Off" (without a black drummer like the Dead Kennedys) to rile up the hostile white-laced crowd. This genre exercise in locked-room horror is masterful and swift, proving Saulnier could direct an episode of *The Walking Dead* with no problem. His script flirts with coupledom and then rejects it, as a nihilist punk horror movie should.

Imogen Poots is excellent as a racist local with a Chelsea haircut who finds herself on the wrong side of the town's white-supremacist criminal gang. Patrick Stewart (Professor Xavier and Jean-Luc Picard himself) plays the leader of the gang in a career-stretching role. He's fine, but dozens of other threatening middle-aged white men could have played it just as well.

British actors like Poots and Stewart have perfected their ability to play not just Americans but American racists. Formerly assigned parts as villainous Romans and Nazis, British actors now populate American films as the worst America has to offer, and sometimes as exemplars of the white working class. What American demons are being exorcised by this kind of casting, and what does it say about how Hollywood views the white underclass that it thinks RADA-trained actors are best at playing them? At the same time, British actors also portray our greatest heroes, from Abraham Lincoln to Superman. All these types and historical figures inhabit a Shakespearean Disneyland in which America is an idea for export, best brought to cinematic life by trained specialists in a brand of good-versus-evil drama set in fictionalized hinterlands or the glorious past. This kind of Anglophiliac casting, glorifying the superiority of the British actor, could instruct actual American xenophobes on how foreigners are taking our jobs. What it does instead is elevate the xenophobes to the level of Captain Picard and Professor X. How flattering, to be played by an Englishman!

The Lobster

Dirty Pretty Things, Never Let Me Go, Under the Skin, and now *The Lobster*—British art-house cinema is obsessed with organ harvesting. Forcing people into strange rooms to rob them of their organs or, in the case of *The Lobster,* to recalibrate their organs and thereby change them into animals . . . I don't think this is something preying on the minds of Americans. Our worries are more immediate. We're more likely to be mowed down by an assault rifle in public than we are to have our organs harvested for use by the upper class or space aliens.

Yorgos Lanthimos's new film is vague and complicated, putting its international all-star cast in situations that portend great metaphoric meaning but end up comparing nosebleeds (false love) with blindness (real love if you're willing to go there). Rachel Weisz plays the blinded woman and narrates the film in caustic tones that convey more emotion than the tamped-down, clipped performances of the other actors. I would gladly listen to Weisz read the audiobook of a Muriel Spark novel, and maybe this film would have worked better as George Saunders–style literary fiction. Instead, *The Lobster* is a Jim Carrey movie stripped of comedy, with Colin Farrell in the Carrey role, an awkward everyman thrust into a sci-fi world resembling our own.

Léa Seydoux plays the heartless leader of the partisans, loners who refuse to be in romantic couples in a society that enforces marriage by law. Her character is the most interesting because her severity and cruel punishments are unexplained. She has loving parents who play Greek music for her when she takes time out from rebellion to visit them, but she insists that her followers listen only to electronic music, which, according to her sketchy ideology, is music for loners. At one point, she brings Farrell's character deeper into the woods to show him an empty grave. "Can you imagine why I brought you to this quiet place today?" she asks. I wondered, too. Maybe to show us the grave of European art cinema?

Chevalier

Athina Rachel Tsangari, who reenergized contemporary Greek cinema with Lanthimos, succeeds in *Chevalier* by concentrating on a group of six men. The title refers to a signet ring over which they compete in an odd contest to determine which of them is "the best in general." Yachting in the Aegean, they find their daily activities don't satisfy them. Spearfishing for sea bream, hunting for octopus, windsurfing, buzzing in circles on a Jet Ski—*Chevalier* presents these as time killers for well-off men with nothing to do. With no adversaries besides fish and mollusks and no women around, they turn to pointless competition and misguided hero worship. Over a tense dinner one night they begin their tournament, which measures everything from their sleep posture to how soon their wives announce they love them during private phone calls, which they play for one another on speakerphone.

The most forlorn of the six (Makis Papadimitriou), a chubby Rubik's Cube expert who is there because he's someone's brother, is the film's Zach Galifianakis. Like *The Lobster*, *Chevalier* sometimes feels like an American comedy minus the comedy. This is what the *Hangover* crew would do on a yacht if they were wealthier and European. At the end, when they slink home, each of the men is humiliated but essentially unchanged, same as in a *Hangover* movie. The trouble begins when the chef and steward, now alone on the yacht, begin to play the game themselves. Tsangari adds politics where Lanthimos subtracts it.

Wrong Move

The second film in Wim Wenders's road-movie trilogy, released in West Germany in 1975, never played in first run in the US until it opened in theaters in advance of the Criterion Collection's DVD release this year. Peter Handke wrote the screenplay, a 1970s update of Goethe's second novel, *Wilhelm Meister's Apprenticeship*, which was published the same decade Jane Austen wrote *Lady Susan*. The film's protagonist (Rüdiger Vogler, who's in all three road films) narrates the film in Handke-speak: *I want to be a writer, but is that possible when you don't like people? . . . I wanted to sleep with her, but maybe it was just an urge to get a grip on things.*

Vogler's Wilhelm starts the film by punching through window glass and then embarks on a journey across the Federal Republic, picking up stray travelers along the way: an old man (Hans Christian Blech) and a girl (Nastassja Kinski), an actress (Hanna Schygulla), and a poet (Peter Kern). The cast and Robby Müller's color cinematography give the film a strange feeling that sets it apart from Wenders's other road movies, which are in black and white and feature actors more closely associated with Wenders, not Fassbinder.

The Germany of *Wrong Move* looks like the present more than today's films set in the 1970s feel like the '70s. It's not just the fashions but the attitudes—the sense of aimlessness and the search for meaning in a fallen world—that resemble our time. Wenders and Handke repudiate Goethe's Romanticism, yet the film feels brighter and clearer than films today, like the air in the mountains where Wilhelm ends up.

Cinematic tropes of the 1970s date from films like this. Children then were casually exposed to things they were supposed to be too young to be around, offered drinks, sexualized, bereft of the special teen culture that would provide the fodder for blockbuster entertainment for the next forty years. Kinski, here a pre–*Wings of Desire* acrobat and 13 at the time, appears nude, dangling herself before Wilhelm as an alternative to a relationship with the adult Schygulla. In overalls and a rainbow sweater, she takes forever to eat an apple, like in a Warhol film. Later the group, exhausted and without a plan, lounges in front of a TV set watching a black-and-white movie, Straub and Huillet's *The Chronicle of Anna Magdalena Bach* (1968)—a tableau of the kind of anomie ignored by jumpy re-creations of this period.

The Thoughts That Once We Had

Thom Andersen, the main proponent of the film-critical essay film as it stands today, meets Gilles Deleuze in *The Thoughts That Once We Had,* which takes its name from a line in the Christina Rossetti poem "Remember," which appeared in Robert Aldrich's late noir, *Kiss Me Deadly* (1955), still the best use of a poem in American cinema.

Andersen's film is a collection of cinephilia's greatest hits, from Miriam Cooper's face in *Intolerance* (1916) up to and including Debra Paget's snake dance from Fritz Lang's *The Indian Tomb* (1959) and scenes from the high points of Timothy Carey's unhinged career as a weirdo heavy. Andersen's interest in the hard-boiled and his terse use of quotations and images-as-quotations allies his film with late David Markson novels. In *The Thoughts That Once We Had,* Andersen uses intertitles instead of narration, mixing his cinephilia semi-mondo style with historical atrocity footage from the 20th century. The film becomes an essay on forgetting as much as a film about Deleuze's breakdown of the cinema into types of images. For Andersen and Deleuze, the cinema is "the space where thought can occur." "To those who have nothing must be restored the cinema," the film concludes.

These hopeful descriptions reminded me of the time the ticket seller at the Elinor Bunin Munroe Film Center told me the theater had "two projection-based spaces," and that the film I was seeing was showing in the one to the right. I wasn't sure if he was joking or what, but I don't believe that is the kind of space Andersen had in mind. This phrase haunted me during the film I watched there, damaging it. I want the cinema to remain "the space where thought can occur," but I'm not sure it can in "projection-based spaces" at Lincoln Center, where thought is assailed by jargon on the way in.

Cemetery of Splendor

Apichatpong Weerasethakul, aware that his films are accused of putting audiences to sleep, inscribes the condition of hypersomnia into *Cemetery of Splendor*. A group of soldiers in a makeshift village hospital, permanently asleep, are treated using colored fluorescent light tubes, as if they live in a Dan Flavin installation. By day, nurses and a kind nurse's aide (Jenjira Pongpas, a Weerasethakul regular who plays a version of herself) tend to them, watching them twitch and dream. Following Jen on her rounds and in her daily life induces a kind of parasomnia in the viewer of this Thai political allegory, in which the past seeps through into daily life even as it is suppressed by authority. Weerasethakul erases the line between dream and reality using only the barest of means. This essential film followed me around for weeks after I saw it. On the subject of another kind of dream, late in the movie Jen speaks with a friend about how she wishes she could have married a European instead of an American. "Americans are too poor," she says. "Europeans are living the American Dream." It takes a filmmaker in Thailand to admit this simple fact, which should be an obvious truth.

Money Monster

Too beholden to the generic conventions of the contemporary action thriller and too in love with television to compete as a film with its nearest corollary, Scorsese's *The King of Comedy* (1983), Jodie Foster's *Money Monster* raises economic issues and the failure of the American Dream in various incisive and entertaining ways, only to abandon them by the end. Maybe the ending is supposed to be ironic: George Clooney's cable-TV news host and his director, Julia Roberts, hug over takeout Chinese while the film's stand-in for the working class, the gunman who had taken them hostage (Jack O'Connell), lies dead in a lobby on Wall Street. Superficiality and blasé acceptance triumph here—they just needed a trial by fire and a dose of magical internet research ("real journalism") to feel better about themselves.

Dominic West and his uncanny hair play the villain, a greedy hedge fund manager who gets his comeuppance via a GIF over which Clooney and Roberts chuckle tastefully. O'Connell and West, both Englishmen, once again show how sophisticated villainy and working-class confusion are imagined as conditions best portrayed by Brits. The exalted plain Americanness of Clooney and Roberts, stars we used to be able to identify with, playing characters with high-salary jobs we'd like to have, is presented as thoroughly relatable in this film about economic disaster made by a director and two stars who collectively have been rich and famous for close to a hundred years.

Maggie's Plan

Not being part of a couple is no more an option in *Maggie's Plan* than in *The Lobster*. This is a screwball comedy of remarriage, and therefore of stasis, but here stasis extends to class issues, not just romance. Greta Gerwig, still unassailable as Our Carole Lombard, stars as Maggie, a young woman who works at the New School in an administrative job. She falls for Ethan Hawke, a writer and theorist teaching there as an adjunct. He's unhappily married to Julianne Moore, a Danish intellectual with tenure at Columbia who enchantingly can't pronounce her *R*s.

The film is beautifully written and directed by Rebecca Miller, beautifully acted by its all-star cast, and beautifully scored. It is full of little surprises that add to its sense of perfection. Kathleen Hanna, for instance, pops up as a Québécoise folkie doing Springsteen. Yet for all its delightfulness, watching it I began to wonder how Miller really feels about the Brooklyn lives she has created for this movie. The stark difference in Gerwig's and Hawke's quality of life after he leaves Moore is telling. They live in some storefront next to the BQE while Moore continues her life of luxury in a huge discount Columbia apartment.

Thus the film's ending seems prescribed, and it strikes me that for Miller this ending is fated because of *sic vivitur* more than true love. The formerly lower-middle-class dude Hawke returns to his wealthy first wife; Gerwig happily accepts the artisanal pickle maker she knew in college who reenters in the last scene at the last minute, and whom she should have been with all along. He's played by Travis Fimmel, an Australian actor doing an American accent who's as close to being British as a Williamsburg pickle maker is to working class.

The dirty secret in *Maggie's Plan* is that in fixing her predicament (her pickle), Gerwig has managed to get stand-ins for her parents back together after fucking her father. An earlier scene in which she and Hawke discuss their childhoods makes this pretty clear, but it never occurs to any of the film's characters. The implicit quality of this aspect of the plot mirrors the uncommented-on class distinctions in the characters' lives. Both are better left unmentioned.

High-Rise

In pounding home its theme of class conflict in a dystopian condo building, this garbage-strewn, rotten film betrays J. G. Ballard's 1975 novel to the max. While its theme couldn't be more timely, *High-Rise*'s incompetent mise-en-scène reduces everything to trash. In its ugly excess, it succumbs, by accident, to Hal Foster's anti-aesthetic: it can't be enjoyed. Artistically, the film is the waste product of income inequality, masquerading as commentary. Its desire to make the 1970s look like vomit is relentless.

High-Rise ends with an audio clip of a Margaret Thatcher speech and The Fall song “Industrial Estate”—an obvious choice because of the title, but the song is about a workplace, not a residence (not sure why the Swell Maps’ “Vertical Slum” wasn’t picked instead). *High-Rise* also features ABBA’s 1975 hit song “S.O.S.” twice, once played by classical musicians at a party where the guests are dressed as French aristocrats, then later in an overwrought new version by Portishead in a music-video-style montage that should have been cut from the film. “S.O.S.” came out the same year as Ballard’s novel, but ABBA’s later hit “On and On and On” would have been better for this film, since the title describes this movie perfectly and the song starts like this:

> I was at a party and this fella said to me,
> “Something bad is happening, I’m sure you do agree.
> People care for nothing, no respect for human rights.
> Evil times are coming, we are in for darker nights.”
> I said, “Who are you to talk about impending doom?”
> He got kinda wary as he looked around the room.

The Nice Guys

This buddy comedy takes place in the same Hollywood-movie 1970s we’ve seen a hundred times since *Boogie Nights*, now with added smog. Ryan Gosling and Russell Crowe play low-life detectives as if they might end up like the soldiers in *Cemetery of Splendor*. Gosling even falls asleep at the wheel at one point, starting an *is it a dream?* sequence. In another strange coincidence, the film begins like Wenders’s *Wrong Move*, with Gosling cutting himself when he punches through a window. And like a Stillman film, the whole thing is, as Gosling announces halfway through, “a porno where the point is the plot.” *The Nice Guys* is worthless, not that funny, far more enjoyable than *High-Rise*, and does nothing at all to justify its existence—a traditional saving grace of the movies. The writer and director of *High-Rise* forgot to make something good, even pretty good, in favor of making something important. Their failure is admirable in this one sense: they didn't let mastery of conventional cinematic form get in the way of shouty commentary about contemporary class relations.

As in *High-Rise,* children in *The Nice Guys* are exposed to swearing, smoking, drinking, drunk driving, drugs, pornography, orgies, violence, crime, and ugly sofas. Only here we see how the exploited runaway teen girl of the '70s has evolved. Angourie Rice, as Gosling's wised-up tween daughter (a demographic category that did not exist then), is the film's voice of reason, exposed to as much vice as any adolescent in a real '70s movie, and now driving the car for her drunk dad instead of the other way around, demonstrating who's really in charge in the audience today.

September 2016

WE'RE NOT UGLY PEOPLE

The Martian

A children's movie about how great science is, *The Martian* has a pragmatic message for budding astronauts: you solve one problem, then another, and see if you survive. The film's obsession with years-long plans imparts a Soviet feel to the space program depicted, but its sunny optimism keeps the movie all-American. Not once do we believe *The Martian* will end with a shot of Matt Damon's skeleton half-buried in sand. Maybe the film is so bright because the days are thirty-nine minutes longer on Mars than on Earth, the same thirty-nine minutes that should have been cut from this Friday-less *Robinson Crusoe*. Kristen Wiig, however, is on hand to show that girls aren't into *The Lord of the Rings*.

Ridley Scott's backlot Mars offers a parable for New Yorkers considering the move to LA. Once you relocate, you're stranded, and the chances of getting home are remote. Yes, you'll have a vegetable garden you can sit near and watch the beautiful sunsets, but you'll be alone, 50 million miles from your loved ones. You'll conduct your social life via text and Skype, make trips to the desert in your electric car. You'll continue to shave every day on the off-chance you get a meeting.

Room

The movies can put a positive spin on anything. Seeing the world anew, or for the first time, becomes an allegory of motherhood and childhood in *Room*, which puts its protagonist (Brie Larson) in a situation not unlike Matt Damon's in *The Martian*, but earthbound, and worse. If *The Martian* is a friendly version of dark Ridley Scott sci-fi, *Room* domesticates repugnant horror with spiritual uplift. Held hostage in a shed with the 5-year-old she's had with her rapist captor, "Ma" becomes a stand-in for every young mother isolated by child care, chained by domestic servitude, and abused at night by a man who's out all day in a world she may never see again. This dismal parody of heterosexual coupling reinforces the idea that it's time to have families in some new way.

45 Years

A tour de force of subtlety and restraint, *45 Years* is the perfect movie to see alone if you've just broken up with someone and want confirmation it was a good idea. No need to waste decades in coupledom if all it amounts to is an unnoticed gesture of frustrated defiance. The film saves that moment for its last shot, which isn't quite the indictment it's meant to be. That's because the film stacks the deck against Tom Courtenay's character, a retiree recovering from a heart attack. Courtenay's performance is a model of invisible acting, even when he's doddering or fumbling an important speech at a party, but the film belongs to Charlotte Rampling, a star presence who can command the screen just by watching the passing landscape from a boat.

The Big Short

The performances in *The Big Short* are carried by wigs, makeup, and bad suits, like in a silent comedy. Adam McKay, Will Ferrell's director, cuts away from everyone's big moments in their big scenes, almost walking away from them. Christian Bale, with a fake glass eye to go with his wig, moves the film along by himself for large chunks of it, often by air drumming, despite the large cast of Hollywood dudes giving it to hedge funders by playing them as self-deluded slickster oafs who will never be Ryan Gosling or Brad Pitt, no matter how many billions they sock away.

The explanatory cameos by Margot Robbie, Anthony Bourdain, Selena Gomez, and Richard Thaler barely work, and the Robbie one is a sarcastic wink-wink insult to the audience that almost tanks the whole movie while, at the same time, referring to *The Wolf of Wall Street*, a better film than this. Even though McKay gives the impression he is using recognizable forms of infotainment to educate us, the film doesn't do that—it's barely in the form of a movie. This disrespect is what makes *The Big Short* so satisfying. It jeers at and burlesques Wall Street for letting the crash happen, using Michael Lewis's book to show there were people who knew it was going to happen. Its slapdash quality reinforces the idea that it needed to be made.

Joy

A fairy tale of lean-in capitalism about a Cinderella without a prince, David O. Russell's *Joy* recasts the crazy family of a Capra comedy with stellar toxicity. Joy's (Jennifer Lawrence's) undermining relatives are the selfish American clan *par excellence*, claiming to know everything about Joy's business while sabotaging her future. Robert De Niro and Isabella Rossellini, playing evil-universe versions of themselves as Joy's father and stepmother, delight in their performances as fickle scoffers.

Joy is a natural inventor prone to epiphanies about household products—the film could be called *A Beautiful Mop*. Her ingenuity and tenacity save her from a life of drudgery, though by the end her victory seems hollow. The film, busy with fake TV soap operas and flashbacks, doesn't imagine another life for her, except maybe settling down with a cable-TV executive (Bradley Cooper) who lectures her and is wrong half the time. The mitigating factors in her struggle are that she can turn a profit, employ her friends, and help younger women manufacture improved lint brushes. Set in the early 1990s, *Joy* suggests these were the consolations working-class Gen Xers could hope for.

Steve Jobs

A series of epic walk-and-talks about the future retconned to be 100 percent correct because they're about our present. For example, the Amazing Steve predicts that journalism will change because of computers. (He says that in 1998, the same year Aaron Sorkin found out.) By the end, when Super Steve tells his estranged daughter he will invent the iPod for her, the movie is indistinguishable from a TV commercial. They should have given *Steve Jobs* away for free without anyone asking for it, like that U2 album. That way, people (users) might have watched it by accident.

Sicario

A nasty film about the drug war on the US-Mexico border that flirts with fascism and artiness, succumbing to the former. The film suggests that the best way for Donald Trump to persuade the Mexican government to pay for a wall would be to tell them it will keep out the CIA.

Benicio del Toro, maybe the last actor from the Robert Mitchum mold, plays an Agency-backed hit man with blasé menace. Del Toro, like Mitchum, is a strange, often indifferent actor who apparently spins a wheel of fortune to choose his roles. Once he settles on one, he's either good or bad in it depending on something no one can figure out, maybe if work starts on a Tuesday. It doesn't matter who directs him. In films by auteurs like Paul Thomas Anderson and Arnaud Desplechin he can range from OK to not good, and then in an overblown thriller like this he shows up with something to prove. In some scenes he stares at Emily Blunt like he's reminding her she is not an American and doesn't work for the FBI, she's just a movie star playing a cop.

The Danish Girl

Tom Hooper knows that eyes are important in cinema, so he has directed the actors in *The Danish Girl* to search the corners of rooms with their glances like they can't find their keys or a mouse just ran by. He makes them doll-like, ventriloquist's dummies, and when they talk to one another they converse in need-speak, as if they're explaining which line to get into at the DMV. The film begins in 1925, so Hooper has imparted a silent-movie feel to *The Danish Girl.* Everyone in this movie's Europe has been hypnotized by Dr. Caligari or tortured like Dreyer's Joan of Arc. Eddie Redmayne, as Lili, plays along, his coyness telegraphing femininity. He puts a flower between his teeth like Chaplin and seems forever on the verge of picking up two forks and sticking them into dinner rolls to make them dance. Since the film is about painters, Hooper hired Jan Vermeer to be his cinematographer.

Ex Machina

Women's captivity is the great theme of most of 2015's Oscar-nominated films, and *Ex Machina* is the most basic and manipulative of these, the tale of a hapless john sent on a bizarre mission by a pimp to see if he can free his whore. The sordidness is made oblique because the characters are a programmer, a genius CEO, and a pixie android, and it's set in a sterile underground lab. This *Taxi Driver* for nerds is heavy with the fear of superwomen empowered by data-driven emotional intelligence and synthetic physical perfection, and hence able to outflank male idiot savants. *Ex Machina* succeeds as a mindfuck stage play for three actors, Domhnall Gleeson, Oscar Isaac, and Alicia Vikander, who were in a total of about a dozen films this year, all less weird and talky than this one. The unavoidable onslaught of virtual reality and artificial intelligence will make stories like this ever more relatable to lonely techies in search of mechanical love in robot form, but not to me. There's not even room in my apartment for a vacuum cleaner.

Creed

Nothing better could have been expected from the seventh film in the Rocky franchise than this flight from Hollywood back to Philadelphia. The savvy, intelligence, and heart of director Ryan Coogler's screenplay equals his achievement in getting an assignment like this after making *Fruitvale Station* in Oakland at age 26. Boxing movies come with built-in emotional manipulation, and this one is no exception, establishing a family for Donnie (Michael B. Jordan) by bringing back a Rocky Balboa stricken with lymphoma. Sylvester Stallone will go down in movie history as the only star of his generation willing to make way for millennials and for black America like this.

Jordan's Donnie, a pro-am boxer, rejects his status as the son of Rocky's rival, Apollo Creed, and exiles himself to working-class

Philadelphia, where he cajoles Rocky into training him. When he finally puts on his father's red-white-and-blue trunks before the big fight, the moment is hokey but astute. He's forced to imitate a father who didn't raise him and who is not there to see what he's made of himself. At the movie's end, Rocky's illness is left uncured and Donnie isn't quite a champion, leaving the story ready for an eighth round. The last scene, on the steps of the Philadelphia Museum of Art, predicts the ending of *Star Wars: The Force Awakens* but undercuts its own myth.

It's clear that Coogler got cheated by the Academy of Motion Picture Arts and Sciences. Is there any doubt *Creed* was as well directed and well written as, say, *Room*? Coming a year after *Selma*'s Ava DuVernay and David Oyelowo were ignored in the Oscar nominations, ignoring Coogler was especially troubling, proof of the problem #OscarsSoWhite exposed—that the Academy consciously ignores black artists. Jada Pinkett Smith's viral video about her husband Will Smith's lack of a nomination for *Concussion* was justified, even if Janet Hubert's response video, reminding Smith that years ago he had refused to stand with other cast members of the *Fresh Prince of Bel-Air* when they wanted a raise, exposed Smith as a victim of karma. The Academy, after all, started out as a union-busting organization. He should have supported his fellow actors in contract negotiations. Yet Smith had played the Oscar game strictly according to the rules by starring in *Concussion*. It was a medical drama about a controversial subject written and directed by a conscientious filmmaker, in which Smith had to change his appearance and his accent—pure Oscar bait. If Sandra Bullock was nominated (and won) for *The Blind Side*, a sappy football drama, Smith deserved at least a nomination for a serious one.

If Will Smith, who has been loyal to Hollywood's way of doing things—loyal to a fault—can't get a nomination, what chance did Coogler have? He made a good sports drama, a big film that made money and that critics liked. The Academy told him only Stallone deserved recognition for it, the same way no one but four white screenwriters were recognized for *Straight Outta Compton*.

Straight Outta Compton

The first half generates excitement as it explores teenage life in 1980s Compton and brings the group together. Then F. Gary Gray's biopic switches gears and splits Eazy-E (Jason Mitchell), Dr. Dre (Corey Hawkins), and Ice Cube (O'Shea Jackson Jr.) into a tripartite version of a Hollywood serious-composer biopic like *Rhapsody in Blue*. When N.W.A breaks up, the film becomes morose, bogged down in cameos, recriminations, and ugly management disputes—a history of beefs—before Eazy-E's sudden illness and death from HIV/AIDS brings it to a close. Eazy-E's tragedy, treated with the gravity it deserves, is not mitigated by Dre's success as a businessman or Ice Cube's prodigiousness. Cube's dignity and conscience extend to the actor playing him, Jackson, his son in real life. Jackson the Younger is a carbon copy of his father who makes him seem even greater than the original; he's somehow more Cube than Cube. Christopher Wallace Jr. set the precedent for this by playing Biggie as a child in 2009's *Notorious*, a film that didn't get mentioned much in relation to *Straight Outta Compton*, which was treated as the first biopic to admit rap's centrality to American culture, maybe because it was from the West Coast.

The Hateful Eight

I used to be a movie-theater projectionist, and sometimes I have an anxiety dream that I'm back working in the booth. I must have been anxious about seeing *The Hateful Eight*, because the night before I saw it I had a booth dream.

In the dream, different machines are in the booth with the two regular 35mm projectors: two 16mm projectors set up next to two 70mm projectors, the gauge Tarantino used for *The Hateful Eight*. These four new projectors crowding the booth—two of them small and two huge—are old models, battered and tarnished. I ask the theater manager why they're there. He tells me the director of the movie we're showing has made sections of the film in these three gauges and the movie is to be projected that way. This director has also specified what make and model of projector each reel must be shown on, down to the year it was made.

As I begin to thread the first reel, I see that the film is old and brittle and has turned pink from age. It has many torn sprockets. I examine it more closely and see it's not a new movie at all, but a western from the early 1960s by the director Joseph M. Newman. The manager tells me to get going, but when I thread the projector I put a twist in the film, which I notice after I start the movie. I tell the manager it's going to break, and he says, "Don't worry. If it breaks we'll show an old cartoon."

There were stories in the news about projectionists flying to distant cities to work in booths for *The Hateful Eight*, valiantly making sure the 70mm roadshow screenings went off without a hitch. When I saw it in 70mm in the East Village, I was happy there weren't any promos for TV shows before it, or ads for soda, or any trailers at all—they couldn't show them with a 70mm print. If Tarantino has done anything, he's given us the experience of watching a new movie by itself, on film, without any extraneous crap beforehand to remind us that movies are part of a universe of media streaming elsewhere. Sitting in that theater watching *The Hateful Eight* put me in the hundred-year flow of people in big cities watching westerns in movie theaters, dreaming of places without skyscrapers and subways.

The Hateful Eight is a reflective film in which the Hawksian Tarantino reevaluates the unfair comments he made about John Ford when *Django* came out. Maybe in rewatching some Ford movies featuring John Wayne in preparation for casting Kurt Russell in a role based on Wayne (and on the constructed authority Wayne brought to his characters—an authority that is questioned and then eliminated in *The Hateful Eight*), Tarantino realized he has more in common with Ford than he thought. Fordian reference abounds:

Russell says "That'll be the day" like John Wayne in *The Searchers*; Tim Roth's character is named Mobray, after an actor in *My Darling Clementine* who, like Roth, plays a part in a saloon; an explanatory flashback subverts the narrative *Liberty Valance*–style. The film's letter from Abraham Lincoln, Ford's touchstone in American history, proves to be false and dangerous, but a beautiful story, held till the end.

Jennifer Jason Leigh spits on that letter. She is the film's destroyer, a poisoner who exists to upend all the stories men tell one another to justify their violence. A Kali figure of the cinema, Leigh's Daisy Domergue, with matted hair and blood in her eyes, fights her captivity with a noose around her neck and the severed arm of Russell's bounty hunter—the arm of the law—dangling from her chains.

I saw *The Hateful Eight* while the occupation of the Malheur National Wildlife Refuge was happening in Oregon. *Malheur*, close to *hateful* in French, was a western, too, with a plot like Tarantino's. Holed up in the middle of nowhere in winter, a group of armed men telling one another bedtime stories about the Constitution threatened to make a bloody mess. Outside, the nation tore itself apart because a large segment of the population refused to give up old myths. *The Hateful Eight* is Tarantino's most timely film.

The Revenant

Swinging hard for the visionary and missing, Alejandro González Iñárritu's *Revenant* combines *Andrei Rublev* with *Apocalypse Now* and *Saving Private Ryan*, unfurling winter panoramas in natural light and adding CGI animals. The heart of the film, the section in which Glass (Leonardo DiCaprio) meets Hikuc (Arthur Redcloud) after the buffalo stampede, rises above Iñárritu's gory conception for a moment, before ending in a hanging and a rape, because if we forget this film's theme for a second we will be snapped back into it as punishment for daydreaming. The rest is a slog, *Klondike Kat* crossed with a Matthew Barney film, dominated by Tom Hardy's distracting-entertaining Appalachian accent. One thing is certain: Iñárritu has finally solved the problem of how to film a realistic bear fight. The next cinematic problem he should tackle is screenwriting.

Mad Max: Fury Road

Tinkertoys in a landscape that's like a painting by Yves Tanguy, while in the foreground the Ed Roth car from the cover of the Birthday Party's *Junk Yard* album drives by at 150 miles an hour. The most cartoonish film in a year of films like Warner Bros. cartoons is also one of the best. How? *Mad Max: Fury Road* is that one-in-a-thousand reboot that will greenlight even more reboots, none of which will justify its existence like this one. Charlize Theron as a one-armed truck driver in postapocalyptic Australia wears black grease as sunscreen under a buzz cut, a look sufficiently removed from her usual perfume-ad glamour, which is displaced onto the women she is rescuing. Tom Hardy is better muttering than pontificating as he did in *The Revenant*. The entire cast seems handpicked for a kind of cinematic glory that has little to do with what goes on in other blockbusters. George Miller has done well to stay away from Hollywood and to switch back from making animated movies to live-action ones.

Miller has also remembered to make the film directly about things, not all subtext begging for explication. The scarcity of water, oil wars, the arms trade, and female emancipation jostle for space with the customized vehicles, coming in and out of focus with the blitz. But when it comes to political subtext, it must be acknowledged that Immortan Joe's demise was predictable from his water-distribution method. Pouring thousands of gallons of water on people's heads from a great height is not the best way to keep them pacified. Better to sell it to them in plastic bottles for ninety-nine cents each.

Star Wars: The Force Awakens

Like J. J. Abrams's Star Trek reboots, his new Star Wars seems crowdsourced and easy to forget, an app you just closed. Kylo Ren's mask sticks in my mind because he doesn't need it and wears it anyway. He's not a disfigured monster like Darth Vader, he's handsome Adam Driver dressing up as Grandpa on Halloween, preprogrammed for redemption. He's not evil, he's just young.

Spotlight

Spotlight joins the thin ranks of good contemporary Boston films (*Mystic River, The Fighter*) and does them one better by offering an explanation for the dark cloud that hangs over the place like the devil looms over the town in Murnau's *Faust*. Set in 2001, during the time of the *Boston Globe*'s exposé of pedophile priests in the Catholic Church, *Spotlight* glorifies investigative journalism and newspaper publishing for a world without newsprint. The film is spare and didactic, an instructional film explaining a disappearing profession. The editors and reporters in the film are saints whose personal lives are secondary to their work, and the Boston they work in is institutionally corrupt—cops and the courts stand between them and the truth as much as the church does.

It captures an essential truth about Boston, that feeling of drabness mixed with hostility and peculiarity anyone who has ever had to knock on a stranger's door in that town has felt. The key scene in this regard is the one in which Rachel McAdams stands at the front door of a disgraced priest, who happily admits to his crimes while his sister barks and snipes, shooing McAdams off. I'm sure that woman puts an orange traffic cone in her parking space in May.

Trumbo

Dalton Trumbo (Bryan Cranston), the blacklisted screenwriter at the center of this earnest-frantic biopic, was pro-Soviet and a member of the CPUSA, his politics formed during the Depression. Called before HUAC in 1947, he served time in jail for refusing to name names and was denied work by the studios. After prison, he wrote films under pseudonyms, including *Gun Crazy*, and won Oscars for two of them. One was *Roman Holiday*—yes, *Roman Holiday* was written by a commie. He couldn't publicly accept or acknowledge his awards until after Kirk Douglas and Otto Preminger broke the blacklist in 1960 by giving him screen credit on *Spartacus* and *Exodus*.

As a true-life version of *Hail, Caesar!* that features many actors familiar from Coen brothers movies, Trumbo hams up the blacklist. The director, Jay Roach, directed the Austin Powers and Fockers movies, and *Trumbo* gets over its awkwardness by focusing on the mechanics of screenwriting under duress, which Roach marvels at. Here is a screenwriter willing to risk everything, including his family, to write B movies for low pay under a pseudonym, without compromising his politics. After *Austin Powers in Goldmember*, that point of view makes sense. Actors play real Hollywood figures with varying degrees of success. Christian Berkel, who plays Otto Preminger, captures his essence, turning the combative auteur into a sly interloper popping up in Highland Park with mordant Viennese panache. *Trumbo* leaves the impression that the '50s worked out for everybody in the end, except for poor Louis C.K., as a left-wing screenwriter who smoked too much.

Bridge of Spies

Also set in the baby-boomer heaven of the 1950s and early '60s, *Bridge of Spies* presents the cold war as genteel and humane compared with the present war on terror. Tom Hanks, a high-powered lawyer but also a middle-class everyman, proves that making deals with our enemies is a better solution than building walls or dropping bombs. Retrofitting the cold war for the end of the Obama era, *Bridge of Spies* combines the negotiation of international agreements with a Trumpist approach: deals are best handled by private citizens who know better than government officials how to get what's best for the country. Today, of course, it is this businessman figure who wants to build a border wall, a bellicose reversal of this film's message.

The Coen brothers cowrote it, but Spielberg's unwavering belief in American values prevents any cynicism from coming through. At the same time, the film is mature, aware that Hanks is aging and could die of pneumonia without his overcoat from Saks Fifth Avenue. The scene with Hanks and Mark Rylance, as a pensive Soviet spy, listening to a Shostakovich piano concerto on a radio in a prison cell was not something I expected to see in a Spielberg movie.

Carol

Set in Manhattan and on the road in the winter of 1952, *Carol* fetishizes the mechanical equipment of surveillance—telephones, cameras, tape recorders. Carol (Cate Blanchett) and Therese (Rooney Mara), soon to be lovers, get into a dove-gray Packard to escape Carol's family but can't avoid the prying men who follow them anyway. Men are confused and pushy in *Carol,* and almost as forcibly drunk and well dressed as Cary Grant in the early scenes of *North by Northwest.* Ed Lachman's cinematography, in Super 16, is by far the most ravishing and understated among these films, a subtle tribute to the medium best suited for the intimacy of furtive glances and hushed conversations. The film is a triumph of art direction and wardrobe, a seductive art object. When Carol tells her husband, "We're not ugly people, Harge," she is telling the truth about a film that finds beauty in bad situations.

Brooklyn

Leaving County Wexford, a rule-bound place where shoe polish is not for sale on Sunday because it's "not a Sunday item," Eilis, a thoughtful girl played with extraordinary composure by Saoirse Ronan, sails for New York. She moves into a boarding house and gets a job at a department store in Brooklyn, across the East River from the department store in *Carol* where Therese works in Todd Haynes's version of New York in 1952.

Eilis meets and falls in love with a handsome Italian-American plumber (Emory Cohen, channeling '50s Method actors) who's as calm and good-hearted as she is. Then she's whisked back to Ireland for her sister's funeral and coaxed to stay there by an equally kind young man played by red-haired Domhnall Gleeson, who's in every movie. Eilis almost makes the decision not to go back to the Brooklyn of 1952, a choice unimaginable to the renters of Brooklyn in 2016, who would take the first boat to that Brooklyn if they could. For all their strenuous effort in vintage bar and restaurant design, they watch a livable Brooklyn drift further off each day. For Eilis, Brooklyn meant freedom from the past. Somebody direct me to a place in this city, besides a movie theater, that represents freedom in the present.

April 2016

THE INTERPRETATION OF SCREAMS

ON DAVID LYNCH

IN 1967, WHEN HE WAS A STUDENT AT THE PENNSYLVANIA ACADEMY OF Fine Arts in Philadelphia, David Lynch, the future director of *Blue Velvet* and *Twin Peaks*, made a mixed-media sculpture, a Rube Goldberg device that, as Dennis Lim describes it in his thorough, compact, and illuminating new book on Lynch, "required dropping a ball bearing down a ramp that would, through a daisy chain of switches and triggers, strike a match, light a firecracker, and cause a sculpted female figure's mouth to open, at which point a red bulb inside would light up, the firecracker would go off, and the sound of a scream would emerge."

This combination of the board game Operation with a blow-up doll and Samuel Beckett's *Not I* (the play featuring only a woman's mouth), plus the sounds of a gunshot and a scream, anticipated the components of the work Lynch has spent the subsequent fifty years making. In film and television, his distinctive oeuvre has obsessed cinephiles, fans of the outré, and film academics, giving rise to the adjective *Lynchian*, a word, as Lim points out, that many have tried to define but that the culture at large has decided means "weird." Lim boils the Lynchian down to "abysmal terror, piercing beauty, convulsive sorrow." Lynch's movies, he writes, "give form to the submerged traumas and desires of our age."

A nicotine fiend and a coffee addict who mixes existential dread with sadomasochism in all-American settings, Lynch is that rare director who makes subversive films without a chip on his shoulder, seemingly without any will to provocation. He is at home with his neuroses and obsessions. His secret is that he proceeds as though he is acting from the most impossible condition of all: normalcy. While directors like David Fincher and Lars von Trier explore similar terrain with grim determination, only Lynch enters nightmare worlds like the Eagle Scout he was, as inquisitive about the depths of human psychology as he is about bugs and twigs.

"There is goodness in blue skies and flowers, but another force—a wild pain and decay—also accompanies everything," Lynch has said. "There's this beautiful world and you just look a little bit closer, and it's all red ants." Like the ones on the severed ear in *Blue Velvet.* Lim connects Lynch to the dark forces that drive the American psyche, the same ones D. H. Lawrence analyzed in his *Studies in Classic American Literature,* and there is more than a touch of "Young Goodman Brown" in Lynch's homespun American surrealism. Like the character in Hawthorne's story, Lynch is drawn to the woods at night, where ordinary people confront the demonic. The Black Lodge in *Twin Peaks* houses America's violent soul.

This view was ingrained in Lynch from the start. His father, a research scientist with the US Forest Service, wrote a doctoral thesis called "Effects of Stocking on Site Measurement and Yield of Second-Growth Ponderosa Pine in the Inland Empire," a title seeded with Lynchian allusion. When a painter acquaintance gave the teenage Lynch a copy of Robert Henri's book *The Art Spirit,* a primer from the Ashcan School that describes art as "our greatest happiness" and encourages its readers (assuming they are male) to "do some great work, Son!," Lynch's path was set.

Lynch grew up in *Leave It to Beaver*–like towns, pinging happily between the Pacific Northwest, Idaho, and Virginia. While his upbringing implanted half his mental landscape, it did not prepare him for Philadelphia, which completed the picture. Lynch was uneasy in northeastern cities after visiting his grandparents in Brooklyn, where he was worried by a tenant in his grandfather's kitchenless building frying an egg on an iron, and recoiled at the hellishness of the subway.

When he arrived in Philadelphia for art school, urban blight overtook him. Lynch moved into an industrial district, a grimy anti-Oz of crumbling buildings and smokestacks. He spent his time there in the neighborhood diner, a hangout for morgue attendants who let him visit their slabs. Soon he was married with a child, working as a printer and living in a cheap house in a bad neighborhood.

"There were places there that had been allowed to decay," Lynch recalls, "where there was so much fear and crime that just for a moment there was an opening to another world." He does not mean the world of poverty he was ensconced in so much as the interior world of psychological trauma poverty underscores. In *Eraserhead*, his first feature, Lynch surrealized that world, aestheticizing it across mental galaxies and inside bodies, heads, and planets. Was that only possible in a place that seemed beyond hope and ungentrifiable—a galaxy far away from us now?

Lynch has called *Eraserhead* "the real *Philadelphia Story*." Completed over a painstaking six years after he was admitted to the American Film Institute in Los Angeles, this "Dream of Dark and Troubling Things" (as the poster's tagline had it) was greeted by *Variety* when it premiered in 1977 with the headline "Dismal American Film Institute Exercise in Gore; Commercial Prospects Nil." Handled expertly by an independent distributor on the midnight-movie circuit during what Lim calls the "year zero for punk," *Eraserhead* proved *Variety* wrong. Lynch's ugly baby thrived in a film economy separate from blockbusters like *Star Wars*, which debuted the same year.

George Lucas, in fact, later asked Lynch to direct *Return of the Jedi*. Of the roads not taken in film history, that was a highway Lynch was wise to avoid. He worked for hire on *The Elephant Man* and *Dune* before he fully abandoned notions of a conventional Hollywood career to make *Blue Velvet* in 1986. The Canadian filmmaker Guy Maddin calls it "the last real earthquake to hit cinema."

Arriving at the height of the Reagan era, *Blue Velvet* rattled audiences, almost molesting them. It had the same effect on film studies, where it became an object of attraction and repulsion, calling across a void to film theorists of all stripes during the time of *Back to the Future* and *Pretty in Pink*, colorful pop films of youthful self-discovery lacking *Blue Velvet*'s sense of menace. Lynch's film shared *Back to the Future*'s Freudian plot and *Pretty in Pink*'s New Wave veneer, but his style of deadpan terror was, to say the least, different. Fredric Jameson, in *Postmodernism, or, The Cultural Logic of Late Capitalism*, was notably discombobulated, seeing the film as an insidious form of "postnostalgia," in which "evil has finally become an image."

Blue Velvet, in addition to providing material for post-structural analysis, is one of those films in which every line is memorable. Lynch's work as a screenwriter is often overlooked in writing on him, but Lim, the director of programming at the Film Society of Lincoln Center, does it justice. Isabella Rossellini was Lynch's significant other at the time, and as the hostage-chanteuse Dorothy Vallens, her line "You put your disease in me" sums up what the film did to people who saw it when it came out in theaters, or later on VHS tapes. Home viewings, Lim points out, in which Lynch's dark vision of small-town America could be watched again and again, paved the way for what Lynch did next.

In 1990, *Twin Peaks* extended the Lynchian into prime-time network television. Lim describes the series as "a mass-culture text that called for communal decoding," and its debut drew thirty-five million viewers, a third of the potential TV audience. *Connoisseur* magazine called it "The Series That Will Change TV Forever," and it did, albeit very slowly. Quality television and its signature genre, the "dead girl" mystery, owe their existence to the story of Special Agent Dale Cooper's investigation of Laura Palmer's murder. Now that Lynch is bringing *Twin Peaks* back on Showtime, he has come full circle, and it's fitting to note that what was once OK for broadcast TV is now only acceptable on premium cable.

After a few years in the pop-culture wilderness, Lynch made *Lost Highway* in 1997, the first movie of his so-called LA Trilogy, which includes 2001's *Mulholland Drive* and *Inland Empire*, the 2006 opus starring Laura Dern he shot on pro-am digital video. While *Mulholland Drive* began life as another series for ABC, Lynch was by then able to secure financing from European sources. Moving beyond the constraints of Hollywood financing and network notes gave him the freedom he needed to contemplate his experiences in Southern California his own way. In those films, Lynch took Los Angeles, Hollywood, and screen acting as his subjects.

Lim points out that these films emerged from the period "of Timothy McVeigh and the Unabomber, the Branch Davidians and Heaven's Gate cults, the televised trials of O. J. Simpson and the Menendez brothers," which created "a potent incubator for apocalyptic thoughts." Lynch's Los Angeles films, in which identity dissolves and congeals into murder, reflect the California sun back on itself. Despite the swimming pools and the modernist houses, he and his characters, living amid palm trees instead of pines, are not out of the woods. By the time of *Inland Empire*, which was partially shot in Poland and is three hours long, the Lynchian Möbius strip had enfolded a new psychic continent.

Those three films, masterworks of anguish and splintered dreams, may be his last. Before his imminent return to TV, Lynch seemed to have given up feature filmmaking for the self-banishment of the Transcendental Meditation foundation he started to promote world peace. Whether it's DV, TV, or TM, Lynch has earned the right to do what he wants. If *Inland Empire*'s closer, an all-female group dance scored to Nina Simone's "Sinnerman," is the last scene of his last movie, it will be the semi-happy end to a career in film that began with a man and his hairdo trudging through a wasteland.

February 2016

STAR WARS IS YOUR GOD

IN DECEMBER, ON THE EVE OF PEARL HARBOR REMEMBRANCE DAY, President Obama spoke to the nation from the Oval Office about the attack in San Bernardino, California, that left fourteen people dead. "The terrorist threat has evolved into a new phase," the President said. The married couple responsible for the attack, he told the camera, "had gone down the dark path of radicalization, embracing a perverted interpretation of Islam that calls for war against America and the West." They were "part of a cult of death," which he contrasted with America's "belief in human dignity." In the battle against the Islamic State's deadly ideology, the President had no doubt that America would prevail.

After his speech, Obama zoomed off to the Kennedy Center to celebrate the artistic achievements of, among others, George Lucas, the creator of the *Star Wars* series. Carrie Fisher appeared in holograph form, beamed to the proceedings from the little droid R2-D2, just as she had as Princess Leia way back in 1977, when the first film was released. A phalanx of Stormtroopers danced their way through the ceremony as the gathered luminaries praised Lucas, who accepted his award by reminding everyone that the "bright side of the Force is love, the dark side is hate." He implored the audience, "Stick to the bright side."

During his time in office, Obama has never missed the Kennedy Center Honors. By attending this year just after appearing on television to quell the nation's fears, he was emphasizing America's commitment to the arts and to the human dignity they affirm. If that human dignity could be hitched to a movie franchise that has brought in billions of dollars from all over the world, and to the imminent premiere of its seventh and latest installment—*Star Wars: The Force Awakens*—so much the better for everyone concerned. In this official setting, *Star Wars* showed that the unparalleled appeal of the American system is bound up with the projection of images that combine innocence with firepower.

It was firepower that at least one commentator, speaking from the dark side, had on his mind as the twin manias for gun violence and *Star Wars* commingled last autumn. "I think I'll wait till *Star Wars* is less a threat scenario," Erick Erickson, the conservative blogger and radio host, mused on his blog, referring to *The Force Awakens*. He was not willing, he said, to see the movie on the day it opened because he had "no confidence in this administration to keep us all safe." Acting on some combination of hysteria and wish fulfillment, he took his anger out on the December 5 edition of the *New York Times,* which featured a front-page editorial calling for gun control. Erickson shot the newspaper full of holes with the weapon he would be prohibited from taking to the movie, then tweeted a photo of his handiwork with a request that his followers do the same.

Perhaps it's no wonder that *Star Wars* is used for such fearmongering. Disney's purchase of the franchise from George Lucas in 2012, for $4 billion, led to an explosion of merchandising options that underscored the way in which *Star Wars*, America's secular, taxable religion, is proselytized from one generation to the next, a form of what Manohla Dargis, a film critic for the *New York Times,* has called "cradle-to-grave entertainment."

A series of Walmart ads called "A New Generation Awakens," which was shown before trailers at movie theaters, depicts parents and grandparents explaining the Force and all it entails to youngsters with the aid of *Star Wars* toys. A creepy TV commercial for HP's expensive printer ink features a father directing and photographing his son and daughter as they reenact the Darth Vader–Luke Skywalker lightsaber duel from *The Empire Strikes Back* for his camera. He prints the pictures and sends them to his own father, proving to this elder that he has done right. In the thirty-nine years of its existence, *Star Wars* has gone from nerdy obsession to full-fledged lifestyle brand. Just as the movies are cradle-to-grave entertainment, the brand offers cause-and-cure tie-ins. Ample Hills Dark Side and Light Side ice cream may cause tooth decay, but Oral-B's and Crest's *Star Wars* toothpastes and toothbrushes will fight it off.

From the beginning, even before the films were available for home viewing, it was Lucas's intention to extend the *Star Wars* experience beyond the theater. The toys became the talismanic figurines of a new faith, totems used to tell the story again and again, with no need for a holy book. (One fan theory postulates that the faraway galaxy in which the *Star Wars* movies are set has dispensed with reading.) When the first film came out, J. G. Ballard, the novelist, identified its inspiration in the "iconography of mass merchandising." The postapocalyptic movie *Reign of Fire,* from 2002, showed adults reenacting the Darth-Luke duel for children in a candlelit church, the conflict sacralized in the waning days of humanity.

Ballard sought a "weird, unintentional parable of the US involvement in Vietnam" in the first of the movies—with the Empire standing in for the United States and the Rebel Alliance for the Vietcong—but he could not quite find one. Ronald Reagan had less difficulty identifying American power with Lucas's 20th-century pop *Nibelungenlied.* Although Lucas objected, Reagan's Strategic Defense Initiative, an antiballistic-missile system, came to be known as Star Wars. Soon after Reagan announced the SDI, in 1983, he applied the term "Evil Empire" to the Soviet Union. The mutability of the Force, which allows it to work for both the dark side and the bright, lends itself to a binary worldview that is readily deployable in geopolitical conflict, even in a time when America is the only empire left. In a postimperial era, it's easy enough for any faction to see themselves as Rebels and their enemies as the Sith.

If *Star Wars* addressed children as consumers, its message of "a new hope" set amid a Freudian power struggle also relieved parental neglect by dramatizing it. For the latchkey kids of the post-Vietnam era, seeing the films with their mothers and fathers provided a central moment of bonding in a world that lacked in children's movies and attachment parenting. The kids who first played with *Star Wars* toys used their miniature Darth Vaders and Luke Skywalkers as a form of developmental therapy. Whether they have grown up or not, those first viewers have aged, like the actors in the original three movies. As Anthony Daniels, who plays C-3PO, the ageless golden droid, told the *Daily Mirror,* "What is funny is C-3PO looks the same—Harrison, Carrie, and Mark, not so much . . . Poor Mark. He was a young lovely looking lad when he was first Luke Skywalker and now . . . well . . . "

IT MUST BE STRANGE to zip around the universe and keep bumping into your family. With *The Force Awakens,* the conflict, and the interbreeding between Empire and Rebellion, now extend to a third generation, even if Darth Vader is only a burnt skeleton kept around for inspiration. (If the children of the Clintons and the Bushes marry, this could be the kind of future we're looking at.) The young protagonists being inducted into *Star Wars* history are reluctant to pursue good or evil—they are more nuanced than their predecessors. With their help, the story has been retrofitted to update it for a post-*Twilight,* post–*Hunger Games* world. Like the children in the Walmart ad, they must be taught how to live in the dualistic *Star Wars* universe.

The film, which is directed by J. J. Abrams, opens with flamethrower-armed Stormtroopers incinerating a village on a desert planet. The scene gestures at the Vietnam allegory that Ballard was looking for in the first episode while also suggesting Iraq, today's version of a never-ending war. One of the Stormtroopers deserts his unit after the rampage. His introduction is ultra-cinematic: before we get to see his face, he is distinguished from the other fighters only by the red blood streaked across his white helmet. This self-emancipated Stormtrooper—played, in a shrewd casting decision, by John Boyega, a British Nigerian actor—chooses to call himself Finn; the name of Mark Twain's white protagonist is suggested by the first two letters of the designation the Empire assigned to him, F-N. (Maybe the characters can read, after all.)

The Empire, now known as the First Order, is no respecter of intergalactic rights. Poe (Oscar Isaac), another new character with a literary name, is a Resistance fighter pilot who gets initiated into the universe of the movies through torture. As all-American in his attitude as any World War II flying ace, Poe mocks the black mask of his lead torturer, Kylo Ren (Adam Driver), which is worn, it seems, in emulation of Darth Vader, Ren's grandfather, not because he needs it to breathe. By the time Rey (Daisy Ridley), the plucky desert scavenger who gives the series a shot of new girl power, takes her turn in the torture chair, we learn that a young woman can use the Force to stop torture as easily as waving off the dentist.

The film's political resonances are as mutable—and as muddled—as those of its predecessors. *The Force Awakens* criticizes American imperialism while also celebrating the revolutionary spirit that founded this country. When the movie needs to bridge the two points of view, it shifts to aerial combat, a default setting that mirrors the war on terror all too well. As the film's *Lawrence of Arabia–Seven Samurai–Triumph of the Will* images (dunes, forests, rallies) coalesce, *The Force Awakens* moves toward a predictable but glorious last scene, which culminates in a monumental image: the bearded, time-battered face of Mark Hamill as Luke Skywalker. He looks ready for Mount Rushmore (and remarkably like Slavoj Žižek). Whatever has happened to Hamill in the years since *Return of the Jedi* came out, in 1983, he wears the ravages of our shared history on his face.

February 2016

THE NONSTOP ZOMBIE BUFFET

WHEN THINGS ARE VERY AMERICAN, THEY ARE AS AMERICAN AS APPLE PIE. Except violence. H. Rap Brown said violence "is as American as cherry pie," not apple pie. Brown's maxim makes us see violence as red and gelatinous, spooned from a can.

But for Brown, in 1967, American violence was white. Explicitly casting himself as an outsider, Brown said in his cherry pie speech that "violence is a part of America's culture" and that Americans taught violence to black people. He explained that violence is a necessary form of self-protection in a society where white people set fire to Bowery bums for fun, and where they shoot strangers from the towers of college campuses for no reason—this was less than a year after Charles Whitman had killed eleven people that way at the University of Texas at Austin, the first mass shooting of its kind in US history. Brown compared these deadly acts of violence to the war in Vietnam; President Lyndon B. Johnson, too, was burning people alive. He said the President's wife was more his enemy than the people of Vietnam were, and that he'd rather kill her than them.

Brown, who was then a leader of the Student Nonviolent Coordinating Committee and who would soon become the Black Panther Party's minister of justice, delivered a version of this speech, or rant, to about four hundred people in Cambridge, Maryland.

When it was over, the police went looking for him and arrested him for inciting a riot. Brown's story afterward is eventful and complicated, but this is an essay about zombie movies. Suffice it to say, Brown knows about violence. Fifty years after that speech, having changed his name to Jamil Abdullah Al-Amin, he's spending life in prison for killing a cop.

The same day Brown was giving his speech in Maryland, George A. Romero, a director of industrial films, was north of Pittsburgh in a small Pennsylvania town called Evans City. Romero was shooting his first feature film, a low-budget horror movie in black and white called *Night of the Living Dead*. Released in October 1968, the first modern zombie movie tells the story of a black man trying to defend himself and others from a sudden plague of lumbering corpses who feed on the living. At the film's end, he is unceremoniously shot and killed by cops who assume he is a zombie trying to kill them. The cops quickly dispose of his body, dumping it in a fire with a heap of the undead, as a posse moves on to hunt more zombies.

Regional gore films were nothing new in themselves; a number had appeared earlier in the 1960s. *Night of the Living Dead*, with its shambling, open-mouthed gut-munchers dressed in business suits and housecoats, might have seemed merely gross or oddly funny in a context other than the America of 1968. But Martin Luther King Jr. had been assassinated six months before its release. The news on TV, which most people still saw in black and white, consisted largely of urban riots and war reports from Vietnam. The My Lai Massacre had occurred the month before King was shot.

Romero's film, seen in the United States the year it came out, had more in common with *Rome Open City* than it did with a drive-in horror movie made for teens—it was close to a work of neorealism. And it was unfunny and dire, much like John Cassavetes's *Faces*, released the same year, whose laughing drunks stopped laughing when they paused to look in the mirror. Romero was a revisionist director of horror in the same way that Peckinpah and Altman were in their career-making genres, the western and the war movie.

Romero cast an African American in the lead, and he shifted the horror genre's dynamic, aligning it with black-and-white anti-war documentaries like Emile de Antonio's *In the Year of the Pig*, also released in 1968, and distinguishing it from the lurid color horror movies Roger Corman and Hammer Films had been turning out up till then. Those films made certain concessions to the film industry; *Night of the Living Dead* did not. This was an *American* horror movie, so it needed no English accents or familiar character actors. It was grim and unflinching, showing average citizens, played by average people, eating the arms and intestines of their fellow townspeople. Romero drove home this central point—that a zombie-infested America differed from the status quo only in degree, not in kind—by ending his film with realistic-looking fake news photos depicting his characters' banal atrocities.

Mainstream film reviewers, including Roger Ebert, were shocked and disgusted by *Night of the Living Dead*. They discouraged people from seeing it, but Romero's images proved to be indelible. The film's reputation grew. In 1978 Romero made the film's first sequel, *Dawn of the Dead*, this time in color. Today, if there's one thing every American knows, it's that zombies can only be killed with a shot to the head. This is common knowledge, cultural literacy, a kind of historical fact, like George Washington chopping down the cherry tree. American-flag bumper stickers assert that these colors don't run, but one of them does. It runs like crazy through American life, through American movies, and now TV, like a faucet left on.

THE *HUFFINGTON POST* HAS HAD a Zombie Apocalypse header since 2011, under which the editors file newsy blog posts chronicling our continuing fascination with zombie pop culture, alongside any nonfiction news story horrible enough to relate to zombies or cannibalism. The infamous Miami face-eater attack of May 2012, which the media gleefully heralded as the start of a "real" zombie apocalypse, contributed to America's sense that it could happen here, provided we wished for it hard enough. Reading through the Zombie

Apocalypse posts, one gets a growing sense that we want the big, self-devouring reckoning to happen because it is the one disaster we are truly mentally prepared for. It won't be the total letdown of the Ebola scare.

The face-eating incident was initially linked to bath salts: ground-up mineral crystals everyone hoped would become the new homemade drug of choice for America's scariest users. It turned out the perpetrator, although naked, was only high on marijuana. He was black, killed by the police as he gouged out his homeless victim's eyes and chewed his face on a causeway over Biscayne Bay. The incident was captured on surveillance video. Here in the golden age of user-generated content, the zombie movies self-generate—much like zombies themselves. The bridge backdrop of this all-too-real zombie vignette neatly summed up both the crumbling condition of America's infrastructure and our more generalized state of neoliberal collapse.

The zombie apocalypse, our favorite apocalypse, seems to unite the right and left. It combines the apocalypse brought about by climate change and the subsequent competition for scant resources with the one loosed by secret government experiments gone awry. Better still, both of these scenarios, as we're typically shown in graphic detail, will necessitate increased gun-toting and firearms expertise.

More than that, the fast-approaching zombie Parousia allows us to indulge our fantasies of a third apocalypse, one that only the most clueless don't embrace: the consumerist Day of Judgment, in which we will all be punished for being fat and lazy and living by remote control, going through our daily routines questioning nothing as the world falls apart and we continue shopping. Supermarkets and shopping carts, malls and food warehouses all figure prominently in the iconography of the post–*Night of the Living Dead* zombie movie, reminding us that even in our quotidian consumerist daze, we are one step away from looting and cannibalism, the last two items on everyone's bucket list.

Still, despite its galvanizing power to place all of humanity on the same side of the cosmic battlefront, the zombie apocalypse, like all ideological constructs, nonetheless manages to cleave the world into two camps. One camp gets it and the other doesn't. One is aware the apocalypse is under way, and the other is blithely oblivious to the world around it.

To confuse matters further, people move in and out of both camps, becoming inert, zombified creatures when obliviousness suits their mood. People blocking our progress on the street as they natter into their hands-free earsets stare straight ahead, refusing to admit that other people exist. At least they don't bite us as we flatten ourselves against walls to pass them without contact. A paradox of the ubiquity of zombie-themed pop culture is how there are surely next to no people left who have not enjoyed a zombie movie, TV show, book, or videogame, yet there are more and more people shuffling around like extras in a zombie film, moving their mouths and making gnawing sounds.

The smartphone-based zombification of street life is a strange testament to Romero's original insight, which becomes more pronounced as the wealth gap widens. The disenfranchised look ever more zombified to the rich, who in turn all look the same and act the same as they take over whole neighborhoods and wall themselves up in condo towers. This, indeed, is exactly what happens in Romero's fourth zombie movie, 2005's *Land of the Dead*, which predicted things as consequential as what happened during Hurricane Katrina in New Orleans and as minor as the rise of food trucks.

The zombie apocalypse is also a parable of the Protestant work ethic, come to reap vengeance at the end of days. It assures us that only very resourceful, tough-minded people will be able to hack it when the dead come back to life. If the rest had really wanted to survive—if they *deserved* to survive—they would have spent a little less time on the sofa. But here, too, the simple and obvious moral takes a perverse turn: the best anti-zombie combatants should be the ones who've watched the most zombie movies, yet by the very logic of our consumer-baiting zombie fables, they won't be physically capable of survival because all they did was watch TV.

WHAT THESE COUCH POTATOES will need, inarguably, is the protection of a strong leader, one who hasn't spent his life in the vain and sodden leisure pursuits that they've inertly embraced—Rick Grimes in *The Walking Dead*, for instance. Why such a person would want to help them is a question they don't ask. With this search for an ultimate hero, the zombie genre has veered into the escapism of savior lust, leaving Romero's unflinching, subversive neorealism behind. In *Night of the Living Dead*, a witless humanity is condemned by its own herd mentality and racism. In latter-day zombie fictions, a quasi-fascist social order is required, uniting us regardless of race, creed, or color.

The predicament of the characters (and the actors) in all the *nouveau* zombie movies relates to this passive consumerism. Both the characters and the actors in new zombie movies have to act like zombie films don't already exist, even though the existence of Romero's films is what permits the existence of the film they are in. Somehow, the characters pull their savvy out of thin air. They must pretend that they have never heard of zombies, even as they immediately and naturally know what to do once their own particular zombie apocalypse gets under way.

This paradox underscores the fantasy aspect of the 21st-century zombie infatuation, in which a fixed set of roles is available for cosplay in a repeatable drama that already took place somewhere else. The difference between Romero's films and the new zombie movies is that the more time that passes since 1968, the more Romero's films don't seem like they were designed as entertainment—even as they are endlessly exploited by the zombie-themed cultural productions that copy them, and even as they remain entertaining. The new zombie films cannibalize Romero's films in an attempt to remake them ideologically, so that we will stop looking for meaning in them and just accept the inevitable.

A PRIMAL FANTASY OF the zombie apocalypse is that when the shit hits the fan, we will be able to kill our own children or parents.

We won't have a choice. The decision to get rid of the generation impeding us will have been made for us by the zombie plague, absolving us of responsibility. We are, after all, killing somebody who is already dead and who, in his or her current state, is a threat to our continued existence.

Against the generalized dystopian entertainment landscape that followed the economic collapse of 2008, the zombie apocalypse made more sense than ever. But YA action-drama dropped it in favor of promoting teen heroes who were stronger than their nice-but-loserish sad-sack parents. This is the uplifting generational affirmation that imbues Suzanne Collins's *Hunger Games* franchise and Veronica Roth's *Divergent* trilogy.

YA comedy, on the other hand, did not ignore zombie movies. Instead, it domesticated the zombie apocalypse, making it friendly. Nonthreatening zom-coms showed young viewers how the opposite sex was really not that scary, that being in a couple was still the most important thing, and that dystopias gave nerds an unprecedented chance to prove they could get the girl or boy. Dystopia, it turns out, is really a best-of-all-possible-worlds scenario for starry-eyed-kids-with-a-disease, or so we learn from zom-coms like *Warm Bodies* and *Life After Beth*.

The latest iteration of this trend, which sets a zombie heroine in a marginally less dystopian world that mirrors our tentative economic comeback, is the CW TV show *iZombie*. The series is brain-eating entertainment for tweens in which they learn you can be OK and have a chill job even if you're a living corpse who's just trying to figure things out. When a zombie gets her own tween-empowerment show on the CW, it's a good indication that zombies don't carry the stern, *unbekannt* stigmas they used to. Zombies, much like corpses in TV commercials, are used as grotesque comic relief in things like animated Adult Swim shows. Such is the diminished status of the zombie; it is now a signifier that can be plugged in anywhere. To paraphrase the undead philosopher of capitalism's own walking-dead demise: first time cannibalism, second time farce.

THE WAY ZOMBIE MOVIES progress, with isolated groups splitting into factions and various elimination rounds as contestants disappear, suggests that *Night of the Living Dead* is also a secret source of reality TV. It makes sense, then, that 2009's *Zombieland*, one of the first YA dystopian zombie entertainments, was penned by screenwriters who created *The Joe Schmo Show* and *I'm a Celebrity . . . Get Me Out of Here!*

Zombieland's protagonist, a college-age dude played by Jesse Eisenberg, is a bundle of phobias, an OCD-style follower of rules who finds himself in a zombie apocalypse after an unexpected date with a hot girl out of his league (Amber Heard) goes wrong. Mentored by Woody Harrelson, who more or less reprised this same role in the *Hunger Games* movies, Eisenberg's millennial character undergoes a reality-TV-scripted makeover. In expiation for his pusillanimity in the opening reel, he winds up rescuing a tough girl (Emma Stone) who also would have been out of his league in the pre-apocalypse scheme of dating. *Zombieland* presents Eisenberg as gutless and Stone as ruthless, but she's the one who ends up a hostage, and he becomes her hero. In fact, one of his rules, "Don't be a hero," changes on-screen to "Be a hero," as we once again learn that millennials really do have what it takes to kill zombies. Earlier in the film, Eisenberg accidentally shoots and kills a non-zombie Bill Murray, playing himself, showing that millennials can also, regretfully, take out baby boomers, including the cool ones who aren't undead.

Edgar Wright's 2004 *Shaun of the Dead*, the first movie zom-com, was a more intelligent version of this same storyline. An English comedy from the "Isn't it cute how much we suck?" school, Wright's film acquiesced to the coupling-up plot rom-coms require, but not without first presenting the routine, pointless daily life of its protagonist (Simon Pegg) as pre-zombified. *Shaun of the Dead* will likely remain the only sweet little comedy in which the protagonist kills his mother, a scene the film has the guts to play without flinching. The joke of Wright's film is that it takes something as brutal as a zombie apocalypse to wake us from our stupor and to show us how good we had it all along. By the film's end, Pegg and his girlfriend (Kate Ashfield) are in exactly the same place they were when the film started, but now at least they live together. A cover of the Buzzcocks' song "Everybody's Happy Nowadays" jangles over the credits, providing a zombified dose of circa-1979 irony.

Wright and Pegg's goofy rethinking of the zombie movie proved how firmly zombies are entrenched in our consciousness, and how easy they are to manipulate for comedic effect. The same month *Shaun of the Dead* came out, a Hollywood remake of Romero's *Dawn of the Dead* was released. It, too, cleaned up at the box office. This new *Dawn of the Dead* seemed like it was made by one of the nerds in the American zom-coms, a jerk desperate to prove he's badass. (The director now makes superhero movies.) Johnny Cash's "The Man Comes Around" accompanies the opening credits, setting a high bar for artistic achievement the ensuing film does not come near to clearing. Jim Carroll's "People Who Died" plays at the end—its placement there as repulsive as anything else in the film.

As all *nouveau* zombie films must, the remake starts in the suburbs, where a couple is watching *American Idol* in bed, underscoring the genre's newfound connection to reality TV. The film's CGI effects, which at the time injected a souped-up faux energy into the on-screen mayhem, dated instantly. They're now the kind of off-the-rack effects featured in Weird Al videos when someone gets hit by a car.

The main point of this new *Dawn of the Dead* is that after the zombie apocalypse, people will spend their time barking orders at each other and calling each other "asshole." The film nods in the direction of loving the military and the police, and totally sanitizes Romero's use of a shopping mall as a site of consumerist critique. Like many films of the 2000s, it postulates that living in a mall wouldn't be a Hobbesian dystopia at all; it would be rad. If the remake had been made five years later, maybe it would have had to grapple with the "dead malls" that began to adorn the American landscape with greater frequency after the economy collapsed. Instead, the mall serving as the film's principal backdrop is spotless and fun. The remake's island-set, sequel-ready, false happy ending makes one long for the denouement of Michael Haneke's *Funny Games*—a longing more unimaginable than any real-life wish-fulfillment fantasy about the zombie apocalypse actually coming to pass.

FANBOYS LIKED THE *Dawn of the Dead* remake and, inexplicably, so did many critics. Manohla Dargis, then at the *Los Angeles Times*, wrote that the film was "the best proof in ages that cannibalizing old material sometimes works fiendishly well," a punny sentiment she might well walk back today.

The next year, when George A. Romero released his first new zombie film in twenty years, it did not fare as well in the suddenly crowded marketplace of the undead. While *Land of the Dead* is fittingly seen as something of a masterpiece now, on its initial release it puzzled genre fans, who had gotten used to the sort of "fast zombies" that were first featured in the nihilistic-with-a-happy-ending British movie *28 Days Later* (2002). Romero's new film was as trenchant as his others, but many fans weren't having it.

IMDb user reviews provide a record of their immediate reactions. "This movie was terrible!" one wrote the month *Land of the Dead* premiered. "The storyline—can't use the word plot as that would give it too much credit—was tedious! Some say it was a great perspective on class? Are you kidding me!!!" Less than a year into George W. Bush's second term, Romero was archly depicting a society much different from the one he'd shown in *Night of the Living Dead*. This new society—today's—was more class-riven, more opportunistic, more cynical. And Romero, even while moving in the direction of Hawksian classicism, was exposing these failings with radical acuity. His dark fable of two Americas at war over the control of the resources necessary to survive was concise, imaginative, and well constructed. Few at the time wanted to consider the film's style, which seemed out of date compared to the *Dawn of the Dead* remake. Fewer still wanted to grapple with its implications.

Ten years later, it is clear that no American genre film from that period digests and exposes the Bush era more skillfully than *Land of the Dead*. Romero's film was uncomfortably ahead of its time, and like his other zombie work, it hasn't dated; it speaks of 2015 as much as 2005. Tightly controlled scenes avoid the pointlessness and repetition of the *nouveau* zombie films, limning class struggle in unexpected ways. Zombies, slowly coming to consciousness, use the tools of the trades from which they've been recently dispossessed to shatter the glass of fortified condos. A zombie pumps gas through the windshield of a limo. The rich commit suicide, only to come back to life as zombies and feed on their children. America, as the original-zombie-era Funkadelic LP taught us, eats its young. To some extent, the rap group Public Enemy had been here before, in their 1988 music video for their song "Night of the Living Baseheads," which redid Romero's *Dawn of the Dead* as a tale of Eighties New York, where stockbrokers get away with doing cocaine while literalized crack zombies roam the streets of Harlem and "rock to a different kind of bass."

As zombie fantasies go, Romero's *Land of the Dead* is much richer than the random, unsatisfying mayhem of the *nouveau* zombie films. Romero, like Public Enemy but unlike his contemporary filmmaking counterparts, does not shy away from race. He shows African Americans pushing back against the injustices and indignities of a militarized police state, thereby completing a circle that began with Duane Jones's performance in *Night of the Living Dead*.

FOR THE LATEST GENERATION of zombie enthusiasts, the zombie genre means just one thing: AMC's massively popular cable series *The Walking Dead*. The show is so much better than any of the recent non-Romero zombie movies that it's among the leading exhibits in the case against the cineplex. The show's politics and implications are widely discussed, and *The Walking Dead* has engendered national debate about all sorts of ethical issues, including something Romero's films raised only in the negative: America's future. But the first problem *The Walking Dead* solved was how to make its own debates about these things interesting: whenever scenes get too talky, a "walker" sidles up and has to be dispatched in the time-honored fashion. At its core, the zombie drama is like playing "You're it!" The show could be called *Game of Tag.*

The Walking Dead debuted in 2010, emerging from a period in US history when, all of a sudden, we found ourselves in a junked, collapsed, post-American environment. New dystopian dramas, especially the YA ones, reflected this chastened reality. *The Walking Dead* looked at first like it might become just another placeholding entry in this cavalcade of glumness, much like TNT's Spielberg-produced, families vs. aliens sci-fi show *Falling Skies.* Zombies were maybe the most dated way possible to dramatize our newly trashed world.

It was *The Walking Dead*'s dated qualities, however, that saved it from becoming cable TV's *Hunger Games.* The show's grunge aesthetic and majority-adult cast situated it elsewhere. And if that particular elsewhere felt like the past as much as the future, that was part of what made the show work for premium cable's Gen X audience. Greg Nicotero, a makeup man who worked under Romero, is one of the show's producers. His presence indicated the people behind the show took the genre seriously, unlike anyone else in Hollywood who had touched it.

Television works by imitating success, by zombifying proven formulas through a process called mimetic isomorphism. When television producers saw *The Walking Dead*'s ratings beating broadcast-network ratings—a first for cable drama—they took notice and began spawning. Copies of copies like *Resurrection, The Last Ship, The Leftovers,* and *12 Monkeys* showed that plague is contagious, but it doesn't have to be zombie plague. Meanwhile, *The Walking Dead* continues its success, and AMC will debut a companion series this summer, unimaginatively called *Fear the Walking Dead.*

If the worst zombie movies unselfconsciously imitate higher-gloss broadcast-network reality trash like *Survivor, The Walking Dead* succeeds by staying closer to the lowest grade of cable-network reality TV.

The world of *The Walking Dead* is closer to *Hoarders* than it is to *Big Brother. Hoarders* presents an America engulfed in mounds of trash that its psychologically damaged possessors can't part with. Mounds of Big Gulp cups and greeting cards and heaps of car parts and instruction manuals overwhelm their homes, spilling into their yards. Shows like *Storage Wars, Pawn Stars,* and *American Pickers* present an America of valueless junk that maybe somebody can make a buck on—if only by televising it for our own lurid delectation. These shows are the opposite of pre-collapse valuation shows like *Antiques Roadshow,* in which the junk people had lying around proved to be worth more than they had imagined. The detritus of *Hoarders* is worthless, the kind of trash that will blow around everywhere after the zombie apocalypse.

IN HIS RECENT BOOK *24/7,* an analysis of the end of sleep and our twenty-four-hour consumption-and-work cycle, Jonathan Crary writes that "part of the modernized world we inhabit is the ubiquitous visibility of useless violence and the human suffering it causes. . . . The act of witnessing and its monotony can become a mere enduring of the night, of the disaster." Zombies, not quite awake but never asleep, are the living-dead reminders of this condition, stumbling through our fictions. When they are not transformed by the wishful thinking of ideology into our pals, they retain this status.

Celebrated everywhere, zombies are the opposite of celebrities, who swoop into our disaster areas like gods from Olympus to rescue us from the calamities that also allow them to flourish. Zombies, far from being elevated, descend into utter undistinguishable anonymity and degradation, which is why they can be destroyed in good conscience. Brad Pitt, one of the producers of ABC's *Resurrection,* also starred in *World War Z,* the most expensive zombie movie ever made. The last line of that odious movie—the first neoliberal zombie movie—is, "Our war has just begun."

Whatever that was supposed to mean to the audience, these fables of the plague years drive home just who the zombies are supposed to be—and who, when the plague hits, will helicopter out holding the machine guns. Col. Kurtz's faithful devotee from *Apocalypse Now,* Dennis Hopper, the counterculture hero who became a Republican golf nut, plays the leader of the remaining 1 percent in *Land of the Dead*. "We don't negotiate with terrorists," he says when he's faced with the choice between his money and our lives.

July 2015

FOR CHANTAL AKERMAN

WAKING FIRST THING TUESDAY MORNING TO THE TERRIBLE NEWS CHANTAL Akerman had died in Paris was awful and distressing, a combination of sorrow, pain, and anxiety all at once. Finding out later that day her death was a suicide made it even harder. She was 65, young for a great director these days; her new film was playing at the New York Film Festival the next day. She made her first film when she was 18 years old, *Saute ma ville* in 1968, forty-seven years ago, and when I saw recent photographs of her or watched her in an interview she didn't seem all that different from how she appeared in black and white as a teenager in a film she made almost fifty years ago. She was recognizably the same person with the same look and sound and attitude. She seemed as melancholy but as calmly defiant as ever, and I never imagined a world where she wouldn't still be making films. Jean-Luc Godard and Michael Snow, the two filmmakers she named as her progenitors, are still working, after all, at 84 and 85.

Her place in cinema history is secure because of *Jeanne Dielman, 23 quai du Commerce, 1080 Bruxelles*, the three-hour-and-twenty-minute study of a middle-aged Belgian widow, mother, and part-time prostitute improbably starring Delphine Seyrig that Akerman made when she was 25, after about half a dozen other films. Yet because her films do not conform to feature-film running times—some are shorts, some are features but under standard feature-film running time, and some, like *Jeanne Dielman,* are quite long—her work is more difficult to exhibit than films by other European auteurs. That is a trait she shares with Marguerite Duras and Agnès Varda, and not with most of the men, better known than her, who have made films in Europe in the same period.

Akerman defied marginalization but not by trying to make art-house masterpieces in a recognizable way. In that respect, the times have caught up with her way of doing things. But since she's not here anymore, it doesn't matter whether the times caught up with her or not. Her last act was to defy a new, post-cinema world of total cinema marginalization by permanently opting out of it. If it makes you sad and anxious, as it does me, that she abandoned her life and her work, perhaps it's because, as with Fassbinder, Truffaut, Tarkovsky, and Cassavetes in the 1980s, she left us when we needed her most.

About fifteen years ago I interviewed Chantal Akerman before a small audience at the French Library and Cultural Center (as it was called then) on Marlborough Street in Boston's Back Bay. She was teaching at Harvard at the time and living in Cambridge. I was a movie theater projectionist and a zine writer, living in the horrible neighborhood of Brighton, and the French Library's media director, Federico Muchnik, hired me to conduct the interview even though there were well-known film critics or film scholars available in Boston. Federico knew I was a fan of her work and I'd mentioned to him how great it was that she was in Boston, how amazing it was, really, that this figure of world cinema was among us, in a town where there was little of cinematic interest going on. I don't think anyone in Boston but a handful of cinephiles even knew she was there. I don't recall the local press taking any interest in the fact that the director of *Jeanne Dielman* was skulking around Harvard Square unnoticed for the towering artist she was, possibly waiting in line for a bad coffee at Au Bon Pain. As far as I could tell, nobody cared.

At the French Library we showed a videotape of *News from Home* and I longed to be in New York and afterward I started the discussion by asking Chantal about what made her want to start making films when she was a teenager in Belgium. I'd read she had cited Godard's *Pierrot le fou* as the film that inspired her to make a film herself, so I added that I'd heard that. She said that was boring to talk about because she had answered that question so many times before, everyone knew she'd said it was because of *Pierrot le fou* that she started making films.

Instead of making me nervous, or more nervous to be talking with her in public, her diffidence put me at ease. It was funny and it made her seem more like a kindred spirit and less like a remote figure of the cinema. Our discussion had begun and Chantal was introspective, calm, and self-deprecating. She did not care what the people there knew about her or didn't know, and she treated the Q&A like something she had stumbled into, which was pretty much the case, so she could just talk about anything. Looking back on it, I wonder why she agreed to do it, and the main things I remember her saying were that she did not like to look at herself on-screen in the films of hers she had appeared in because it made her too conscious of her physicality, and that when she worked in video she had to try to make the image look worse than it would otherwise because if she didn't video looked too clear and boring, like everything it captured was understandable and normal, there wasn't enough interference.

After the Q&A I took her to a cheap Vietnamese restaurant on Brighton Avenue in Allston. I drove her there in my junky car and we ate pho and spring rolls. It was winter, as I remember, and Brighton Avenue was a nowhere strip back then; it had a certain classic northeastern American urban nothingness to it, but sucked nonetheless, a dirty street in a crappy neighborhood in a boring town. She deserved better. All the restaurants in Boston back then were bad in my opinion, Pho Pasteur was the only one I liked, and sometimes I ate there twice a day. Chantal did not seem to mind that she was eating in a place with photo menus and plastic tablecloths. She told me a story about working with a celebrated actress who was hard to deal with because her head had gotten big since she'd become famous, and she mentioned how much she liked the Samuel Fuller film *Shock Corridor* and how if that had been the only film he'd ever made it would have been enough. While we spoke I could not look directly into her very pale blue eyes. She treated me like somebody she would talk to anyway, but I was dazed. Chantal Akerman was eating with me in the only restaurant I could stand.

Sitting in the window of that restaurant with her had a real Edward Hopper feel, I can see that now. It really was like something in her film *Toute une nuit*. I didn't realize it at the time. When we left the restaurant, Brighton Avenue was deserted, as it usually was at night, lit by dim streetlights, and cold. I drove Chantal back to Harvard Square and dropped her off, and I never saw her or communicated with her again. She had given me her address in Paris but I didn't feel like I had a good reason to write her. I thanked her through the French Library and went back to life as I lived it then, trying to make enough money to pay my rent and find a way out of Brighton, Massachusetts. ("Why do they call it *Brighton*?" an old Frenchman with a heavy accent I'd often see on the Green Line B train used to ask no one in particular. "They should call it *Darkton*. It is never *bright*.")

It is fitting to remember that *Pierrot le fou*, Chantal's touchstone that she did not want to discuss, ends with the lead character's suicide. Belmondo blows himself up with dynamite at the film's end, but not before trying to put out the fuse in a last life-affirming moment of doubt. In Michael Snow's *La région centrale*, the three-hour landscape film Chantal also cited as central to her work, there are no people, just nature and electronic sounds Snow added to accompany the camera movements. *News from Home* is something like that, but Chantal added the people of New York to it, riding the subway and walking the streets, along with her own voice and words from her mother's letters to her. The film ends with the city seen from the Staten Island ferry receding into the background as she goes away unseen, present but not present.

There's an interview with her conducted by Nicole Brenez that appears, in David Phelps's translation, in the online film journal LOLA.

Brenez calls this piece "The Pajama Interview" because Akerman talks about how she spends so much time asleep in bed, how periods of depression confined her to it. Brenez points out that Akerman would sometimes direct her films in her pajamas. Maybe the Akerman film most like her life, then, is *The Man with the Suitcase*, in which she plays a character so irked by her ordinary-seeming male roommate that she confines herself in her room and ends up monitoring the outside world with video cameras. This short feature is hard to see today. If one thing comes out of Chantal's death I hope it's that films like that one, along with the amazing *Portrait of a Young Girl at the End of the '60s in Brussels, Night and Day, I'm Hungry, I'm Cold, Les années 80*, and *Golden Eighties* (two different films) become more widely seen and better known. To me these 1980s and '90s films represent a neglected period in her work between her essential '70s films and her more recent work, which she also showed in various forms in art galleries and museums.

In his book *24/7*, Jonathan Crary, without mentioning or probably even knowing about her hypersomnia, describes her 1993 film *From the East* as one poised between two worlds, one that is ending and one that more and more we all have to live in whether we want to or not. This landscape-with-people film tracks groups waiting in long queues in the former Eastern bloc after the collapse of the Soviet Union. Crary writes that the film, in its "extended portrayal of certain textures of everyday life," cinematically preserved a world of collective public spaces and sheltered domesticity where actual encounters can occur, a world disappearing into an all-encompassing, inescapable system dedicated to destroying time and community. The "suspended, unproductive time" (in Crary's phrase) of ordinary people was Chantal's subject. She has ended up a Simone Weil of the cinema, as her film *Je tu il elle* seems in retrospect to predict she would, an artist hyperaware and sensitive to the world around her, one she apparently couldn't take anymore.

In remembering Chantal Akerman I combine the wistfully happy, emotionally confused long twilight strolls through Paris the protagonist (Guilaine Londez) takes in *Night and Day* with Chantal's own manic sugar-eating in *Je tu il elle*. To me, these are the unforgettable extremes of Akerman's cinema more than the repressed, unhappy violence of *Jeanne Dielman*. A few years ago a couple I know, a translator and a painter who did not know who Chantal Akerman was and had never seen one of her films, gave me a poster for *News from Home* they had found because they thought it seemed like something I would like. It's hanging in a frame on the wall over my kitchen table as I finish writing this.

October 2015

WELLES LETTRES

ONE DAY IN 1974, ORSON WELLES, JOHN HUSTON, AND THE COMEDIAN Rich Little were sitting in a Denny's near Carefree, Arizona, about to order a meal. Huston and Little were acting in Welles's new film, *The Other Side of the Wind,* which is still unfinished and unreleased and was then in its fourth year of production. Welles was living in a desert house nearby, a rental in which he was also shooting his movie, something he had neglected to tell the owners he'd be doing.

Rich Little was a television star at the time, a popular nightclub impressionist seen on an ABC variety show called *The Kopykats* and on Dean Martin's TV roasts, which often included Welles. Welles had hired Little to play the second lead in *The Other Side of the Wind,* a choice that raised eyebrows. Welles wanted Little because he needed someone who could do voice impressions of Hollywood stars, not because he thought Little was a great actor himself. His character in Welles's semiautobiographical film was based on Peter Bogdanovich, the young director of *The Last Picture Show* and *Paper Moon* and a Welles acolyte known for his ability to mimic the voices of movie greats.

A waitress approached the table where the three men sat. She recognized Little right away. After bantering with the impressionist for a bit, she nodded toward Welles and asked Little, "Who's your fat friend?"

Huston, saving the day, answered for Little with a straight face. "You know, we don't actually know this man," he said, indicating Welles. "We picked him up on the highway and he seemed undernourished. We're going to feed him and then send him on his way."

The story comes from *Orson Welles's Last Movie*, a recent book by Josh Karp. It's one of many anecdotes designed to show how low the mighty director of the greatest movie ever made fell after completing what was supposedly his first and only masterpiece, *Citizen Kane*, in 1941. See the Boy Genius three decades later, fat-shamed at Denny's.

Further passage of time, however, has put stories like this one in a different light. Welles's detractors have been trying to punish him for his uncompromising approach to filmmaking—a directing style that looked, especially to Hollywood traditionalists, unorthodox—since before *Citizen Kane* was even released. By 1942, the year RKO butchered his second film, *The Magnificent Ambersons*, and blamed Welles for his own film's disfigurement, the myth of the self-destructive auteur was already in place. But now when we look back on Welles's work in Hollywood in the early 1940s, his real problems become clear: his dark vision of American capitalism was out of tune with the gung-ho years of World War II. That Welles pursued his original vision, even as he worked in a state of hand-to-mouth auteur financing into the '80s, looks from our vantage point like a sign of strength and integrity. The director of *Citizen Kane* and the director of *The Maltese Falcon* sitting in a Denny's in Arizona with Rich Little in 1974? That is a picture of dignity in the face of adversity, not a picture of failure.

It's been difficult to get beyond the mocking portrayals of Welles in part because so many critics and pop film historians have adopted Hollywood's conformist notions of success. Welles's story of unambition and lack of concern for studio approval has functioned as a cautionary tale: a lesson in how not to succeed in show business. Writers of the early '70s, such as Charles Higham and Pauline Kael, worked hard to knock Welles off a pedestal Hollywood had already smashed. Other writers have scraped away at the great man's self-image, marring it the way scratches on film tear into the emulsion and make it harder to see. Some continue to punish Welles. For a recent example, check Peter Biskind's introduction to the book *My Lunches with Orson*, a series of transcripts from tape-recorded conversations the filmmaker Henry Jaglom had with Welles in the LA restaurant Ma Maison between 1983 and 1985, the year Welles died. Biskind can't resist reveling in Welles's last days, when Welles "had ballooned to the size of a baby elephant" and survived by appearing in "B movies produced by fly-by-night producers in no-name countries" and "odds and ends like soaps, game shows, and TV commercials."

But this year, the Welles centennial, an appreciation for Welles—even the late, bloated, talk-show-guest Welles—is gathering force. Karp's book, along with Patrick McGilligan's remarkable, eye-opening biography *Young Orson* and A. Brad Schwartz's *Broadcast Hysteria*, provide a deep, nuanced portrait of the director at the start and finish of his career. By skipping his better known and much studied years as an actor-director in Hollywood in the heyday of the studio system, and his years in the '50s and '60s as a nomadic filmmaker in Europe, these studies offer a new image of Welles, one that re-radicalizes him as an artist and sets him against the backdrop of the Depression and the early days of World War II. Focusing on his work in the theater and radio in New York and elsewhere in the '30s, then cutting, *Kane*-like, to the New Hollywood of the '70s reveals an unwavering Welles, committed to a kaleidoscopic vision that was also a style of work and a way of being in the world. If he failed to find a way to direct his films with Hollywood funding and approval, he went elsewhere—a rebuke the movie industry saw as disrespectful, self-sabotaging, and grotesque.

While the cautionary Welles is a great source of internet listicle kitsch ("16 Hilarious Examples of Orson Welles's Late-Career

Slumming," flogged a headline on Newsweek.com earlier this year), it is not the Welles we need in the 21st century. The Welles of TV talk shows and wine commercials is in fact an indictment of how the second half of the 20th century failed to live up to the promises of the first half. In reality, it wasn't that Welles did not fulfill his promise. The times let him down.

In that sense, Welles's career started as it ended. When he was 5 years old, he got a gig dressing up as the White Rabbit at Marshall Field's department store in Chicago, hopping around and announcing, "Oh, I must hurry—or else it will be too late to see the woolen underwear on the eighth floor!" Welles called doing advertisements "the most innocent form of whoring," and even on radio the sponsor-free *Mercury Theatre on the Air* eventually became the *Campbell Playhouse*, introduced by long ads extolling the virtues of hot soup. Welles went on to become, as one historian quoted in McGilligan's book describes him, "the American Brecht, the single most important Popular Front artist in theater, radio, and film, both politically and aesthetically." But he never seemed to worry about maintaining a claim to purity: in some ways, he was always willing to step back into the bunny suit, if it could make him the money he needed for his next film or theater piece, or if it fit his strange view of American entertainment.

Welles recalled his childhood as "one of those lost worlds, one of those Edens that you get thrown out of." He grew up in idyllic towns with names like Oregon, Wisconsin, and Wyoming, New York, places that sound like they were invented by Franz Kafka for his novel *Amerika*. Welles's politically progressive mother and father encouraged his precocity and indulged his dramatic bent, taking him to the theater, magic shows, and concerts. As a child, Welles had seen on the stage many of the actors he later cast in plays and in his movies. Agnes Moorehead, who played Charles Foster Kane's mother and George Amberson Minafer's aunt in Welles's first two films, acted with Welles in the radio series *The Shadow*. Fifteen years older than him, she remembered seeing

Welles as a 9-year-old in the lobby of the Waldorf Hotel in New York City after Igor Stravinsky's American debut and listening to him pontificate on Stravinsky's music to his father. With his "shock of black hair," Moorehead remembered, "he was fantastic, the way he kept explaining his feelings about the concert."

"Less than a year after the death of his own mother," McGilligan observes, "he had met her fictional counterpart." Welles's childhood, so like a Wes Anderson movie, was shaped by his parents' divorce and their early deaths. His mother, a pianist, elocutionist, and suffragist, died of a liver ailment when Welles was 9. His father, the inventor of an automobile headlight and a successful businessman who retired wealthy and young, slipped into alcoholism after he divorced Welles's mother, and it worsened after her death. He died when Welles was 15, leaving him a trust fund Welles would collect in full when he turned 25. A family friend, Dr. Maurice Bernstein, an eccentric surgeon and musician who provided the name for a character in *Citizen Kane*, oversaw the trust, doling out $100 a month.

Welles, established as his prep school's resident artistic genius, declined a scholarship to Harvard and set sail for the Gate Theatre in Dublin. He convinced the artistic directors there, Hilton Edwards and Micheál MacLiammóir, that he was 18. Sensing, in MacLiammóir's words, "some ageless and superb inner confidence," they cast the 16-year-old Welles in a play, setting a template for the rest of his career by assigning him the role of a man in his fifties. Welles's entrance onto the stage was greeted, MacLiammóir wrote, with "a flutter of astonishment and alarm, a hush, and a volley of applause." Welles took six curtain calls on opening night and his performance was reviewed favorably across the ocean in the *New York Times*.

Welles was in a whirlwind, spinning at its center and gathering more force. After stints back in the Midwest, in New York City, and then in Spain, where he fought four professional bullfights (McGilligan confirms this much disputed claim), Welles settled, at age 19, in Manhattan with his 18-year-old bride, Virginia Nicolson, also an actor, also from a prominent midwestern family. They lived in a one-room apartment with a bathtub in the middle of the room, which they covered with a board at night to turn into a bed.

IT ALL SOUNDS VERY ROMANTIC, and it was. McGilligan's Orson is a Welles for a new generation. His book has a quality more in tune with Patti Smith's *Just Kids* (albeit a *Just Kids* that is eight hundred pages long) than with McGilligan's similarly lengthy and authoritative biographies of Alfred Hitchcock and Fritz Lang. Like Patti Smith and Robert Mapplethorpe in their New York, Welles was hyperaware of his own status as a fledgling artist setting out to conquer the town. McGilligan's book vibrates with uncertainty and risk, and it hums with the possibility that talented people actually can realize their dreams in the forms they choose. In the words, once again, of MacLiammóir, the book speaks of a time when "Orson had not yet found his true métier, which was a preoccupation with restless grandeur and intoxication, a view of life wholly American and welling up from the soil of the huge territory which had given him birth."

Young Orson's urgency is also a function of the kinds of theater and radio Welles was making in those years. McGilligan writes that he has tried to produce a book that is scrupulous but sympathetic to Welles, and his sympathy extends to the social-justice causes that animated the artistic life of young New Yorkers in the days of the New Deal, the WPA, and the Federal Theatre Project. The sources of Welles's achievement in the cinema are there, but the roots of his later problems with authority, with the right wing, and with mass culture are there, too. Reactionaries lurk at every turn, ready to disparage Welles's accomplishments and seal his fate.

Welles's initial struggle was to earn enough money acting on the radio to pay for what he wanted to do in theater, and this he managed to do. His mad scramble, however, began a cycle that became the pattern of his life. His first success on the American stage came in late 1934, as Tybalt in a high-end but conventional production of *Romeo and Juliet*. It was there that John Houseman, who would become the Mercury Theatre's producer and Welles's lifelong nemesis, first saw him, reacting to his performance with a homoerotic thrill that later led to jealousy and resentment, and which replicated and reflected the older man/younger man dynamic of so much of Welles's work. Welles's first radical or avant-garde success came three months later in a production of the poet Archibald MacLeish's play *Panic*, "a blank-verse autopsy of the US banking crisis of 1933, complete with Greek chorus." The 19-year-old Welles, in his performance as a middle-aged banker, was "bluff, defiant, bullock-like and brutal," according to a newspaper review. Houseman, in one of his memoirs, describes Welles's voice in *Panic* as "an instrument of pathos and terror, of infinite delicacy and brutally devastating power."

It was a voice for radio. Welles made good money as an anonymous actor on news shows like *The March of Time*, playing figures from the news of the day in staged re-creations of world events. At CBS he met actors like Joseph Cotten and Ray Collins, who later followed him to the Mercury Theatre and Hollywood. Even after the success of the Mercury Theatre on the stage and on the air, Welles continued to act for radio news. He had the strange honor of playing himself, uncredited, after the *War of the Worlds* panic became international news on Halloween in 1938.

The two years before the *War of the Worlds* broadcast were the most eventful of Welles's life. Working with Houseman for the Federal Theatre Project's so-called Negro Unit in Harlem, Welles directed a black-cast version of *Macbeth*, popularly known as the "Voodoo *Macbeth*." Employing many nonactors from the neighborhood, this African American production was not the minstrel show some feared it might become, but a landmark production in American theater. (You can find footage of it on YouTube.) A cause célèbre, it attracted audiences from all over the city and solidified Welles's reputation as a fighter for racial equality, a position that hurt him later. As an arch-lefty but noncommunist, Welles faced a soft exclusion from Hollywood that was conveniently attributed to his mythical unreliability.

The Mercury Theatre's "fascist" *Julius Caesar* followed, by all accounts a staggering, even frightening production featuring Welles as Brutus that received but one mean review, from Mary McCarthy. Fearing attacks from anti–New Deal Republicans, the Federal Theatre Project then shut down Welles's production of Marc Blitzstein's prolabor musical *The Cradle Will Rock*, padlocking the door to keep out the audience. Welles moved the crowd twenty blocks to a vacant theater and put on the show in the aisles with Blitzstein at the piano onstage.

A year later, Welles had too many plays in rehearsal, was doing too many radio shows, was taking Benzedrine to stay awake, ignoring his marriage, sending telegrams to ballerinas in an early version of sexting, and pushing his actors to work around the clock. He was overextended by the time the Mercury Theatre's radio production of H. G. Wells's novel *The War of the Worlds* hit the air. Changing the setting to contemporary New Jersey and presenting the radio play as a fake news broadcast panicked about a million listeners who had tuned in late, according to Schwartz in *Broadcast Hysteria*, causing them to believe a real Martian attack, or at least some kind of invasion or disaster, was under way.

Schwartz is careful in his excellent book to untangle the facts of what happened that night from the ways newspapers distorted the reaction, blaming it on hysterical women and residents of rural areas, or claiming Welles's sci-fi drama was a hoax. *Broadcast Hysteria* studies the almost two thousand letters people sent to Welles, to CBS Radio, and to the FCC, many in appreciation of Welles's show, but many outraged and condemnatory. One reader from the South wrote in to say Welles should be lynched.

This 1930s version of the comments section included much praise for Welles, too. A listener wrote that he had "put to shame the alleged master-minds of Hollywood and now they will be beseeching you with offers." In fact, they had already called. Soon Welles was flying back and forth between New York and Hollywood, earning his status as TWA's most frequent flier that year, to do his radio show once a week while also preparing his first movie for RKO, under a contract that gave him complete control over the finished product.

McGilligan follows him through that process, presenting excerpts from his bold first-person (and later abandoned) script for *Heart of Darkness*, based on the Joseph Conrad novel, chronicling the writing of *Citizen Kane* with Houseman and Herman Mankiewicz (an account that should finally lay to rest Pauline Kael's assertion that Welles wrote none of that famous film's screenplay). The book wraps when Welles calls "Action!" on the first day of shooting *Kane*.

Welles started his first film that day; he never finished his last. In May 2015, thirty years after his death, an Indiegogo campaign sought to raise $1 million to complete *The Other Side of the Wind*, now that the film's labyrinthine rights issues have been cleared up. The campaign page featured testimonials from well-known contemporary directors who were not giving money of their own, and offered premiums at different donation levels, including a white terry-cloth bathrobe with Welles's signature and face emblazoned on the chest. The drive fell several hundred thousand dollars short of its goal. The producers say they will finish the film anyway. It is imperative that they do.

In the mid-1980s, Steven Spielberg bought a Rosebud sled from *Citizen Kane* at auction for $60,500. At the same time, Spielberg denied Welles the opportunity to direct an episode of his NBC television series *Amazing Stories*, instead opting to hire directorial talent such as Burt Reynolds and Timothy Hutton. According to Joseph McBride, who has written several books on Welles and also *Steven Spielberg: A Biography*, Spielberg, after buying the prop, said he saw it as "a symbolic medallion of quality in movies. When you look at Rosebud, you don't think of fast dollars, fast sequels, and remakes. This to me says that movies of my generation had better be good."

Maybe that's why there has never been a *Goonies* sequel. Meanwhile, back at Denny's, the summer 2015 menu features a pancake entrée called the "Invisible Woman Slam," "drizzled with a clear citrus glaze," part of a promotion for the new *Fantastic Four* movie. In Hollywood, Welles once said, they "make the kind of movie producers want to produce," the kind written in invisible pancake syrup.

That was not Welles's goal in life. Whether we see him as an outcast or a genius, his story is the biggest argument against that system's idea of genius.

September 2015

EXPERIENCE MACHINES

STAN VANDERBEEK AND MOVIES ON AIRPLANES

WE LIVE SURROUNDED BY MOVING IMAGES IN AN ENVIRONMENT WE CAN escape only with difficulty, and then just for short periods. Yet it isn't really accurate to say we live surrounded by moving images. We are not merely surrounded by them. We inhabit a content environment. Moving-image content is what we live in and deal with every day, whether we want to or not. We move through it with more ease than we move through weather. If we bother to turn off the screens in taxicabs as we pass the LED billboards outside, it's usually only to better concentrate on our smartphones.

When all moving-image production is reduced to the level of content, and understood as such, it feels like it isn't there. Like weather, there is no reason to pay close attention to it, unless all of a sudden it becomes threatening, or we want to bliss out during a sunset. Even then, it's just more information, instructing us how to react. We like to think we have more control over content than we do over smog, rain, or drought. We call it up and put it to use, and the rest of the time it just looms or lurks, waiting for us to notice. Meanwhile, we're checking our weather app.

The possibility now exists that everyone on earth can be a content producer of some kind. If you share a photo on Instagram, you are one. At the same time, every environment can also be a retail environment, subject to a barrage of marketing content. Brands from Prada to Chipotle hire cinema auteurs and feature-film animation studios to make long-form ads, little movies with recognizable stars and styles that can be viewed anywhere. Content is shown at gas pumps, there to help you not think about peak oil or anything else. 7-Eleven even has an in-store TV channel to show ads. It could also produce original television and movie content, like Amazon does, and stream it instead of selling it in bins of DVDs. Why not? 7-Eleven's TV shows would probably be just as good as what's on ad-supported broadcast TV.

How did we get to the point where a chain store that sells hot dogs might also subject us to content that's comprised of more than just ads? Two recent books, which undertake very different projects, but have fascinating points of contact, help answer that question.

The Experience Machine: Stan VanDerBeek's Movie-Drome and Expanded Cinema, by Gloria Sutton, a professor of contemporary art history and new media in Northeastern University's Department of Art and Design, positions the polymath American avant-garde filmmaker Stan VanDerBeek as the progenitor of media performance environments that exist where do-it-yourself filmmaking and installation art meet corporate and institutional sponsorship, and then, like VanDerBeek's films, go digital. *Cinema Beyond Territory: Inflight Entertainment and Atmospheres of Globalisation,* by Stephen Groening, a professor of cinema and media studies at the University of Washington, traces the history of movies on airplanes, following in-flight content from early experiments with film projection and television transmission to today's seat-back screens and Wi-Fi-enabled cabins. Each book carefully and thoroughly investigates its subject, analyzing how motion pictures have been integrated into digital environments. VanDerBeek's work, which emerged from a bohemian milieu that encouraged group collaboration and aimed to counter alienation and expand minds as well as cinema, fits in surprising ways with how airlines have painstakingly reimagined the spaces they control and which then control us.

Domes link the two conceptions. VanDerBeek's *Movie-Drome,* a large-scale domed assemblage built from an aluminum barn-silo kit, in which he projected his films and slides to a recumbent audience in upstate New York, was unveiled to the public as part of the 1966 New York Film Festival. Attendees, including critic-theorist Annette Michelson and filmmaker-artists Shirley Clarke, Andy Warhol, Ed Emshwiller, and Agnès Varda, were bussed to Stony Point, New York, to experience this installation-machine firsthand, lying on its floor as VanDerBeek projected film onto the dome's inner surface and ceiling above their heads.

VanDerBeek, who coined the term *expanded cinema,* wanted to create a kind of civic art that was also a prototype for similar domes he envisioned as linked by satellite, which could then share visual presentations, including scientific ones and breaking news. The *Movie-Drome,* therefore, envisioned many of the ways we communicate and share information now: livestreaming, YouTube, teleconferences, Skype, TED Talks, et cetera. By bringing festivalgoers to the *Movie-Drome* upstate, VanDerBeek was also linking the cosmopolitan to the rural, showing his audience how places that seem far apart could be linked and communicate.

In 1966, American Airlines also unveiled a dome, called the Astrosphere, which the company moved from shopping mall to shopping mall in suburbs across the United States. The Astrosphere, as Groening explains, was part thrill ride, part science demonstration, in which potential travelers who feared flying were put at ease as they experienced what it was like to be in the first-class cabin of an American Airlines jet. This corporate experience machine existed for the same reason in-flight movies are shown on planes: to soothe potential consumers of air travel, who naturally experience varying degrees of anxiety flying over the clouds in a metal tube at six hundred miles per hour. American Airlines designed the Astrosphere to placate consumers and study their fears, just as today's seat-back screens record and report what you watch, when you watch it, and who you are, so that airlines can better determine what kinds of entertainment calm you. American Airlines, at the same time as VanDerBeek, was using their dome for very different reasons and exhibiting it to a different audience, but these multimedia approaches were not dissimilar, joining science, theater, and art to the dissemination of content meant to change minds.

Another VanDerBeek piece Sutton describes, his *Cine Naps,* which were performed in planetariums in Philadelphia and Florida in the early 1970s, also has strange corollaries to the goals of in-flight entertainment. VanDerBeek projected his sounds and images but encouraged his audience to sleep during these presentations. Afterward, attendees were given a phone number to call, so they could report any dreams they'd had during their nap, which VanDerBeek recorded on an answering machine. Since lulling travelers to sleep is one of the goals of the edited movie-and-TV content airlines show on long-haul flights, and since airlines pester travelers with post-flight email surveys, we are led to wonder if someone in the airline industry went to art school before getting an MBA. In any case, from now on I plan to report whatever dreams I had on the plane instead of answering whether or not I liked the snacks.

Sutton adroitly places VanDerBeek in the milieu from which he emerged: art studies at radical-experimental Black Mountain College, the influence of architect Buckminster Fuller and media theorist Marshall McLuhan, and collaborative work with composers, dancers, and painters, including John Cage, Claes Oldenburg, Carolee Schneemann, and Merce Cunningham. VanDerBeek died too young, at age 57, in 1984, and therefore did not get to witness the total digital content environments Groening presents in his book, including the strange tale of JetBlue Flight 292, which in September 2005 was rerouted to Los Angeles after a malfunction and forced to circle the runway for three hours before pilots decided it was safe to land. Onboard, passengers had live TV on their seat-back screens and could follow their plight on the news, knowing, as Groening puts it, "that as long as they were viewers they were still alive." The emergency turned out to have been overblown, a nonevent, and the plane landed safely, not before at least one passenger had recorded a video farewell. As an added bonus, since this was an LA–New York flight, many of the passengers were media professionals who reported on the event as it happened and wrote about it later.

Such events (and nonevents) are the stock-in-trade of cable-TV news, a non-experience machine that has linked the world like airplanes have, during which we are stationary, as on an airplane or in VanDerBeek's *Movie-Drome,* while everything around us moves. Groening places in-flight entertainment firmly in the context of neoliberalism, demonstrating that as we come to rely on our own personal digital devices, airlines give business-class travelers more and more and the rest of us in coach less and less. He glosses over the hell air travel has become for most people, which now too closely resembles the Jolly Fats Weehawkin Airline scenes in Jerry Lewis's *Cracking Up.* Instead, he proposes a new, more well-adjusted way of analyzing the world of total digital content that he terms a "meteorology of media."

That, it's true, is necessary, since no one today gets research grants for just complaining about air travel. On the other hand, as someone who saw his first movie (it was *The Love Bug)* on what was also his first airplane flight, and witnessed the entire world of the present and the future opening before his eyes, and at six hundred miles per hour thirty thousand feet in the air, I still hope for an approach closer to VanDerBeek's. Sutton is careful not to position him as a man against the system, and explains how he survived on institutional grants, by working for TV, and with places like Bell Labs. But she also points out that despite a resurgence of interest in his work that has included rebuilding the *Movie-Drome* in New York's New Museum for a show in 2012 (which I'm glad I saw), his estate is represented by his family, not by the kind of gallerist who jets around the world first class.

September 2015

DEPICTION IS NOT ENDORSEMENT

Argo

The new CIA-rehab thriller, as a genre, is anticonspiracy. Unlike the domestic spy thriller of the 1970s, today's CIA apologist thriller does not reveal how official truth is an illusion, an elaborate cover-up constructed to hide abuses of power.

Instead, the newer, sunnier CIA thriller shows how failure in the intelligence community is merely the result of human error. Overthrowing the democratically elected Mosaddegh government in Iran in 1953, for instance, and installing a corrupt puppet government headed by an absolute ruler, is something that could have happened to anyone. Years later there's a little blowback. Sadly, someone from the Agency has to pick up the pieces.

Ben Affleck's *Argo* shows that even movies that don't exist are more fun, and possibly more real, than the struggle of a nation. *Argo* is more like a 1970s heist movie than a paranoid espionage film. If it were a Robert Redford '70s movie, it would be *The Hot Rock*, not *Three Days of the Condor*.

Disguising themselves as a film crew allows the cast of *Argo* to put one over on Iranians who are by turns wily and childish. Confronted by cartoon storyboards for the fake movie (supposedly drawn by Jack Kirby, they look more like the placemats in a Big Boy restaurant), Iranian guards react with delight when one member of the fake crew makes whooshing sounds and jet-plane hand motions. Since this is the exact post–*Star Wars* position American filmgoers have been put in for decades—in fact beginning around the same time as the Iranian hostage crisis—it's a little unnerving to find Iranian soldiers standing in for the American audience like that.

Argo puts into practice the cinema-meets-military theories of Paul Virilio in an unpredictable way. We see the CIA as a creator of fantasy here, but that's all to the good: American lives are saved, no one gets hurt. Our enemies are fooled, not killed. The desire to believe in the movies, Affleck tells us, is universal. Happy endings depend on the success of the ruse, even when the ruse has geopolitical implications.

Argo is a much better film than the previous two Affleck directed, and his performance in it is low-key and self-effacing. The entire cast is good, including Clea DuVall in black glasses and black hair, here at least doing something worthy of her talent, and Adrienne Barbeau, wandering through the Hollywood script-reading scene as a cheeseball actress and producer's ex-wife.

It's noteworthy that the selection and reading of a film script plays such an important role in *Argo,* even if the whole point is that the script is derivative and lousy. That's another comment on the era in which *Argo* takes place. The existence of *Argo,* which could not have been made back then because its story was classified by the CIA, is more proof that that era is over, historical. Part of the fascination in watching *Argo* is wondering whether this caper could work today. The friendlier, humanized CIA of the Carter Era this film asks us to trust relies on fake mustaches, not enhanced interrogation techniques.

Zero Dark Thirty

All Kathryn Bigelow's *Zero Dark Thirty* asks us to believe in is the brute presentation of facts. Whether or not the film is a torture film is therefore, the film implies, beside the point. Torture happened, the film says, and here's how. So of course *Zero Dark Thirty* is a torture film, but we are expected to understand that now we are beyond the moral question of whether torture is right or wrong. The CIA got various kinds of information from torturing various people. Regardless of whether that information was good or bad, information is power. You sift, you put the pieces together, just like the Iranian schoolchildren in *Argo* put photographs back together from documents the US Embassy shredded in Tehran. Eventually you get a clear picture and if you're lucky human error doesn't enter into it and you are allowed to act on what you've learned and kill the guy you need to kill.

The film is in three parts. Part One: Torture. Part Two: Intelligence. Part Three: Execution. Each is a separate film that struggles between being quality television and something more cinematic, defined by Jessica Chastain's film-hero poker face and go-it-alone refusal to succumb to backstory, or do anything but work, grimly, at her job. Chastain's Maya, we later learned from news stories about the film, is a composite character meant to represent the hard work done by many women in the CIA in its effort to find and kill bin Laden. At the same time, she stands for every American woman today, who can succeed if she works day and night, if she stares into her computer for as long as it takes, if she makes the mean face but doesn't complain when her boss doesn't understand she's right, and is willing to relocate.

Bigelow wrote a piece for the *Los Angeles Times* in which she explained that when it comes to torture in *Zero Dark Thirty*, "depiction is not endorsement." But as always in the movies, the problem is not in the what but the how. *How* torture is depicted is more important than that it is depicted. Since Bigelow used to work for Semiotext(e) back in the day, maybe some French film criticism will come in handy here.

In 1961, Jacques Rivette, writing on the 1959 Gillo Pontecorvo film *Kapò*, which is about the inmates of a concentration camp, singled out one shot that ended on the hand of a character played by Emmanuelle Riva (Emmanuelle Riva who stars in *Amour*) as she died on an electrified barbed-wire fence. To Rivette, the preciosity of this shot was contemptible. Earlier in the piece, Rivette noted that this mixture of easy "realism" and spectacle was inherently immoral, because "that which [the filmmaker] dares present as 'reality' is physically tolerable for the viewer . . . but ultimately not *intolerable*. . . . At the same time everyone unknowingly becomes accustomed to the horror, which little by little is accepted by morality, and will quickly become part of the mental landscape of modern man; who, the next time, will be able to be surprised or irritated at that which will in effect have ceased to be *shocking*?" (The translation is David Phelps's and Jeremi Szaniawski's.)

This is the exact effect of the torture in *Zero Dark Thirty*. In 1983 Kathryn Bigelow played a feminist revolutionary working for a newspaper in Lizzie Borden's film *Born in Flames*, which imagines a socialist America and ends with a bombing at the World Trade Center. Questions of depiction come down to whose side you are on. If that seems too simple, it is no simpler than saying that "depiction is not endorsement," an evasive notion that lets any film director off the hook entirely, every time. After the "firsthand account" of torture in *Zero Dark Thirty*, it is hard not to conclude that Bigelow, like Maya, is working for the Man.

Skyfall

James Bond has always been the Man, that is the whole point of James Bond movies. *Skyfall* is a movie for a confused era, a digital, data-driven era, where killing is done by remote control. At first the film seems to admit it no longer makes sense to keep Bond on the payroll in this new world. The film starts with a radical move: Bond is shot and killed by another agent who happens to be a black woman (Naomie Harris). The story of *Skyfall* is the story of this character. First she kills Bond. Later she seduces him but is thrown over for an Asian temptress. She comes back at the end as the new Miss Moneypenny, Bond's boss's secretary, whose role is to lust after Bond but never get him, an underling he constantly teases. She wears a tight dress and sits in an office looking at Bond with big eyes while admitting she wasn't really cut out for fieldwork in the first place—she accidentally shot him, after all!

So much for empowerment. The theme of *Skyfall* is that the world must remain safe for white Englishmen to run around shooting people who aren't white and English. The film ends in Scotland, the ancestral home of Bond and the emotional heart of the upper-class Great Britain Orwell identified in "Such, Such Were the Joys," a domain of shotgun blasts and heritage-brand hunting togs, where large stags still wander, imperiously and symbolically, like they did in *The Queen*, with Helen Mirren, in 2006. It is here that the film's one good moment emerges, as Daniel Craig's Bond and Javier Bardem's pan-ethnic (but paradoxically ultra-pale) villain chase each other across the moors until Bardem, exasperated, needles him: "Do you see what comes of all this running around, Mr. Bond? All this jumping and fighting, it's exhausting."

The Avengers

Recruited into the secret agent game by Samuel L. Jackson's Nick Fury, Agent of S.H.I.E.L.D., American superheroes in *The Avengers* fight to protect New York from total destruction. It is no longer enough for one superhero to fight a single villain while dealing with his own personal problems, apocalypse must now enter into it. This apocalypse comes in the form not of climate change, the real menace to New York we witnessed firsthand in 2012, but in the form of mechanized aliens who must be stand-ins for our new enemies, the Chinese, because when they attack it looks like the sky is shitting endless orders of steamed whole fish.

Les Misérables

Tom Hooper directs every scene and composes every shot in this bloated, reactionary musical as if he were trying to express a new idea every time any actor moves a fraction of an inch. At the same time, this version of *Les Misérables* depends on absolute familiarity with the songs from the stage musical to produce the tears that are its reason for existing. Hugh Jackman's performance eventually moves even the uninitiated to cry, not because he is so moving—often he sounds like Walter Brennan singing "Old Rivers"—but because he had to endure so much just so two insufferable teenagers could get married.

Hooper's approach to revolution in the streets is to telegraph how doomed it is from the start, but also to show that it is completely justified—every character in the film is so exploited that he or she is a clear argument for immediate radical change. This sickly paradox puts the viewer on the side of getting the inevitable over with. Long before a little boy (Daniel Huttlestone), the mascot of the revolution, is killed by soldiers, his status as the most annoying Cockney urchin in the history of cinema made me want to see Russell Crowe's Javert beat him to death with Leonardo DiCaprio's hammer from *Django Unchained*.

Lincoln

Daniel Day-Lewis's animatronic performance in Spielberg's film underscores how Abraham Lincoln is like E.T., appearing among human beings to make things right before going back to the mysterious place he came from. He is also the perfect contemporary dad, reading to his little son about bugs while Congress debates the Thirteenth Amendment. *Lincoln* performs the important function of getting Americans to think about the terrible legacy of slavery in this country, and to reevaluate the influence of the South on national affairs. It is a political movie in every way, and has a science-fiction aspect: it posits white people as alien oppressors. White people are so white in *Lincoln*, which photographs them as grayish and pale under a winter sun, that sometimes it testifies to the lack of tanning salons in Washington DC in 1865.

Day-Lewis's pronunciation of the word righteous as "right-ee-ous" left an indelible mark on me, and it is no doubt historically accurate. But as someone from a small town near Hartford, I resent the film for claiming that the abolitionist Congressional representatives from Connecticut voted against the amendment to end slavery. That bothered me when I saw the film, but I never bothered to check whether it was true, and when Maureen Dowd wrote in her *Times* column that it wasn't, and that Tony Kushner dismissed his mistake by equating it to showing Lincoln wearing blue socks instead of green socks, I became doubly annoyed, because now I was in the position of defending a state I'd be happy never to see again and admitting I'd learned something from Maureen Dowd.

There's another thing Kushner left out of his screenplay that would have been good to include. When Lee surrendered to Grant at Appomattox, a Native American colonel on Grant's staff named Ely S. Parker was there, too. Parker, who is played in *Lincoln* by Asa-Luke Twocrow, drafted and wrote by hand the terms of surrender delivered to Lee, and in the film we see him on the porch with Grant as Lee approaches. This is not in the film, but when Lee saw Parker, he thought he was black, and made some remark to that effect, which he had to apologize for when told Parker was a Seneca Indian. "Well," said Lee. "I am glad to see one real American here." Parker responded by pointing out, "We are all Americans, sir." Not including this great moment implies that there was something Spielberg and Kushner thought was too corny for this film.

Django Unchained

Django Unchained is not so much the evil twin of the saintly *Lincoln* as its nasty, more clever kid brother, fighting the favorite for recognition, acting out. If I prefer it to *Lincoln* it's because I prefer the Tarantinian project, flaws and all, to Steven Spielberg's entire career. *Lincoln* may be the culmination of the Spielberg–Lucas reimagining of the American cinema as family entertainment, a transcendent work beyond the blockbuster form that reimagines the official national myth of an official national father for current and future generations.

Tarantino is more interested in a pre-consolidated cinema that predates Spielberg, in which national myths were put to use in tawdry, violent, and grandiloquent ways, and myth was open to interpretation by genre filmmakers outside the US. So however Tarantino has failed the actual history of slavery in the United States, the way he has opened it up for discussion strikes me as far more remarkable than the storybook of Spielberg's *Lincoln*, which closes with a thump and sends us off to bed.

People forget how sick, not anemic but twisted and ugly, the cinema had become before Spielberg and Lucas made movie theaters safe for families again. Tarantino looks to the minor glories of that era, which were amoral and provocative and not designed to last forever on any storage medium other than film. Maybe if you were never dragged by an adult to see an end-of-Hollywood/end-of-America movie like *Hustle*, with Burt Reynolds and Catherine Deneuve, you can't truly understand how warped it was. That film came out in 1975, the same year as *Mandingo*, a repellent, brutal film about slavery that is a touchstone for Tarantino.

Spaghetti westerns questioned the underpinnings of civilization. They examined sick societies through the eyes of tight-lipped, one-dimensional antiheroes surrounded by manic, cruel, and jaded characters who played terminal games of cat-and-mouse and growled dubbed insults at each other. The tense dinner scene at the Candyland plantation in *Django Unchained* captures their tone. When Christoph Waltz, as Dr. King Schultz, demands that the harpist sitting behind him stop playing Beethoven, Tarantino shows us the hypocritical European elegance spaghetti westerns layered underneath their operatic gunfights. That scene, and the one at the beginning with Schultz holding his lantern looking for an honest man, and the blood on the cotton, are as original as moments in Leone or Corbucci.

Beasts of the Southern Wild

Certain liberal-minded film critics judged *Beasts of the Southern Wild* harshly, were outraged by it, describing it as racist, shamelessly manipulative, and like advertising. That, putting it mildly, is a stretch. The film is such a convincing, fully realized, and overpowering achievement that begrudging its popular and artistic success is feckless. The film understands an America that is divorced from social services and beset by environmental collapse, but understands those things at the level of fable. It's not a documentary of Katrina and Louisiana any more than *The Wizard of Oz* was a documentary of the Dust Bowl and Kansas, and expecting it to reflect the exact political reality of its time, or any kind of progressive politics, is like hating *The Wizard of Oz* because it's not propaganda for the New Deal. Quvenzhané Wallis is *Beasts*' Judy Garland, and her narration is as emotional and devastating as Garland singing "Somewhere Over the Rainbow." Her hopes for the future and for the people in her community are no different from Garland's at the end of *The Wizard of Oz*. That's not a crime, and she's not running for office.

Hitchcock

Anthony Hopkins as Hitchcock convinces us that he is not Anthony Hopkins without convincing us that the lumpy man he is playing is Alfred Hitchcock. His portrayal lacks the sly charm of Hitchcock's TV introductions and seems overly interested in telling us Hitchcock was sad and weird. It does succeed in reminding us that there was a time when film directors had different body types, weren't all at least six-foot-three, didn't go to the gym, and didn't all wear sweaters with zippers.

Hitchcock also does two other noteworthy disservices to the master. One is that it eliminates his daughter from his marriage to Alma Reville (Helen Mirren). Since Patricia Hitchcock has an acting part in *Psycho*, which this film details the making of, that is a pointed omission designed to further question Hitchcock's marriage. The second is that every time Hitchcock takes a drink—and this film has him drinking wine and scotch frequently, including on the set—the soundtrack accompanies his imbibing with impolite slurping sounds. Hopkins's prosthetic lips seem wine-stained throughout. I've read a few Hitchcock biographies, some of which impugn him mightily, but I don't recall reading this fastidious man was a slurper.

The Master

This low-key but agitated antiauthoritarian film often comes off like a buddy movie about two very different men who like to get together to drink paint thinner and antifreeze. *The Master* is puzzling at all times, ignoring our desire to decipher it as it's unspooling (if you saw it on film). It creates a weird mood, as if in a dream *The Shining* got mixed in with Altman's *Popeye*. It keeps verging on the horrible and the cartoonish without quite getting to either. Joaquin Phoenix's performance successfully combines Marlon Brando with Moe Howard, while Philip Seymour Hoffman looks on, occasionally getting irritated but indulging him all the same. Amy Adams, as Hoffman's Lady Macbeth–ish wife, puts the brakes on the Phoenix–Hoffman relationship by masturbating Hoffman in front of a bathroom sink and uttering threatening, nonexplanatory lines like, "This is something you do for a billion years or not at all." When Hoffman sings the entirety of the song "Slow Boat to China" to Phoenix, it's clear the film is ending and that Phoenix will now be free of his demons, but why "Slow Boat to China"? Because Phoenix was in the navy in World

War II? Because they met on Hoffman's boat? Because the intense, repetitive, ad hoc, and perhaps meaningless process Hoffman has put Phoenix through has "melted his heart of stone"?

Flight

Flight is an excellent, hard-hitting, sleazy movie about an alcoholic airline pilot (Denzel Washington, really great here) who, hungover and right after surreptitiously downing three vodka nips, crash-lands a malfunctioning plane during a storm, saving everyone onboard except the flight attendant (Nadine Velazquez) he'd spent the night with. It is so good, except for the syrupy last ten minutes, that it is hard to believe Robert Zemeckis, who directed it, has spent the last twenty-five or so years since he made *Back to the Future* directing the things he's directed. *Flight* contains many riveting scenes, but one, with Washington alone in a hotel room the night before he faces a hearing about the crash, is especially riveting, and does not sell out the film. Its climax comes on a shot of a nip bottle, the kind he drank on the plane, sitting on top of a mini-fridge, one of 2012's best shots, so to speak.

Life of Pi

I went to the Sunday matinee of *Life of Pi*, in 3D, at the Regal Union Square Stadium 14 and paid my $18.50 to get in. Since it was Sunday morning I had stopped on the way and bought a large coffee to drink while I watched the movie. As I approached the escalator to get to the floor where the movie was playing, a ticket taker stopped me and told me I could not go in with coffee. If I wanted to see the movie, I would have to finish it before I went in or throw it out. I asked why. He said it was the theater's policy. I suggested that since the cineplex was almost empty because it was eleven in the morning, he might just look the other way if I brought the coffee in. No way, he said, they watch me on cameras. So I went back downstairs and got my money back. Sorry, Ang Lee. That coffee was more important to me that morning than seeing a movie in 3D.

Instead of seeing it, I walked over to the Strand, which is nearby, and looked at the discount books out front while I drank the coffee. I picked one up and opened it randomly, where I read something that seemed related to *Life of Pi* because the movie has a tiger in it. Reading it also had the virtue of being free and allowing me to drink the coffee while I read it: "Rapt/I dwell in this thorn and my claw alights/ On the sweet breasts of poverty and crime." Momentarily I considered stealing the book because it mentioned crime and I wanted to get back at the world for the movie theater's absurd policy. I bought it, though, and that and the coffee together cost over ten dollars less than seeing *Life of Pi*.

Moonrise Kingdom

Making a film featuring the music of Benjamin Britten and a biblical flood so you will get the chance to see a 12-year-old girl dancing in her underwear is a perfect example of going the long way around the barn. And the barn is the perfect color.

The Impossible

The Impossible is too one- or two-note to succeed as a prestige film. It lacks subtext or metaphor, or any subtlety at all, and deals with climate change head on. It is a horror film about Western tourists, directed by a horror director (Juan Antonio Bayona), without any of the genre trappings of a horror film.

Note one, the first half of the film, is the tsunami that struck countries on the Indian Ocean and the Andaman Sea, including

Thailand, where the film takes place at a pricey resort, in 2004. Note two is the aftermath of the tsunami, during which a family searches for one another across a vast, devastated landscape. Bayona's staging of the tsunami without (seemingly without) digital effects is relentless, convincing, terrifying, non-stupid, and without Hollywood wonder. The second half features Naomi Watts, the mother, in a hospital bed, mostly unable to move, mostly unattended, and slowly dying. The film has a message: Welcome to the vacation of the future.

Fans of Jacques Rivette, Carlos Saura, Robert Altman, and Alan Rudolph will appreciate Geraldine Chaplin's out-of-nowhere appearance in *The Impossible* as an elegant older woman, also cast adrift by the tsunami, who briefly and somewhat enigmatically shows up to speak to one of the two lost sons. *The Impossible* is a more trenchant and realistic film about the future of English people in foreign countries than *Skyfall*. The two films should play as a double feature.

Amour

The fate of African Americans in the South, the CIA, great floods, and immobilized bodies: these were the themes that got films nominated for Oscars in 2012. Michael Haneke's crossover hit, *Amour*, begins with the corpse of Emmanuelle Riva, decomposing on her bed and surrounded by flowers. Through Riva, the star of Resnais's *Hiroshima Mon Amour*, one of the French films from 1959 that changed everything, Haneke freezes the European art film in history, immobilizes it, while delivering a poignant film about aging and dying that will please a mainstream audience. Somehow this comes off as typical Hanekian perversity and slightly annoying "last modernist" pretentiousness. Jean-Louis Trintignant, who has worked with almost every great or even interesting European director, from Rohmer, Chabrol, and Truffaut to Kieślowski, Corbucci, and Costa-Gavras, ends the film, and with it, Haneke implies, a whole world of film, a whole era.

He does it in a way that will ensure viewers unfamiliar with Haneke understand he didn't make *Amour* for the Hallmark Channel.

The Sessions

I was prepared to feel awkward while watching *The Sessions*, a noble film about a poet (John Hawkes) immobilized by polio who hires a sex therapist (Helen Hunt) to guide him through the first sexual encounters of his life. I was not prepared for the combination of Helen Hunt nude plus a Boston accent. The fact that the poet's first name is Mark added to my discomfort. "Mock, Mock, it's time to get stotted. Mock, we should stot." It was the first time sex in a movie made me want to cover my ears.

Silver Linings Playbook

This shrill movie, which features lots of yelling, reinvents the screwball comedy for a post-collapse America by thoroughly deglamorizing its genre. Set in a lower-middle-class Philadelphia suburb, it is a *Philadelphia Story* in which the female lead (Jennifer Lawrence) dresses only in black, and the male lead (Bradley Cooper), no Cary Grant, works out wearing a garbage bag. The craziness of screwball is literalized in *Silver Linings Playbook*. Both characters are, to varying degrees, mentally ill, on meds, or in therapy. The story contains standard rom-com elements, but David O. Russell and cinematographer Masanobu Takayanagi shoot the film in a self-consciously gritty, shaky, and underlit way that deflects any resemblance to, say, *Friends with Benefits*.

Silver Linings Playbook is difficult to like, and too long, with a climactic dance scene that is filmically botched, which is fine with the movie because according to the plot it did not have to be good to succeed. The chatty, exasperating qualities of Cooper's pathology, which Russell understood so well in *The Fighter*, are equally present here, but Cooper seems more violent and unhinged than Christian Bale did in that movie because he's nicer and closer to normal. Just as this movie is closer to the romantic experiences of many, many people than the standard-issue Hollywood rom-coms it has stylistically left behind.

April 2013

FILM-LIKE

THIS SECOND EDITION OF THE *N1FR*, *N+1*'S FILM REVIEW, IS VERY LATE. ITS lateness has nothing to do with *n+1* or with any of the contributors, or with our generous sponsor, IFC Films. It's entirely my fault. I wish I could say the delay in the appearance of a new *N1FR* was the result of some kind of considered process, that it was an example of the kind of "Slow Criticism" practiced at *De Filmkrant* in the Netherlands. I wish I could say I've been spending all my time since the last issue carefully mulling over developments in the movies before committing anything to print. I wish I could say I had not made this issue's excellent (and timely) contributors wait for me as I slid out of frame.

But I can't. I have not spent all this time attending international film festivals with Dutch people. I have not been reconsidering and revising and trying to get things right. The difference between this Late (or Tardy) Criticism and other people's Slow Criticism is the difference between taking your time and not having any time.

In the last year and a half my day job has taken over my life, and while it has brought me to fascinating places, from fortresses of the entertainment industry to video rental stores for truckers, it has not taken me to even one international film festival. It has provided me with a living, but not with enough time to edit and write.

My consumption of cinema has decreased proportionally. I missed dozens of new films last year. Did I see *Martha Marcy May Marlene*? I did not. Did I miss the entire New York Film Festival? I did. Did I see *Melancholia* on the internet? I didn't even see *Bad Teacher* on the plane. I've had a Netflix DVD of Mia Hansen-Løve's *Father of My Children* sitting next to my TV since last June 4.

Most of what cinema I did take in I got from DVR'ing movies on TCM and then mainlining them into my neck on my way out the door. *White Shadows in the South Seas*? I've got that covered. Abel Gance's *J'accuse* and *La roue* are going to be on soon, too, I hear.

You can see I've only fallen about ninety-five years behind. Like an abandoned cineplex I visited in Indiana that had been turned into a church by an Assemblies of God splinter group, I have descended below the cinema of attractions into a pre-cinematic state. Even if I download an app that will let me watch the new *Ghost Ride*r film on an iPhone in 3D, I'm not sure I could catch up.

FILM PRODUCERS IN AMERICA, from the highest to the lowest, constantly tell us how much film critics don't matter. Recently, via YouTube, Kevin Smith announced the debut of a new cable-TV reality show he hosts and shoots in a comic-book store he owns. During the video he took the time to remind viewers that film critics are irrelevant, and that nothing brings out their irrelevance more than explaining to them how irrelevant they are. If only it were that easy.

Since most working film critics don't make enough money to feed themselves, much less the families they don't have, it has become increasingly mysterious to me how they are able to watch what they watch and then write film criticism (of whatever speed) at all. One of the most telling cinematic events of last year came in the form of a letter: the reply David Denby sent to Scott Rudin last December after Rudin got mad at Denby for ignoring his command against publishing reviews of *The Girl with the Dragon Tattoo* (which Rudin produced) until after the film was out, even though critics like Denby had already seen it in press screenings. Denby had agreed to this embargo, and embargoes like that are a common practice in the film industry, and then he went back on his word.

Rudin called the publication of Denby's review in the *New Yorker*, which was a positive review, "a very, very damaging move," and in a subsequent email to Denby told him he had "very badly damaged the movie," and that he had done something "deeply destructive" and "immoral."

In his email, Denby pointed out something that is true: "The system is destructive"—"the system," not positive reviews of blockbusters. By "the system," in this case, Denby meant the way studios release their serious, quality, or award-getting movies all at the same time, near Christmas, forcing film critics to madly rush from one film to another, in an attempt to keep up, seem professional, write long pieces on things presumably worth writing about, and take part in voting for yearly awards as part of whatever professional bodies they belong to.

"Grown-ups are ignored for much of the year, cast out like downsized workers, and then given eight good movies all at once in the last five weeks of the year," Denby wrote to Rudin. (I'm not sure how he arrived at the number eight, I would have said twenty, because Denby is only thinking of big-studio releases here, when in fact a lot of worthwhile smaller films also flood the market at the same time.) Denby speaks the truth, and could have gone further: at the end of the year a horde of disenfranchised, semi-disenfranchised, and soon-to-be disenfranchised American film critics are forced to work overtime for film producers, people who do not sign their paychecks. They are not only forced to work for them by writing promotion for their films in the form of reviews, but by following their instructions to the letter about when they are allowed to publish—in essence, about when they are allowed to speak.

That is the system that is destructive. It's destructive to the cinema, it's destructive to film criticism, and finally and ironically, it is destructive, of all things, to Christmas. Film critics are forced to contemplate drear like *J. Edgar* and *The Iron Lady* instead of spending time with their loved ones and forgetting their cares at holiday parties and not letting old acquaintances be forgot. But for film producers it is an exciting time, the kind that makes life worth living—a time to worry about skimming the cream. Rudin can release two movies at almost the same time: a serious drama with Tom Hanks and a cute kid like *Extremely Loud and Incredibly Close,* and a rape thriller like *The Girl with the Dragon Tattoo,* and every possible person who could want to see a movie during the Christmas season should be happy—except critics, who, given the circumstances, naturally rebel. It is not immoral to agree to and then disregard an immoral command. More critics (and their editors and publishers) should just say "*Yeah, yeah*" to these things and then do whatever they want. Critics are not Christmas elves working in Santa's factory so the children of the world can see *We Bought a Zoo.*

IF THE OSCAR SEASON that is now upon us proves anything, it is that Scott Rudin probably should have asked critics not to write about *Extremely Loud and Incredibly Close,* instead of *The Girl with the Dragon Tattoo.* On the other hand, what does it matter? *Extremely Loud and Incredibly Close* was nominated for a Best Picture Oscar even though critics didn't like it, an honor it shares with two or three of the other eight nominees for Best Picture.

This new practice of over-nomination—couldn't they have just rounded the number of nominees up to ten?—reflects what most Hollywood movies and other American culture products have become: dollar-store items piled in heaps, undifferentiable from each other, sold clear-wrapped together on skids, advertised the same way food is advertised in supermarket circulars, in little square color pictures you need a magnifying glass to see.

Until very recently you could go into a chain store and find a wire spinner-rack of discount DVDs for sale. Then the spinner changed into a trough, then a barrel, and now it's the size of an aboveground swimming pool. This flood of discount DVDs overflowing its bin isn't just at Walmart or in home-electronics stores anymore. Now you go into a corner convenience store or a gas station on the highway and find them, too. The complete movie careers of everyone from Jennifer Aniston to Mark Wahlberg to Sarah Jessica Parker and Bruce Willis are bundled together into two-fers and three-fers as studios try to unload these unwanted pieces of plastic onto late-night potato-chip buyers and other people too confused to know what they want. I will never forget the time I saw a man in a parking lot scraping the snow off the windshield of his car with the DVD of *Independence Day* he had just bought.

THE COMBINED AGES OF James Franco and Anne Hathaway are a year less than Billy Crystal's. Crystal's return to the Oscar telecast as host this year after an eight-year absence reflects something beyond the failure of last year's attempt to instill some youth appeal into the proceedings by using Franco and Hathaway. He's there to remind the people in charge of their glory days, when Crystal could insert himself into parodies of blockbusters secure in the knowledge that those blockbusters were real and big. Kidding them proved how important they were to the culture at large and to the people who made them. Do we really want to see Crystal lovingly chiding *War Horse*?

During the last time of great cultural confusion in this country, the late 1960s and early 1970s, the Oscars had no hosts at all for three years in a row. Back then, there was also a three-month gap between the Superbowl and the Oscars. This year, there are three weeks between the two. That gives us an opportunity, if we watch them both, to recall all the commercials for upcoming movies that aired during the Superbowl—for movies like *Battleship*, *John Carter*, and *The Avengers*, which are not the Superbowl commercials people think about but ones they get anyway—and compare what Hollywood really is today to the face it puts on during the Oscars.

And if you watch the trailer the Academy made to advertise Crystal's return to the Oscars, the one where Megan Fox and Josh Duhamel from the *Transformers* movies go to Mongolia Indiana

Jones–style to search for Billy Crystal, the ancient sage of the Oscar telecasts, this last human they have to bring back to digital Hollywood, you will see that the trailer is described on YouTube as "film-like."

I'm not sure how that term is related to *life-like*, but I think, now, it is. *Film-like* means "the way films used to be" the same way *life-like* means "almost convincingly alive." In this issue of the *N1FR*, which because of my lateness does not cover even one film nominated for an Oscar this year, we cover other, better films by disentangling the two terms, too slowly, but here it is. In future issues we will move to a more regular online model, with pieces appearing one at a time, but that's a story for later.

February 2012

CALL TO YOUTH

ON JONATHAN ROSENBAUM

IN THE FIRST PARAGRAPH OF HIS INTRODUCTION TO THIS COLLECTION OF career-spanning essays, Jonathan Rosenbaum, the essential American film critic of his generation (but one who works hard to transcend his Americanness), divides his "friends and colleagues" in half. He places those who "think that we're currently approaching the end of cinema as an art form and the end of film criticism as a serious activity" on one side of the divide. On the other he locates those who "believe that we're enjoying some form of exciting resurgence and renaissance in both areas." Most of "the naysayers," he notes, are people in their sixties like him, or older, while the optimists are mostly in their twenties.

Leaving aside for a moment the three-decade middle group of people in their thirties, forties, and fifties Rosenbaum neglects, which reflects a generalized baby-boomer neglect of the interim generation in favor of their grandchildren, it is important to note that, consciously or not, Rosenbaum has always addressed himself to the future. He has done so in a way that is admirable and rare in a film critic working regularly in American journalism. That sets him apart.

Instead of writing only about what's playing now, Rosenbaum concentrates on what we might be able to see *at some point,* and works toward making a world where hidden movies come to light.

If he is on the side of the optimists in his new book, it is because he is living in a world where this has actually happened, and in his lifetime. Although it has not happened for the most part in the way most cinephiles wanted it to, which is in movie theaters where 35mm film prints are projected on large screens to more than one person at a time, we are nevertheless living in a new world of new possibilities.

Goodbye Cinema, Hello Cinephilia is therefore not a polemic like *Movie Wars,* Rosenbaum's book from 2000 about the limits studios and distributors impose on what we are allowed to see. Things have changed in ten years. Nor is it an exercise in canon-making, like 2004's *Essential Cinema.* In this book, which is a summa of his best work on his favorite films, filmmakers, and film critics, Rosenbaum resists criticizing the fragmentary aspects of digital culture, opting to become a Virgil leading us out of distribution hell into a downloadable purgatory where films are unfrozen.

I experienced the Rosenbaum call-to-youth firsthand. I began reading him in my late teens and early twenties after buying, on sight, knowing nothing about it, and right when it came out, a copy of *Midnight Movies,* a book he wrote with J. Hoberman. *Midnight Movies* covers something that was on its last legs when the book was published in 1983, the then widespread practice of exhibiting *outré,* trippy movies after-hours at revival houses and art theaters—really more of an activity than a practice. Midnight screenings have never completely gone away, but they are nothing like they were in the dress-up, drug-fueled 1970s heyday of *The Rocky Horror Picture Show,* a phenomenon of its time whose echoes have faded.

The mania for *Rocky Horror* provided an excuse for Rosenbaum and Hoberman to write an engaging, intelligent book on the films of, among others, David Lynch, George Romero, John Waters, Jack Smith, and Andy Warhol, a group united by weirdness whose films were best seen in the double darkness of a movie theater after decent people had gone to bed. As a teenager, I lived near enough to a couple of college towns to see *Eraserhead, Night of the Living Dead,* and *Pink Flamingos* under conditions close to the ones described in the book.

Totally unlike the blockbusters that had begun to dominate cineplex screens, these films rescued me and many others from a moviegoing life of infantile blandness—*E.T., Return of the Jedi,* Reaganoid films for the "morning in America" pep rally we confronted by day.

If *Midnight Movies* was high school, Rosenbaum's solo book from the same year, the eye-opening *Film: The Front Line 1983,* was college. It was also collage. The mix of filmmakers in the book was a revelation. It was amazing that Rosenbaum thought to put them all together—Chantal Akerman, James Benning, Manuel DeLanda, Yvonne Rainer, Rivette, Snow, Straub and Huillet. Reporting from inside many kinds of non-mainstream filmmaking, mixing difficult European art films with various strains of North American and British experimentalism, *Film: The Front Line 1983* described a world that was going out of fashion as the one-size-fits-all mainstream solidified in malls across the land, and it proposed an avant-garde that would someday counter and maybe replace that. The book had a dated quality, because art and underground films did not provide a career path in the age of *Risky Business,* and a futuristic aspect, because who knew what would happen if people could see films by the forty or so filmmakers he included in the book?

Film culture, for the most part, caught up with it only recently; the book was twenty-five years ahead of its time. Reading it plunged me into a world more cerebral and enticing than the dirty-glitzy, ugly-beautiful one exposed in *Midnight Movies.* Attracted and confused by the intimidating structuralist-materialist principles of Peter Gidal, wondering what Jackie Raynal's *Deux fois* would really be like were I actually able to see it, *Film: The Front Line 1983,* a mini-encyclopedia and map, pointed me toward places I barely knew existed.

Please excuse the foray into autobiography. It is hard to resist when writing about Rosenbaum, for among his contemporaries he is the most autobiographical film critic, maybe the only American film critic who has fully let autobiography enter his work. I admit that sometimes I get frustrated reading again about his childhood in Florence, Alabama, among a family of movie theater owners. Then

I reread an essay like "'The Doddering Relics of a Lost Cause': John Ford's *The Sun Shines Bright*" (included in *Goodbye Cinema)* and I remember how autobiography leads him to connect Ford's film to an unexpected series of other films—*Pickup on South Street, Stars in My Crown, Gertrud,* and *Playtime*—taking him on tangents that broaden and deepen understanding of *The Sun Shines Bright,* and Ford in general, in remarkable ways. And unlike other writers who took the opportunity after Susan Sontag's death to memorialize their encounters with her, Rosenbaum's Sontag piece, "Goodbye, Susan, Goodbye: Sontag and Movies" (also in the book), acknowledges her influence, then treats her affectionately—his Sontag plays the jukebox and sashays over to the cigarette machine, Godard-style—even though she was as prickly with him as she was with others. Part of Rosenbaum's appeal is his ease and comfort in a world of arts and letters he is confident and gracious enough to put to good use.

Having essays like his 1977 piece on Luc Moullet from *Film Comment* and his 1974 Erich von Stroheim piece from the same magazine between covers is invaluable, but it is the book's first section of newer essays, which Rosenbaum calls "Position Papers," that justifies its title. It is this section, along with the introduction, that investigates and ultimately affirms a new world of digital media that makes obscure films more accessible and shareable than ever. Rosenbaum quotes Tag Gallagher, whose video essays for the Criterion Collection and other DVD companies are changing the ways we study movies. "For a movie lover," Gallagher says, "there's no better time to be alive—with all due respect for those who claim that only nitrate is worth watching."

While these new formats help exemplary critics like Rosenbaum and Gallagher finally get their due, the one thing neither answers is how anyone is going to make a living as a film critic anymore, outside the ever expanding world of infotainment. For two writers commendably concerned with issues of social justice in the movies, neither has much to say about how this new generation of super-knowledgeable, cinema-at-their-fingertips optimistic twentysomethings is going to get paid. The generation Rosenbaum leaves out of his introduction has learned the hard way that film criticism is a tough dollar, and Rosenbaum and Gallagher know it themselves. Do they really look forward to a world where the majority of people keeping the cinema alive have boring day jobs, download movies at home, watch them on computer screens at night, then blog about them as the sun rises, with an expanded sense of community their main reward? Rosenbaum sought to change film criticism, and he did, making many people aware that there is more to the movies than commercial interests let on. Now what?

One filmmaker Rosenbaum turns to again and again is Jacques Tati, an artist as melancholic and optimistic as he is, who also works to help us see everything at once and to understand how it is all related. I am optimistic, too, and I don't want to rain on his *Parade,* but I wish Rosenbaum would offer an answer to that question. At the same time, I don't want to criticize an excellent book I came away from whistling the theme from *Mon oncle.* Just like in Tati's film, it is the play between the old world and the new that makes *Goodbye Cinema, Hello Cinephilia* so valuable and unique.

March 2011

127 HOURS IN GASLAND

Black Swan

It makes sense that *Black Swan* came out around Christmas because *Black Swan* is like a fruitcake. It is a cake, but not any kind of cake you'd like to eat; it's heavy; and you find out too late it's filled with gooey red clumps made out of God knows what. With dialogue like silent movie intertitles, its sunless expressionism is not so much reminiscent of *The Red Shoes* and *Carrie* as *The Cabinet of Dr. Caligari*. It recasts ballet as a masculinized competition between broken dolls and maniacs that takes place inside a Freudian fairy tale, making it a film for today—incoherent and unsatisfying, it leaves you battered and confused.

True Grit

I keep reading how much the new *True Grit* is like the John Wayne original, but what's more interesting to me is how much it's like *Tron: Legacy*.

In both, Jeff Bridges plays a cool old dude (grizzled and fat in *True Grit*, sleek and smooth in *Tron: Legacy*) who reluctantly shepherds an adolescent through a maze of conflicting allegiances in a frontier space that has more to do with baby-boomer self-image than it does with the historical reality of the Choctaw Nation or what it's like inside a computer.

In *True Grit,* Bridges is a father who has abandoned his son and who reconnects with his parental side by protecting a girl young enough to be his granddaughter, while she avenges the murder of her own absent father; in the *Tron* sequel he becomes Zen-hippie grandfather to his abandoned son, whom he reconnects with after disappearing into cyberspace (i.e., up his own ass) during the son's formative years.

These Bridges roles aren't very different from those in *Crazy Heart* and *Iron Man*. The *Crazy Heart* Bridges, a fat Southern alky like *True Grit*'s, abandoned his son and sought to be a father to the child of a woman young enough to be his daughter (Maggie Gyllenhaal). In *Iron Man* he was the appointed father substitute for Robert Downey Jr.'s rambunctious eternal adolescent Tony Stark, who like the son in *Tron: Legacy* sees the world through a computerized mask.

This quartet of Bridges efforts shows how this laid-back and exemplary actor—good in every role he plays, the consummate Southern California hippie professional; he is, after all, the Dude—has become aging Hollywood's classic-rock version of its best self, the medium through which it explains and shows its paternity to the world. It is Bridges who should be hosting the Oscars, with James Franco and Anne Hathaway as cute grandchildren he can smile on and guide as they give out trophies to their peers.

The Social Network

David Fincher solved a problem no director has ever been able to solve before: how to make Cambridge, Massachusetts, look glamorous. You do it by setting almost every scene at night and bathing everything in chartreuse light. Watching *The Social Network* was so epic it was like watching the Superbowl, except it was a Superbowl in reverse, where the game appears like a commercial in the middle and the main part is all ads, clever people yapping at each other while they try to sell you something. The Thames rowing set piece interrupted the movie like the most exciting Superbowl commercial ever made, in which we learn that physical mastery and bodily perfection will no longer be enough to win the game in this new world of internet brainiacs. And like many a Superbowl, the last ten minutes needed a rewrite.

Restrepo

This matter-of-fact documentary was made by the writer Sebastian Junger and news photographer Tim Hetherington while they where embedded with a US infantry regiment in Afghanistan's Korengal Valley. The regiment hunkers down at the bottom of the valley while the Taliban, who completely surround them, shoot at them with AK-47s, machine guns, sniper rifles, and rocket launchers four or five times a day, month after month. After a slow, painstaking effort, the soldiers manage to take a mountaintop and establish a fort there called Restrepo, named for a fallen comrade, a doctor they admired.

The film is so dry it doesn't bother to explain why or how the fierce, staring village elders who sometimes meet with the commanding officers dye their beards and eyebrows red and black while leaving the close-cropped hair on their heads gray. This gives them an unsettling look that, while normal to them, seems more foreign than anything else in this film. If these are the old men, you wonder what the young ones who spend their days shooting at Americans look like.

The King's Speech

This cold and stylized yet oh-so-warm movie seems like it is going to show us something really interesting about the difference between sound and image, then becomes a parable about how, whoever we are, colonial or king, we have to turn our loose upper palates into stiff upper lips and learn not to stutter so we can face the coming global threat (Nazis). Geoffrey Rush is his usual endearing self, a whirlwind of acting in a world of under-players and technicians. But as an American who recoils from monarchy I am compelled to ask, what if we solved the king's problem by cutting off his head? It's exactly that kind of thinking that is not called for, says *The King's Speech*, a movie set in a gray-blue-brown past that seems like both the future and today.

Alice in Wonderland

Tim Burton uses every digital tool there is, but to little effect, because he has forgotten the most basic things about cinema: where to put the camera, how long a shot should go on, where a character should look. Do his characters look at anything at all?

No amount of production design can make up for directorial laziness. This *Alice in Wonderland* would be better if it were shot in black and white on VHS tape with actors in furry mascot costumes. Burton should push himself a little. He is not just stuck in the childish creepy-arty phase that made him who he is; he has actually regressed to the point of being where he can defang any material he tackles, no matter what it is, and dress it up in girly striped stockings. Roald Dahl, Washington Irving, Topps bubblegum cards, Stephen Sondheim, *The Planet of the Apes*, Lewis Carroll—Burton can make anything family friendly. The hobbled dance that Johnny Depp, miscast as the Mad Hatter, performs at the end of this film is a pathetic reminder of Winona Ryder's joyous "Jump in the Line" number at the end of *Beetlejuice*, twenty-two years ago. Seeing Depp hop in 3D does not help.

127 Hours

Danny Boyle's best film (maybe because it's so simple) is a male *Eat Pray Love* set in a tiny crevice. It includes all the usual vulgar Boyleisms—aggressive music, brain-beating editing, a concentration on bodily wastes (urine instead of shit for a change), lots of flashbacks, video, and dream sequences—but here they culminate in a nice gory scene of a guy cutting off his own arm, and are more excusable because the setting is so limited. James Franco gives a performance that at first seems like a parable for much larger global issues. He's an average zesty American dude—a Phish fan!—without a care in the world who suddenly finds himself in over his head, trapped by his own foolishness.

Franco gives a workmanlike performance that seems normal, regular, not like manic dabbling in a profession not his own. He could be Any Actor instead of the Boy of Every Medium, the Spokesmodel for Everything. While the coming years will probably see him appointed US ambassador to Fiji while he's simultaneously appearing as the nutty new astrophysicist on *Big Bang Theory* and preparing his scrimshaw exhibit for the Whitney, here he gives us hope that maybe someday he will stop displacing water in other media. It's good to know he has something to fall back on.

Blue Valentine

You know it's a feel-bad movie when your first thought when it's over is, she should have had the abortion. She doesn't have the abortion for the same reason John Ford said the cavalry doesn't kill the Indians in the first reel: if they did, there wouldn't be a movie. That may explain a lot about the way abortion is treated in American movies these days.

Blue Valentine, a glum film of intertwined backstories revolving around a claustrophobic scene in a sex motel, never coheres, despite the mighty struggle of Michelle Williams and Ryan Gosling to make it work. Derek Cianfrance spends too much time on nice things that don't matter, worrying over the pleasant Grizzly Bear score and the end-credits sequence informed by American avant-garde filmmaking. Cassavetes never worried about touches, even when his characters were at their most hyper, muddled, or lost. By the end of *Blue Valentine*, Gosling seems like a dupe, smoking alone in a windowless room, Williams like a hard-ass who never wanted to marry a guy who could sing like Tiny Tim anyway. The film is non-illuminating. It depresses you but doesn't change your life.

The Town

How many helicopter shots of Charlestown, Massachusetts, can one film hold? Was *The Town* directed by Google Maps? And if there has ever been a woman like Rebecca Hall working as an assistant bank manager anywhere in Boston, I will eat writer-director-star Ben Affleck's three-season Red Sox cap for lunch and his winter knit Bruins hat for supper, unless lunch and supper are the same thing where he grew up. Jon Hamm, playing a character who should not have existed in the script, gives a performance so bad he looks as puzzled to be there as Jeremy Renner looks pissed.

The Fighter

On the other hand, *The Fighter* captures its working-class Lowell, Massachusetts, milieu with depth and accuracy. A feel-good yet crack-ruined movie, this boxing film overflows with good performances that are scary and over-the-top and stand in relief against dense, cluttered backgrounds where people are drunk, smoking, scabby, and could use new hair. Mark Wahlberg is the film's anchor, its one stable point. Christian Bale dances and chatters around him like a monkey, a squirrel, or an unraveling mummy. David O. Russell has managed two impressive things in his direction of this movie. He's found a way to shoot boxing that feels like boxing on HBO in the 1990s but also adds something newly cinematic to the genre, and he keeps the film's ending uncertain even though it's based on a true story boxing fans know well. There's something powerful and real about *The Fighter.* Like *127 Hours,* it makes getting away with only permanent damage into a triumph.

Animal Kingdom

This Australian film places its crime-family characters in the same kind of environment several of this year's Oscar-nominated films do—a sordid, violent, polluted-looking city or near-city sprawl, where people do not participate in anything resembling normal family life. These are all films that announce the world has changed. *Animal Kingdom* is quieter than the others, with sneakier, more menacing performances, especially Ben Mendelsohn's oldest brother, an amoral middle-aged Johnny Rotten of crime who is low-key and disaffected to the point of being in a fugue state. The film has the best two or three opening and closing minutes of anything nominated for an Oscar this year, with the possible exception of *Dogtooth.*

Biutiful

If *Animal Kingdom* has the best opening and closing minutes, *Biutiful* has the worst. Is now really the time for a comforting reunion set in a wintry afterlife? These framing scenes are offensive not because of their pseudo-spirituality but because they are unnecessary. The two characters—Javier Bardem and his father, who is younger than Bardem because he died earlier—talk inscrutably about owls, but they might as well be making a snowman.

The rest of the film is the best work Alejandro González Iñárritu has done. Although, like his previous films, it has peculiar notions about animals and the afterlife and globalism, it's much simpler and smarter, and a real turnaround after the deadening pointlessness of *Babel.* Bardem's Uxbal, an ex-junkie dying of prostate cancer, provides luxury-goods forgers with Chinese factory workers to make their wares and African street vendors to sell them. He also has an ill-defined spiritual gift that allows him to speak with the recently deceased. Strange as it sounds, this aspect of the film does not dominate or become tedious. Instead, Iñárritu pays very close attention to people and to background, creating a detailed portrait of the people who live in Barcelona's margins.

Bardem deserves his Oscar nomination, and if you have ever wanted to see him in an adult diaper, now's your chance. But if he deserves to be recognized, so does Maricel Alvarez, who plays his sometime wife, a bipolar massage therapist who cheats on him with his scumbag brother, beats their son, and likes to party more than work or feed their kids. Alvarez makes this character tender and believable instead of easy to hate, and she has the best nose in movies this year.

Gasland

Documentaries now do what both TV news and horror movies used to do—break real stories and scare the shit out of you. *Gasland,* a documentary and personal essay film about hydrofracking, provided the year's scariest image—water from people's faucets bursting into flames. This one image of tap water on fire should be able to bring down Halliburton and reverse the legislation that allows corporations to destroy the environment in secret. There should at least be a law that gas company executives have to drink people's water if they've declared it safe. Josh Fox, who made this film, has an eye for nature and industrial degradation—at times *Gasland* calls to mind

Bruce Baillie or *Red Desert.* He also has an ear for music and a way of getting people to talk. He contrasts an environment of total industrialization with the pristine waterways he grew up knowing, showing us an America that's now scarred and ruined, and in which too many people are sick and even brain damaged from industrial pollution. This is the new American landscape, where George Romero meets Henry Thoreau.

Jean-Luc Godard

Godard received an "Academy Honorary Award" this year, "for passion, for confrontation, for a new kind of cinema." While the Academy may be interested in passion and confrontation when giving out honorary awards, it was in no way interested in Godard showing those qualities live on TV. Since last year, honorary awards have been presented at a private ceremony in November. It seems they are not even letting Francis Ford Coppola get his honorary award on TV this year—not even the man who made *The Godfather,* Hollywood's favorite proof that it is capable of greatness.

Denying the world the potentially coruscating scandal of watching Godard get an Oscar, then saying whatever it is he would have said, is a missed opportunity of the highest order. How bad could it have been, Academy? Even if Godard had excoriated Hollywood, he probably would have thrown in a few good words for Hawks and Hitchcock, for Nick and Sam. Godard himself has been quiet about the whole thing, not even deigning to acknowledge that he received the award. His uncharacteristic silence speaks volumes; Anne-Marie Miéville acknowledged he was annoyed. Will he at least get booed by someone when they read his name, or will it pass by to polite applause and baffled looks? Can we cut to a shot of Megan Fox?

February 2011

BAD INFLUENCES, BAD PERSONALITIES

Exit Through the Gift Shop

What begins as an interesting documentary about how Banksy and other famous graffiti artists make their art soon turns into a semi-mockumentary that plays into people's desire to believe the art world is too easily manipulated and therefore something they don't have to pay attention to; that, in fact, they would be idiots to pay any attention to it at all. What they should pay attention to is Banksy, who doesn't credit himself or anybody else as the director of this film, but who appears on-screen to speak to us from the shadows, if that's really him, next to a monkey mask with ping-pong balls for eyes.

Much of the film takes place in Los Angeles, which Banksy sees as an art-deprived suburb of Disneyland. When he brings his site-specific op-ed cartooning to a Los Angeles gallery, the film acts like this is a revelation to the locals, who (presumably after years of taking in everything from Ed Ruscha to Raymond Pettibon to Mike Kelley) are easily wowed by the live elephant he has on hand.

We are told the film was originally meant to be assembled from thousands of hours of footage shot by a kooky Frenchman. The film's rejection of this footage as incoherent and unsalvageable is a normalizing strategy that forces literal meaning on us by finding a regular documentary inside a mess—we are supposed to believe that because of someone else's incompetence, Banksy had no choice but to make something anyone could understand. Banksy's own coy self-definitions, for which he apologizes in a recessive friendly-macho way, pull him into the back of the frame and out of the film. His will to absence makes the monumental daring of his work all the more impressive, especially since it's a pleasant kind of art that brightens the urban landscape and cheers people up.

Chase

Twenty folding chairs in an unair-conditioned screening room on a humid night in Chelsea. The artist is present. She is Liz Magic Laser (her real name—the question must come up a lot), here to introduce *Chase*, her two-and-a-half-hour film of Bertolt Brecht's *Man Equals Man*, a play first performed in Germany in 1926.

Laser shot *Chase* on digital video in the ATM vestibules of banks in New York City. She worked without permission, gaining access like anyone else would, by swiping a bank card to open the door. In the film, her actors perform next to customers using the ATMs, among security guards and cleaning ladies. The actors declaim Brecht's words while bystanders, a built-in audience, make withdrawals and deposits or wait around. Usually people ignore the actors, but some, roped in, play along for a moment before they leave. Whenever a new customer opens the door, a burst of unmixed sound from the outside world floods in, then the door closes and cuts it off again. One actor, Max Woertendyke, struts and works the crowd like he was born to act in foyers backed by a chorus of beeping machines. At one point, without breaking character, Woertendyke nonchalantly takes a gummy bear from a package a bystander is holding and eats it.

Laser gets a lot of good angles in these small spaces no one who isn't homeless or an architect ever thinks about or studies. She does it without resorting to off-kilter framing or wide-angle lenses—the spaces are not distorted or dramatized, and the film is free of production value and art direction. Another of the many strengths of this brilliantly conceived film is how Laser does not have to fuzz out any of the corporate logos that fill the backgrounds, because this is art for an art gallery, which is granted a freedom the movies and TV don't have and should demand. *Chase* shows us the world as we actually see it, festooned with advertising that isn't product placement.

Each actor performs separately in a different ATM lobby. Laser cuts the film as if they were together, talking across the void of the ATM monitors. (She explained this by mentioning Eisenstein.) Much of the cutting doesn't match, the sound cuts don't match, and some of the acting, like the camerawork, is amateurish. The actors, alone in their vestibules, never quite agree on the pronunciations of certain names, including that of the play's protagonist, Galy Gay. It doesn't matter. *Chase* is one of those rare films that benefits from its flaws and limitations, getting better and more interesting as it goes along.

Brecht's play, which takes place in the northern reaches of a farcical, Kipling-esque India ("where the tiger asks the jaguar about his teeth"), attempts to demonstrate how soldiers are created. The simple raw material of human personality is easily broken down, Brecht says, and it readily adapts to combat and killing. Part of *Man Equals Man* is set near a treasure-filled pagoda, which may have suggested an ATM to Laser. One side effect of having her actors perform opposite ATMs is that we get to see how much money they have in their bank accounts (not much) when they make withdrawals to use cash as a prop. That's not something that happens in *Salt*. Here, the money is on the screen.

Sex and the City 2

A group of Americans, weighed down with equipment, is airlifted into a Middle Eastern country on a pointless mission. Once there, they live in a protected environment separated from the local population. On their forays away from the karaoke nights at their base, they screw up everything they attempt, alienating the natives and getting more confused the longer they stay. For reasons impossible to understand, their time in this country drags on and on, yet they can't seem to end it. Finally expelled from this quagmire of their own making, they leave behind a mess and some money for the help.

Just as there had to be a second Iraq war after the unfinished business of the first, there had to be a *Sex and the City 2*. For in the first, Carrie (Sarah Jessica Parker) did not get what she really wanted, just like the first Bush Administration did not get what it really wanted in the first war.

In the first movie, Carrie pretended to learn that a big diamond ring wasn't what love and marriage were all about. In the second, she gets her ring, a sinister black diamond symbolizing the war-for-oil aspects of this shameless movie. Carrie's Pyrrhic victory, a consolation prize, caps a movie that is a form of debasement before the Arab world. It shows Americans as grasping whores who make endless justifications for their lameness and greed, who are bored with their lives yet incapable of learning. The film is a low point in the history of American pop culture, but to mock specific scenes in it would be a waste of time. One image lingers: Sarah Jessica Parker shoving Pringles potato chips in her mouth on an airplane.

I Am Love

Of all the things that are influential about Hitchcock's films, who would have guessed that in the end it would be the hair that was the most influential of all? It proves the triviality of influence, something *I Am Love* goes out of its way to make us understand. Whether striving for a Viscontian lushness, an Antonionian loneliness, a Sirkian catharsis, or a Hitchcockian precision with hair, *I Am Love* revels in notions of provenance, which it relates to qualities of real experience and feelings of true luxury, pleasures the film lets us know few people truly understand, even if they can afford them.

One of the main ways it does that is through food. The meals prepared by the young locavore chef, the adulterous lover of Tilda Swinton's married Emma, are transcendent, enigmatic, yummy. While the two make love in a meadow by his organic farm, we get close-ups of bugs that are reminiscent of the life-changing prawns he served Emma, not ants at a picnic or worms in an apple.

"The Recchis are exploiters!" someone blurts in this movie about the family of upper-class Italian industrialists it dismantles. It shouts what it has only partially managed to show. Emma's husband, for instance, a cold fish who quickly turns on her when the time comes, does callous things like change the channel when she's trying to watch the movie *Philadelphia* on TV. That way we know he's a real *bastardo.*

The film is too much in love with beauty to be anything but pretty, and by the end it's corrupted by the system it indicts. Before a bizarre, inappropriate happy ending featuring Emma and her chef curled up in a cave, Swinton has effectively left the film, running out in a tracksuit like she's late to the set of the next *Narnia* movie.

The Kids Are All Right

I have not been everywhere, and I have never lived in Los Angeles. But as far as I know, there is no corner of the universe where a guy like the unmarried restaurateur played by Mark Ruffalo in *The Kids Are All Right* would dump a girl like the crazy-haired hostess played by Yaya DaCosta for the married lesbian played by Julianne Moore. It boggles the mind more than *The Last Airbender* in 3D.

Let's examine this character, Paul, whom Ruffalo plays. Paul has such an air of manly skill about him he makes the author of *Shop Class as Soulcraft* look like Truman Capote. He owns a motorcycle he fixes himself. He listens to X in an old truck he drives. He has his own house with a tiered backyard and his own restaurant where he is the head chef. He grows food for his restaurant on his own organic farm; when he picks vegetables there he politely ignores the come-ons of a hot helper girl who wants to roll around in the chard with him.

Even though Paul shrugs off the farm girl, we are supposed to see him as a sexual opportunist. Paul is nice, and sometimes even wise, and he genuinely likes the two teenagers who were conceived by the married couple Jules and Nic (Annette Bening) with sperm he donated years ago. But *why* is he so nice? To what end? *Why* is he so pleasant and helpful to these people who were strangers to him until just the other day?

The Kids Are All Right joins a line of recent movies that portray unmarried men over 40 as lonely, confused, and adrift—appearances to the contrary notwithstanding—because they don't have families of their own. Evidently it is inconceivable—excuse the pun—to the makers of American feature films that a man could be content without a wife and children.

On the higher end of this bachelor scale we find George Clooney in *Up in the Air.* He may seem suave, carefree, and capable, but no. He is a husk, only going through the motions as he flies around the country ruining people's lives. He, too, will end up staring through a window at someone else's happy family. On the low end of the scale we find Ben Stiller in *Greenberg.* Maybe it's better not to think about him.

Before I get too personal I should look at other aspects of *The Kids Are All Right.* This heartwarming family comedy is the first film I have ever seen in which T-shirt choice so thoroughly dictates character. At times the movie seems like satire, but by the end, when Bening's crotchety Nic blasts Paul with a "go make your own family, buster, and take your stinking paws off mine," it reveals itself as only slightly less conservative than Steven Spielberg's *War of the Worlds.*

Strange lapses puzzled me. Why do we never learn what college young Joni is going to, even though it keeps coming up and eventually we even visit this unnamed institution? Is it to make the film more generic? Why is it never established that Jules has used Paul's hairbrush before Nic goes into his bathroom and finds the incriminating tangle of hair? Is it important that the film can't mention in passing the legal status of gay marriage in California (illegal when the film was made), or would that have been tendentious and therefore not about how hard marriage is for everyone, and therefore not about how everyone is the same? And why does a bartender, who has just poured Nic a glass of wine, ask her if she's going to drink it? In my experience, once it's poured it's a done deal. In California, do they pour it back in the bottle if you've just silently realized you're kind of an alcoholic?

Dogtooth

Stills and trailers made *Dogtooth* look like an art film starring white people posing for emptied-out art photos influenced by Fairfield Porter paintings. It's not like that. It's something more harrowing and exciting. *Dogtooth* is simple and restricted, maybe in the end confinement wins out over austerity, but it is not a frosty film about pent-up people who can't show their emotions. It's more about people who aren't allowed to understand anything.

Dogtooth is a Greek film directed by somebody named Yorgos Lanthimos. I would see anything else by him after seeing this amazing film, the best of the summer. With much less at its disposal, it out-Cronenbergs Cronenberg by way of a sunny creepiness that insists on its normality even as it turns incestuous and bloody. Primarily about language and the family, it should be seen by homeschoolers everywhere.

The mother and father in *Dogtooth* restrict their children—two daughters and a son in their late teens—to their house and yard. The kids know nothing of the world outside, and have been taught that any word that describes something not found at home—*motorway, gun*—has a meaning from the natural world—*wind, flower, bird.* The teens get together to watch videos on TV, but they only watch home movies of their younger selves; as they sit on the couch, they mouth along to things they said years ago. When they do good, their parents reward them with stickers they put on their headboards.

The outside world enters in the form of a young woman the father hires to have sex with the son. This goes badly: she ends up beaten in the head with a VCR wielded by the father, who curses her: "I hope your kids have bad influences and develop bad personalities!" The father (Christos Stergioglou), a fat Grinch who looks like he has no business being in movies, is boring yet scary, especially when he mouths words to his wife in the kitchen so the kids won't hear, has his daughters cut his toenails, or explains that "in two months your mother will give birth to two more children and a dog." The actors who play the daughters, Angeliki Papoulia and Mary Tsoni, deserve special recognition for their willingness to do anything, including frenzied dancing inspired by *Flashdance* and intra-family bathtub groping.

A Short History of Cahiers du cinéma

Cinephile reviewers attacked this slim book by Emilie Bickerton, a writer for the *New Left Review*, when it was published by Verso several months ago. They justifiably seized on errors of fact, some of which showed an unwillingness to check simple things; others revealed an unfamiliarity with the history of cinema in general. In tracing the decline of *Cahiers du cinéma* from aesthetic radicalism through political radicalism and into market-driven acquiescence and subsequent irrelevance, Bickerton does not appear to have seen many of the films she brings up.

Calling John Ford's *Two Rode Together* by translating its French title into English—she called it *The Two Cavaliers* in advance copies of the book, which were corrected before publication—tipped off movie-loving reviewers that there was something wrong. Defending that mistake as a proofreading error, as Bickerton did in response to a negative review in *Film Comment*, did not help her case, especially since equally odd mistakes stand in the book as published. She names many French New Wave films using titles they have never been called outside of IMDb.com—Godard's *Vivre sa vie* is *It's My Life* and Chabrol's *Les godelureaux* and *La rupture* are *Wise Guys* and *The Breach*. (She also dismisses Chabrol's 1970s films as "poor" apparently without having seen them herself, because someone at *Cahiers* said that about them at one point, and Truffaut backed him up.)

She has to use a footnote to describe the plot of Godard's *Weekend*, citing somebody else to explain a seminal film she could have easily seen, and should have before writing this book. She describes Alfred Hitchcock as an exile in Hollywood like Fritz Lang, equating a career move on Hitchcock's part with Lang's flight from the Nazis. Bickerton's most boneheaded goof will cause spit takes all over the world, but especially in France: she implies that *Grand Illusion* was made under Vichy. By the end, she has described Arnaud Desplechin as an '80s filmmaker and Jean-Jacques Annaud as one from the '90s. I ignore her errors of emphasis and tone only because they're not as fun to list.

Does it sound like I don't like this book? Because that's not the case. I like it very much—it was completely engrossing—and I think anyone interested in the French New Wave, and especially anyone interested in film criticism, should read it. And I think cinephiles offended by it, including the cinephile in me, should get over it and take heed. Bickerton's basic message—that starting in the '80s film criticism caved in without a fight—is undeniable.

Bickerton writes that *Cahiers du cinéma* started life in the early 1950s with a high-minded goal: "the destruction of prevailing value systems and the elevation of the *film maudit*." Thirty years later, as "various factors combined to create an environment that was hostile to the free exploration and critique of cinema outside the market logic," the magazine devolved into praising M. Night Shyamalan movies as if they were today's undiscovered artistic equivalents of films by Hitchcock and Hawks, sidestepping at the same time any kind of politicized readings that might counter their appeal.

Bickerton quotes Jean-Louis Comolli, an editor at the magazine during its most radical phase in the '60s and '70s. Film criticism and filmmaking, he wrote, must make "a political choice to stop seeing the audience as an inert, amorphous mass open to all sorts of manipulation by advertising," and instead must "bank on the existence of an audience that is lucid" and "ultimately as creative as the filmmaker." Bickerton argues that *Cahiers* switched tactics as the film industry changed during the Reagan–*Star Wars* era, dumbing down in order to please a new kind of consumer and to drive flagging sales.

Only Serge Daney, the magazine's most vital film critic since the days of Bazin and Truffaut, held fast, admitting that while "the times themselves [had] grown more feeble, in terms of thought," film critics still had to discover and explain "what was cinema's 'specificity,' given the proliferation of images through advertising and television. . . . And how should the critic conceive of his or her role within this transformed landscape of images?"

How many film critics have taken up this challenge since Daney's death? In her sections on him, Bickerton points a way forward. To make up for the fact-checking errors, Verso could show a real commitment to a genuinely radical film criticism by publishing Daney's work in English translation. For a long time, his English-language readers have had to rely on blogs collecting stray translations. That would be a start.

Winter's Bone

This harsh film, set in gray Ozark forests, represents a step forward in screen depictions of the rural South, and in the career of its writer-director, Debra Granik. The stripped and collapsed world brought to the screen in *Winter's Bone*, which was adapted from a novel by

Daniel Woodrell, stands in stark contrast to representations of similar territory in indie films from the Bush era, like the odious *Junebug* (2005). *Junebug* painted small-town Southerners as humble and lovable God-fearing folks, gentle losers even if they were racist nuts. In *Winter's Bone*, people are poor and dangerous, which is to say they have dignity. Plus they're all on meth, the driver of their economy.

All the performances in this film work. The teenage lead (Jennifer Lawrence), a semi-parentless Renée Zellweger look-alike with no future, carries the film easily. The mountainous, unlistening crime patriarch, who rules from a huge shed that's like a barn for monster trucks, comes across as intractable, ignorant, and deadly. He didn't talk much, but he was convincing. Even the guy playing the most thankless role, a weak-willed state cop, was good. But it is Dale Dickey as Merab, the wife of the criminal patriarch, who steals the film. With her deeply lined face and mean, squinty eyes, Merab cowers and thrives in this methland, scaring the shit out of anyone who dares to ask her a question. It is a cliché for an actress in a countrified film to look as hard as the country where the movie is set, but Dickey's performance is something else. She looks as choppy and blasted as the terrain, but she doesn't slip into *Tobacco Road* parody mode.

Cyrus

A drab comedic love triangle between a mother (Marisa Tomei, a sexy chipmunk), her son (Jonah Hill, a poison toad), and her new boyfriend (John C. Reilly, a catcher's mitt). Directed by Jay Duplass and Mark Duplass, *Cyrus* was produced by Ridley Scott and Tony Scott to atone for their sins while showing support for a younger pair of director brothers.

Cyrus depicts the lower rungs of media employment as lackluster and low paying—Reilly's character is some kind of TV editor and lives in the shabbiest apartment I've seen in movies for a long time. Wherever it goes, it is excessively drab for a movie set in LA—a peach nightgown Tomei wears is the same color as her skin and the walls at her place—but it lacks the mortifying intensity of an Elaine May movie, which it at times seems to be going for and really needed.

Henri-Georges Clouzot's Inferno

This documentary partially reassembles a big-budget, ambitiously experimental film Henri-Georges Clouzot, the director of *Diabolique* and *The Wages of Fear*, left unfinished after suffering a heart attack on location in the Auvergne in 1964. The film, *L'enfer*, meant to push cinema to the breaking point, broke Clouzot instead—his heart gave out while he was shooting a lesbian kissing scene between Romy Schneider and Dany Carrel. Whenever Clouzot's footage takes over, the film comes to glorious, decadent life; other times, it gets bogged down in talking-head interviews with the original crew and cringe-worthy reenactments featuring two uncomfortable actors on a soundstage.

L'enfer, an international coproduction meant to top Hitchcock, adopts techniques from lurid Italian genre films and the surrealistic avant-garde; it looks like a more starkly modern Mario Bava or Kenneth Anger movie. To make the water in a lake appear bloodred on film, Clouzot's actors are painted green or blue like real-life Na'vi—in 1964, Clouzot had already exposed the superfluity of CGI. Much of the footage consists of camera tests of the alluring Romy Schneider. Her skin spangles and glitters while dots of light roll and spin in her eyes. She exhales cigarette smoke backward, appearing to breathe it in—smoking in reverse, she inhales smoke from the air. In a purple slip, wearing purple lipstick, she licks her lips with a purple tongue. Trying to find "the improbable colors of madness," Clouzot predicted a lurid psychedelic world still three or four years away.

The sound track, edited together from the film's electro-acoustical music cues and a *musique concrète* score, competes with kinetic-art-inspired lens effects that bend figures into primitive sculptures seen in fun-house mirrors. Several long scenes are cut together. In one, the film's protagonist (Serge Reggiani), Schneider's jealous husband, desperately follows her from a twisting highway above the lake as she gyrates back and forth on water skis in the foreground—mesmerizing footage from a film that was never made. It calls into question the category of the "late masterpiece," usually seen as radically austere and stripped down. It makes you want to see other excessive late-career works plotted in the 1960s and never made, like Fritz Lang's *Death of a Career Girl* and Hitchcock's *Kaleidoscope*, which in a reworked version became 1972's *Frenzy*, not exactly a sane and mild film, but not the freak-out Hitchcock planned.

Around a Small Mountain

Somber or apprehensive moods or tones in this movie about summertime, the countryside, clothes, and the little agonies of failing circus performers save *Around a Small Mountain* from being too light, making it strange and buoyant. The way Jane Birkin pauses in a sunny graveyard demonstrates Jacques Rivette's interest in stopping his performers short at moments of reflection. Rivette does this in an unobtrusive, subtle way within simple long takes that do not call attention to themselves the way they do in the work of younger art-house directors. Similarly, the film's lack of a music score isn't noticeable until Pierre Allio's Tati-esque jazz returns over the end credits, after a final shot of the moon, large in the frame, that makes it look balanced in the air, with a weight we can feel.

It is to the honor of Sergio Castellitto that he appears in Rivette's late films. With his Humphrey Bogart–Leonard Cohen looks, this classic-style film star shows great aplomb even when confused or doing nothing. He contrasts stillness with abrupt motion, enacting the mental agility of Rivette's mise-en-scène. The way he pulls out a chair and sits down mirrors the way he talks and listens. He wears a different suit in every scene, which he carries off more impressively than Tilda Swinton's wardrobe changes in *I Am Love*, and which, as in that movie, also seem to be part of the point. Here it is an entertaining point, free from histrionics or indictments of society. A nighttime scene in front of a café puts Castellitto and others on an impromptu stage and goes through several on-off light changes in one shot, plunging the actors in and out of silhouette, reminding us that simple effects in movies are the most sublime.

Inception

Something about *Inception* confused me. I know it's a head-scratcher in general, but after I saw it there was one thing I wanted to understand more than anything else: How did Christopher Nolan come up with the name "Dom Cobb"?

Was it because "Dom Cobb" sounds like something you say when you're just waking up but you're not really awake yet? And you're making that jaw motion where you open and close your mouth like a fish trying to talk while you mumble some incoherent *om, om* syllable because your lips are sticking together? And the person next to you goes, "What was that, honey? Dom Cobb?"

Maybe Dom Cobb is a metaphorical name like Ariadne or Mal, other characters in this turgid crowd-pleaser, and I just didn't know what the significance was. A lot of people who have seen it will tell you that *Inception* is one big metaphor—a movie about making movies, about how movies work, about what it's like to see movies, and how close they are to dreams and how life is like a dream and like a movie, too. "It's a movie about movies!" these fans insist, giving special emphasis to the word *movies* the way sometimes people used to say something meaningful was about life. Then they tell you how it was about movies. What they don't tell you is that it's about bad movies.

"Always imagine new places," Dom Cobb (Leonardo DiCaprio) instructs, but *Inception* refuses to do that. It presents instantly recognizable non-places, swanky hotel bars in world capitals, vistas from James Bond movies with skiing in them, postapocalyptic landscapes from comic books. Suffused with an ahistorical sensibility, this insta-remake of *Shutter Island* combines the washy metaphysics of Nicolas Roeg films with *Where Eagles Dare*—a range of unsmiling British unfun. Terrible dialogue fights to the death with bombastic music meant to pound a "militarized subconscious" into further submission, which it does.

Inception succeeds in convincing us for two and a half hours that somehow our dreams and lives are exactly like all the bad action movies we have ever seen. The film has none of the vivid unpredictable banality of dreams or life. Instead it has the kind of banality found in *Speed 2*—it puts dreamers on cruise control, lays them out on gurneys, runs them up and down elevators. I can't recount the plot of *Inception* or tell you what it means, but I can tell you this: People whose dream movie is a bad movie about dreams that are like bad movies are fucked.

August 2010

WE NEED TO CONFIRM THAT YOU KNOW GREGORY ARKADIN

MR. ARKADIN'S DECADENCE LOOKS LIKE VITALITY NOW; ITS POVERTY LOOKS like riches; what William S. Pechter called its "half-baked profundities" don't jar and clash so much as fall like snow falls in the film. If *Mr. Arkadin* once seemed sad because it seemed amateurish and like a comedown for Welles, what is sad about it now settles into it like the cold. If for some people the film used to be terrible, now it points in the direction of something terrible outside of it.

The film has had defenders since it came out in 1955, but misgivings accompany their praise. In 1958 *Cahiers du cinéma* called *Mr. Arkadin* Welles's greatest film and one of the twelve best films ever made, but for André Bazin it was "a film of only secondary importance." We owe Jonathan Rosenbaum a debt of gratitude for all the work he has done in bringing the various versions of *Arkadin* to light, but for him the film's problem is Welles himself. Welles's performance in the title role is "debilitating," defined by falseness, variability, and silly moments. Richard Brody, in the *New Yorker*, has recently been "struck by the anguish and self-loathing that the film displays" and identifies "the film's intense confessional pathos, the drama of a man who doubts that he could be loved for the person he knows himself to be." These key observations bookend the comments of another *New Yorker* writer, who, between the two Brody write-ups, called *Mr. Arkadin* "Welles's unfinished botch of a film."

In contrast to glossier cold war paranoias that came later, like *The Manchurian Candidate*, Welles's version is sewn by hand or nailed together; it's crafty. *Arkadin*'s black-and-white images, shot through an 18.5mm lens, pop big heads into the frame. The 18.5mm lens provides great depth of field in vistas with Spanish castles in the background and in small rooms that are extra cluttered or that house only one old chair. The most modern things—airplanes, telephones, speakers, sunglasses—compete with the junk-shop detritus of a broken Europe more splintered and random than *The Third Man*'s Vienna.

A typical camera move follows a worn-out character—one of Arkadin's old friends—and reveals a bed pole capped with a swastika across from an upside-down portrait of Hitler. Welles doesn't linger over these things, yet he makes us expect them. Then he gradually removes them until, at the end, he disappears, too, a bulky mannequin thrown overboard so that the film can rise into an empty gray sky.

The film is self-consciously a fable; Arkadin is a king. The fable goes like this: Gregory Arkadin, an international financier with a shady past and a beautiful daughter, sits atop a fortune. He claims he can't remember anything that happened to him before a night in 1927 when he woke up in a Zurich street with pockets full of cash. He hires an American grifter named Van Stratten to dig into his past, telling him he wants to find out who he is and where he's from. Traveling the globe, Van Stratten uncovers a frowsy network of aging criminals living quiet, sometimes weird lives—Arkadin's ex-cronies. Murdered by Arkadin one by one as Van Stratten locates them, the detective realizes his investigation is a manhunt Arkadin has started so he can eliminate anyone who knows his secret; Van Stratten will be his final victim.

The tragedy, or the joke, is that Arkadin's old friends and ex-lovers are past caring; ignoring them would have been enough. Arkadin laughs when he finally comes face-to-face with the last survivor. Akim

Tamiroff's tragicomic Jakob Zouk, an ex-con hiding in a bed in his underwear, shivers alone in a small room, Arkadin's whole world shrunk down to a pinpoint, a black dot like a flea in the flea circus we visited earlier. "So what's funny?" asks Zouk. "Old age," Arkadin answers. "Old age," he says again as he glides out Zouk's door. Which doesn't stop him from killing Zouk later.

Time has added a new layer to this film's encrustations. *Mr. Arkadin* looks different in the age of digital social networking. We don't lose track of people from our pasts like Arkadin did, and if we have lost track we can find old friends just by typing in their names and "friending" them, and they can find us, too. If we want to eliminate them we can defriend them and with a keystroke they disappear. The internet has replaced the need for a Van Stratten to find people for us, and we can get rid of them by ourselves. It's a form of "murder by remote control," as Humphrey Bogart says in *The Big Sleep*, describing a hired gun. Where Gregory Arkadin needed a vast system of spies with binoculars hiding behind trees and on parapets and a staff of secretaries to keep files in rows of black file cabinets, the internet has eliminated the need for a staff and made us all into little Arkadins.

In *Mr. Arkadin* we can feel Welles trying to do away with a younger version of himself, embodied in the "cornball" Van Stratten and in the way Welles disguises himself as the Neptune-like Arkadin. This basic Wellesian theme starts in *Citizen Kane*. The overconfident Wellesian protagonist forgets his younger self even as this earlier version is always present; tragedy strikes; surrounded by doubles and mirrors he ages before our eyes; the past catches up with him and engulfs him. "I drag my myth around with me," Welles told a critic, explaining why he could never make a new start, why preconceptions and misconceptions about him hurt his career.

"Oh, I've been photographed," Arkadin explains to Van Stratten. "But usually I *break the photograph*." What does it mean, to *break the photograph*? To break the photograph instead of the camera? We accept that without thinking about it when Welles says it in

Arkadin's Russian accent. His accent deflects the strangeness of the phrase *break the photograph*. Is it some kind of crypto-allusion to film editing, to cutting out of the scene?

We see a couple of photographs of Arkadin before he was Arkadin, when he was still Waclaw Athabadze, youngish criminal on the make. These photographs come back to haunt Arkadin like the high school photos people post of us on Facebook, or ones from last night's party. The photos they post give the lie to whichever photo we choose for our profile picture just like they do to the carefully constructed face of Arkadin—one constant of *Arkadin* criticism is how phony Welles looks in it. We drag the past around with us whether we want to or not, getting tagged like in *Mr. Arkadin*'s game-of-tag plot. Until we do, we sit there unknowing, waiting, shimmering somewhere in cyberspace without names to go with our faces.

It makes sense that in the age of social networking, vampire movies would become popular again. When we accept these email requests from the people who have found us, we become members of a new clan. Poor Bella Swan, who frets about aging while her boyfriend stays 17 forever, is like someone who can't decide whether to join Facebook or not, because quitting would be awkward. The teenage vampires of the *Twilight* saga aren't carriers of evil infections like the vampires of the past. Today's vampires are more of an after-school club that has lots of rules and regulations about membership. They confer a kind of Facebook immortality on each other and get defriended not with stakes through the heart so much as by not observing social cues and being careful about boundaries.

New Moon, the second movie in the *Twilight* series, gurgles with an unintentional Wellesian undercurrent. The characters recite Shakespeare and wander moors. The film is moody, self-conscious, and aimed at the arty kids. There's even an Arkadinian jet plane to Europe in it. It could use more Mercury Theatre and less *X-Men*, however, because it lacks drive and purpose. *Arkadin* is eventful. It's filled with commentary, quips, maxims, stories within stories; the camera follows Van Stratten and Raina, Arkadin's daughter, along fences and past ruins like it has somewhere it has to be. *New Moon*'s emo-gotho-depresso pop-hits sound track replicates the experience of someone listening to music while working on a computer who isn't really concentrating on anything, just updating her status to read: "It's raining outside. Dating a monster is hard. I am sad right now," like maybe the movie is based on a haiku, not a six-hundred-page novel. Its unformed characters lack the sweep of any kind of history, even though some of them have supposedly been around for hundreds of years. They are tied to dreary Forks, Washington, even though they can defy space and time.

Around the time I saw the *Twilight* movie and rewatched *Mr. Arkadin* I was reading a book I found on the street, a book by Ryszard Kapuściński called *Travels with Herodotus*. Near the end, Kapuściński quotes a passage from T. S. Eliot's 1944 essay on Virgil. For me it summed up the link between *New Moon* and *Mr. Arkadin* in the Facebook era, so I'm ending with it too:

> In our age, when men seem more than ever prone to confuse wisdom with knowledge, and knowledge with information, and to try to solve problems of life in terms of engineering, there is coming into existence a new kind of provincialism which perhaps deserves a new name. It is a provincialism, not of space, but of time; one for which history is merely the chronicle of human devices which have served their turn and been scrapped, one for which the world is the property solely of the living, a property in which the dead hold no shares. The menace of this kind of provincialism is, that we can all, all the peoples on the globe, be provincials together; and those who are not content to become provincials, can only become hermits.

Arkadin jumped from his plane, Bella Swan will become a vampire, I'm posting the link to this article on Facebook.

April 2010

A COTTAGE FOR SALE

ON THOMAS KINKADE

Our little dream castle
With every dream gone . . .

THE CHRISTMAS COTTAGE, A BIOPIC ABOUT THE ARTIST THOMAS KINKADE, famous for the quaint-scary-ugly paintings he sells in shopping malls, is a cinematic portrait of the multimillionaire artist as a young man. Kinkade coproduced the movie, which went straight to DVD when it came out in 2008. In a pivotal scene, the budding "Painter of Light," home from college, gathers with his mother and younger brother on Christmas morning.

It's the mid-'70s in Placerville, California, a small town in the foothills of the Sierra Nevada. The Kinkades are a poor family living in a run-down house. Kinkade's mother, divorced from Kinkade's father, has lost her job, and because she is generous to other people in the town—"she loaned people money, she gave people things"—and because she refuses assistance from anyone else, the Kinkades are about to lose what they call "the cottage." The bank is foreclosing. They've only got a few days left to pay.

Young Thom—the grown-up artist spells the short version of his name that way—and his brother have been working hard to raise money for their mother's overdue mortgage payment, but they haven't put together enough cash. They can't save the house, so understandably they don't have store-bought Christmas gifts to exchange. Instead, Thom (Jared Padalecki, from *Gilmore Girls*) presents his mother (Marcia Gay Harden) with a picture of their house he's drawn himself, so she'll always have something by which to remember what they're about to lose.

At that moment, in bursts the rest of the film's cast, made up of character actors from old TV shows—Charlotte Rae from *The Facts of Life*, the guy who played Bull on *Night Court*. Are they there to save the day and end the film the way *It's a Wonderful Life* ends? Not exactly. They don't come bearing money to make things right with the bank the way the townspeople do in Capra's film. They arrive carrying tools and cans of paint. If the Kinkade cottage can't be saved for the Kinkades, they figure they can at least fix it up so it can be sold for more money than it would have if it remained broken down and leaky. They arrive in the nick of time not to save Maryanne Kinkade but to help her flip her house, and possibly to make sure its appearance doesn't drive down their own property values. They quickly get to work, and in a jiffy the cottage looks brand-new.

But Maryanne is still stuck in the same sinking boat—it just looks nicer. That afternoon, true economic salvation arrives in the form of Peter O'Toole, decrepit but still more powerful than a troupe of yesterday's sitcom stars. The former Lawrence of Arabia, playing an old, dying painter who inhabits the barn next door, drags himself across the snowy wastes of the Kinkades' yard carrying an unknown masterpiece. At Christmas dinner, the painter, a renowned artist who has retired to Placerville, unveils what will be his last work on canvas. "You will sell it!" he thunders. "It should bring you enough to keep this cottage *forever*!"

And it does. The Kinkades save their house. The painting, the film's narration tells us, "is now owned by a museum in New York." Never mind that that isn't true—on the DVD commentary track Kinkade says he doesn't know the whereabouts of the painting that saved his childhood home. What's important is that in Thomas

Kinkade's originating myth, two things happen. First, he substitutes a picture he's drawn of a house for the thing itself, giving the representation to his mother to replace the real thing; second, it is not community that saves the house, but the sale of a painting, which is worth much more. Young Thom learns a lesson the film pretends it isn't teaching. Community only goes so far; art is money in the bank.

> Whoever has no house now, will never build one.
> —Rainer Maria Rilke, "Autumn Day"

THE DAY BEFORE I SAW *The Christmas Cottage*, I saw Charlie Kaufman's film *Synecdoche, New York*, which begins with that line of Rilke's heard over a radio. The two films have a lot in common. Both are about painting, theater, old age, and death; both are about real estate. In *The Christmas Cottage*, young Thom paints a mural of Placerville in the town square while his mother rehearses a Christmas pageant at her church; in *Synecdoche, New York*, a theater director rehearses a play after his wife, a painter of miniatures, deserts him. *The Christmas Cottage* is a meta-movie like *Synecdoche, New York*—its alternate title could be *Being Thomas Kinkade*—but it's a meta-movie for God-fearing grandparents. It ends with Kinkade himself daubing a fleck of yellow on a painting of the cottage whose story we have just seen, the kind of painting Kinkade sells to old people in his mall stores.

Of the themes the two films share, it's real estate that seals the Kinkade-Kaufman connection. In fact, real estate links *Synecdoche, New York* to Thomas Kinkade's work in general, not just to *The Christmas Cottage*. In Kaufman's film, one character buys and lives out her life in a house that is always on fire. It's even on fire the first time a real estate agent shows it to her. The fire isn't explained; it's just part of the package. We have to accept it, just as we have to accept that the violent orange glow that emanates from the interior of nearly every house in a Kinkade painting merely indicates that the house is warm and inviting, not burning to the ground.

The appearance Kinkade houses have of being on fire is something that glares from his paintings. It's unsettling, but it's something people who like Kinkade paintings don't notice or don't mind. Others recoil. Joan Didion mentions Kinkade in *Where I Was From*, her memoir of California. A Kinkade painting, she writes,

> was typically rendered in slightly surreal pastels. It typically featured a cottage or a house of such insistent coziness as to seem actually sinister, suggestive of a trap designed to attract Hansel and Gretel. Every window was lit, to lurid effect, as if the interior of the structure might be on fire.

It's a passage that has become permanently associated with Kinkade; it's included in his Wikipedia write-up. On *The Christmas Cottage*'s commentary track, the artist tells a story he'd probably rather have people recall when they look at his work. He says that as the son of a single mother who worked late, he often came home to a house that was dark and cold, especially in winter. The "Kinkade glow" represents what he wished was there instead. He tells the story more than once, which raises a question or two: Didn't he maybe just want to burn the place down? Is his art really a form of arson?

The way Kinkade sells his paintings certainly bespeaks a desire to make people pay. At a time when massive numbers of homes are going into foreclosure all over the country, Kinkade's sales method seems designed to drive buyers further into debt. A big sign in the Kinkade gallery in Placerville promises WELLS FARGO FINANCING—12 MONTHS INTEREST-FREE—$0 DOWN—15-MINUTE APPROVAL.

Kinkade's sales system is confusing. It includes licensed gallery stores, their websites, his own website, and other venues as well. As I write this, Kinkade's main website is offering "*Sizzling Summer Deals—Up to 70 Percent Off*!" Does that indicate a new understanding of the plight of the people he calls "my collectors," or is it a Kinkadian fire sale intended to unload stock that isn't moving in a bad economy?

When I visit the Placerville showroom, exalted in the system because it's his "Hometown Gallery," I notice a painting called *Sunday Outing* selling for $150,000. Kinkade's cottage paintings don't usually have people in them, but this one does. The family in it looks like they're fleeing a burning house. The price is written on the wall tag in ballpoint pen over another price that had been covered with Wite-Out. I ask the saleslady working in the gallery if they'd lowered the price of *Sunday Outing*, which was not one of the touched-up reproductions Kinkade is known for but an original signed with "John 3:16" next to Kinkade's Norman Rockwell–like signature. "Uh, no," she replies, with just a hint of the scorn you expect in an art gallery. "We actually raised it."

Why not? Kinkade can afford to dream. The one uncheckable factoid everything written on him can't fail to include is that supposedly one in twenty American homes has a Kinkade hanging in it. "What the heck, I'm a romantic," he says on the *Christmas Cottage* commentary track, explaining that he paints "an art that comforts your heart and reminds you of foundational things, a very sentimental kind of art." When Oscar Wilde wrote that "a sentimentalist is simply one who desires to have the luxury of an emotion without paying for it," he didn't know that someday an American painter would find a way to make sentimentalists pay for it in monthly installments.

The plate-glass display window of the Kinkade gallery on Main Street in Placerville features a big painting called *NASCAR Thunder*. The painting is detailed and complicated, featuring a termite-like mound of NASCAR fans filling stands that recede into the horizon as jets and a blimp fly in formation overhead and fireworks explode in the sky. This painting is in Kinkade's lucrative-commission style, not in the gemütlich-unheimlich style of his cottage paintings. It's a vast fictional panorama that uses items from reality to gauze up a location of idealized American spectacle that never was and won't ever be. Kinkade moves further into the realm of Hansel and Gretel fantasy with his series of Disney commissions, one of which is called *Snow White Discovers the Cottage*.

What do these paintings mean in Placerville, a town that has seen better days as recently as 1852, the year the California Gold Rush ended? Outside the gallery, stores sell funny postcards of shacks reading "For Sale: California Home Bargain—Only $999,950.00." Postcards like that predate the mortgage crisis; out-of-whack real estate prices have long been a subject for humor at the funny-postcard level of American culture, and so have postcards of dilapidated shacks; you can find them in every state. They keep disaster and unaffordability at arm's length. In Placerville these postcards remind me that the houses Kinkade paints were inspired by ones he saw in this town growing up, and that in a sixteen-point manifesto Kinkade wrote for the crew of *The Christmas Cottage* that was leaked to *Vanity Fair*'s website, he advised the filmmakers to "favor shots that feature older buildings, ramshackle, careworn structures," to avoid filming "shopping centers and contemporary storefronts" like the kind in which his paintings are sold, and to "avoid anything that is shiny." In the windows of a nearby real estate agency, half the fliers note the houses for sale are bank owned!! Half the storefronts on Main Street are for rent. None of them is shiny.

The Christmas Cottage was not shot in Placerville (because of "logistics," says Kinkade in the DVD commentary track). According to the film's credits, it was shot in British Columbia, Canada, "in the Historical City of Fort Langley." A thorough search of Placerville's walls and hoardings turns up no mural of the town like the one young Kinkade paints in *The Christmas Cottage.* The woman who runs the Placerville Historical Museum tells me the mural does not exist and never existed. The closest thing, she says, is the painting he gave to the town's library. She hands me a xeroxed copy of a skeptical article about Kinkade from a 2002 issue of *Newsweek* she saves for tourists who inquire about the artist. "Given that art's value is predicated on scarcity, how can anyone create an appreciating market for mass-produced 'limited editions'?" the article asks, before letting readers know that Kinkade's factory "churns out 10,000 pieces a month, each signed by a 'DNA pen' containing drops of Kinkade's blood."

The closest things to outdoor murals in Placerville are the crude mountain-snow and duck-pond scenes painted on the boarded-up windows of a Main Street building that once housed a bar and a tae kwon do school. Both are out of business, and the building is falling down. Across the street an Original Mels Diner, filled with blown-up photos from *American Graffiti* printed with George Lucas's autograph, offers a competing, more specific nostalgia to the nebulous kind that informs Kinkade's cottage paintings. I have lunch there, wondering if I should order cottage cheese.

> And the people lived in marvels of art—and ate and drank out of masterpieces—for there was nothing else to eat and to drink out of, and no bad building to live in; no article of daily life, of luxury, or of necessity, that had not been handed down from the design of the master, and made by his workmen.
>
> —James McNeill Whistler, "Ten O'Clock"

THE THOMAS KINKADE COMPANY has licensing agreements with more than fifty companies to produce various Kinkade-branded items. These include everything from books, clocks, night-lights, calendars, and candle holders to more elaborate-sounding artifacts: live flower arrangements, glow-in-the-dark puzzles, fuzzy posters, and "coasters made out of natural sandstone and/or dolomite/gypsum." You can get a Kinkade-branded checkbook cover and a book of Kinkade-branded personal bank checks and use them to pay for his paintings, or maybe for the mortgage on your house in the Kinkade-inspired Village at Hiddenbrooke, a gated community within a gated community in Vallejo, California.

When you look at Hiddenbrooke on a map, it hovers to the northeast of Vallejo like a stray kidney, an errant jellyfish, or a comic-strip thought bubble. The day I drove to the Kinkade village the gates were stuck open: the roads were being repaved, and the pavers had broken the gate. When the Village at Hiddenbrooke opened in 2001 and the houses there were selling for about $400,000, it got a lot of press, much of it sarcastic and disappointed because the development wasn't sufficiently Kinkadian and horrible.

While the houses superficially resemble those in Kinkade's paintings, they are not the fantasias you would expect. They are on small lots, each lot about a tenth of an acre. They stand close to each other, huddled under brown hills, not nestled alone in forests or by the seashore. The skies in Vallejo are blue and hot, not dramatic and variable like the skies in Kinkade's paintings. The houses feature details taken from Kinkade's work—turrets and dormers and exposed stonework—but they don't differ substantially from the other houses in Hiddenbrooke, except that many of those are bigger, built in a faux-Craftsman style on bigger lots, and set in the hills to give them a bird's-eye view of the development's golf course and the Kinkade village below.

In the early afternoon on the summer weekday I choose to visit, the Village at Hiddenbrooke has a deserted, eerie feel, like the set of a David Lynch film. It is quiet as I walk past the gate, save for the yapping of a small dog coming from inside one of the houses on one of the village's seven little streets. I walk down the middle of these streets; no cars come by. None is parked by the curb or in a driveway, either. Being there is like being in a Children's Fairyland version of *The Omega Man*. The place is as depopulated as one of Kinkade's cottage paintings.

After wandering around for a while, I come to a cul-de-sac and meet a lone man standing in front of his house with a poodle. He identifies himself as Mr. Jensen. He moved to the Village at Hiddenbrooke with his wife when the development opened, he says, because she's a Kinkade fan. They have some Kinkades they've put on their walls. He tells me most of the people here decorate with Kinkades.

There were two foreclosures in the Village and two short sales that Mr. Jensen knew of. One Village short sale I investigated was for a four-bedroom, three-and-a-half-bath model the owners bought in 2005 for $675,000 and were selling at the insistence of the bank for $333,000. I ask Mr. Jensen about the school featured on the map of Hiddenbrooke that I hadn't been able to find as I drove around. The school was never built, he tells me, because the residents were afraid the city would force it to take local children from Vallejo. Hiddenbrooke residents do not want locals "coming over the hill," Mr. Jensen explains. "Ninety-five percent of the kids here go to private school, anyway," he says. "We don't need a school." What's wrong with locals coming over the hill? I ask. The explanation Mr. Jensen offers didn't exactly answer the question, but he made his meaning clear: "Vallejo is a dump."

> Some sympathy was wasted on the house,
> A good old-timer dating back along;
> But a house isn't sentient; the house
> Didn't feel anything. And if it did,
> Why not regard it as a sacrifice,
> And an old-fashioned sacrifice by fire,
> Instead of a new-fashioned one at auction?
>
> —Robert Frost, "The Star-Splitter"

EVERY WEEKDAY THE CITY of Vallejo holds three auctions of foreclosed houses on the steps of the city hall. For as little $40,000, investors and developers buy up houses that sold for as much as $400,000 four years ago. They often pay in cash. Whatever doesn't sell goes back to the bank. One morning while I watched the auctions, a twitchy, skinny teenager in denim board shorts and a goatee tried to sell me "smoke."

The City of Vallejo is bankrupt. It went bankrupt in May 2008, the first city in California to declare bankruptcy since the economic downturn and only the second in the state's history. Inside city hall, an out-of-work contractor tells me "there's nothing. There's no new houses starting." He comes to the Planning Division once a week to check anyway. When he asks me what I'm doing there, another out-of-work contractor overhears me tell him I'm looking into foreclosed houses in the area. Without saying much he hands me the card of a loss-mitigation and loan-modification specialist named Vienna Train Bertolano.

I give her a call, and we meet the next day. We meet in a Mexican restaurant Bertolano co-owns. In addition to her work as a loan specialist and restaurateur, she also works as a legal assistant for a bankruptcy lawyer. Bertolano, who tells me to call her Vienna, is a petite Filipina in her midfifties with a slight accent. "Vallejo," she tells me, "was going to be the new Silicon Valley. It was a thriving market. People could buy investment homes here and see them go up 30 percent right away. When the bubble burst in late '06, middle- and lower-income buyers who could barely afford $1,500 a month in rent were stuck with $350,000 homes they'd bought with no money down. In 2005 there were never houses here for less than $300,000. Now there are over 2,000 houses selling in Solano County for less than $100,000, many of them for around $35,000. The only people buying them are investors. And it's going to get a lot worse. It's going to be bleak."

I ask her about Hiddenbrooke. "Thirty to forty percent of homes in Hiddenbrooke have been foreclosed or short-sold," she says. "People were buying those places three or four years ago for around $750,000. Those people are out of those houses. Agents are trying to sell them for $350,000. Maybe they can get $250,000."

In Vienna's office we prepare to visit foreclosed properties in Hiddenbrooke by looking them up in a local real estate database. "Homes in Hiddenbrooke have lost 50 percent of their value or more!" Vienna exclaims in surprise as she scrolls through the listings. The first one we visited, a four-bedroom Kinkade house that had been on the market for six months, was going for $350,000.

The house has a short patch of grass out front that refers to a yard more than being one, like a display bed in a department store. A tiny patio out back overlooks the golf course parking lot. When we get inside Bertolano looks around. "This is all standard stuff, no upgrades. This is a first-time homebuyer house. The previous owners didn't do anything. It doesn't look like anyone ever lived here. These are the cheap cabinets and countertops the place came with. There are a lot of houses in Hiddenbrooke better than this," she concludes.

We went to one, a giant pile right on the golf course with five bedrooms that sold for $1.3 million in 2007. It's now going for $500,000. There is a golfball-shaped hole in one of the garage windows, and I glimpse the white of stray balls through the shrubs out front. Although the house has been on the market for more than two years, inside it looks like whoever lived there left an hour ago, and in a hurry.

The house is filled with stuff. Dozens of toys are strewn about. There are Spider-Man bedclothes balled up in a corner of the living room and a Superman standee lying flat in the family room. Each bedroom has a DVD player in it, with videogame boxes nearby. The case for a DVD called *Ghetto Brawls 2* sits on the kitchen counter. A bookshelf in the foyer holds a passenger safety card from Alaska Airlines. Dozens and dozens of real estate agents' cards are scattered on the kitchen counter and in the entranceway, each one with the smiling face of an agent printed on it.

The two-car garage is filled with dead houseplants, abandoned strollers, and baby seats. "Only a two-car garage?" asks Vienna. "These people lived lavishly," she points out. "You can tell they over-extended themselves. I call them over-livers."

On the drive back to her restaurant, Vienna tells me a story about her neighborhood in Vallejo, which she describes as a nice place where mostly older people live. There was a bank-owned property across the street from her house, and a few weeks ago she'd noticed a white, middle-class family had moved in. "I was surprised to find out the house had sold or rented," she says. "But it hadn't." Her new neighbors were a family of squatters. "It takes two weeks to evict them," Vienna explains. "Last week they were fined for throwing beer cans into the street. Police came and gave them a ticket but couldn't tell them to leave."

> Without this fatal spiritual flaw, he was capable of becoming one of the greatest of our artists; but instead he only became one of the strangest of our madmen.
>
> —Théophile Gautier, "The Painter"

IN *THE CHRISTMAS COTTAGE* we learned that Thomas Kinkade is no stranger to economic hardship. Nor is the Painter of Light a stranger to lawsuits. In 2001, when Kinkade's then publicly traded company, Media Arts Group, began liquidating Kinkade product at deep discount prices, owners of Kinkade gallery franchises began to wonder if they'd made wise investments. As the value of the company's stock plummeted, some speculated that the artist was deliberately driving down the price so he could buy back the company. In early 2004 he did just that, taking the business private for $32.7 million. Investors lost a lot of money, but now the business is owned solely by the Thomas Kinkade Company, an entity that has turned *light*, according to its company profile, into an acronym for "Loyalty, Integrity, Growth, Honoring God, Trust." Like the acronym, it almost worked.

The FBI has reportedly been investigating Kinkade since 2006. According to news reports, the bureau's probe began after "at least" six former Kinkade Signature Gallery owners sued the Kinkade Company for fraud. They claimed the company persuaded them to invest in galleries and then undercut them by selling Kinkade reproductions direct to consumers for less than the galleries charged.

After years of appeals, Kinkade gallery owners have lately started to win their lawsuits. A gallery-owning couple from Virginia claims Kinkade executives rooked them by creating "a certain religious environment designed to instill a special relationship of trust" between them and the Kinkade Company; a judge recently awarded them $2.1 million. Another couple, in Michigan, was awarded $1.4 million.

It is hard to feel sorry for these people. After all, they put their life savings into the work of a man whose best-known public utterance came when he got drunk at a Siegfried and Roy show in Las Vegas and repeatedly yelled the word "codpiece" at the magicians until he was calmed by his mother.

New owners of Kinkade galleries also have reason not to be thrilled. In March 2009, several months before a couple in Prescott, Arizona, bought a Kinkade gallery there, the Painter of Light himself made an appearance before five hundred fans to give a motivational talk and raise money for charity by drawing a sketch, maybe one not that different from the one he gave his mother that Christmas back in the '70s. The drawing was auctioned for $12,000. According to the Prescott *Daily Courier*, the audience believed the $12,000 would be split between two charities. They didn't know that Kinkade had arranged to keep 80 percent of the sales price himself, with the charities receiving only about $2,000.

Why was a wealthy painter like Kinkade using these charities' good names to collect a measly $10,000? The new gallery owners don't know. What they do know is that since the news of Kinkade's 80/20 split leaked in late August, disgruntled Prescottians have been phoning their gallery and threatening to throw bricks through the window.

> Obsessed by a fairy tale, we spend our lives searching for a magic door and a lost kingdom of peace from which we have been dispossessed by a greedy swindler.
>
> —Eugene O'Neill, *More Stately Mansions*

THE HOUSE THAT WAS TO BE the playwright Eugene O'Neill's final harbor, the Tao House, sits in the hills above Danville, California, about 120 miles southwest of Placerville and 35 miles southeast of Vallejo. O'Neill and his wife purchased the Tao House and the ranchland around it in 1937, and the couple lived there until 1944, when O'Neill became too sick to write. While he was living there, he wrote many of his best plays, including *The Iceman Cometh* and

Long Day's Journey into Night. The house is now a National Historic Site administered by the National Park Service.

Visitors can tour the Tao House Wednesdays through Saturdays. To get there, you wait for a bus in front of a supermarket and a park ranger drives you up the hill. In O'Neill's time the land was clear. Now there's a gated housing development there. After the housing development was built, the National Park Service had to ask permission to drive through it to get to the O'Neill site.

On the ride to see the study in which O'Neill wrote *More Stately Mansions*, the park ranger driving the bus points out some of the sights of the gated community. "Have you ever seen a house worth $1.85 million?" he asks. "That house on the left was valued at $1.85 million!" He doesn't say what it's worth now. We travel farther into the gated community and the driver points out another place. "You see that house on the right?" he asks. "That house has an infinity pool. Have you ever gone swimming in one of those? That's a pool that looks like it just falls off into space, like off the side of a cliff."

The tourists I'm with seem a little let down when we arrive at O'Neill's Tao House. It's just a two-story house. It's not even that big. Looking at O'Neill's Bessie Smith records and his book collection is a disappointment to them after almost seeing an infinity pool. Studying his tiny handwriting through a magnifying glass the Park Service provides doesn't excite them, either. Even the grave of O'Neill's dog, Blemie, doesn't move them very much, and they barely stop to look at themselves in the strange black mirror in the master bedroom.

Weep for what little things could make them glad.
Then for the house that is no more a house,
But only a belilaced cellar hole,
Now slowly closing like a dent in dough.

—Robert Frost, "Directive"

O'NEILL'S CONTEMPORARY Robert Frost is a counterbalance to Kinkade more than any other American artist. In poem after poem, Frost writes about abandoned houses, arson and fire, debt and loss. When he writes about a cottage, he writes about it because there's no one there anymore. His cottages are haunted by memories of the people who lived and died in them, or built them and lost them. They aren't glowy; they're cold, and they speak of a time in the life of this country when people earned their houses instead of getting them with no money down. The word *subprime* does not appear in his work.

Frost is associated with New England, but he was born out here, in San Francisco. As I write this, California's seasonal wildfires are turning the sky over Oakland black. "The best way is to come uphill with me," Frost wrote, "and have our fire and laugh and be afraid." While the fires rage in California this August, that strikes me as the best way to look at Kinkade too. Whatever his value as an artist, he has used his own experience to create a business that predicted, and in some ways replicates, the current mortgage crisis. His paintings of quaint houses with burning interiors substitute nostalgia for values and hope for community. The idea that these reproductions, gobbed with points of light, are a good investment isn't any different from the idea that flipping gated, golf-coursed mansions is the way to get rich. Kinkade is a living testament to how the triumph of kitsch values has repercussions in the marketplace, outside the world of taste.

Meanwhile, in a safer part of California, Kinkade is still sitting on his gold mine, at least until the FBI and the courts decide to take it away.

When I was getting ready to leave California, a news story broke in a town close to Placerville that made people forget about the fires. Phillip Garrido, who ran a printing and graphic design business out of his home, was arrested for abducting a girl in 1991, when she was 11. He held her hostage for eighteen years in a makeshift compound in his backyard, and while she was his captive he fathered two children with her. Garrido, a religious fanatic, gave interviews after his arrest. "Wait till you hear the story of this house," he told a reporter. "You're going to find the most powerful story coming from the witness, the victim—you wait. If you take this a step at a time, you're going to fall over backwards, and in the end, you're going to find the most powerful heartwarming story."

There are a lot of houses in this country with Thomas Kinkade paintings in them, so when you tell people you're writing about Thomas Kinkade, you often find out their lives have been touched by his work; "highlighted" by it, you might say. I spoke with a young woman named Katie who works as a waitress at a California Pizza Kitchen in San Francisco. She told me her grandparents are Kinkade collectors who have left her and her siblings one Kinkade painting each from their collection. The paintings are reproductions they had highlighted at a Kinkade gallery, and they bought the proper gallery lighting equipment so they could display them the way Kinkade meant for them to be seen.

Katie says that if her grandmother were to die today (her grandfather has passed on), she wouldn't display her Kinkade where she lives, which is in a one-bedroom apartment in the Mission she shares with her girlfriend. The painting doesn't fit into her lifestyle right now, she tells me. It's too fancy and valuable. Maybe if she had a big house she would, but she doesn't, and she doesn't expect to anytime soon.

December 2009

Postscript

THOMAS KINKADE DIED IN BED on April 6, 2012. A lethal combination of alcohol and Valium killed him. He was 54 years old. His death was ruled accidental, but it has the feel of something closer to suicide. The artist had been drinking at home all night, said his girlfriend, Amy Pinto, with whom he'd been living. His wife, vacationing in

Australia, claimed Kinkade died of natural causes. Pinto, who was there, explained that Kinkade "died in his sleep, very happy, in the house he built, with the paintings he loved and the woman he loved." It doesn't sound like he was all that happy.

Pinto produced two handwritten wills Kinkade scrawled in the months before his death. The wills, described as "squiggly notes" written in a hand made shaky by drink, left Pinto the house and $10 million. She was supposed to use the money to open a Kinkade museum, featuring paintings valued (by her lawyers) at $66 million. Nanette Kinkade posted a guard at the house after her estranged husband's death to make sure Pinto didn't steal anything.

The two women settled Kinkade's estate eight months later, "after months of name-calling and finger-pointing," according to an article in the December 19, 2012, *San Jose Mercury News*. The settlement is secret. Pinto "accepted a deal in return for her silence."

Few details of Kinkade's last days have emerged. The *Mercury News* reported that the artist was a "fixture at local bars." His brother told the paper that "mean-spirited criticism of Kinkade's work and his estrangement from his wife and four daughters had taken its toll on the artist and factored into his alcoholism."

It was a dark ending for the Painter of Light, a Romantic ending in the 19th-century sense, something that could fit into the *Lives of the Artists*. It is sordid, tragic, and sodden, with women fighting over his possessions.

On the other hand, Kinkade overcame the disadvantages of his youth to scale the heights of American capitalism like no other artist of his time. A laughingstock in the big cities, he was the art hero of the hinterlands. He got there by eagerly resorting to questionable business practices that make the unregulated shenanigans of the legitimate art world look lazy and uncreative.

Because Kinkade is dead now, the quotation from Gautier's "The Painter," printed above, means more than it did when I wrote "A Cottage for Sale" in 2009. Kinkade's "fatal spiritual flaw" seems like what killed him. His greed, which expressed itself in his desire to leave his mark on anything and everything, allowed him to spread his bad taste over every surface he could. His alcoholism may have been inherited; the spiritual malaise of his death speaks of something else. It indicts his relentless uglification of the world, the end result of his licensing deals, and the way he got people to pay for his crap with their nickels and dimes a little at a time, preferably with interest.

One gets the sense that Kinkade saw himself as a figure for the ages. Now the internet offers endless parodies of his work. No obituary published after his death failed to mention how worthless the "highlighted" factory-made Kinkade paintings really were, and how they will not appreciate in value. Their value, it turns out, really was purely sentimental.

Kinkade's paintings are still produced and sold, although those squiggly wills make one wonder who painted some of the last ones to come off the line. His *Disney Dreams Collection*, for instance, one of his last commissioned sets, is still offered on his company's website. There's an anecdote I did not include in what I wrote in 2009. Once, while drunk at the Disneyland Hotel in Anaheim, California, Kinkade urinated on a statue of Winnie the Pooh while shouting, "This one's for you, Walt!"

A *Winnie the Pooh: So Much Better with Two* set of matched paintings, part of the Disney collection, was "published" in November 2013 by "we at the Thomas Kinkade Studios." The reproductions retail for $710 each, $1,020 for a foil-stamped limited edition. I wonder if Kinkade left something of himself behind in the paint that went into them? After all, we know that while he was alive his reproductions were auto-signed by a DNA pen containing drops of his own blood.

January 2014

THIS PLANET IS NOT YOURS TO RULE

Funny People

The pathos of comedians used to be that they were funny because they wanted everyone to love them. They were motivated by their psychic wounds, their difficult personalities, their inability to tolerate the world as they found it. Gags and jokes were a way to triumph over brute physical reality and the intractability of the human race.

In this movie, comedians beg for something new and different: "Love me because I'm not that funny," they plead. "Love me because I'm only funny enough to be on a sitcom. Love me because the movies I'm in aren't any good." "And by the way," Apatow adds, "aren't my daughters cute? These are my *real* daughters!"

The movie is lugubrious, like a Chekhov play about comedians in Los Angeles, a Chekhov play with hundreds of dick jokes, in which Jimmy Fallon might show up in a cameo as himself.

A side effect of *Funny People* is that now I am prepared for the death of Adam Sandler. It's an eventuality I hadn't thought about much. Really I didn't think about it much while I was watching the film. As Sandler swam alone in the pool on his big lonely estate where he thought he was dying, mostly what I thought was, I wish I had a pool like that. I want to swim alone in the morning. If I was supposed to question the values that led his character to that mansion and that pool, I didn't. I wanted the pool and I wanted to be alone in it, instead of in a theater watching this long movie that had all the sincerity of a Dean Martin roast and none of the laughs.

Away We Go

This mild, charmless comedy is not the provocation critics made it out to be. Reading their reviews, you'd think they wanted to throw ink at the screen, like the fascists who went to the premiere of *L'age d'or* in 1930. "Smug! Cynical!" they screamed at *Away We Go*, like two out of three movies released aren't smug and cynical. I guess they expected whatever the opposite of smug-and-cynical is.

Even if it's not so terrible, the "Oh! Sweet Nuthin'" scene stands out for its terribleness. It's probably unplayable by any actors, and Sam Mendes does nothing to help. He directs it like he's never seen a film he didn't make. Coming after scenes of great familial love in a house full of adopted, multiracial children, it is confusing. Determining its intentions is a fool's game. It is mysterious and offensive, but not like *L'age d'or*.

In the "Oh! Sweet Nuthin'" scene, Melanie Lynskey, playing a character named Munch, has to dance around a stripper pole in a bar, slowly and fully clothed, while her husband (Chris Messina) delivers a maudlin speech to the film's protagonist about Munch's miscarriage. The Velvet Underground's "Oh! Sweet Nuthin'" plays as Lynskey silently twirls around the pole with what is either a faraway look of deep loss in her eyes or an intense stare of abiding married love.

It turns out Munch and her husband, who we thought had it all, don't have it all. They have failed to have a child of their own; those other kids aren't enough. "She ain't got nothin' at all," sing the Velvets. The film builds up this attractive, fun-loving couple, then tears them down. We believed in their happiness, which was a sham, and now we are asked to believe in their emptiness, which is pathetic.

How about if we don't believe in either? This scene punctures the film and lets the air out, not a good thing to happen to a road movie.

Whatever Works

If people overthink a film written by Dave Eggers and Vendela Vida, they don't think about a film written by Woody Allen at all. Woody Allen turns critics into people who honk their horn as soon as the light turns green. Once they go through the intersection, they forget they're the kind of people who honk like that.

No matter what Woody Allen does in a new film, people say the same things about it they said about the last film he made, and the one before that. The reviews write themselves; you switch out the title and the names of a couple of the actors.

Whatever Works is a vituperative, hostile film that mellows after a great painful-looking shot of Larry David lying on top of a woman he's landed on while trying to commit suicide by jumping out a window. David does not play Woody Allen in this movie, which was what everyone was afraid of. He plays one of those disheveled, scowling old men you see limping down Houston Street, the kind who makes you think, how does that guy have an apartment? I can't afford anything, and that guy gets to live here?

If the film's subject is happiness in a hopeless world, Allen and David express it only through disgruntlement and contempt—happiness is ignored, like it is in real life. What film of recent years has blasted conservative America as thoroughly and relentlessly as this one? It's an unending string of insults and a summation of the last period of American history, which sent Woody Allen into exile like Chaplin.

A scene set in Madame Tussauds—a light, throwaway scene filled with complaining—contrasts wax statues of George W. Bush and other political creeps with living, breathing people from George Bush's America, who as the film progresses change for the better by coming up against New York City. If this is a fantasy, so be it. Allen is right, they are better off living as New Yorkers, New York changes people for the better, that's all there is to it, as far as he's concerned. It takes a lot of not caring what other people think to make a film as mean, nitpicky, unlovable, and unfair as this one, which is the opposite of *Funny People* in every way.

John Hughes

John Hughes was only 59 when he died on a Manhattan street last week, but he'd been retired as a director since 1991, and really since 1989—for twenty years. It is not a fitting coda to his work that his last credit was a pseudonymous one as one of the writers of *Drillbit Taylor.* His directorial career spans the mid- to late '80s, the sequel period from *Indiana Jones and the Temple of Doom* to *Ghostbusters II.* His movies are remembered and loved because in a bleak period they really stood out. They were warm and they gave young actors and character actors well-written, endearing parts to play. They believed in people, not concepts.

By the time he was making *Ferris Bueller's Day Off* in 1986 (his best film), he was already letting lesser directors handle films he should have made himself—*Pretty in Pink* and *Some Kind of Wonderful.* Those films are good, but they suffered because Hughes was directing them by proxy. By the time he made *Uncle Buck* in 1989 (his last good movie), he had in some sense given up and had cynically if good-naturedly descended into writing and producing but not directing childish movies like the *Home Alone* series and *Baby's Day Out.* He was moving backward in human development from the adolescence of *Sixteen Candles* and *The Breakfast Club* into films whose logical extension should have ended in movies about cute amoebas, or eggs and sperm.

Young actors thrived in the parts he wrote for them; they became definitive as teenage types: brain, basket case, princess, athlete, and criminal. But the Brat Pack was a generation of underachievers Hughes and the movies abandoned. They are loved because they are only semi-iconic, not stars, people lost to Hollywood. Jennifer Grey and Charlie Sheen, lesser lights of *Ferris Bueller's Day Off*, are the real poster children for the Hughes oeuvre, not Molly Ringwald. Sheen's character doesn't even have a name. Grey, as Ferris's unhappy sister who lives in his shadow, tries to make up for that by having two. She's Jean but she calls herself Shauna.

Transformers: Revenge of the Fallen

This second *Transformers* film is garbage, a big pile of useless scrap in every way, but there are shots of plastic beauty in it that use Megan Fox's stress-tested porno face like an element in a James Rosenquist painting of car parts and spaghetti. But so what? James Rosenquist paintings already exist.

The film satisfies a young man's desire to make and build machines at the same time as it tells him that he'll never be allowed to. It's not just that the film turns its audience into passive viewers of pseudo-mechanical spectacle, it's not just that the main kid in it doesn't do anything more than sprinkle fairy dust on a machine to make it move again, which subverts the idea of what a machine is. The very nature of the Autobots and Decepticons is nonmechanical, they're form-shapes, CGI-generated non-things. They have no materiality, they're junky and fragile. The film dangles them every which way, like trinkets hanging from a rearview mirror in a car crash, just to yank them away. Or it holds them over a crib like Mommy.

The US Army, so present in the film, does nothing. The film is entirely militaristic but the army is useless. The Autobots control everything. Army men fill up the screen, which would seem empty without them. This is a film in which a lot of frantic running around, all over the world, shows us that neither civilians nor soldiers have a say in anything. Optimus Prime, a monolithic blowhard good-guy slab, calls the shots, and what interesting lines there are go to the evil Decepticons, who at least get to call people weak ("*You . . . are . . . so . . . weak!*") and tell Optimus, a drive-in speaker blaring instructions, that the world is not his to rule, which should be true but isn't.

Roger Ebert, in his review of this film, said it was the last of its kind, that the genre had reached a terminal point of stupidity and could not continue. I said that too, when *Jurassic Park* came out.

The Limits of Control

Jim Jarmusch's nonchalant and precise *Limits of Control* moves through real landscapes in Spain, city and nowhere, his two favorite places. It is an antidote to the *Transformers* movie or any of the summer's militaristic blockbusters, holdovers from the Bush era this film repudiates.

Looking and listening—paying attention—replace the hysterical yelling and flailing of big-budget action in this anti–*Bourne Identity*. For something so minimal the performances are flashy—Tilda Swinton in a white wig and cowboy suit, Bill Murray as a rogue Dick Cheney in a toupee and bunker, a soulful John Hurt pointing out the difference between consumer bohemianism and the kind in Aki Kaurismäki's poverty-soaked movie *La vie de bohème,* which he describes without naming.

At junctures in the film, the nonaction fully stops to let Isaach de Bankolé's hit man contemplate three different paintings. Jarmusch mixes the subjects of these paintings into the film, relating them to objects, people, and landscapes. Paz de la Huerta is probably the most lingered-over nude in any American film; the Andalusian locations have a felt presence the deserts trashed in the *Transformers* movie don't achieve before they're destroyed.

Revenge of the Fallen claims to be about memories: "I send this message so that our past will always be remembered, for in those memories we live on," broadcasts the profundo telephone tower

Optimus Prime, trying to implant a memory to control us. But "the best films are dreams you're never really sure you had," counters Tilda Swinton in Jarmusch's film, neutralizing him.

The Hurt Locker

Far from being nonideological or apolitical, *The Hurt Locker* is actually pro-war, and it's not a contradiction that it's the best American film made about the war in Iraq so far. Kathryn Bigelow's film explicitly states that it is better to spend every day of your life risking getting blown to pieces defusing IEDs in Baghdad than it is to spend even one day in the US shopping for cereal at Costco with your family. While many films have tried to present the American family's consumerist nightmare before, Bigelow's film is one that really makes you feel it. She does not shy away from the lower-income status of her hero by ennobling it, nor does she make it shameful. It is stated as fact.

Maybe it's implicit in the film that the freedom the United States is supposedly helping Iraq achieve will, if successful, lead to the construction of a giant Costco in Baghdad. Bigelow makes sure that's only a fleeting thought, favoring long scenes of stupid daring, quiet psychotic bravery, and misguided adventure, which to the film's credit are often numbing and hard to fathom. Jeremy Renner, who gives the best performance by a Hollywood actor in any Iraq war film, makes no concessions to likability or heroism. In this Iraq war movie, Baghdad actually looks war-torn, full of rubble and garbage strewn, and America is gray-brown and rainy.

Looker

All week things went wrong. You know a week isn't going to go well when it starts with food poisoning at a casino in Pennsylvania. I couldn't concentrate when I tried to work, the laundry lost my socks, the place where I eat breakfast burnt my toast, that bird that makes a sound like a rusty gate chirped outside my window nonstop. Forces in the world conspired against me.

I couldn't get into the movies. I went to see the Iraq war comedy *In the Loop* Saturday night, which was playing on three screens where it was showing, but when I met my date there the next three shows were sold out. We decided to go to Do Hwa, a Korean restaurant where they make good drinks and show movies in the bar.

I bet *In the Loop* is funny—I heard somebody calls somebody else "Horse of the Year" in it—but this is a review of *Looker*, a sci-fi thriller starring Albert Finney that Michael Crichton wrote and directed in 1981. That's what they were showing on the wall at Do Hwa.

While waiting for the subway on the way into Manhattan, I had studied a giant, aggressive ad on the platform wall for a new TV show called *Addicted to Beauty*, a reality show about a plastic surgery clinic. The posters make the show look like the clown hospital scene from *Pee-wee's Big Adventure*, but with a white background instead of a black one.

In the poster, the cast, ostensibly real people, look like surgically altered vultures with polished beaks. Their faces are shoe shiny, like heads on a Jeff Koons sculpture. Predatory women with mad faces and deep cleavage hold syringes while effeminate men hold their hands to their open mouths in "no you didn't" gestures, all of them refugees from a Fellini film, glaring at commuters to make them uneasy. *You probably need plastic surgery,* they say. *We're going to get you.*

In the clown hospital scene from *Pee-wee's Big Adventure*, it's not Pee-wee but his bicycle that's operated on, then scrapped. That low-tech scene, lit with the kind of multicolored fluorescent tubes in a Dan Flavin installation, is as far removed from the false mechanics of the *Transformers* movie as *Looker* is from *Addicted to Beauty.*

People who work in fashion and beauty always like entertainments about their industry to be dystopian. They want them to portray fashion and beauty as murderous and fascistic. Somehow that flatters them.

Looker, on first glance, looks like maybe it was directed by John Carpenter or David Cronenberg. Its surfaces are glossy and shallow, the camera concentrates on people's hair, and it has a knowing, threatening, mind-control-alert quality, especially when Finney puts on big sunglasses or aims his time-stopping ray gun at empty rooms framed like photos from late 1970s furniture catalogs.

Do Hwa showed *Looker* with the sound off and music by Au Revoir Simone playing in the background. The choice added to the matter-of-factness of the film's images: models falling to their deaths from windows, crashing onto car hoods. It de-dramatized them but made them poetic.

In *Looker,* Finney is a plastic surgeon who stumbles on an ad agency scheme to surgically perfect a group of young models, scan and digitize them, use their digitized images in TV commercials, then kill them. With the sound off, it was unclear why the models had to be killed. I think it was so the agency could use their images for free. Now that's done with contracts. Isolated parts of women's bodies appear in the rifle-site targets of optician's instruments and where floors should be there are black grids outlined in 1980s computer-display green. The ad agency is called Digital Matrix. Finney tries to stop them when he meets Susan Dey, one of the models.

At the end of *Looker,* Finney and Dey stand on one of the floor grids, two actors who have no reason to be together and who aren't really anywhere. They look around, then walk out of frame, into a future world where computer-generated imagery and cosmetic surgery are normal.

Outside the bar people go by who look like the actors in *Looker.* It's good to look like people from that era, its flat brightness has been stylish for a while. These good-looking people live in the buildings we walk by in the West Village. What do they do for a living? Are they models, actors, surgeons? We walk through them and descend past the *Addicted to Beauty* posters into the subway. The bucket drummers are out in full force, pounding on hard plastic, drowning out the sound of the trains.

August 2009

ALIEN LAND

THE GRAPES OF WRATH

> The anger of a moment, the thousand pictures, that's us.
>
> —John Steinbeck, *The Grapes of Wrath*

SOMETIMES IN THE 1980S, WHENEVER SOMEONE ASKED ME WHAT MY favorite science-fiction movie was, I would just say *The Grapes of Wrath* out of exasperation. Back then, people used to ask that question a lot, because sci-fi movies were still a little unusual then. They weren't quite mainstream. They were getting there, though, as nerd culture came to the fore, and already you were expected to have a finely tuned opinion. I didn't care about George Lucas, whose movies took place in some distant past that never happened. To me, it was John Ford's 1940 adaptation of John Steinbeck's novel that had the quality of being a film from the past that seemed to be about the future. *The Grapes of Wrath* was predicting something.

Since I first saw it around the time *The Road Warrior* came out in the US, that made sense to me. *The Grapes of Wrath* had more in common with that movie, or with another postapocalyptic dystopia, *Escape from New York*, which also came out around then, than it did with movies about the contemporary rural poor. I shunned rural-poor movies as preachy and boring, overly emotional and fake-actorly. *The Grapes of Wrath* is preachy and boring and those other things, too, but in a way wholly unrelated to something like *Norma Rae* (1979). The relative artistic conservatism of *Norma Rae* makes *The Grapes of Wrath* seem like *Ivan the Terrible,* which also seems like science fiction now. Black and white used to be a signifier of greater reality. Now it makes movies seem fantastic and otherworldly.

The Grapes of Wrath, with its trip through a blighted, alien land, has a Jules Verne side—it's a trip to the moon. Like John Ford himself, the film seems a product of the 19th century, explicitly concerned with production instead of consumption. Travel in *The Grapes of Wrath* is in no sense leisure. Today the film is as much Méliès as Lumière, although on the surface it is pure Lumière, documentary not fantasy, and clearly influenced by trends across the political spectrum of 1930s documentary, from Ivens to Riefenstahl.

Or maybe since Ford's film was such an obvious influence on Orson Welles we should say it has an H. G. Wells quality. Gregg Toland's photography makes it seem like time travel, like *La jetée* (1962). Many of the people in *The Grapes of Wrath* have the get-in-and-get-out quality of 1950s science-fiction-movie bit players. *The Grapes of Wrath* is filled with petty officials using great catastrophe as an excuse to hector bug-like, semi-anonymous lumpens. It is not a Wellesian/Wellsian Martian invasion that causes them to scatter and scurry in *The Grapes of Wrath,* or organize themselves into protective camps. It's man-made natural disaster, the destructive changes brought on by the sharecropper system of over-farming that was so easily exploited by land companies, farming conglomerates, and banks. Today we call it climate change or global warming. In the 1930s it was drought and floods.

Steinbeck plays up this dystopian aspect in his novel. Huge Caterpillar tractors manned by insectoid drivers in goggles and face masks plow over fields and shacks. The film's one montage sequence is based on Steinbeck's description of those tractors, and Sovietized by Ford. But these aren't the heroic tractors of Soviet films. The "Cats" raze everything in their path. They are destructive machines from a mechanized future in which tiny humans like the Joads have no place. The tractors are alien overlords commanded by banks so far away from Sallisaw, Oklahoma, they might as well be on another planet. The Joads are powerless against them.

In its time *The Grapes of Wrath* was a film about the recent past—the soil erosion and windstorms of the Dust Bowl, a period in the history of the American prairie that lasted through the 1930s and up to the time of the film's release. That had seemed a quaint era in US history, wrapped up in WPA photographs that had become art pictures used to decorate the white walls of suburban homes and city condos, part of our visual heritage on display in chain-store coffee shops along with Bob Dylan CDs. Even if Bruce Springsteen tried to keep the Woody Guthrie tradition alive by writing a song about Tom Joad—and Ford's film was an influence on Guthrie—by the 1980s *The Grapes of Wrath* seemed hopelessly dated. It appealed to a small minority concerned about the disappearance of family farms or people who loved scratchy music transferred from 78 rpm records. It appealed to John Ford fans, but not like *The Searchers* (1956).

The film's message in the Reagan era was completely out of step with the times. The famous speeches in the film, which are lifted directly from Steinbeck's novel, echoed in the culture only in the vaguest way. People knew those speeches and sometimes repeated them, but they said them the way Bible verses are intoned, without thinking what they meant, just knowing they had something to do with "the people" and helping the poor and downtrodden. It's true they were said a little more reverently than the Schwarzenegger catchphrases that defined that era. They were used to invoke gravitas, the kind of fake gravitas "I'll be back" didn't have.

"Wherever a cop's beatin' up a guy, I'll be there." In the last thirty years, that "I" became a video camera. We abdicated responsibility to our machines and put what they captured on TV news and then on YouTube. Reality became novelistic, reversing Steinbeck. Just now we are starting to deal with the legacy of that abdication.

Until recently *The Grapes of Wrath* seemed quaint. But like all good science fiction, it has come true again. "I'll be there," said Tom Joad. Not "I'll be back" but "I'll be there in the dark."

Reading the novel now, you realize that if every eighth grader in the US had had to read *The Grapes of Wrath* instead of Steinbeck's *Of Mice and Men*, which is what I had to read in eighth grade, probably because it's shorter, we might live in a different country now. *The Grapes of Wrath* was still banned in certain municipal libraries as late as the 1990s, and many incidents in the book are still deemed unsuitable for young people to know about. Read today, *The Grapes of Wrath* is practically *The Communist Manifesto.* The novel seems exactly like that—its anti-capitalism, not to mention its socialism, is blatant and powerful. Even the Nunnally Johnson–Darryl Zanuck screenplay, which tries hard to downplay the story's radicalism, can't bury the book's inherent hatred of bosses, cops, and the faceless rich, its disgust with the unfairness and stupidity of a system that benefits only a tiny fraction of society.

That comes through in the film, and Ford, in what's really an act of hostility, extends it more deeply into the characters than Steinbeck did. Ford is much less loving than Steinbeck. His eye is more machined and his Joads have an inhuman, tiresome edge. At times we want them to die. When some of them do, the way the remaining Joads move on from their grief is different than it is in the novel. They just go on to the next scene, to more humiliation and confusion, terser and less reflective than Steinbeck makes them. Born of an ignorance that Ford observes but doesn't have time to explain or to be kind about, the Joads' cockroach resilience becomes as threatening as the Californians trying to keep them at bay imagine it is, but in an entirely different way. We begin to picture a world inhabited entirely by Joads, displaced zombie farmers sliding into dementia and starving to death.

This is subversive to the screenplay and to certain of the actors' performances, specifically to Jane Darwell's Oscar-winning turn as Ma Joad. Darwell rolls through the film like a slow-moving cannonball getting closer and closer to the lens. She is Eisensteinian in the worst way, and gets the last word—a quiet speech she grinds into us—after Henry Fonda's Tom Joad has departed the film alone, like a regular Ford hero. Much of the film is a long breakup between this mother and son. Tom has to escape many things to try to make a better world, and one of them turns out to be his monstrous, speechifying mother, endlessly stirring up mush.

The film has never been as controversial as the book, and in fact it is one of those movies that has to be saved from its status as a masterpiece. The screenplay is a distillation of the novel, "factory liquor" that lacks the afterburn of Steinbeckian rotgut. It is concise but it is not a model of concision. The Johnson-Zanuck screenplay is essentially ameliorationist and Hollywood-ized. Ford works against that, sometimes successfully, sometimes not. Although it is not well constructed, Ford's *Grapes of Wrath* has the virtue of seeming to have been made quickly with an eye to keeping down the running time.

On one side we have Zanuck-Johnson-Darwell, producer-screenwriters and an actress who was imposed on Ford over his choice, the scrawnier, less lovable, less maternal Beulah Bondi. On the other side, we have Ford-Toland-Fonda, director, cinematographer, and the only actor in 1930s Hollywood who could have played Tom Joad with the haunted dignity the part required. The film lurches between these two competing groups, one section dominated by one, the next by the other almost schematically.

The first reel is all Ford-Toland-Fonda, with contributions from John Carradine's preacher Casy and John Qualen's Muley Graves, a man who has gone crazy by staying behind on his land when everyone else has left; he calls himself a "graveyard ghost." Carradine and Qualen were never better than in *The Grapes of Wrath*, and 1940 is also the year Qualen played another lost soul, the hapless killer Earl Williams in *His Girl Friday*. Both seem to have given themselves over to a higher power here, to have momentarily escaped their theatricality and character-actor elbowing, although for a film considered naturalistic, this section of *The Grapes of Wrath* is highly theatrical, stark, austere, and lonely.

The film's greatness rests on this first section, which begins with Fonda walking down a road alone, the same way the film ends before the Zanuck-imposed coda of Darwell's "we're the people, we keep a-comin" speech. (*Searchers* fans, she does not add "sure as the turnin' of the earth.") Toland makes the blacks very black—black telephone poles jut into the scene at angles—and he and Ford frame everything funny, with heads too low or too big. The composition, seen from inside a truck, in which Fonda gets out, says "homicide" to the truck driver who has given him a lift and pronounces it *ho-micide*, is the first indication that the film can be better than the novel. Yet Ford-Toland-Fonda almost throw the scene away. The truck door slams, adding a period, not an exclamation point to Fonda's three syllables. This is a triumph of mise-en-scène over whatever Zanuck and Johnson had in mind.

The shots switch between location work, a set at Fox, even a stock insert of a storm a-brewin'. Fonda meets Carradine. The two men share a pint of bourbon, and when they're finished, Fonda throws the bottle out of frame. When it lands and smashes that's another kind of subtle punctuation. Fonda's hand goes out of frame; we don't even see the bottle leave it, because Ford refuses to cut into the shot or even to pan away from the two actors. It is a gesture, and it seems radical today, and not because the scene is too good to mess with but because Ford didn't do something that was unnecessary, he refused to do something he didn't have to do.

So Fonda and Carradine move through this post-tornado–*Wizard of Oz* farmland in black and white and come upon Fonda's old house and then Muley Graves. Never have three actors with more haunted eyes shared a night interior. Ford plays all this for as long as he can, but we get the sense of Zanuck's hand in the editing room. There are things missing, but it works here. This long section of the film is too short; the night is long, but before we know it it's morning and we're meeting the rest of the Joads.

Ford's *Tobacco Road*, which he made the next year, deals in hillbilly antics and seems like some kind of revenge on the more outré aspects of the Joads' domestic life. After *The Grapes of Wrath*, comedy became the way American culture dealt with the more unsettling aspects of Southern rural poverty, its decrepit old age, too-close quarters, and too-young pregnancies. From Ma and Pa Kettle to *The Beverly Hillbillies* on TV, this kind of material had to be made funny to be looked at at all. When Granma and Grampa Joad die on the road we are not far from the death of Aunt Edna in *National Lampoon's Vacation* forty-three years later or *Little Miss Sunshine* twenty-five years after that. The death of an older relative on a western road trip haunts our national psyche and begs to be turned into comedy, it seems.

This journey west is pure Ford, as is the dance scene at the nice Department of Agriculture camp where Tom and Ma have their farewell dance to "Red River Valley." Both are in the novel and it's amazing how Fordian Steinbeck's book already was. The difference between this journey west and other ones in Ford films is that *The Grapes of Wrath* takes place in the present, so road signs direct the Joads and tell the audience where they are at every moment. So insistent are these signs that when Fonda walks by a sign at the government camp instructing people to turn off a water faucet after use, he turns it off even though he hasn't seen the sign, which is facing us, the audience, not him, who approaches it from behind as he walks toward the camera.

People are crowded into small spaces in the vast landscape of the West in *The Grapes of Wrath*, and this is uncharacteristic of Ford, as is the way the camera is mounted to the Joads' truck as they pull into a Hooverville. We see out-of-work migrants moving aside as we travel through the crowd in this striking shot that shows how Ford and Toland knew the West they were depicting was not the West of *Stagecoach* (1939) and had figured out how to show it, how to expose it in every sense of the word. The scene ends in a kind of urban violence removed to the West. A deputy—not a deputy in the western sense, he's just a cop—accidentally shoots a woman in crossfire and she falls to the ground. Another cop gets dialogue out of Steinbeck: "Boy, what a mess them .45s make." In the book, the fingers were blown off her hand, like in *Taxi Driver* (1976), which reverses the Ford-Toland process by reimagining the Fordian West in New York City.

More than any other, *The Grapes of Wrath* is the John Ford film that most deserves to be revived today. The world it predicted has come to pass. *The Grapes of Wrath* proves George W. Bush was another Herbert Hoover as much as anything does. Bank foreclosures have forced people out of their homes. We are going through a depression marked by catastrophic climate change, which is the one aspect of the previous depression everyone has forgotten in the recent wave of predictable Thirties nostalgia. Man-made natural disasters like Hurricane Katrina have forced populations to relocate. Maybe we don't pay as much attention to the people displaced by that catastrophe because they are not white like the Joads—20th Century Fox, now owned by Rupert Murdoch, has not made that into a film like Zanuck decided to do with Steinbeck's novel. The Depression was not just an urban phenomenon limned in Warner Bros. gangster films and *Gold Diggers* musicals. It was a rural phenomenon, too, and hit the rural poor as hard as anybody. Anyway, let's not forget that in 1938 John Ford also directed *The Hurricane.*

One of very few films that has come close to dealing with the world as it is today is another science fiction, George Romero's *Land of the Dead* (2005), which predicted the world of Hurricane Katrina two months before it happened and went on to describe a world we are now beginning to glimpse. It is as anti-capitalist as *The Grapes of Wrath* and deals with a small band of people escaping an untenable community against the backdrop of a vast migration of Okie-like zombies into a city. As a side note, I feel compelled to mention that the ending of Steinbeck's novel, which was considered obscene, improbable, and unfilmable in 1940, actually happened this year, and with a real actress. In the book's last paragraph, Rosasharn, a Joad daughter who has just delivered a stillborn baby, offers her breast to a starving man to feed him so he won't die. In February of this year, Salma Hayek did the same thing for a starving baby in Sierra Leone and allowed the TV news show *Nightline* to film it.

May 2009

OEDIPAL MULTIPLEX

ON DAVID THOMSON

"I ONCE SHOWED *RED RIVER* ON A COURSE FOR AMERICAN STUDENTS," David Thomson wrote in his *Biographical Dictionary of Film*, back in the pre-blockbuster 1970s, "and at the end—like Charles Foster Kane at the opera—I stood up alone to applaud." For thirty-five years Thomson's readers have watched him retreat from that moment. In more than a dozen books, in countless articles in newspapers and magazines and online, Thomson's enthusiasm for the movies has drained—not in a trickle but in torrents, like an emptying ocean.

Unlike the horde of cheerleading critics whose hollow praise blights the film pages, Thomson alone has made bitterness a career, mourning Hollywood's decline and fall. A genuine litterateur, he has elevated himself above ordinary movie reviewing in a way someone like Roger Ebert has not. As he's become darker and more defeatist, alienated from the cinema and preoccupied with celebrities and power, he's gained in respect. The *Atlantic* calls him "probably the greatest living film critic and historian."

Thomson has seen his *Biographical Dictionary*, a collection of erudite essays covering everyone from Anouk Aimée to Darryl Zanuck, become a standard reference and an updatable franchise, like *Raiders of the Lost Ark*. The *New York Times Book Review* described it as "one of the most probing accounts ever written of a human being's engagement with the movies," adding breathlessly that Thomson's "ambition is to probe nothing less than human illusions."

Accustomed to praise, Thomson is also forgiven his trespasses. His 2006 tome *Nicole Kidman*, a hymn to the actress in the form of a picky mash note, raised eyebrows. But it was forgotten when the weirdly titled *"Have You Seen . . . ?" A Personal Introduction to 1,000 Films* came out last year, prompting the copresident of Sony Pictures to call Thomson "the foremost film writer of our time." Yet it's the Kidman book, with its fantasies of made-up movies in which Kidman does not appear, along with 2005's *The Whole Equation: A History of Hollywood*, that seem like quintessential David Thomson: high-toned, windy books concerned not with movies or directors but with The System and David Thomson's "personal" fantasy of what it does to people.

Thomson maintains his preeminence by pleasing on two fronts. For literary baby boomers, traditionally suspicious of the movies, he laments the passing of cinema's glory days. For seekers of inside dope, he exposes the spiritual corruption of the blockbuster industry, submitting to its fall as predestined. In his adopted homeland, the USA, the Englishman Thomson spreads pessimism over our illusions like orange marmalade, and he's been thanked for it more than any film critic could expect.

One gets the feeling, however, when reading his books, that no reward is great enough for this chronicler of the movies' decline. His prose exudes a sense of wounded disappointment beyond praise. With the release of his new memoir, *Try to Tell the Story*, an account of his boyhood and teenage years in London after World War II, we begin to see why. Postwar London, as Thomson describes it, looked and felt defeated. He grew up among bombed-out buildings in a nation victorious but wrecked, a child with little privacy in a house shared by three generations and a boarder. Lonely but never quite alone, his childhood was dominated by someone who wasn't really there—not "Sally," the slightly older and wiser girl he invented to be his imaginary friend, but his father, who abandoned his family to live across town with another woman. His desertion, however, was incomplete: he remained married to Thomson's mother, showing up two weekends out of three to live with the family he'd left. Thomson's father hit him, took back gifts, failed to support his decision to study film instead of going to Oxford on a scholarship, and made a point of leaving him nothing in his will.

This unorthodox situation was quietly accepted in the Thomson household. Thomson's father owned the house; his mother lived there, too. As she aged, her daughter-in-law looked after her. Thomson's mother cannot have been happy about her life, but we can't really know. She is a quiet presence in *Try to Tell the Story*. Thomson acknowledges her absence in a coda: "My mum is not quite there, not like she was in life. And in a way, that is the final mark of Dad's influence. That he left us was a gesture that claimed our story as being lived in his shadow."

This is a coming-of-age story that will make sense to other cineastes. Left to figure out the world for himself, the young Thomson turned to movies, jazz, and cricket, and his memoir calls back to life the films, music, and sports of a London that has disappeared. Many of the best sections of the book deal with movies and music, and that makes sense; Thomson is a critic. His memoir echoes a recent film, Terence Davies's *Of Time and the City*, a documentary about the director's youth in Liverpool. *Of Time and the City* is an aggrieved work, narrated in tones of extreme disdain, but in *Try to Tell the Story*, Thomson for once leaves bitterness behind, to see the past more clearly. Davies stayed in England; Thomson eventually left for America. Even before he went away, Thomson left his past behind by trading his father's shadow for the shadows on the screen.

If Thomson's story is inherently dingy and sad, he takes pains to make it vibrant instead of maudlin. Because he is reliving his first encounter with Hollywood movies, before he was jaded by encounters with the real Hollywood, everything seems fresh. His memoir describes the real melancholy Thomson overcame, unlike the melancholy he sells today as the real tinsel beneath Hollywood's fake tinsel. To quote the Christina Rossetti sonnet that features prominently in

Kiss Me Deadly, darkness and corruption have left a vestige of the thoughts that he once had.

Oscar Wilde wrote that "the highest, as the lowest, form of criticism is a mode of autobiography." A film critic's autobiography is the story of his response to certain films. For Thomson, those films were made in Hollywood in the 1940s and '50s, when he was young. Thomson's taste mirrors that of the critics at *Cahiers du cinéma* who became the Nouvelle Vague. Like them, and in the same years, he loved *Citizen Kane*, James Dean in *Rebel Without a Cause*, Howard Hawks. Every critic has that one film that changed everything. For Thomson it was Hawks's *Red River*.

"I remember all these pictures, and many others," Thomson writes, "but nothing was like the experience of seeing *Red River*. . . . This was the first story I had encountered that I knew was meant for me. So I could not give it up." Right after seeing it for the first time, he stays for a second show. The prolific Chilean director Raúl Ruiz writes that when he first saw Edgar Ulmer's 1930s horror movie *The Black Cat*, for him it was like a father calling to his son: "Now at last recognition came to me, and as in an old melodrama, I exclaimed: 'Father!' and he replied 'My son!'" Quentin Tarantino has said that as a boy growing up without a father, his constant viewing of Howard Hawks films taught him how to be a man.

Let me confess that I, too, was raised by *The Big Sleep*, *To Have and Have Not*, *His Girl Friday*, *Twentieth Century*, and Hawks westerns in lieu of a father who wasn't around. *Red River* is Hawks's most overt film in this respect. It deals explicitly with the difficult, sometimes hate-filled relationship between a surrogate father, John Wayne, and son, Montgomery Clift. *Red River* still exerts so much power over Thomson that he refuses to give away the film's ending in his memoir.

I will respect Thomson enough to say only that *Red River* ends unexpectedly, maturely, and happily. John Wayne is absent from much of the film's action, but this father figure haunts every moment of the film just the same, the way art isn't always there in the movies, but the promise of art always is. For young men without fathers, the film fulfills a wish of reconciliation but also shows how fathers can be wrong, dangerous, and necessary to remove.

Which is how Thomson seems to feel about movies today. Cinema is a vagrant art and it travels from country to country. Instead of looking for the cinema as he found it in the late 1940s, which meant looking for it wherever it might appear, Thomson kept looking to Hollywood, seeking the same kind of affirmation he got from *Red River* as child. Is it any wonder he's been disappointed? While Thomson may have worked himself out of a fix by writing *Try to Tell the Story*, for a long time his readers have had to put up with the soured feelings that got him there. For too many years before this book, Thomson has harrumphed his way through his gossipy prose like he's Colonel Mustard in the billiard room with the candlestick, beating the movies to death in his own personal game of Clue.

"No good American ever seriously questions an English judgment on an aesthetic question," H. L. Mencken wrote in 1920. Thomson has thrived on Mencken's sardonic axiom. Once he realized Hollywood wasn't going to deliver another *Red River*, he began telling a certain kind of sophisticated reader what he or she wanted to hear. In the bleak age of the weekend box office gross he reminded us that Cary Grant is spotless, that producers care more about money than the script, that Nicole Kidman is a honey but not getting any younger. Nobody thought otherwise, but it was comforting to hear somebody say it in such a cultured way.

I, for one, will never forget the queasy sensation I felt when I first picked up a copy of his book *Warren Beatty and Desert Eyes*, another half biography, half novel, and read this excerpt on the back cover: "And like any Narcissus, he will keep his looks so long as desire moves him. If that ever goes, if it becomes a mere idea, then youth will be replaced by something like Dracula's haggard smile." It reminds me of the last two lines of that Christina Rossetti poem from *Kiss Me Deadly*: "Better by far you should forget and smile / Than that you should remember and be sad."

Today David Thomson lives in San Francisco, where he sits in judgment north of Hollywood. *Try to Tell the Story* returns him, and us, to a more generous time in his life, when he was putting the world together instead of tearing it apart.

February 2009

NATURE WILL REGULATE US

Encounters at the End of the World

Encounters at the End of the World gratifies on three levels: it is apocalyptic, it has cute penguins, and it stars a man with a German accent berating us because we are inadequate. It is an animal show, end-of-the-world adventure travel, and a trip to a German dentist. Herzog's impatience with people has become palpable. He can't wait to tell whoever he meets that "nature will regulate us," that "the empire has started to fade into the abyss of history." Saying these things in Antarctica gives them a weight they'd lack if you said them on DeKalb Avenue.

Revolutionary Road

Revolutionary Road shows something people think they want to see but really don't: what happens if Leonardo DiCaprio and Kate Winslet survive the *Titanic*.

WALL-E, Kung Fu Panda, Bolt, Waltz with Bashir, et cetera

Carbon-free, cruelty-free, cage-free. I've decided to live my life *cartoon-free.* I spent too much time last year listening to otherwise normal adults describe the plots of animated movies. As someone with no children and no nieces or nephews, as a free man who does not have to take kids to matinees, I hereby declare my independence from cartoons.

Are you an adult? Adopt my program! If the urge to see an animated feature creeps up on you, have a drink instead. A drink costs less than a movie. Got a date? Skip the movie, cut to the booze. While you enjoy it, you can invent what the movie you didn't see was about. Your inebriated version of *Bolt* will be better than the animated one you missed.

Listening to people talk about *WALL-E,* it struck me that it was a version of Mike Judge's great satire *Idiocracy,* but without live actors. *WALL-E* made millions and was loved by everyone who saw it, while *Idiocracy* was deemed unreleasable by the studio who paid for it. We prefer our dystopias cute.

As for drawing over actors' faces, why? Did actors become actors so somebody in front of a computer could color over their faces? The hostility inherent in that is a form of violence I reject as much as any in *Waltz with Bashir.*

Slumdog Millionaire

I don't like movies that cover their heroes in shit. But covering a little boy in shit and having him go up to Amitabh Bachchan to ask for an autograph is audacious even for a filmmaker as crass as Danny Boyle.

Slumdog Millionaire is a torture movie, which I didn't know going in. The Islamic protagonist is a stand-in for all the Muslims tortured since September 11. They are offered *Slumdog Millionaire* as a redemption—a torture movie is about to win an Oscar for their trouble.

We learn being tortured is worth it. If you give the right answers it's like winning the lottery: they'll set you free and pay you off, you get the girl, a dance sequence where you're the star.

Part of the torture is that you have to turn every experience you've ever had into a mnemonic device that could save your life in a deadly game of Trivial Pursuit. It's no longer enough just to spin the cylinder in Russian roulette like in *The Deer Hunter.* Now somebody has to ask you what's the capital of South Dakota first.

Frost/Nixon

If *Slumdog Millionaire* offers a reward to the tortured, *Frost/Nixon* substitutes Nixon's admission that he let the American people down for George W. Bush's failure to admit anything he did was wrong. Nixon, our last verifiably criminal Republican President, sits in for the latest.

Australia

Sometimes the critics are wrong. *Australia* was dismissed as dumb and bad but it's an important film. The reason it's important is because now the cat's out of the bag about Baz Luhrmann. No worse or better than Luhrmann's other films, *William Shakespeare's Romeo + Juliet* and *Moulin Rouge!, Australia* finally beat critics into submission and they cried uncle. And it did it without the provocation of a plus sign or an exclamation point in the title.

Jerry Lewis

In 2005, when AOL and the Discovery Channel determined who was the Greatest American, Ronald Reagan came in first, beating Abraham Lincoln and Martin Luther King Jr. George W. Bush was sixth, but Jerry Lewis did not even make the top 100. He didn't even make the list of nominees. When the director of *The Nutty Professor* and star of *The King of Comedy* strides across the stage at the Kodak Theatre to receive his Jean Hersholt Humanitarian Award on February 22, in his familiar, distinctive walk, I will consider him vindicated.

Happy-Go-Lucky

Sally Hawkins's Polly is a lot like Jerry Lewis. She's kooky. She prefers bright colors. She needles shop clerks. She wants everyone to love her even while she's sucking the air out of the room.

She moves like Jerry Lewis and even kind of looks like him, with her black hair and big open mouth. Like him, she places herself beyond criticism. She gets the same look of confusion on her face about how mean everybody is, or about how sad things are. Then: another outburst.

Last summer was a time for trampolining. When I saw Sally Hawkins jumping in the air in *Happy-Go-Lucky*, that confirmed it for me. I was surprised there was trampolining in *Happy-Go-Lucky* because until last summer I wasn't conscious of it at all. I only found out it was a real sport watching Russian and Chinese girls compete in women's trampoline on TV during the Summer Olympics. I loved the overhead shot the TV directors used, with the big red cross in the middle of the white field of the trampoline and the trampolinist tumbling toward me in the foreground above it, like a pinball about to crack the glass. I attributed Russian, Chinese, and Canadian dominance of this sport to cold acrobatic winters spent trying to hit the ceiling from the bed. It reminds me of the opening credits in a Jerry

Lewis movie called *The Patsy.* Jerry falls out a hotel window, freezes in crazy poses on the way to the pavement, then hits a canopy and bounces back into the room. Lewis achieved the effect by jumping on a trampoline.

It was an optimistic sport for an optimistic time, like *Happy-Go-Lucky* was an optimistic movie, but now we're all business again.

Tropic Thunder

Ben Stiller is the Mel Gibson of comedy. Everyone acclaimed the post-racism casting of Robert Downey as an Australian Method actor playing a black soldier, but Tom Cruise's disturbing anti-Semitic portrayal of a Jewish producer was more heartfelt, sicker, and funnier. Stiller wisely let him take over the film. The movie wasn't just post-racism. The trailers for the imitation–Eddie Murphy fat-people movies Jack Black was supposedly in were post-weightism or something, post-grotesque.

Tropic Thunder was post-everything, including entertainment. It's a white-boy version of a Wayans brothers movie, made long after satirizing Vietnam War films could possibly matter. With the war in Iraq still going on, it's cowardly and weird, like making a comedy version of *Uncle Tom's Cabin* during the Battle of Corregidor.

The Curious Case of Benjamin Button

In a series of bad dreams, Brad Pitt combines with Forrest Gump, E.T., Oliver from *The Brady Bunch,* the baby from *Eraserhead,* Tom Waits album covers, *Dr. Zhivago,* Dick Cheney/Donald Rumsfeld, on and on, like robot locusts eating the inside of the movie theater for three hours.

Milk

A noble, unobjectionable film, detailed, entertaining, and it goes by quickly. An interesting thing about *Milk* was the way it used grainy, washed-out color photography to make San Francisco look like Buffalo, New York. Everything was in shades of light brown and industrial green. I guess that's what people think the 1970s looked like, like the faded Eastmancolor print of a movie that's been run five thousand times. To me it was like the opening credits to *WKRP in Cincinnati*, which would have been pretty arty if that was what Van Sant was going for.

The film's flatness and desaturation imply without showing it that it was only after gay people got political representation that San Francisco became a place where residents could paint their three-story Victorians purple or lime green. Like many a nostalgia trip, it stops at the moment the style it's rejecting is about to begin.

In Bruges

The trailer made it look like a hit-man comedy directed in the style of Baz Luhrmann, starring an Anglo-Irish Laurel and Hardy. But it's not like that at all. *In Bruges* is a serious film with great performances written and directed by someone who knows what he's doing. One of the strengths of this film, which is one of the year's best, is the way it gets more dire and nuanced with every character it introduces, especially Ralph Fiennes's yuppie attack dog of a mob boss.

The Wrestler

People so loved seeing Mickey Rourke get whomped and Marisa Tomei take off her clothes they couldn't sit still for the scenes with Evan Rachel Wood as Rourke's daughter. To prefer two middle-aged people to Evan Rachel Wood is a sign of progress in the cinema. Despite all the mayhem and nudity, the best scene is one of accommodation: Rourke trying to enjoy his job as a deli clerk and make the best of it. For that alone he deserves an Oscar.

May 2009

INSOLUBLE FARBER

WHEN MANNY FARBER DIED LAST AUGUST AFTER A LONG LIFE OF PAINTING, teaching, thirty-five years of writing film criticism, then thirty years of not writing film criticism, American film reviewers rushed to their blogs to eulogize him. Farber had become a writer no one didn't like, a figure of American culture like Johnny Cash or Philip Guston who all thinking people agreed was excellent, unmatched, et cetera.

When Pauline Kael died, the old arguments about circles and squares were rehashed one last time. There were no arguments to retrieve when Farber died. There was no controversy about Farber's greatness; his film criticism was intact and no one wanted to shoot holes in it. The terms he invented—*underground films* (a slippery term the way he used it but a favorite), *white elephant art, termite art, the gimp*—were trotted out by critics to show they knew them. Knowing them proved Farber was an influence. Whether their work or anyone else's really had any of Farber's spirit was not a question to ask at a sad time.

For film critics interested in the history of cinema, deaths are commonplace, eulogies frequent. Every day another immortal dies, today Antonioni, tomorrow Ingmar Bergman—actually it was both of them the same day. This summer Farber was gone. Tomorrow Cyd Charisse, Richard Widmark, or Charlton Heston would go, and it would be time for another blog post to patch on to the official obituaries linked from newspapers' websites. But on August 19, 2008, everybody could agree: nobody writes like Manny Farber wrote. They didn't mean a specific nobody. They just meant Farber was an original. Whether there's a reason nobody writes like he did was another question they didn't ask.

There is a reason for it. Farber was not a publicist or a cheerleader. In the interview that ends the expanded edition of *Negative Space*, the only collection of his work published so far (although we keep hearing another is on the way), Farber worries that some of his later pieces cross a line. "The Herzog article from *City* irritates us now for its promotional tone," he says, the "us" being him and his writing partner Patricia Patterson, who began collaborating with him in the 1970s. "At this point," Farber insists, he and Patterson would do it differently, they'd concentrate on something else, Herzog's "apparent cruelties to dramatize the space."

Although the Herzog piece in question does contain the worst line ever to appear in a Farber piece (even if it's true)—"There is nothing quite like *Fata Morgana*!"—by the standards of today that poster-ready blurb is so ambiguous it practically constitutes a dis. And the exclamation point, in Farber's case, humanizes it instead of making it a gush. Here is Farber being awestruck. He's being normal, reacting to *Fata Morgana* like anyone else. It is endearing or inspiring that Farber, a critic whose offhand, sometimes bizarre cruelty was not out of sync with Herzog's, would worry about being too nice, too commercial. Maybe he *was* too nice in that piece. Worrying like that makes him seem tougher, a tough old bird, even though he said that thirty years ago, back when he was only 60—and about to stop publishing.

Had Farber mellowed too much to keep writing? After that interview, he devoted himself to painting, and teaching what is called cinema studies. He was still doing criticism but he wasn't writing it anymore. He talked it, breathed it, painted it. It no longer came to readers in the form of prose; it no longer came to readers at all. Interested parties had to go to San Diego for it, had to climb the mountain to talk to this holy man who had rejected prose and mass communication.

In 1945, other writers, even ones who seemed to like him, weren't so sure about Farber. As part of the Farber eulogizing, some film critics brought up a piece S. J. Perelman published in the *New Yorker* that year. It's not quite the praise they made it out to be. "Hell in the Gabardines" references anti-Farber sentiment from unknown, presumably literary quarters, which Perelman both undercuts and trumps.

"It has been suggested by some that Mr. Farber's prose style is labyrinthine; they fidget as he picks up a complex sentence full of interlocking clauses and sends it rumbling down the alley. I do not share this view," Perelman explains, separating himself from these anti-Farberites. "With men who know rococo best, it's Farber two to one." S. J. Perelman knew rococo all right, but he wasn't about to let Farber off that easy, with just a backhanded compliment squeezed from the advertising of the day. "Lulled by his Wagnerian rhythms, I snooze in my armchair, confident that the *mystique* of the talking picture is in capable hands," he concludes, dismissing Farber without even getting up while using the phrase *talking picture* to mock the silent-movie purism that still hung around revival houses in 1945.

For the ex-Paramount screenwriter Perelman, snoozing, film criticism, and moviegoing all went together. Thirteen years after "Hell in the Gabardines," Perelman published a piece in the *New Yorker* called "Small Is My Cinema, Deep My Doze." Mostly a takedown of art-house ambiance, the piece takes a swipe at the kind of film critic Farber was not. Toward the end of the piece, Perelman and his wife are strolling by the marquee of a "little cinema." "Look," she exclaims. "They're showing *Acrid Fruit* with Gérard Philipe, Danièle Delorme, and Danielle Darrieux! Jesse Zunser of *Cue* gave it five mangosteens!"

Jesse Zunser, by the way, was a real person, not some invention of Perelman's. He was a working film critic in New York for thirty years, like Farber was. At the end of Zunser's career in the mid-1960s, he claimed he'd reviewed twelve thousand movies. Farber, the ultimate non-giver of mangosteens, said in the *Negative Space* interview that he thought it was "obscene and degrading for criticism" that a review should "add up to four stars or a hit movie." How many films had he reviewed in his career? Maybe one-twentieth the amount Zunser had, maybe less. Farber's collected work gives the impression of tackling the same two hundred films again and again, many of them *Only Angels Have Wings.*

Farber is in a sense not part of film criticism. Film criticism today is even more what Perelman said it was. Farber is apart from that, next to it, somewhere below it, always above it. He comes at it from the hidden position he admired in a filmmaker like Hawks, and he's always looking for a way to work in a dig at the "daily and weekly reviewers" he accused of making the audience dumb. In "Blame the Audience," Farber calls audiences of 1952 "the worst in history" but later exonerates them. He shifts the blame to "snobbism on the part of most of the leading film reviewers," which he says makes filmmakers dumb along with the audience by encouraging them to repeat the successes of the bad "prestige" (Farber puts the word in quotes) pictures critics love.

By the mid-1970s Farber knew what he wanted from audiences. He wanted them to be Farber. "The audience," he said, "should be fantastically dialectical, involved in a continuing discussion of every movie." He wanted the same from filmmakers: "The person making the movie should be held responsible for everything that's said and shown, and so should the audience seeing it." If this seems a long way from the pure pleasure Kael-ite critics accuse him of deriving from "underground" movies by directors like Hawks, Walsh, or Aldrich, it's not. It's just that Farber feels those directors were aware of a certain kind of responsibility. Ours is a cinematic age of auteurism without responsibility. Every film is A Film By and no director is ever held accountable for making bad movies and no audience is ever ridiculed for liking them. Farber's direction for audiences and filmmakers makes more sense than ever, even as it becomes less possible for working film critics and film directors to follow it.

For the American film critics of the past we still read today, writing film criticism was not a lifelong profession. Today it has become a sinecure for certain writers. It traps them and forces us to witness their long, long, *long* slides into irrelevance. Because he could paint, and because for him painting and writing film criticism were inextricably linked, Farber escaped this fate. He did not write film criticism his whole life nor did he make it his nine-to-five job, but it was something woven into both. When he said "I can't imagine a more perfect art form, a more perfect career than criticism," the word *career* must have had a different meaning for Farber in 1977 than it does for us today. His definition of *underground* in movies—"it is as though the film has a life of its own that goes on beneath the story action"—applies to his career as well, which sometimes seems as mysterious as Edgar Ulmer's.

Asked whether his painting and his criticism had things in common, he answered, "The brutal fact is that they're exactly the same thing." He did not accept the idea there was a difference between artists and critics. ("I get a great laugh from artists who ridicule the critics as parasites or artists *manqués*— such a horrible joke.") In fact, his prose equals the subjects he wrote about and often surpasses them. While this may be true of some film critics writing today, saying their prose equals the subjects they write about is not a compliment.

Farber states that he is not interested in pronouncing movies *good* or *bad*, but he is still always *for* or *against* something. If we see his influence in the nonjudgmental quality of our film critics today, who celebrate the great diversity of the regime of image-making practices, choices, and options we all live under, what we look for and don't find is anyone being *for* or *against* anything they see.

They can't even describe movies anymore because they take them for granted like water or grass, which now that I think of it are in jeopardy through the paradox of overuse and neglect, too. Farber wrote at a time (the 1960s) when everybody was just beginning to study every kind of movie. He lists them: "Czech films, Underground films" (by then he meant the avant-garde, not *White Heat*), "Hollywood films. . . . skin flicks, TV commercials, scopitone." Undaunted by this proliferation, he worked them all in.

After reading a review today we are usually still in the dark as to what a movie looks like. This is never a problem with Farber. "The texture of a Panama hat is emphasized to the point where you feel Huston is trying to stamp its price tag on your retina," he writes about John Huston's films in general. He describes the documentary locale of a film called *In the Street* as "an uptown neighborhood where the adults look like badly repaired Humpty Dumpties who have lived a thousand years in some subway rest room and where the kids have a wild gypsy charm and evidently spend most of their days savagely spoofing the dress and manners of their elders."

Everybody already knows what *The Third Man* looks like. They think they know what it sounds like, too. Farber does the work of capturing these things together, there are shortcuts but no shorthand in a Farber review: "Reed's nervous, hesitant film is actually held together by the wires of its exhilarating zither, which sounds like a trio and hits one's consciousness like a cloudburst of sewing needles. Raining aggressive notes around the characters, it chastises them for being so inactive and fragmentary and gives the film the unity and movement the story lacks." This is an example of why we have to write about films as they happen, before they become classics that shut us up.

Farber doesn't skimp on these descriptions. Slightly pithier when describing actors—Eleanor Parker is "a tremulous actress with a genius for finely shaded whimpering," Kirk Douglas's "mad-dog style of acting is bound to make any character into a one-sided surface of loud-pedaled ugliness"—Farber's strength as a critic resides in the things he leaves out, the things he refuses to do. His refusals are radical, political, which he explicitly recognized in his *for* or *against* remark. These refusals spit in the face of commerce but give readers a lot of credit.

One thing he doesn't do is plot description. You can read a Farber piece on *The Graduate* and have little to no idea what it's about. He waits until the last possible second to bring up a director's name, and when he does sometimes he only uses the last name, as if maybe "Tourneur," in a piece on Val Lewton that had not previously mentioned any director at all, is a household name everybody knew in 1951. A piece called "Clutter" covers *China Is Near* and gets around to mentioning "Bellochio" [*sic*] six paragraphs in. He can barely bring himself to write "Mike Nichols." In praising Pierre Clémenti's performance in *Belle de jour*, praising it very highly, he doesn't mention Clémenti by name at all.

In one of Farber's most hilarious sentences, a real shocker, this late-intro style extends to using the word *late* itself. "The late work of certain important directors—," he writes, "Cukor's *The Chapman Report,* Huston's films since *The Roots of Heaven,* Truffaut's *The 400 Blows . . .*" The first half of a Farber sentence giveth, the second half taketh away: "Movies have seldom if ever been as subtle as these scenes, or as depressing in the use of outrageous elements to expedite ambiguous craftsmanship."

Farber always lets in the outside world. Describing what it's like to see "termite" films in inner-city theaters, he lets us know that "the spectator watches two or three action films go by and leaves feeling as though he were a pirate discharged from a giant sponge." At the same time, no one bears down on the screen like he does. In his piece on Godard, the first film he mentions is *Les carabiniers.* He can't get this film out of his head, it prompts the key phrase in all his work, the one that stamps a certain kind of cinema for all time: "long stretches of aggressive, complicated nothingness." He writes an entire piece on Godard without mentioning *Pierrot le fou.* Did he even see it?

Somehow, *Les carabiniers,* maybe Godard's best film, which Farber works hard to make central, gets Farber to realize that *The Exterminating Angel* is Buñuel's great achievement, his *Les carabiniers.* These observations seem so obvious in retrospect, yet to be able to dig them out of movies takes years of prep. To cap it all off,

Farber compares Buñuel to Westbrook Pegler—in 1969, in the pages of *Artforum,* no less. He's less harsh on Godard, but, like Perelman was to him, not exactly straightforward. Godard, he writes "sees the world as a spiky place, the terrible danger of brassiere ads, the fierce menaces of Coca Cola and Richard Widmark, the corruption implicit in praising a Ferrari when in the character's heart-of-hearts it's Maserati all the way." *Spiky* and *spiking* often seem like his favorite words.

"The sentences are swamps that are filled with a suspicious number of right-sounding insights," Farber wrote about James Agee's film criticism. He admits Agee might be as good as people say, "if his whole complexity of traits is admitted in the record." This is true of Farber just as much. When he wrote about Agee he was writing about himself. His foibles, as unremarked as the things he leaves out of his work, are the other source of his strength.

He gets titles wrong—Val Lewton's *Death Ship*? John Ford's *Last of the Mohicans*? Hawks's *G. I. Joe*?—he gives away endings; he repeats the same joke or observation twice in the same piece (the tunnel comparison in the Huston piece, the "handmade/homemade" thing in the Herzog piece); he is doggedly dedicated to certain actors he loves or hates: Kirk Douglas, Lee Marvin, Jeanne Moreau, "Pat Neal," like he used to ogle her from across the hall when they were neighbors. His affection for Frankie Darro compels him to compare *Mouchette* to a bad Frank Capra–Bing Crosby horse-racing comedy called *Riding High,* in which Darro plays a jockey. The most unexpected comparison in film criticism; maybe it's also the greatest. To think of connections like that without looking for them because they come naturally to you is not an ability most film critics have.

More quirks. Whenever he can, Farber compares something to a Winslow Homer painting or a comic strip. His love of comic strips melds seamlessly into his disdain for movie reviewers: "As in the Dr. Rex Morgan comic strip, life is a horrible mess that transpires in the speeches of upright citizens who seem to be glued against a gray backdrop that is always underlit and hard on the eyes. . . . For this reason, many people, including the critics of the *New Yorker* and *Time,* think [these] movies are full of 'ideas'—'disturbing,' 'offbeat,' and even 'three-dimensional.'" He loves the extra adjective: "Every Hitchcock-style director should study this picture if he wants to see really stealthy, queer-looking, odd-acting, foreboding people."

And as for his great distinction between dreaded "white elephant art" and admirable "termite art," has anyone noticed how close his definition of white elephant art is to his definition of a "minimal underground classic"? The three sins of white elephant art are, he writes, "(1) frame the action with an all-over pattern, (2) install every event, character, situation in a frieze of continuities, and (3) treat every inch of the screen and film as a potential area for prizeworthy creativity." MUCs, meanwhile, must meet these conditions: "that the shape of a film be discernible in any single frame; that a single-camera strategy be the basis for the movie's metaphysic and any situation within the film; that the repetitions of the camera, which is always obviously present, creates a spirituality; and that the field of examination be more or less static, durational, and unromanticized."

In the introduction to *Negative Space,* he asks a pertinent question: "Why even invent two such categories: white elephant and termite, one tied to the realm of celebrity and affluence and the other burrowing into the nether world of privacy?" Maybe today he'd answer the question differently, because today, how much difference is there between the two? A Farber jeremiad sums up his time and ours: "The mess we are facing in movies and other media promises to be the worst era in the history of art. Not even the ponderously boring periods, similar to the one in which Titian and Tintoretto painted elephantine conceit and hemstitched complication into the huge dress-works affair called Venetian painting, can equal the present inferno of American culture, which is so jammed with successful con men." Farber was ahead of his time and at odds with it, a condition he shrugged off as normal.

It is tempting to quote Farber again and again. Despite his assessment of it, he speaks to us from a great period in film history, roughly the Raoul Walsh–and–*Wavelength* era, a time he captured like no one else. He stopped writing about two seconds before *Star Wars* came out, a real shame but understandable. Only his students know what he thought of films made in the last thirty years.

It makes sense that Farber ends his career as a publishing film critic by writing about Chantal Akerman, the most underrated filmmaker alive, who works in no known system. If you walk the New York streets at night after reading Farber (when you'll be able to see why he was attracted-repelled by *Taxi Driver*) you walk them with new eyes, you see things differently, the light looks different, the night is like the night in Akerman's *Night and Day,* and everything slides past like it does in *News from Home*. Finally you feel like you remember what it means to think and see.

In 1967, the year Farber wrote a piece called "Cartooned Hip Acting," Susan Sontag wrote "The Aesthetic of Silence." "So far as he is serious, the artist is continually tempted to sever the dialogue he has with an audience," writes Sontag. "By silence he frees himself from servile bondage to the world, which appears as patron, client, consumer, antagonist, arbiter, and distorter of his work. . . . More typically, he continues speaking, but in a manner that his audience can't hear." Farber stopped writing but continued to paint, and it is in his paintings we will find his last works of film criticism. "I think the point of criticism is to build up the mystery. And the point is to find movies which have a lot of puzzle in them, a lot of questions," Farber says in the interview that ends *Negative Space*. "Whatever is wholly mysterious is at once both psychically relieving and anxiety-provoking," Sontag replies. Her remark lacks the "poignant, voluptuous cynicism" of Hildy Johnson's exit line at the death cell in *His Girl Friday,* but it will have to do for now.

October 2008

JESSICA BIEL'S HAND

THE WAR ON TERROR

FOR TWO MONTHS THIS SUMMER THE ONLY MOVIES I WATCHED WERE movies about the war on terror. While other moviegoers were enjoying cinematic treats like *You Don't Mess with the Zohan* and *The Happening*, or the revival of Kobayashi's *The Human Condition*, or that Norwegian movie about Norwegian yuppie writers that everybody liked so much, I was immersed in the backlog of global war-on-terror movies released since 2002. The only summer blockbuster I saw was *Iron Man*, a war-on-terror movie and therefore allowable.

I watched three dozen of these movies and maybe 15 percent of them were any good. The rest, like the war itself, represented an enormous waste of manpower and resources that would have been better spent on something good for people, like entertainment. When I say this I do not mean any disrespect to the three thousand men and women who died on September 11, 2001, or the over four thousand American soldiers who have died overseas, or the tens of thousands of Iraqis who have been killed, or the unknown number of detainees who have been tortured in prisons. But watching these movies was like being buried under rubble while working in an office, like being stuck in the desert far from home, invaded by an occupying army, left tied in a stress position for days.

You ask why I put myself through this. Like some kid fresh out of high school sauntering into a recruitment center just to check it out, I wasn't exactly coerced. I wasn't drafted. A suggestion was made, I volunteered, I didn't want to seem like a wuss. Here was the story of our time, they said, told cinematically. Wasn't it my duty to cover it? It might be, I answered. So they signed me up, they put my name on a contract.

Fortunately for me, I cannot be stop-lossed. American soldiers continue to die in Iraq with no power to make it end, but I can simply file this report, turn my back on the cinematic quagmire and walk away. I know it's unfair. It's criminal. But if there's one thing we've learned these past seven years, it's that fairness has nothing to do with it.

THE FIRST IRAQ WAR MOVIE was *Fort Apache*, a western John Ford made in 1948. It was also the first Vietnam movie. A thinly veiled retelling of Custer's defeat at Little Bighorn in 1876, *Fort Apache* holds up the ordinary cavalry soldier, represented by John Wayne's Captain York, against an oblivious commander, Henry Fonda's Colonel Thursday, who foolishly leads his men to doom at the hands of Apache warriors. In *Fort Apache*, the soldiers of the Seventh Cavalry do their duty, "riding the outposts of a nation," as it says in another Ford western, while a commander who refuses to listen to his officers charges blindly into death.

Wayne's York gives what amounts to a press conference after the defeat. He doesn't lie to the assembled reporters who consider the dead Thursday a hero—we can't picture John Wayne lying in a movie made in 1948—but he doesn't tell the truth, either. What he does is let the reporters believe what they want to believe. The reporters don't really listen to what York says, anyway. Instead, they tell him what happened in the battle, even though they weren't there and he was. York's response, a soliloquy about dead soldiers and the permanence of the US Army, delivered by John Wayne as he looks out a window, ends the film.

The Apaches carry *Fort Apache*'s moral weight, rejecting peace to fight with honor. The movie preserves the dignity of the US Army, however, which is portrayed as separate and apart from Thursday's stupidity even as it's subject to it. Ford shows Thursday was wrong; he shows how regular soldiers get killed. What makes the film tragic is that it doesn't matter. In their victory the Apaches remain the enemy, in defeat Thursday remains a hero. After a while nobody remembers the dead soldiers' names.

John Ford fought in World War II and filmed the landing at Normandy, but *Fort Apache* was not about the war just ended. It was about a much longer war. What we see in movies about the war in Iraq and Afghanistan, in movies about the so-called global war on terror, is that we are still playing the *Fort Apache* game—cowboys and Indians and reporters.

MAYBE ANOTHER FILM, made closer to the events at hand, a film with no moral weight at all, is really the first Iraq war movie. In 2001, less than four months before the destruction of the World Trade Center, *Pearl Harbor* came out, to much fanfare, on 3,200 screens.

Brought to us by the men who made *Armageddon*, *Pearl Harbor* existed to celebrate, in costly and spectacular fashion, the fliers who avenged the attack that got us into World War II. But it also existed to do away with the very idea of moral weight, to make war look like late-'90s action-adventure, something that happens while Ben Affleck and Josh Hartnett argue over a girl. In *Pearl Harbor* Michael Bay and Jerry Bruckheimer celebrated war from the sky, a kind of war like the first Gulf War, the kind Jean Baudrillard could claim didn't really take place because the soldiers fighting it were never in any danger.

Who wants to remember *Pearl Harbor* now? After seven years of this new war that isn't so new anymore, nobody does. Looking back on that obnoxious and innocent time when *Pearl Harbor* was the first blockbuster of 2001, and being able to see the last blockbuster of that summer looming on the horizon, *Pearl Harbor* becomes an insult to everything—life, death, war, the movies. Why was that entertainment?

The truth is it wasn't entertainment. Is any summer blockbuster? Summer blockbusters are civics lessons, collective work we do for the economy, grim torture-filled slogs like *The Dark Knight* or the war in Iraq. The lesson of *Pearl Harbor* came in the form of dialogue delivered by Colonel Jimmy Doolittle, played by Alec Baldwin in the last role he had where we were supposed to take him seriously as an authority figure. "Victory belongs to those who believe in it the most and believe in it the longest," he says in *Pearl Harbor.* "We're gonna believe. We're gonna make America believe, too."

In the year or so before 9/11 that's what all our blockbusters were telling us, from *X-Men* to *Bring It On*. It was a message we were ready to hear. Boys and girls had to get together as a team, learn from the old dudes, and kick some ass. Why? We didn't know why. But it's good to be prepared.

Soon enough we found out. And pretty soon after that, just like in *Duck Soup*, we had a war we were promised would be both easy to win and endless.

RIGHT AWAY ENTERTAINMENT began to take over. Already there was no other way to see anything. Everything had to fit into the world of entertainment, even though TV, the source of entertainment, kept saying the world had changed forever.

On September 11, 2001, two French brothers, Gédéon and Jules Naudet, who were working on a documentary about a firehouse in downtown New York, filmed the destruction of the World Trade Center right from Ground Zero. They caught the planes going into each tower, the initial rescue efforts, with the sound of bodies thudding on the pavement outside. Jules Naudet, trapped with firemen inside the North Tower when the South Tower collapsed, continued filming.

It was like filming the exact moment of the Big Bang, but in reverse: the end of the world. The buildings were gone, there was nothing but white smoke and sirens. Spreadsheet confetti fell endlessly, like volcanic ash. "The building collapsed to dust," says one firefighter in *9/11*, the TV movie that emerged from the Naudets' footage. "No desks, no chairs, no telephones, no computers . . . you find a foot."

The scenes are frightening and tragic, put together in a thoughtful way that gives every firefighter his due, and yet something's missing. You feel bad for even thinking so, but it's true: something's missing. The Naudets' footage, as essential as anything that's ever been filmed, became the basis for a TV special. Set within the context of TV it strives to be really good TV, and it is really good TV, and now who ever thinks about the Naudets or their footage anymore?

WHILE JULES NAUDET WAS filming in the North Tower, a thousand miles away, in Sarasota, Florida, George W. Bush was sitting in front of an elementary school classroom reading along with second graders as they followed a story called "The Pet Goat." After his chief of staff whispered to him that a second plane had struck the Twin Towers, the President just sat there for over seven minutes. He continued to read silently or stared into space.

This footage is as essential as the Naudets' footage of the end of the World Trade Center. It too deserves to be seen in its entirety. Instead, it was taken over by Michael Moore, who was afraid we would be bored by it. So instead of letting us see this thick chunk of dead time in which the President of the United States squirmed, he spoiled it in *Fahrenheit 9/11* by showing only sections of it, adding an on-screen countdown clock to time the President's inaction, and talking over it, telling us what we were already seeing: "Mr. Bush just sat there."

Whatever we would have thought about this footage on our own was not good enough for Michael Moore. He ruined it in the name of entertainment, encouraging us not to think while he showed pictures of a man he claimed wasn't thinking.

THE FIRST TWENTY-FIVE MINUTES of Oliver Stone's *World Trade Center*, which take place on the morning of September 11 before the first tower was hit, are an evocative and even beautiful remembrance of New

York City—evocative and beautiful because we know what's going to happen. Haunted shots accumulate and create a strange tension the rest of the film can't sustain. Stone wisely introduces the towers from the deck of the inbound Staten Island Ferry; we see that romantic view that is gone forever. Soon the shadow of a plane passes over the side of a building with a billboard for the movie *Zoolander* on it.

World Trade Center has the unintentional effect of reminding us how much TV we watch. So much of the film consists of families of trapped policemen watching TV that you begin to see this as a fundamental part of Stone's view of humanity. History is a slag pile they stare at without understanding. (The firemen called Ground Zero "the Pile.") Stone forces regular people to watch and rewatch the catastrophe over and over, as if he's saying, "See? See?" He makes his characters submit docilely to TV news, then presents the rest of their lives as a series of Hallmark moments that weren't worth filming.

THESE ARE THE TROPES of war-on-terror movies: fake Middle Eastern music, constant TV news and radio commentary, scenes of combat shot in Morocco instead of Iraq, actors we don't recognize speaking Arabic with subtitles, videos of men in ski masks proclaiming in Arabic while they hold a Westerner hostage, American soldiers accidentally killing an Iraqi woman or child, vets losing their shit in their hometowns, a constant resort to cell phones, a scorpion fight, titles identifying every location change, a cut to black to avoid showing something horrible, a precredits wrap-up crawl that tells us what happened later, blonde wives back home. It's amazing how everyone has a blonde wife back home. You'd think al Qaeda made these movies.

Shaky-cam always reminds me of TV cop shows or coffee commercials, things that are on in the background. There's a lot of shaky-cam in *United 93*, so like TV it has an ambient quality. It's almost calm. A storm is brewing but all people do is look at computer screens and talk on cell phones. Then they turn on CNN. Back on the plane, a hapless passenger is buttering a muffin while one of the hijackers puts together a bomb in the restroom.

The hijacker's bomb is a fake meant to frighten the passengers into submission, a prop in the movie but a prop in real life, too. It makes you think about how all the cell phones in the movie are props. The actors scream and cry into their fake phones, yet they are not famous actors, maybe not actors at all, and you put yourself into their situation so much you can't believe they actually made a movie about this. If Kevin Costner were on the plane, you might have cheered it on its way, wanting it to crash as he calmly dialed his wife. His presence would have contradicted this strange radio commentary from the Naudets' *9/11*: "What you see here is right out of one of those movies you would see in Hollywood: people walking around with cell phones in tears." The cell phones cried that day and it seemed like Hollywood.

United 93 is an exploitation film in the form of a safety-instruction manual. It manipulates us mercilessly but blandly. When Flight 93 crashes the screen cuts to black. The only decent thing to do at that point would have been to end the film right there and flip on the lights in the theater. But miles of credits roll like they always do.

ROBERT REDFORD'S *LIONS FOR LAMBS* is as close to the purely didactic as Hollywood gets. Yet since it doesn't quite know what it wants to say, this salutary didacticism is really a lost cause. It's like a play that examines every viewpoint it can think of in the most boring way possible. I admired that about it, but if it were a person doing that instead of a movie, you'd leave the room. Maybe the same thing does happen with the movie. It's hard to imagine someone watching it. It's like an art installation called "Robert Redford Political Movie."

Tom Cruise is exceptional as a US senator who wants to escalate the war. For some reason, he's very good at playing very serious self-convinced loonies. Redford, however, gives the scariest aging-star performance since *What Ever Happened to Baby Jane*? At one point, while calmly discussing something with a student in his office (he plays a college professor), he suddenly jerks his hand upward to reveal a huge scar on his forehead, then barks out lines about getting "fifty-four stitches protesting in Chicago" after he came home from Vietnam. That was as harrowing as the plane crash in *United 93.* It was so unexpected and frightening I jumped out of my seat like it was wired. I know he's an actor playing a part and all, but in the 1960s Robert Redford was a handsome movie star who made a lot of money by not being in Vietnam. I don't know if he was at the 1968 Democratic National Convention, but somehow I doubt it. Wasn't he filming *Butch Cassidy and the Sundance Kid* then? He thinks we all have short memories. That's probably why we allowed another Vietnam to happen.

THE AMERICAN CINEMA has been producing bullshit for so long now it's no longer capable of dealing with a situation like this. That's the message of *Home of the Brave.* The vets in this movie who return home and have trouble adjusting to civilian life are a sad mirror for Hollywood's inability to cope with the war in Iraq. In *Home of the Brave,* one of the vets even gets a job selling tickets at a cineplex. "I sell these stupid tickets to these stupid movies," he says. "But I don't go see any of them."

In 1946, right after the war, William Wyler cast a man named Harold Russell in *The Best Years of Our Lives,* a movie about the problems vets faced returning to their hometowns. Russell, an army vet, was a nonactor who lost both hands in an explosion during the war and was fitted with prosthetic hooks. When you watch the movie you can tell Russell is not a professional actor yet his performance as sailor Homer Parrish is unsentimental, affecting, and unforgettable.

In *Home of the Brave,* pretty Jessica Biel plays a vet who has lost one hand. The actual Jessica Biel, it goes without saying, has both her hands. Her stump, which we see, is a prop stump she covers with another prop, a fake hand. When a coworker at the school where she teaches gym tries to help her with something by saying, in all seriousness, "Hey, let me give you a hand," the audience laughs. If somebody had laughed at Harold Russell in 1946, he would've gotten his head bashed in. That is the difference between then and now—not just in terms of how we think about veterans or about the current war, but about the movies, too, about whether acting is taken seriously and about the way actors move through the frame or are moved through the frame by directors. The story in 1946 was that Harold Russell's Homer was a good guy who faced his problems the only way he knew how, by trying to get through life like everybody else. In the film from 2006, there is no story; there is a message. The message is that if you lost a hand in Iraq, Jessica Biel might play you in a movie. Any veteran who laughed at her deserves a medal.

THERE IS A DIFFERENCE BETWEEN acknowledging that many veterans come home with post-traumatic stress disorder and wanting them to come home with it. Fortunately for Hollywood, many vets do come home with psychological problems, emotional adjustment issues that lend themselves to drama. *In the Valley of Elah*, which is based on a true story, is noteworthy for how sordid and amoral it is, how sordid and dull.

Paul Haggis, who wrote and directed it, seems to have consciously drained the film of all the effects that ruin contemporary filmmaking. *In the Valley of Elah* is quiet, low-key, precisely framed and carefully lit, shot in long takes. It has things besides Tommy Lee Jones in common with *No Country for Old Men*: its brutality and its southwestern setting. Jones is better in this than in the Coens' film. He gets to be typically authentic but also an uptight asshole. He's got a face like a dog, with black beady eyes, jowls and lines, and he looks shrunken, pale, and mottled. An excellent actor named Victor Wolf, who plays a Latino soldier from Jones's son's unit, gets to spit a question in Jones's face: "Wouldn't it be funny if the devil looked just like you?"

When the film sticks to amorality it's pretty good. When it gets to lecturing Salvadoran janitors about raising American flags upside down to signal distress, it gets pretty bad. The film refuses to condemn the war outright. It does so instead by equation. The war must be wrong if it turns a soldier's best buddies into psychos who will kill him for no reason, then chop him up and set him on fire to get rid of the evidence. This is a case where "based on a true story" really works for Hollywood. It gets you to shut up and keep your complaints to yourself.

EMPIRES IN DECLINE need imaginary cads who are also superheroes. They send them out into the world preening and being casually brutal so we can all pretend the empire's doing fine. The English have James Bond, a 1960s import to the movies from postwar British fiction, and now America has Robert Downey Jr.'s Tony Stark, a.k.a. *Iron Man*, an import from our literature created in the Vietnam era and updated for the war in Afghanistan.

Because of Robert Downey's charm we care only about Tony. When he puts on the *Iron Man* suit we lose interest; he becomes a steroidal C-3PO and he's gone. But Tony Stark fascinates. He needs a fake heart to keep him alive, the fake heart powers a superhero carapace that makes him all-powerful—he's a metaphor for how Hollywood movies work at the box office. The metal suit is as much an excuse to give Robert Downey a good part as it is a touching industrial fantasy. Tony Stark and *Iron Man* are two separate things. When he's out of the suit, he's free, he can act, do interesting things other actors don't do when they play superheroes because they are always too much the costume. What's also touching is Tony Stark's very American desire to make everything right in the world, a desire he doesn't share with James Bond.

To the extent that *Iron Man* is a war movie about how Yankee ingenuity and super-technology will make things right in Afghanistan, it's interesting. When it becomes a clash between competing business executives in giant metal suits, it's boring. And when Tony Stark returns home and asks for a hamburger after being tortured and held captive in the caves of Tora Bora, and somebody gives him one from Burger King, and Robert Downey has to act like he likes it, you have to wonder what's the point of being a billionaire playboy at all.

GRACE IS GONE IS A CURIOUS FILM. It had the potential to be the best of the homefront Iraq war movies—certainly it's the best acted. It's under eighty minutes long, but that's not its problem. The problem is that it gives every indication of having been tampered with or left slightly incomplete. Scenes seem truncated, and actors in the cast list aren't really in the movie. It emerges as a film that was worth making, wasn't fully made, and is only half worth watching.

Another problem has to do with one of the film's locations, a small amusement park that to me was clearly a substitute for Disney World. It's too bad Disney World would never let a film like this be made there. That would be something, a poignant indictment more to the point than a lot of documentaries. It's too bad in general that although going to Disney World is a big part of a lot of people's lives, it's an experience that can't be represented cinematically outside of home movies. God forbid we should see somebody unhappy on the spinning teacups.

John Cusack plays a schlumpy, tentative Home Depot manager in the Midwest who doesn't know how to tell his two young daughters that their mother, a soldier, has died in Iraq. He decides to put it off as long as possible by taking them to Enchanted Gardens, the Disney World substitute. As the three drive through a landscape of big-box stores, motels, and chain restaurants, we see the beige landscape our soldiers are fighting for in Iraq. The only other recent film I can recall showing this landscape is *The Brown Bunny*, the film in which Chloë Sevigny gives Vincent Gallo a blow job. I don't necessarily recommend pairing them as a double feature.

In Cusack's other wartime effort, the near-future satire *War, Inc.*, he plays a weary corporate hitman going through the motions in a war-torn country named Turaqistan. It's to his credit that Cusack wants to make movies that investigate or indict contemporary reality, but *War, Inc.*'s satire is hesitant and chaste. It gets lost in set pieces that only try to replicate the things they're supposed to be mocking.

A meal Cusack shares with Marisa Tomei (canny left-wing reporter) and Hilary Duff (whorish Turaqistani pop star) at an abandoned château should have been a Renoiresque highlight, the heart and soul of the film. Here we get the first inkling the trio constitutes some kind of sexually tense family. Instead, it turns into a tribute to the torture scene in *Reservoir Dogs*, which is emerging as the primal scene of all Iraq war–era movies and maybe the entire era in general.

I SAW THE DOCUMENTARY *The War Tapes* on DVD and made the mistake of watching the bonus features first. One of the bonus features turned out to be résumés for director Deborah Scranton and producer Chuck Lacy. Scranton is a former director of network-TV sports who graduated from Brown with a degree in semiotics. She's also a former member of the US Ski Team who lives on a farm in the mountains of New Hampshire. Lacy, the former president of Ben & Jerry's, runs a venture capital fund and in his spare time breeds grass-fed cattle and imports yerba maté from Paraguay. After I read that I had to take a day off before I watched the film so I could evaluate it without prejudice. Also to reassess my life.

Scranton and Lacy made *The War Tapes* by giving small video cameras to soldiers in a New Hampshire National Guard unit stationed in Iraq in 2004. The film uses footage shot by three of the soldiers: Mike Moriarty, an unemployed forklift operator who would like his kids to see him "as a good man who was brave"; Steve Pink, an acerbic carpenter whose graphic letters home reveal a good writer; and Zack Bazzi, a serious-minded liberal who moved to the US from Lebanon when he was a child and wants to be a career soldier.

All the footage these men shot is riveting, even when it's boring. Sometimes little is going on and the men just horse around or complain about KBR and Halliburton. Then comes the poetry of burning trucks, then sickening incidents. Riding in their Humvee one night, the men strike and kill an Iraqi woman as she's crossing the street carrying a box of cookies. Scranton and Lacy are not content to let the soldiers' footage speak for itself. They add ominous music and turn it into an Iraq-based episode of *Ice Road Truckers*, abusing the pact they seem to have made with these soldiers when they gave them cameras.

The three men are inherently interesting, even after they return from the war. Bazzi remains unflappable, opposed to the war but not the military and concerned about the way the media portrays vets as PTSD-addled head cases. Moriarty takes a lot of pain medication for injuries he sustained in Iraq and goes through a couple of jobs before settling down into a good one with the town where he lives. Pink seems bitter about his experiences. He rants about how the war is about money and oil, "and somebody better get some pretty soon besides Dick Cheney or none of those lives were worth it"—1,800 soldiers had died when Pink said that and gas cost $2.23 a gallon.

THE GROUND TRUTH TAKES US through the process of joining the army, going to war, and coming home with your face burned off or without your legs. Although this documentary is unapologetic about emphasizing the last part of the process, it doesn't neglect the first part. *The Ground Truth* exposes US Army recruiting as a form of unregulated advertising and Marine Corps recruiting as out-and-out fraud. The film portrays basic training as psychological torture designed to obliterate personality. It shows how new recruits, naturally opposed to taking lives for no reason, learn to enjoy singing songs about killing, with ethnic slurs that make them easier to memorize.

Once they were in Iraq, one soldier notes that "the killing of civilians started to pile up." Another points out that "peer-pressure group killing is not necessarily courage." They are different people when they get home. A 23-year-old veteran hangs himself because he can't stop thinking of himself as a murderer. Another laments, "Even if I become a Muslim, if I read the Koran every day," it wouldn't bring back the woman he accidentally killed.

This grim film ends on a heroic note when a soldier named Camilo Mejía decides his conscience won't allow him to return to Iraq for another tour of duty. Mejía defies the rule that once in the armed forces you must continue to fight in an illegal war. Patricia Foulkrod, the film's director, does not defy the rule that documentaries must include sentimental music, photo montages, and stock footage.

The Situation claims it was the first fiction feature to deal with the war in Iraq. The film is set in Morocco, the pretend Iraq, and features fake Middle Eastern music. The strapping, apple-cheeked Danish actress Connie Nielsen plays a courageous war correspondent caught between two men. In crucial scenes, I was distracted by a large silver ring she wears. *The Situation* has an air of Hollywood glamour and self-congratulation that it tries to efface at every turn. And it's not even a Hollywood film. A couple of lines in the end credits sum up these problems. Special thanks go to *Sa Majesté le Roi Mohammed VI, Roi du Maroc* and Cynthia Rowley Sunglasses.

The Kingdom is unabashed overkill entertainment. Made during wartime and dealing specifically with the global war on terror, it seems more like a prewar film, straight-up Hollywood action-adventure fantasy from another time. It's far too gruesome for what it wants to be, and too late.

A crack FBI team goes into Saudi Arabia to investigate the bombing of an American workers' city. Two of the team are mock-squabbling Jennifer Garner and Jason Bateman. Chris Cooper, the senior guy, rubs team leader Jamie Foxx's chest: "Feels like you got a beast in there." Later Jeremy Piven feels Foxx's chest, too. This was written by the screenwriter who wrote *Lions for Lambs*, a unique talent. Some of his dialogue, post-bombing: "My five-year-old boy, when I got home, had a box of Band-Aids and was trying to put his mama's mouth back on."

Rendition asks us to oppose something everybody is already opposed to, the torture of innocent people. If the Egyptian-American who's whisked away to an unnamed Middle Eastern country (Morocco) to be tortured had in fact been a terrorist, this film might have worked. We would have had to ask ourselves if we were opposed to the torture of viable suspects in the war on terror. But in *Rendition* we get the torture-porn thrill of watching an innocent man be interrogated—blonde Reese Witherspoon's husband, no less—at the same time as we get to deplore that this happens.

Jake Gyllenhaal, an unlikely CIA bureau chief, watches with increasing desperation as interrogation techniques become enhanced. His subplot mirrors *The Devil Wears Prada*. When he finally quits his demeaning job, he throws his cell phone in the water, just like Anne Hathaway did in that movie. Maybe next he goes and gets a job at the *New York Sun* or the *Village Voice* or wherever it was supposed to be in *Prada*.

Even though *Ghosts of Abu Ghraib* came out more than a year before Errol Morris's *Standard Operating Procedure*, which covers the same subject, I saw the Errol Morris film first. It's striking how similar the two films are, not just because they both deal with the torture of prisoners at Abu Ghraib and the scandal that broke when photographs of the abuse appeared in 2004. The main difference between the two films, and this is not to Morris's credit, since *Ghosts of Abu Ghraib* is straightforward, TV-style documentary and not great art like Morris makes, is that *Standard Operating Procedure* is obsessed with infographically investigating the photographs and has Lynndie England in it.

Rory Kennedy's film, more of an exposé than an investigation, is the better of the two. That Morris's film got a theatrical release and Kennedy's premiered on HBO says something about what is deemed worthy of theatrical release in this country, and why. Kennedy's film uses the same techniques as TV news shows, which makes her film more overtly cheesy than Morris's, which, with its barking-dog and creaking-chain reenactments, was also cheesy. But in Kennedy's film we get the sense that she feels these techniques are being put in the service of finding out the truth, whereas in Morris's film we get the sense that he's looking at people like they are bugs, *then* finding out the truth. They are stand-ins for Bush, Cheney, and Rumsfeld, whose victims they are. It's these higher-ups who are guilty—and here the sound editor cuts in the loud thwack of a rubber stamp—GUILTY! Morris's attitude raises the question of why he doesn't make a film about Bush, Cheney, and Rumsfeld, and of course the answer is that he can't because they would never talk to him. So *Standard Operating Procedure* tortures Lynndie England with Morris's Interrotron camera, using her (and her fellow soldiers) as replacements for the people he'd really like to pin down.

Ghosts of Abu Ghraib takes the visual simile of "ghost" detainees—detainees brought in off the books so they can be tortured in secret—too far. But so did Morris's film. Why do all American films, even American films made by intelligent documentarians, have to literalize everything? Maybe that has something to do with why Morris used Danny Elfman for his score. We automatically associate Elfman's music with Tim Burton, the great literalizer of childhood imagination. The problem is that scary music—and the music in *Ghosts of Abu Ghraib* is pretty scary—makes too much obvious sense. Abu Ghraib may remind us of certain scenes in *Carrie*, but it is not *Carrie*, it is real, and that's the point. What happened at Abu Ghraib may be the product of a culture formed by Stephen King, but in making films about it, serious filmmakers would do better not to indulge their inner *Cujo*.

Certain people appear as interview subjects in a number of different war-on-terror documentaries—the prison guards from Abu Ghraib, anti-abuse navy men Alberto Mora and John Hutson, legal scholars and authors like Scott Horton and Alfred McCoy, the infamous John Yoo, who is always bland and calm. Their various appearances in these films were shot probably only months apart, but seeing each of them one after another in different films, in different jackets under different lighting, we watch them age before the camera with the strain of telling their stories again. Meanwhile, we see the same clips of George W. Bush saying he's going to "smoke 'em out and get 'em runnin'," or Donald Rumsfeld saying he was only kidding about standing up eight to ten hours a day. They are frozen in those moments when they appear stupid and evil, yet these clips take them out of life and into some timeless realm of official TV where no one is ever punished. Maybe punishment is what happens on home video, then on YouTube, like it did to Saddam Hussein.

If, by July 2007, you had not heard there was a war going on in Iraq, then *No End in Sight* was the documentary for you. The film had a real audience of maybe two people—two people, by the way, I would be happy to meet. The film is meticulous in establishing that the war was a botched job from the beginning, and it gets a lot of well-known people to appear on camera to support that extremely noncontroversial viewpoint. Then it concludes that, since American soldiers have died in this war or were horribly maimed or crippled for life, we have got to find something good about it. It is easy to get confused and emotional when you are dealing with veterans whose lives have been permanently altered for the worse, but you've got to figure things out a little more than that before you make a movie.

A DOCUMENTARY FROM the early 1980s called *The Atomic Cafe* changed everything. It introduced the idea that history could be told via stock-footage fiesta, a fun combination of clips strung together for maximum hilarity at the expense of the people who shot them. Industrial films, TV commercials, military films, TV news footage, scenes from B movies, home movies—detritus from the lower rungs of film history could be marshaled into formation to make glib points about things we are against.

Most documentaries do this now, even if that's not all they do. So for instance in *Why We Fight*, a documentary on the militarization of our culture and how that led to the war on terror, if the narrator mentions "cities" and "work" we are treated to sixty-year-old stock footage of people flooding into the lobbies of office buildings.

What we are seeing when this happens is America's Greatest Hits, an exercise in nostalgia that shows up our era in favor of a time when the average person dressed a little better and his most cherished goal was not to grow up to be Jimmy Fallon. This is lazy filmmaking, but it can be pretty entertaining. In *Why We Fight*, we get to see a Halliburton promotional film from 1951 in which the original narrator chirps, "There she is—oil! That's what all the fuss is about."

One of America's Greatest Hits was President Dwight Eisenhower's farewell address, which he delivered live from the Oval Office on January 17, 1961. The former general warned the country about the creeping influence of what he called the military-industrial complex. The country, the film notes, didn't listen. Of course we don't see the whole speech—that would be boring. Instead, we get to see bits of it photoshopped into TV screens in stock footage of 1950s living rooms. As Oliver North once said: *Neat!*

It's not that *Why We Fight* is wrong. It's a collage, but it's not wrong. No, it invites us to contemplate its rightness even as it contemplates its rightness itself. Given the subject matter, it does that in a pretty serene way. It demonstrates that there is no point of radicalism from which it could do anything else. So "*why we fight*" also means "why we don't fight," why we are passive, why we don't rebel.

Today people are very concerned about where their food comes from. They want to know that the ingredients in it are fresh, organic, locally grown, all that stuff. That's how I feel about documentaries. Where did all this footage come from? Wouldn't it be better if the director made it all himself? Or maybe making films like this is like making your house out of straw, sticks, and brick, and then putting aluminum siding on it and columns out front. Funny, yes. A little scary. I wouldn't want to live there.

Taxi to the Dark Side overwhelms you with detail so repellent and frightening that by the end of it you are fully convinced that no punishment could be painful enough for the Bush Administration. The film calls them murderers and makes the charge stick. It too often relies on ominosity (the American cinema has become an ominosity machine) but the depth of the information presented here excuses the film's excess. Who knew Guantánamo Bay had a gift shop where you could buy T-shirts that say GUANTANAMO BAY BEHAVIOR MODIFICATION INSTRUCTOR CUBA? Who knew the enhanced interrogation techniques used there included forcing detainees to wear pointed birthday hats? Alex Gibney, the film's director, covers his subject more thoroughly than any book or article I've read. It is without question the grimmest film on the war, and that's saying something.

It's best, however, when it sticks to its main story, essentially an on-screen autopsy. Dilawar was a taxi driver who was stopped by Afghan warlords in December 2002 and turned over to US forces for money. Chained in the prison at Bagram, he was beaten for days until he died. His legs were so "pulpified" by the beatings that had he lived it would've been necessary to amputate them. His guards beat him so he'd shut up because he was screaming in pain and continued beating him after he'd died because they thought he was faking immobility. They jumped on his back until they were tired, took breaks, then beat him some more. He was shackled the whole time. Dilawar didn't have a last name but back in his village he got one on his gravestone: the martyr.

Gibney traces these techniques up through the chain of command, where Donald Rumsfeld stands all day and tells reporters "life goes on." A lieutenant general explains enhanced interrogation techniques, inadvertently describing the war on terror at the same time: "It was California avocado freestyle. I mean, it was just a free-for-all."

Iraq in Fragments is so good I'm surprised people even recognize it as a movie. It's devoid of the clutter other documentaries rely on for visual interest. (Most documentaries are radio with pictures.) The person who made it, James Longley, also shot it, recorded the sound, and edited it. His cinematography is so superior to the cinematography in any of these other documentaries that he must be a Martian. Longley made his film in Iraq, not in a TV studio or in Morocco. He does not have to thank *Sa Majesté* or Cynthia Rowley for anything. The film's stars are the Mahdi Army and the people of Baghdad and Kurdistan.

If only for the way the movie reveals Iraq as a country of colors instead of just the tan dust we see in other Iraq war movies, this film would be exceptional. These vibrant images switch between the tranquil—fruit and vegetables for sale in a market, fish in an aquarium—and the violent—the scarves covering the faces of the Mahdi Army vigilantes kicking the alcohol sellers, the strings of colored lights lining the streets at night as flagellants parade by, beating themselves with metal chains.

Longley lets things play out, even speeches and the harangues of clerics. The sound in the film is unlike that in other films, too. Longley makes sure the sound always works in tandem with the images to evoke the places where they were shot, not to explain them. In the film's final third, shot in Kurdistan, where the sky is full of smoke from brick kilns and the fields are covered with sunflowers, Longley's filmmaking pares things down to an elemental level reminiscent of Dovzhenko: images of fire, the moon, snow, bones, and blood. The film ends in twilight with a Kurd reminding us that "nobody can escape America's reach" and that when it's all over, the winners always let you know God was on their side.

Brian de Palma's *Redacted* aroused controversy when it came out in late 2007, the kind of ridiculous controversy that is the hallmark of our time. The film found no audience and played on few screens, but the right-wing media howled.

Bill O'Reilly and others called for De Palma and the film's producer, TV and sports magnate Mark Cuban, to be arrested for treason and sued for defamation. In an attempt to hit them where they live, right-wingers demanded fans boycott the Dallas Mavericks, one of Cuban's properties. Later it emerged that Cuban had in fact cut the film's final scenes, fearing they would cause "emotional distress" and result in lawsuits from the families of real soldiers. TV personalities getting together to decry a basketball team because of a movie that's already been expurgated by its producer—we don't have censorship in this country, we have synergy.

Redacted fictionalizes the Mahmudiyah rampage, in which five American infantrymen gang-raped and murdered a 14-year-old Iraqi girl after killing her parents and her sister, a toddler. De Palma goes for a new kind of annoying realism by showing how this played out in various media, including the ones that went on to attack him, yet at the same time *Redacted* feels stagy. The film is a clunky combination of De Palma's Vietnam movie *Casualties of War* and the amazing "Be Black, Baby" section of his underrated *Hi, Mom!* For a film of such urgency, *Redacted* is inferior to the De Palma movie that preceded it, the trashy *Black Dahlia*, also a fictionalized account of an infamous real-life rape and murder.

Shot in Jordan, not Morocco, *Redacted* moved in the direction of Iraq, not Hollywood. *Battle for Haditha*, also the reenactment of a war atrocity, also shot in Jordan, moves even closer. Improvised around the story of how marines murdered twenty-four innocent Iraqi men, women, and children in al-Anbar province in November 2005, *Battle for Haditha* is the best Iraq combat film yet made, which is to say the only good one.

The British director Nick Broomfield, known in this country for documentaries like *Kurt & Courtney* and *Biggie and Tupac*, interlaces three stories in a way that owes more to neorealism than "hyperlink" cinema, that already forgotten term for movies like *Syriana* and *Babel*. Broomfield presents a middle-aged ex-Baathist, the insurgent who plants an IED that leads to the bloodbath, as an irked, confused speechifier without reducing him to pure villain status. I didn't get the name of the actor who plays this difficult, thankless role. The names of Arab actors are too easily buried and forgotten, like the names of the Arab dead. Elliot Ruiz's portrait of a competent, intelligent 20-year-old soldier who is nonetheless guilty of murder is flawless. To successfully improvise a part this grueling without going over the top is a sign of real distinction.

A throwaway scene in *Battle for Haditha* sticks in my mind: a marine forced to drop and do push-ups while chanting "I will not be funny anymore." For me, this quick scene encapsulates something real that it's glib to acknowledge: the war on terror is one group of Americans punishing another for the 1990s—in another country, with lots of collateral damage.

You can shoot a reenactment feature where it took place, even if it took place in Pakistan and Afghanistan. But what if part of it took place in the prison cells and interrogation rooms of the Guantánamo Bay detention facility? Michael Winterbottom and Mat Whitecross, British directors like Nick Broomfield, knew they would not be allowed to film in Camp X-Ray and Camp Delta, so they re-created the Guantánamo center in a hospitable country near where they were already shooting: Iran.

The Road to Guantánamo, one of the essential war-on-terror films, begins unpromisingly as extreme-travel TV or the first episode of *Real World: Guantánamo Bay.* We meet the Tipton Three (although they are not called that in the film), young British men of Pakistani descent who were kidnapped by the United Front in Afghanistan. Quickly the film shifts tone, the story becomes more and more harrowing as the photography of landscapes and faces becomes more beautiful. Thoughts of *Harold & Kumar Escape from Guantánamo Bay* dissipate well before the three (now played by actors) are trapped inside a truck that's filling up with blood as dozens of prisoners scramble over each other to avoid the bullets Afghani soldiers shoot through its walls.

Once in Cuba, the three are subjected to abuse that includes the nonstop yelling of their fascistic American guards, whose evident fear of being looked at tends to impart demonic power to the boys' collective gaze. "Don't let 'em look!" and "Face away from us!" are the commands of powerless people who are afraid to be seen because they know what they're doing is wrong. Two years later, the guards still harangue them as they are driven by bus past the HONOR BOUND TO DEFEND FREEDOM sign and taken out of the prison camp to be set free: "Don't look out the window!" The film makes those five words as sickening as anything that's happened in the war on terror.

In 1981, the English band Au Pairs had a song called "Armagh," about an Irish woman tortured in a British prison. The first lines went:

> We don't torture, we're a civilized nation.
> We're avoiding any confrontation.

Is their country's experience in Northern Ireland the reason British filmmakers are making better films about the war on terror than Americans?

Maybe. But right after *The Road to Guantánamo,* Michael Winterbottom, without Mat Whitecross, made *A Mighty Heart,* from Mariane Pearl's book about the kidnapping and murder of her husband, the journalist Daniel Pearl, by terrorist jihadis in Pakistan in early 2002. Shot in Pakistan and India, the film strives for the kind of grainy shaky-cam realism on which *The Road to Guantánamo* did not rely.

A Mighty Heart stars Angelina Jolie as Mariane Pearl. The first half of the movie is like a documentary about Jolie playing Mariane, the reenactment of a reenactment like *The Road to Guantánamo.* We watch her acting, she walks around with a prosthetic pregnant belly, underplays her phone reaction to Daniel's boneheaded parents, who think everything is going to work out fine. The third quarter of *A Mighty Heart* is a very good episode of *Karachi Vice*—"I love this town," an American intelligence agent exclaims. The last quarter is back to Jolie. Her lower lip is dry, later almost split, illustrating the film's arc of emotional destitution.

Mostly she's on the phone. Not just her; everyone in *A Mighty Heart* is on the phone. The film is an investigation into cell phone use among Westerners who live in big houses in Karachi; it's a film about manners. The cell phone is the instrument the Westerners use to control the world around them, a world where they make everyone their servant. Even when Daniel is out working, his nice-guy unctuousness gives him away as a privileged Westerner. He might as well be ordering organic pizza in a restaurant in Brooklyn. He's always all "Yeah, no, I'm good" and "I'm gonna let you go, OK?" Still, he depends on his cell phone less than the others, and the film implies he's punished for it. When he's kidnapped, Mariane loses phone contact with him, a sign of grave danger. In bed at night, with little hope, she continues to send texts he'll never read: "I love you."

What Winterbottom intended is unclear. He does the best he can under the circumstances, working with the biggest star in the world to help her tell the most important story on earth, ambiguously undercutting it with repetitive actions showing Americans as both all-powerful and ineffectual. Were the Pearls really like this? By the film's end, after Mariane gives birth, we see her and her child as a unit complete without Daniel. Wistful music from the band Nouvelle Vague plays. Is this supposed to be melancholy, or is it a testament to the superfluousness of the Western male, or both?

A Mighty Heart ends with a birth, *The Hills Have Eyes II* starts with one. A cinematic coincidence, but maybe it's in trash like this that we'll find the truth of the situation. After all, it's the torture porn of the *Hostel* and *Saw* franchises, made concurrently with the prisoner abuse at Abu Ghraib, that exposed certain truths about American culture before the Abu Ghraib photos did.

Even better, *The Hills Have Eyes II* is explicitly a war film. National Guard troops on a training exercise in the New Mexico desert, which we're initially led to think is Afghanistan or Iraq, run around yelling "America number one, bitch!" Soon they begin to get picked off Indian-style by relatives of the mutant family from the first remake of *The Hills Have Eyes.* This is a promising start, but the movie ends up being less effective than it should be. Too bad producer Wes Craven assigned it to a director of videos for Nickelback and Sisqo when it needed a John Carpenter. One gory image lingers, a dead man with his wallet shoved into his head.

WOULDN'T IT BE FUNNY if it turned out that World Wrestling Entertainment had made one of the best films about the war in Iraq? That's the kind of dumb hope I had going into *The Marine.* John Cena, the professional wrestler, a bulky Matt Damon delivered by forceps, plays the title role, a veteran of the war in Iraq. Returning to his blonde wife in South Carolina, he finds the only job he can get is security guard. After he's fired for throwing somebody through a plate-glass window, he goes home and confesses his biggest fear: sitting around at home doing nothing.

Triton (that's the marine's last name) is like the United States. He's never learned that all men's miseries come from not being able to sit quietly in a room alone. The couple decides to take a road trip in their Lincoln Navigator, a preposterous vehicle for them to own, but I guess not more than it is for anybody else. A gas station blows up, Triton's wife is kidnapped—significantly, he is robbed at a gas pump. Now Triton is back in his element, once again doing what he was trained to do in Iraq. For the rest of the movie he is shot at thousands and thousands of times and not hit once.

With the exception of trash movies, war-on-terror films are so grim, dismal, and tragic that when you have contempt for one, you feel bad about it. *Gunner Palace*, a documentary in the form of a music video, promotes the war in Iraq as crazy fucked-up shit that nobody but the grunts and a few hajji good guys understand—and the film's director, who narrates in a cool-guy whisper that sounds like he's auditioning to dub *2 or 3 Things I Know About Her* into English.

Right off, this sub-Godardian voice-over is childish and filled with hokey attitude. "Most of us don't see this on the news anymore. We have reality TV instead—*Joe Millionaire, Survivor.* Well, survive this: a year in Baghdad without changing the channel." When the filmmaker tells us, "Unlike a movie, war has no end," we don't bother to sort that out because we are glad that at least movies have an end. In a piece from 1955 on Soviet films, Robert Warshow wrote that "the commentator is one of the diseases of our time and must be endured; he will be there at the end of the world to say into a microphone: 'This is the end of the world.'" But Warshow didn't know the commentator would be hip.

Making a film this bad helps no one. It's also inappropriately lame. When a soldier shows an Iraqi orphan a SpongeBob SquarePants doll, a title appears over the image: SPONGEBOB. The film becomes human when the soldiers *Gunner Palace* follows around are allowed to speak for themselves. The hilarious slacker SPC Stuart Wilf tells us that it's better to be in Iraq than to be a loser in his hometown, where he'd be doing nothing because there's nothing to do. This 19-year-old combat veteran speaks for everyone who's from a place like that, and the sanity of his position is only bolstered by the way he dances around in a Saudi robe he bought on leave in Qatar. Wilf comes across as all-American and a total fuckup, a much more appealing figure than John Cena's ludicrous marine, and more heroic.

Kimberley Peirce's 1999 feature debut, *Boys Don't Cry,* was as assured and fully achieved as Nicholas Ray's debut was fifty years earlier. Like *They Live by Night, Boys Don't Cry* showed a flair for drama that was intimate but explosive, and had a true understanding for the pain outsiders feel in love. Why, then, nine years later, is Peirce imitating *Gunner Palace*? *Stop-Loss* had the potential to be the best movie about the war in Iraq. The combat scenes early in the film are the best-directed combat scenes in any war-on-terror movie. When they end, *Stop-Loss* resorts to an MTV-inspired version of media realism—soldiers' video diary footage and interludes of rap—that has nothing to do with the story Peirce wants to tell, and has everything to do with keeping the attention of her perceived audience so she can tell them an important story. The film has to jerk itself out of this mode whenever it wants to be a film at all.

When actor-director Liev Schreiber and his producer on *Everything Is Illuminated,* an adaptation of the Jonathan Safran Foer novel, go to the airport to pick up an intern coming to work on their film, we are witnessing not just a historic first in the history of interning but also the beginning of one of the best movies about the war on terror. Nina Davenport's documentary *Operation Filmmaker* is only tangentially related to the actual war in Iraq, but it has more to say about the issues animating it than most films dealing with it directly.

Having seen a young Iraqi film student named Muthana Mohmed interviewed in Baghdad by MTV, Schreiber gets the genius idea to hire Muthana and fly him to Prague, where Schreiber's film is shooting. Soon Muthana, the Stuart Wilf of international film production, is charged with tasks like mixing vegan snacks in little plastic cups for producers who must constantly be treated like babies. Producer Peter Saraf, unhappy with the slacker Muthana's attitude, schools him: Muthana has to learn to make himself invaluable to his bosses. He must fawn over his producer and director. For instance, to ingratiate himself, he should bring them coffee in the middle of meetings—but discreetly and quietly.

That's how we do it in America, Saraf explains. Nothing demeaning about it. Totally normal. We all came up that way.

A better portrait of how people who think of themselves as Good turn the disadvantaged into their slaves has never been put on film. *Operation Filmmaker,* the entire thing a subtle metaphor for the way America helps Iraq by occupying it, damns everyone it touches, including Muthana and the filmmaker herself. After Muthana expresses his admiration for George W. Bush, the producers of *Everything Is Illuminated* pretty much abandon him to fend for himself. He stays in Prague, gets a job on a movie based on the video game *Doom,* and convinces its affable star, Dwayne "The Rock" Johnson, to pay for him to go to film school in London. The Rock may have been conned by Muthana, but why should he care? The Rock's a movie star, he's got money, and he can give it out any way he chooses. In *Operation Filmmaker* a professional wrestler really does come to the rescue, and Davenport has the grace not to make the ironic but obvious point that the Rock is a Republican and Saraf and Schreiber are Democrats.

MAYBE IN MOVIES RIGHT NOW the war is best approached obliquely. *Full Battle Rattle,* by Tony Gerber and Jesse Moss, documents what happens at the National Training Center at Fort Irwin, a thousand-mile tract of the Mojave Desert comprising thirteen replica Iraqi villages. The army sees this as a stage set where soldiers learn how to handle themselves in the real theater of war. A Lieutenant Colonel McLoughlin, training there, explains: "Our number one priority is to provide hope to the people. All our bright thinking here is all for naught if we don't control the crowd."

These soldiers learn to control the crowd by playing cowboys and Indians in a landscape where Indians used to be. The center employs 250 Arabic-speaking Iraqi-Americans, who are given character biographies and scripts so they can portray townspeople, insurgents, and Iraqi policemen. In one scenario, the son of the deputy mayor is accidentally killed by American firepower. Negotiations begin that are more like *The Price Is Right* than a war movie. American soldiers carry around $2,500 in play money to pay off relatives of the dead. Then the brass steps in for further smoothing, awkwardly rehearsing for the real thing. "I have a contract for a sewage system," says Lt. Col. McLoughlin. "It's worth over $280,000—*approved*!" He seals the deal: "Have some fruit. This is our best fruit."

It's not just the soldiers who believe in this fiction the army's created. The middle-aged Iraqi man who plays the deputy mayor longs to be promoted to the status of full mayor. At work in the Mojave his dignity is restored. Later we see him at his other job, manning the cash register at a liquor store in a desolate San Diego neighborhood.

This beautifully composed documentary provides the most human and balanced view in any of these films. It's a hopeful, even utopian film that takes place far away from the Green Zone and Abu Ghraib, strangely touching and sad. A doctor shows us mannequin limbs with carved plastic wounds. "These injuries are exact replicas," he says. The limbs snap back into place. By the time the film was edited, five of the soldiers in it were already dead.

Dick Cheney has told us this war will not end in our lifetime. An era of endless war chokes off the kind of evaluation that in the past has produced the best war movies. If the war on terror never ends, those films cannot be made. Evaluation will be left to movies like *The Dark Knight*, which indulge our longing for relief from war at the same time as they replicate its stasis and reconfigure its atrocities as blockbuster entertainment.

You always hear conservatives say Hollywood hates America. To me, what proves Hollywood hates America is the way they keep making Batman movies. Meanwhile, no Hollywood filmmakers have gone to Iraq. All the 1990s World War II films Hollywood made, the *Saving Private Ryan*s, with their Pentagon advisers and Department of Defense equipment they got at the cost of script approval, were made by people pretending they wanted to go to war. *If only we had a war*, they seemed to moan. *Ach, we were born too late*!

Here was your chance, Hollywood, to emulate the Greatest Generation filmmakers you professed to admire so much. What you made instead were things like *War of the Worlds*, a film that reveled in the destruction of New York, then hightailed it through the woods to grandmother's house. Sleep tight.

September 2008

SAY SOMETHING IN CHINESE

The Alameda Theatre

For a few weeks every summer I escape the humidity of Brooklyn and go to Oakland, California. I stay on a street that runs off an iron drawbridge into the town of Alameda. Alameda sits on an island in the San Francisco Bay. To me, Alameda is an enchanted place. It is everything you want America to be but never is. When I retire, I'd like to move there and run for mayor.

Alameda is Spanish for "tree-lined avenue." The town's wide streets are also lined with Hawaiian barbecue joints and uncrowded cafés, shops that sell used furniture, and bars with neon signs that open at 9 AM. The streets end in shopping centers anchored by giant new supermarkets filled with brightly colored produce. The newest one, according to a circular I picked up, offers "personal watermelons," perfectly round watermelons a little smaller than a basketball. I think the phrase *personal watermelons* sums up California. It should be on the California license plate, the same way it says famous potatoes on license plates in Idaho.

Alameda also sits on a major fault line. It could be swallowed by the sea at any moment. There used to be a Coney Island there called Neptune Beach, where the popsicle and the snow cone were invented, icy novelties as all-American as Nathan's hot dogs.

Alameda has a history with the movies. The film producer Robert Lippert was a native. He got his start as a movie theater projectionist there, then bought his own movie theater, then moved to Hollywood to produce cheap westerns. In the late 1940s and early 1950s he released Samuel Fuller's first films and introduced the cinema to the Garutso Balanced Lens, a split diopter apparatus invented to compete with 3D by heightening screen realism. It kept foreground and background in focus at the same time. Fans of Brian De Palma or Raúl Ruiz know the effect well.

A lot of Hollywood movies are shot in Alameda. *The Net*, with Sandra Bullock, features scenes filmed on the bridge near where I stay. There's a huge soundstage in town, at a decommissioned naval base. *The Matrix* movies were shot there; Alameda is where the Wachowski brothers unleashed bullet time.

Bullet time and the livin' is easy. Summer in Alameda is pretty idyllic. It only lacked one thing: a movie theater. The previous two summers I watched with anticipation as the Alameda Theatre, an abandoned art deco movie house in the middle of town, was slowly turned into an eight-screen cineplex.

The theater, with its three-story neon sign, is the town's centerpiece. I'd watched the summer before as workers restored the lobby. Photos on boards in the construction office showed how the theater would be made into a palace again, with oriental motifs throughout, carpeting patterned with an intricate design, golden balusters on the mezzanine.

This was great. I wouldn't have to drive into Oakland or Berkeley to catch a movie anymore. I'd be able to walk to the Alameda Theatre. My vacation spot would be complete. I was looking forward to seeing a movie on each screen, no matter what it was. I'd see *WALL-E*, if that's what it came to, even though I lose interest in cartoons over ten minutes long. I'd watch *Mamma Mia*, if that's what they were showing, even though I find it hard to relate to anyone for whom ABBA is historical.

I landed at the Oakland airport in late July with a vision of the new Alameda Theatre fixed in mind. I saw myself on Central Avenue at night, gazing up at the theater's neon sign, lit for the first time in years. I saw myself marveling at the new lobby as I went in, looking for a seat in the plush auditorium. I pictured myself settling in as the first trailer began, ready to be overwhelmed by the new sound system and underwhelmed by—I didn't know by what. *Hancock*? I didn't care. The cinema lived again in Alameda.

Reader, it was not to be. Right when I got into town a headline blared at me from a newspaper box on a street corner. "Alameda Labor Dispute Hinges on Skills of Projectionists," read the front page of the *East Bay Express*, the area's alt-weekly. The projectionists at the Alameda Theatre were on strike. The theater's owner refused to hire union operators. Shows were starting late and breaking down, prints were scratched and dirty. Audiences were leaving with black clouds over their heads. Incompetents were manning the equipment and the owner didn't care. He offered no excuses. Digital projection would replace film projection any day now, any second, he said, and "when I convert to digital there is no projectionist. There's no projectionist anymore. I am trying to make them understand that."

He was dreaming about a day when the machines would run themselves at the same time as he was talking out his ass. I walked by the theater to make sure the strike was on. It was, in a California way. Some guy was sitting in a folding chair with flyers in his lap. There was no blow-up rat, no pickets that night, nobody chanting slogans. Still, I couldn't go in. I used to be a movie theater projectionist. I couldn't cross the line.

The City of Alameda poured over $30 million into bringing the Alameda Theatre back to life, partnering with an owner who was now barking at reporters. He didn't care about the quality of presentation in the town's new showplace. He had no interest in hiring skilled labor and wasn't concerned with the future of the medium to which his boondoggle was a shrine. The Alameda Theatre was a glowing airplane hangar with fancy carpeting and a parking garage attached, a monumental excuse to sell Milk Duds under a glass counter. The films showing there—*Swing Vote* with Kevin Costner, *Journey to the Center of the Earth* with Brendan Fraser—weren't worth paying to see.

The city used taxpayers' dollars so its citizens could pay to see *Swing Vote*. Even for $30 million they couldn't buy their way out of that. The circus of superheroes, Batman and the rest, had come to town. But who pays the circus to come to town? You pay the circus to leave.

Would the ghost of the projectionist-turned-showman Lippert be proud or disgusted, wondering why he couldn't get the city to hand over $30 million back in his day, before he left for Los Angeles? Maybe crappy Hollywood movies are the God-given right of every medium-size city now, like a fourth-place hockey team, but there are other movies to see. Just not in Alameda.

Free Movies That Matter

But where? The people of the East Bay could tell I was looking. At the farmer's market at Lake Merritt, where the produce is so abundant they force samples on you, somebody handed me a leaflet. "Free Movies That Matter," it read. "You're invited to Free Evenings of Pizza, Film, and Conversation."

Twice each month on Friday nights, the leaflet said, the Harmony Center for the Joyful Spirit hosts movies at the "Home of Gwendolyn and Daniel." The mission of Oakland's Harmony Center is to bring "Joy and Inspiration into our lives." "What better way to do that than to get together with friendly people for an informal meal, enjoy a great film, and then have a lively discussion of the ethical and spiritual lessons of the film?" the leaflet asked. It described Gwendolyn and Daniel's "24th floor penthouse apartment with a 'top of the world' view" where "movies are shown on our 58-inch plasma HDTV with Dolby Digital Surround Sound." Instructions followed: "If possible, please call or email with your choice of pizza, meat or veggie. Please note that we maintain a shoeless household." Now I knew I was in California. And I knew what being in California meant: no matter how spiritual the discussion, the pizza would suck.

The next great film planned for G and D's was a movie from five years ago, *House of Sand and Fog* with Ben Kingsley and Jennifer Connelly, "a gripping exploration of the American dream gone awry" that I'd missed on purpose when it came out. Was this what moviegoing in the Bay Area had become, a shoeless pizza party "Celebrating the Divine in Each of Us" around a big TV? I decided this vacation movies were best avoided. I'd tour the countryside instead.

Crockett

California is death haunted compared to New York. Everything is still and spooky, the grass along the highways north of Oakland is dry and brown. New York moves in the frame-skip fast-forward of digital video. One thing replaces another, they build an IKEA in no time by paving over cobblestone streets in Brooklyn, and they demolish buildings from the 1850s to do it. In New York, even the ghosts get priced out. In the quiet counties of Marin and Contra Costa, they linger.

Crockett, a town of about three thousand people under the massive Carquinez Bridge on the Carquinez Strait, was once home to forty-six bars. The imposing C&H sugar refinery was running at full swing then when all those bars were open. It still operates, but at half capacity, and still looms over the town, which the sugar makes smell like candy. Railroad trains stop in Crockett to load white sugar, but passenger trains don't. There's one bar left, the Club Tac, a hall too large for the lunchtime drinkers who assemble there. The little railroad station in town is now the Crockett Museum.

Old Crockett men, veterans of World War II and Korea, spend their days at a big table in the main room of the museum, chatting amiably with visitors who wander among pictures of them as younger men dressed for war. An accordion in a glass case is the same one you see in pictures of a local man named Babe entertaining fellow soldiers in the South Pacific. A giant sturgeon nine and a half feet long, the world record, was caught in Crockett and inhabits another glass case, a small-town version of Damien Hirst's shark.

In one corner of the museum there is a memorial shrine to another veteran of World War II, a favorite son, Aldo Ray, the Hollywood actor. Ray grew up in Crockett and served as town sheriff before Hollywood discovered him while a film was shooting there. A signed 8 × 10", Ray's Hollywood headshot, greets visitors: "The best of life to everyone looking at this photo."

Ray, an underappreciated actor, was one of the best of the 1950s. Solidly built, with a large square head and short, sandy hair, he spoke in the tough, gravelly voice of the sugar-refinery stevedore and navy frogman he was. He looked capable of punching a hole through a door but played light comedy opposite Judy Holliday, the toast of Broadway, in George Cukor movies like *The Marrying Kind* and *Pat and Mike*. In *We're No Angels*, a Michael Curtiz comedy with a touch of '50s Renoir to it, Ray out-acts Humphrey Bogart and Peter Ustinov. Aldo Ray seems like the model for a James Ellroy character, a non-stupid ex-boxer who's seen too much and looks good in a suit. If Ray is remembered at all, he's also remembered for his portrayals of unstrung soldiers in war movies like Anthony Mann's *Men in War* and two Raoul Walsh films, *Battle Cry* and the Hollywood *Naked and the Dead*, which I like better than the novel.

Ray had a difficult time in Hollywood. He was married three times by the time he was 33—there's a photo of him with his 21-year-old British sweetheart, his third wife, in the museum. Evidently he drank heavily, a habit he must have picked up in some of those forty-six bars after shifts at C&H. Before he returned to Crockett to die in a VA hospital in 1991, he became unlikely friends with Ed Wood in Hollywood, and would share bottles with the transvestite director at his apartment. The Crockett Museum is silent on that.

How often do Aldo Ray films show anywhere, even on TCM? One was showing while I was in Oakland, though, at the Pacific Film Archive in Berkeley. The film was Jacques Tourneur's black-and-white film noir *Nightfall*, from 1957, screening as part of a series of adaptations of David Goodis novels. I hadn't seen it in years, but in keeping with my vacation so far, I couldn't go. I had a freelance deadline the same night it was playing. *Nightfall* costars a young Anne Bancroft as a model and Ray as a commercial illustrator, a melancholy couple who get mixed up in a bank robbery. There's a still of Ray and Bancroft from *Nightfall* at the Crockett Museum. I remember *Nightfall* for its scenes in the snow in Wyoming and for the song "Red River Valley" Ray and Bancroft listen to on a transistor radio while riding a Greyhound bus.

Bolinas

Bolinas is about fifty miles southeast of Crockett, but this gothic hippie town that smells like compost is really a world away. Sweet-smelling Crockett was a cheery place where residents were fixing up storefronts on the town's two main streets. Bolinas exists on a lagoon in a brown-acid time warp like a fenced-in brackish Vermont. It turns out if hippies live in isolation too long, they become the Addams Family. This tiny town, where the residents are known for tearing down the highway signs leading to it that the State of California puts up, is the post-bohemian enclave where the hippie writer Richard Brautigan killed himself in 1984. The author of *Trout Fishing in America* ended his life in a house in Bolinas's creepy tall trees and his body wasn't discovered for days.

The Brautigan death town is the anti-Crockett. In an organic grocery store in Bolinas I overheard a girl in black dreadlocks arguing with a clerk about some kind of orange coffee filters she wanted.

Why was the store out of them? Outside, a well-to-do-looking older hippie dude sitting at a table kept asking passersby if they wanted a bite of his burrito.

At the town's unmanned used bookstore there's a chart next to a lock box with a slot in it for money. The chart tells book lovers to leave whatever they think a book is worth in the box—$10 for great books down to $1 for ones that are just OK. You pick out a book, shove in a dollar or two, then turn around to confront a sign reading something like this store is under constant video surveillance. California über alles, I thought, as I left with a volume of S. J. Perelman's letters.

At the Bolinas post office another aging hippie was leaving a Netflix envelope in the mailbox outside. They watch DVDs here? What movies do these rich old hippies like? Since Netflix lets you look up local favorites by zip code, when I got back to Oakland I punched in Bolinas's and found out that the most popular film there was *Surfwise: The Amazing True Odyssey of the Paskowitz Family*, a documentary about a surfer named Doc who had nine kids and instead of allowing them to go to school raised them in a camper on the beach. Maybe no one would believe that *Surfwise* is Bolinas's local favorite, but it's true.

Bruce Conner: *Mabuhay Gardens*

I forgot to mention the name of the owner of the Alameda Theatre. It's Kyle Conner. With his complete lack of interest in the celluloid *matériel* of film, I doubt Kyle Conner is related to Bruce Conner, the great assembler of collage films from scraps, but maybe he is. Maybe he's just scratching and dirtying prints for future use by crunchy *bricoleurs* like the filmmaker he shares a name with.

There has been a great revival of interest in Bruce Conner's work since his death in July. A show called *Crossroads: A Tribute to Bruce Conner* goes up at Light Industry in Brooklyn this October.

In Cambridge, Massachusetts, at the Harvard Film Archive, a large-scale retrospective of his film work starts around the same time. While I was in Oakland, I saw a show of Conner's punk-rock photographs at the Berkeley Art Museum (BAM) called *Bruce Conner: Mabuhay Gardens.*

Even though Conner was a little old for the crowd, starting in 1976 he began acting as house photographer at the San Francisco equivalent of CBGB, a former Filipino nightspot called Mabuhay Gardens scenesters turned into a punk venue. Conner's black-and-white photographs, originally published in the zine *Search and Destroy,* are essential documents of punk as it happened, just as vital as the ones in Jim Jocoy's *We're Desperate* or Byron Coley's *No Wave.*

In these pictures, bands like the Avengers, Crime, U.X.A., and Negative Trend throw themselves around onstage before crowds who still don't look quite punk. They're a mix of Ramones-style leather and tight jeans and feathered Seventies hair and button-down shirts. The bands themselves are super stylish but seem to emerge from a void (aided by the deep black of Conner's underlit backgrounds) where they can do whatever they want because nothing's possible, nothing's going to happen. This is the opposite of a local scene today, where scenester musicians do very specific things and everything is possible, at least musically.

Jim Campbell: *Home Movies*

Another gallery at BAM featured a piece by someone named Jim Campbell called *Home Movies.* Campbell, according to BAM, is "a leading developer of high-definition television" and also an artist, which, I assume, they all are. You enter a vast slightly darkened room. Opposite your entrance you take in a series of LED strips running up and down the entire wall, projecting pulses of white light. Standing far away from them, you can just make out blurred moving images. These images were grabbed from home movies, but blown out to the point where they aren't recognizable. The effect was like viewing a giant shower curtain on display at a Sharper Image bankruptcy sale.

Campbell's images were opaque and boring, an uncommunicative dot matrix of nothing. But I enjoyed his writing. The artist's statement is one of the emptiest forms of our time, but Campbell filled it with evocative phrases. His LED installation, he says, "brings us emotionally close without sentimentality . . . to the unshareable quotient of memories." It "flickers with the seductive familiarity of the cinema." Did his words have anything to do with his work? Maybe they were randomly generated by it.

Kaleidoscope Jazz Chair

Abstraction used to be abstract. It wasn't hidden home movies you had to stand across the street to make out. At the surprisingly pleasant and well-designed Oakland Museum, with its labyrinthine series of galleries and concrete passageways and balconies overlooking neat, wide gardens, a show called *Birth of the Cool: California Art, Design, and Culture at Midcentury* returned me to the non-representational, the metaphorical instead of the literal. One of the painters in the show, Lorser Feitelson, a painter of "Magical Space Forms" worthy of the name, explains, in an artist's statement from sometime in the middle of the last century: "I have tried to create a wonder-world of formidable, mood-evoking form, color, space, and movement: a configuration that for me metaphorically expresses the deep disturbance of our time: ominously magnificent and terrifying events, hurtling menacingly from the unforeseeable."

In the 1950s, Feitelson hosted a show on art that aired on NBC, probably the only serious painter who ever had a network series. Even Bob Ross was just on PBS. I would like to see Feitelson on that show, saying things like that. He sounds like he was introducing an episode of *The Twilight Zone*. The show was a grab bag of things from midcentury California, presented kind of eBay style: jazz album covers on one wall, TVs and paperbacks on another, chairs and vases on a shelf in the middle. These objects kept bringing me back to the movies. Over here, a photograph of Richard Neutra's house for Josef von Sternberg in Northridge, California; over there, scenes from *North by Northwest* on a flat-screen TV, featuring James Mason's house near Mount Rushmore, a movie house, not a real house like von Sternberg's.

Movies were part of the show. In a short film from 1960 by Ray and Charles Eames called *Kaleidoscope Jazz Chair*, abstract shots made through a kaleidoscope cut to scenes of Eames plastic chairs animated in stop-motion. In this six-minute film, the romance of industrial design blips by, filmed in a cartoon Soviet style, in colors available only in the USA of 1960—candy reds, calm pinks, many shades of gray, mint green, and deep black.

Another screen showed a four-minute-long abstract electronic animation made with an oscilloscope and an optical printer. The photographer Hy Hirsh made it in 1959 and cut it to Thelonious Monk's "Evidence." Lines the color of Eames chairs dance against a black background, creating an eerie-happy Atomic Age mood that does without cartoon characters, something I wish the literal-minded animators at Pixar, which is based near Oakland, would consider sometime.

Why is animation always about anthropomorphized spatulas and talking bugs voiced by TV stars? Pixar has created a look all of California now aspires to. It's crisp yet gummy, sharply molded, but not like an Eames chair, which is a real object you can take a picture of, then move and take another picture of, then you can cut the two shots together, and repeat until the chair is moving on its own. To give the chair a mouth and make it talk would be childish.

The Birth of the Cool show was so good I wanted to buy the book. But, like at the Bruce Conner show, the museum was sold out. Either that's a sign of wild success or it's a California thing—they don't think anybody reads.

The Earth Trembles, the iPhone Rings

Outside the Oakland Museum, my friend from Brooklyn who's visiting me in California answers a call on his iPhone. After he's finished, he tells me he's figured out how to copy movies from DVDs and put them on his phone. He doesn't explain why he wants them there. Instead of asking him, I ask what movies he's got. "*La terra trema*," he answers. "*La terra trema*? You have *La terra trema* on your iPhone?" "Yeah," he says. "But the subtitles are a bitch." Then we go to a Vietnamese restaurant. There are a lot of Vietnamese restaurants in Oakland, and they're all better than the ones in New York. I never found out why he brought *La terra trema* to Oakland on his iPhone. Maybe because there are earthquakes there.

The Last Mistress

Habits die hard, even when you're out of town. After hurting my head thinking about Italian neorealism on an iPhone, the siren call of Asia Argento lured me back into a theater.

The real title of *The Last Mistress* translates as *An Old Mistress*—another case of American distributors afraid of a French film's actual title. "Even if your heart is loftier than your morals . . ." one character starts a sentence in this inscrutable tale with an important lesson: if you've got a hot mistress you really love, forget about your wife no matter what. Reminiscent of the period pieces of Eric Rohmer or Benoît Jacquot, Catherine Breillat's lukewarm film, based on a mid-nineteenth-century novel, lacks Rohmer's love and charity or Jacquot's enigmatic throb. It stays in the mind for its clammy stare and its costuming, which at one point makes Asia Argento look like she's auditioning for a silent-movie *Carmen*.

Mongol

Genghis Khan is hot in the West. All of a sudden everywhere you look you see him. There are nonfiction books and novels about Genghis Khan, TV shows and museum exhibits, and evidently he's also big in Japan. People never tire of repeating that supposedly some huge percentage of people in Asia share his genes. Clearly, he's a celebrity. What is this fascination with an illiterate conqueror from a brutal society who militarized most of the world?

Sergei Bodrov's *Mongol* is one of at least two Genghis Khan films made in the last year or so, and there are more to come. Tadanobu Asano, costar of Uniqlo billboards with Chloë Sevigny, usually appears in art or genre films by directors like Takeshi Kitano, Kiyoshi Kurosawa, Takashi Miike, and Hou Hsiao-hsien. Now Russians have tapped him to play Temüjin, which was the Khan's real name.

Bodrov and Asano turn Genghis Khan into Jesus with a real sword. This is the Russian-icon version, flat and suffering—*The Passion of the Khan*. In this bloody story, Genghis is a martyr. He struggles with his absent father to bring law to his people and emerges as a Jewish Japanese mystic kicking everyone out of everywhere.

Yet *Mongol* isn't kosher at all. The film indulges our current passion for meat and the parts of animals we didn't use to eat. *Mongol* serves up a platter of bones in soup and shanks on spits, accompanied by New Carnivore advice like "you can't cook two ram heads in one pot." The film is as milky as it is meaty. Genghis's father drinks poisoned milk, the rest of the milk in the film has blood in it, the rain on the steppes looks more like milk than water. The groaning music on the sound track undergirds a culture that ate nothing but meat and dairy, the sound of stomachs that built an empire and conquered the world.

The Exiles

Maybe the one essential release of the summer was *The Exiles.* Kent MacKenzie's shoestring black-and-white drama from 1961 exists at the same level as *Shadows, Killer of Sheep* and *My Brother's Wedding,* and *Stranger Than Paradise,* which shares a poker scene with it. MacKenzie's film, which never really had an official release back when it was made, follows a group of Native Americans through a dark night of the soul in a Los Angeles that vanished not long after the film was made. It really has more in common with *Faces* than with *Shadows.*

The Exiles spends most of its time on men drinking in bars and drunk driving. They live in a world where every song sounds like Link Wray. MacKenzie's film exposes this world's desperation and also traps these men there. Although it's a fiction film, it's also a documentary about how everything looked in Bunker Hill in the early '60s, the men's work shirts, haircuts, cigarettes, and bottles of beer. Its characters have escaped what one describes as the ordered freedom of life on the reservation for the completely disordered freedom of bad jobs, tiny apartments, and cheap booze.

The actors in the film are nonprofessionals from the Native American community in Los Angeles at the time. They use their own names for the parts they play—Homer, Mary, Tommy, Cliff, Rico, Yvonne. Playing versions of themselves, the men are tough and unapologetic, the women tender and sad. One of the women abandons the men at a gas station on Sunset Boulevard, just gets out of the car and leaves the film behind. Another sits by herself through intermission at a double feature showing of Sirk's *Imitation of Life.* The "Intermission Time" song she listens to silently and alone exposes all the tawdriness and inadequacy of entertainment.

Pineapple Express

Pineapple Express sets out to prove that in a country where pot is illegal, daily life will be humiliating and violent. This theme runs through current American cinema like stems in a fifty. The movie takes place in a nondescript county somewhere in Generic America that's as crappy as any locale in a 1970s John Waters film. In this milieu, people's only bond is their mutual desire to get high. Every junk-stuffed, washed-out frame traps the film's wounded losers into deadly situations they can escape only because the movie is a comedy. Tim Orr's cinematography, the ugliest since *Before the Devil Knows You're Dead*, deserves an Oscar for being so bold and unremitting in sticking to what it set out to do.

Vicky Cristina Barcelona

If you grew up reading *Archie* comics, you learned that the ultimate choice Archie has to make in life is not what to do for a living, not where to live, not where to get health insurance. Archie's ultimate choice is: Betty or Veronica? In real life, Betty and Veronica have their own choices to make. It's to Woody Allen's credit that he shows this situation from the perspectives of women, close to the way Catherine Breillat showed it in *The Last Mistress* and close to the way Ingmar Bergman does it—*Vicky Cristina Barcelona* is like one of the Bergman summer films Woody Allen likes so much.

But getting back to the Archies, here Betty is Scarlett Johansson's Cristina, Veronica is Rebecca Hall's Vicky, except sometimes she's Penélope Cruz's Maria Elena. I guess Barcelona is Riverdale. Except Bardem is more like Boris Karloff than he is like Archie Andrews.

When Johansson's amorphous blonde turns to photography in *Vicky Cristina Barcelona*, the film at first appears to be letting her off the hook. She doesn't know what she wants in life but at least she's an artist. Yet her photos are only kind of good, and I think

Allen made them that way on purpose. Cristina faces the problem of having average talent, which is a much more baffling problem for people than being talented or untalented.

Rebecca Hall is the daughter of Peter Hall, the British stage director who founded the Royal Shakespeare Company. Her portrayal of an American—specifically a Woody Allen American, which is not quite the same thing—is better than an American would have done. Why is it that the children of acting royalty in England are Rebecca Hall and in America they're Jake Busey?

Allen shows a subtle contempt for Cristina's go-getter New York fiancé, who's overly proud of how normal he is. When he starts to tell a joke in one scene, Allen cuts out the sound so we don't hear his punch line. At one point the film gets too comfortable with itself. Then Allen brings in the fearsome Maria Elena, who we've been hearing about like she's Harry Lime. Offended by Cristina's American version of worldliness, which involves studying a language she'll never use, Maria Elena snaps "Say something in Chinese!" at her, the most aggressive line of the summer. Allen doesn't leave it at that. Maria Elena goes on to insult the very idea of Chinese, expressing incredulity that anyone, including Chinese people, would want to speak it at all.

Something to Talk About

Godard says the cinema is valuable because it gives us something to talk about. So it makes sense there's a movie called *Something to Talk About*. What doesn't make sense is that I had to see it on an airplane. On JetBlue, every seat has a TV embedded in the back of the seat in front of you. I don't like to watch TV on airplanes so I usually turn it off. Sometimes I check out the flight-path channel, which shows the plane over a map and tells your altitude.

Returning from Oakland, the person sitting across the aisle and ahead of me to my right was watching *Something to Talk About* on one of the JetBlue channels. Sometimes when I'm in a bar and a TV's on, I can't take my eyes off it, regardless of what's showing or who I'm with. That's what happened, but I couldn't sit facing away like you can in a bar. Whenever I put my nose in a magazine, *Something to Talk About* drew it out. I'd try to concentrate on what I was reading and this useless movie from the mid-'90s with Julia Roberts and Dennis Quaid would catch my eye and I'd start watching it again. Julia Roberts has this power, like a road accident.

I couldn't even hear the sound. The movie looks like it's about people who own horses. Gena Rowlands and Robert Duvall are in it, which helped reel me in, and Kyra Sedgwick flails around in it for reasons I couldn't understand. I think she was mad she was in *Something to Talk About* and was trying to wave me away.

The Brooklyn-Queens Expressway

People like to quote *The Wizard of Oz*: "There's no place like home." I prefer to get my homilies from somebody a little more disabused than Dorothy Gale, in this case the jazz pianist Andrew Hill: "There is no refuge. There is no place to hide. No matter where you look, you're still the one who's looking." I was still looking at the world through a screen, right now a window in a car-service car on the BQE taking me home to South Brooklyn from JFK. I love driving on the BQE watching the dirty buildings go by. I know I'm home when I'm on it, even though I live so close to it the noise and fumes are probably killing me. I see the youth moose graffiti on that building in Williamsburg and know in a few minutes I'll be unlocking my door.

September 2008

THE HUMAN PYRAMID THING

Standard Operating Procedure

America has a dark secret, one it's unwilling to face: Errol Morris's films are boring. His "interrotron" technique is supposed to be penetrating but it makes everybody look like they're on a job interview.

Maybe he's auditioning people to find out if they're worthy of being in one of his important works of nonfiction. But no one is worthy of the form he's devised—he wants to expose the banality of evil but insists banality prove its humanity, and vice versa.

Enter Lynndie England, American nightmare imp, cigarette-smoking Abu Ghraib leash girl. *Standard Operating Procedure*'s real subject is not torture at Abu Ghraib so much as the confrontation between people like Lynndie England and digital cameras. Morris is more interested in the pictures she's in than in England herself. He didn't need her in person to make this film. Yet there she is, dragged in to redeem herself so she can be admitted into humankind.

Standard Operating Procedure concludes that prison-guard soldiers like England photographed the abuse they dished out because they were improperly supervised—they resented their neglect. The uninterviewed Chuck Graner and "Chip" Frederick, torture ringleaders now in prison, instigators of "the human pyramid thing," stand in for Cheney and Rumsfeld, supervisors of the larger debacle still on the loose.

Danny Elfman's score implies that any minute Iraqi prisoners are going to be interrogated by Edward Scissorhands, who doesn't appear either.

Harold & Kumar Escape from Guantanamo Bay

In the first one, white people were clueless idiots; in the sequel, Harold and Kumar face a world where the war on terror has turned everybody into idiots. The film dispenses with the torture angle early, after an interlude with prison guards that brings out all the psychosexual hypocrisy ignored by other discussions of American torture, including *Standard Operating Procedure*. Later, this stoner comedy reverses Abu Ghraib by having a rich Arab kid at a pool party force American girls to walk around with their pants off. Of course the girls are into it—the Arab kid has to restrain them from taking off their tops.

When Harold and Kumar travel through a completely Bush-ified American South and then head to Amsterdam, the film's message couldn't be clearer. You can't find freedom here—escape to a place where it's legal to smoke pot.

A dream

I'm hurtling through icy clouds toward Earth. I'm standing in what appears to be the gondola of a balloon, except it's more like a cheap plastic wastebasket, flimsy and thin, a detached bucket with just enough room for one.

I have a red-and-white Netflix envelope in my hand, sealed and ready to be returned. I must have watched the movie in it, but I can't remember what it was. The ground rises to meet me; this appears to be one of those dreams where you experience your own demise.

I crash and feel my bones break. The DVD inside the Netflix envelope shatters, but the envelope remains intact, not even torn. With great effort I pick myself up and limp to a mailbox on the street. I pull open the blue door and deposit the DVD. The shards inside rattle lightly as the envelope falls to the bottom.

Baby Mama

Baby Mama belongs to a small group of films, maybe larger if you live in New York: films you see because they were shot in your neighborhood. Which is strange, because my neighborhood is in Brooklyn and *Baby Mama* takes place in Philadelphia. Evidently Brooklyn is the new Toronto.

Since this part of Brooklyn is exactly like the gentrified, baby-obsessed Philadelphia described by the movie—in fact, it is more like that than Philadelphia is—it was a puzzle to me why the film was set there.

I thought and thought about this. I remembered how *The Departed* was shot across the street from me in Brooklyn even though it was supposed to take place in Boston, where I used to live until I escaped. I got pissed off all over again at Martin Scorsese, the ultimate New York filmmaker, for bringing Boston back to my doorstep when I hoped I'd never see it again. The irony!

Then I realized *The Departed* doesn't take place in Boston at all. What does Martin Scorsese care about Boston? He just wanted to show he could make a movie about gangsters that didn't take place in New York. No, *The Departed* takes place in a city called *Not New York*, a movie city that—even though it is New York—exists to reassure the perceived audience of non–New Yorkers that the New Yorkers who made the film they're watching don't actually hate America and don't hate leaving New York to work out of town.

So it is with *Baby Mama*. You could tell the producers were worried the whole film might be seen as an insult to regular America.

They were afraid that if it took place in Brooklyn, where it was shot, it would be construed as mean to the white-trash people it gets so much fun out of.

Changing it to Philadelphia deflected that potential criticism by setting the film among non–New Yorkers in the city of Not New York. If Tina Fey's wealthy yuppie was a Brooklyn mommy-wannabe everyone would know she was a snob; Amy Poehler's good-hearted Tastykake eater would be seen as condescended to. But make them Pennsylvanians and they're both lovable dopes. Problem solved.

Except for the problem that by any objective standard, the film takes place in Brooklyn, not Philadelphia. And the other problem is that the only thing marking Poehler as trashy is that she doesn't have to kiss her boss's ass all day like Tina Fey does. Other than that Poehler is regular, like any other girl you'd meet around here.

My Blueberry Nights

It never occurred to me that I'd rather see Lynndie England in a movie than Norah Jones. Nothing works in *My Blueberry Nights.* Even Wong Kar-wai's famous ability to pick music deserts him. Regardless of what's playing on the sound track, it's "After Midnight" you hear—the film looks like a ten-year-old beer commercial starring Eric Clapton.

What has Wong Kar-wai been doing for the last eight years? None of it makes sense. He seems more lost than any of his characters. Today we live off revivals of *Days of Being Wild* or *As Tears Go By,* but when *In the Mood for Love* came out in 2001 it was a film you pressed close, you looked into its eyes, it was tragic, true, and hot. Its sound track got us through many nights or car rides home—"*Quizás, quizás, quizás.*" Seven years later, it's over. The thrill is gone, the nights are cold.

Flight of the Red Balloon

While everyone was loving Wong Kar-wai in the 1990s, Hou Hsiao-hsien became this flashpoint director film critics could get fired for liking. It wasn't that his films were controversial because of what happened in them, it was that his films were controversial because nothing happened in them.

It was assumed that the public, hostile to boredom, was also hostile to proponents of boredom, so praising Hou was frowned upon. No responsible film critic—meaning no film critic who liked to eat—would bother saying good things about a Hou Hsiao-hsien film unless he absolutely couldn't avoid it. Fortunately for the working press, Hou films appeared infrequently in first run and many jobs were saved.

Those days are over and everybody knows better now. For one thing, most of those jobs are gone. Their disappearance had little to do with Hou Hsiao-hsien. For another, Hou keeps making great films. Now he's only hated by the kind of critics it's fun to have hate you. Kurt Loder, the guy who used to read the news on MTV (maybe he still does?), called *Flight of the Red Balloon* "monumentally boring" and "intensely frustrating" on VH1.com, which I swear I saw by accident when I was doing a search to find out what the piano music in the movie was.

Like in *The Errand Boy*, puppets express the theme of *Flight of the Red Balloon*: "How angrily fate treats each of us differently." The film is about how friendships run out and how people coldly move on. It takes place in Paris—it's a remake of *The Red Balloon*, although that doesn't matter—where Juliette Binoche works doing voices in a Chinese puppet theater. The balloon, this red circle that gets in front of things and blocks your vision like Julie Delpy's eye problem in *2 Days in Paris*, floats across the screen and somehow never gets hokey or irritating.

What irritated the person I saw the movie with was the way the character of Song, Binoche's Chinese nanny and an aspiring filmmaker, kept saying "*d'accord.*" "I wanted to slap her if she said '*d'accord*' one more time," my friend told me after the movie. When Hou's film *Millennium Mambo* came out, another woman I know saw it, then said, referring to the heroine played by Shu Qi, "If that girl lit one more cigarette I was going to have to slap it out of her face." What's with these white chicks who want to slap the Chinese girls in Hou Hsiao-hsien movies? It's true that all the characters in *Flight of the Red Balloon* are kind of irritating, not just Song; the film is a documentary on Paris.

Trailer Reviews

No one has time to go to the movies anymore but because of the internet they have plenty of time to watch trailers.

Son of Rambow: The cinema has become such an unsophisticated medium that now even 4-year-olds can make a Rambo movie. *Indiana Jones and the Kingdom of the Crystal Skull*: The cinema has become such an unsophisticated medium that now even old people can make an *Indiana Jones* movie. *Sex and the City*: Terrible, like watching dinosaurs fight—the fake dinosaurs at the beginning of *Robot Monster* that are really just lizards dressed up.

May 2008

SCARY CREATURE ACTION

Paranoid Park

The film is washed away by the quirky music choices Van Sant made for the sound track. They turn *Paranoid Park* into a pleasant mix tape made by somebody with OK taste. It doesn't help that his mix tape is offered to teenagers.

Van Sant's teenagers are mostly numb objects. They're no James Deans, they don't act out, and Van Sant has a Warholian view of them. The girls come off better than the boys, which is strange because the girls appear to be professional actors and the point seems to be how beautifully natural everything is, or naturally beautiful.

It doesn't work for me because it doesn't jibe with my memory of adolescence, which for me was a time of turmoil and emotional confusion not spent in Portland, Oregon. Even when I was trying to appear indifferent I was still boiling inside and horrified by everything around me. I don't see that in Van Sant's teenagers; I don't recognize them.

Boarding Gate

Olivier Assayas thinks globalization is a cacophony of bad acting styles. For him, people's inability to be genuine or know what they really want is an indictment of the system. Ultimately, says Assayas, globalization turns everyone into a sad sack; the movie itself is pathetic.

There's no reason to watch it when you could watch a Johnnie To or a Michael Mann movie instead. Their films are serious about being existential confrontations between criminals and their times. They mean it, even if they're even cheesier than this cheesy film. And Assayas probably knows that. He has good taste but the things he likes are better than the movies he makes.

Only Asia Argento, a half-drunk dream girl who falls asleep in bars, makes it through untainted by the film's irrelevance. At one point she gets a new passport with an "anonymous" American name: Flavia Trapizano or something, the kind of name you hear in the US all the time if you never leave Nino's Pizzeria on Henry Street in Carroll Gardens.

On Taste

When talking about Van Sant and Assayas we have to talk about taste—their films are the sum of their tastes. They are the cinematic equivalent of record-collector bands like Sonic Youth. That's why they both have Kim Gordon in their films. They couldn't go on if they had to be silent about other people's work, and something compels them to get their fingerprints on everything they love.

Doomsday

Doomsday does for the 1980s-style postapocalypticism of *Road Warrior* what *Grease* did for the 1950s. It turns it into a kiddie musical. The difference is that people liked *Grease.* They had affection for it and it meant something to them. *Doomsday* doesn't even mean anything to the people who made it. It's filled with decapitations, burnings alive, and cannibalism, but it's more like *Rent* than *Escape from New York.*

The modern-primitive characters in *Doomsday* shout and shout, begging to be killed. The main character, a counterfeit Beckinsale, chooses to live among them rather than go back to plague-free London. She'd rather rule in Hell (Scotland), but the Hell is plague-free too, no different from London except David O'Hara (a great actor) doesn't live there. The film is dedicated to the suspicion that in the future we will have to be total assholes just to survive. Unlike now.

Married Life

Thinking about *Grease* reminds me that I've been watching new films set in the 1950s my whole life, even though I wasn't alive in the 1950s. I'm not looking forward to watching new films that take place in the '50s when I'm in my fifties.

If *Married Life* doesn't take place in the 1950s, it takes place around 1949, and that's close enough. A couple of years ago, the director of *Married Life*, Ira Sachs, made an excellent film called *Forty Shades of Blue*. Part of what made it so good was that it took place in the present. It was about a beautiful Russian woman married to a successful, belligerent music producer in Nashville. It wasn't afraid to set its drama today and to go for it—the film was impassioned and not phony.

Married Life, Sachs's follow-up, is the opposite: enervated, stylized, boring. It falls into the reactionary tradition of movies like *Far from Heaven*, which retreat to the 1950s to flirt with significance by crypto-commenting on today. Movies like that are coy and cheats—anti-repression but repressed themselves, too much in love with Tupperware. It's impossible to care what happens in *Married Life*, a movie about living room furniture Pierce Brosnan does everything he can to save.

Funny Games

The most brutalizing thing about this movie is the title. *Funny Games* is not a phrase in English. You can't go around pretending it is. Has any natural-born English speaker ever used it? For the remake, Haneke should have translated the title into English. Repeating the same mistake twice is an example of the film's redundancy.

The Duchess of Langeais

That reminds me: Why isn't *The Duchess of Langeais* called *Don't Touch the Axe*, an exact translation of its French title and the name of the Balzac story it's based on? It's a clueless US distributor who thinks Americans would rather see a movie called *The Duchess of Langeais* than one called *Don't Touch the Axe*.

A conversation with my aunt

I was talking to my aunt about movies on the phone the other day. She was telling me about a friend of hers who sees a lot of movies for free. "He gets free tickets because he knows people," she said. "He's a prison guard."

The Spiderwick Chronicles

Feeling unwell and without health insurance, I visited a walk-in clinic in my neighborhood, Red Hook. While sitting in the waiting room with about twenty other people, half of them children under ten, a security guard wheeled in a TV and a DVD player on a stand. He popped open the tray and put in a DVD so everyone waiting would have something to watch.

An MPAA warning appeared on the screen: "Some material may not be suitable for children for scary creature action and violence, peril and some thematic elements." Then the movie started, but it was strangely framed and hard to see. The color was washed out, everything had a brownish tinge. At first I thought the main actor was Dustin Hoffman, but as the film went on I realized it was David Strathairn. The movie was loud and obnoxious, featuring realistic sword fights between children and computer-generated goblins.

It was like a zombie movie for 11-year-olds, relentless and terrible, something no one should watch, especially in a health clinic in a poor neighborhood, especially me when I was sick and maybe dying. Why was this on?

The TV was so loud I couldn't read the book I'd brought. Pretty soon I realized I was watching a Canal Street bootleg of *The Spiderwick Chronicles*, a movie currently playing in theaters. I saw eighty minutes of it before a doctor called me in. *The Spiderwick Chronicles* sucks. Don't go see it and don't show it to kids.

You may think it's unfair to judge a movie based on seeing eighty minutes of a pirated DVD in a health-clinic waiting room. The banks of fluorescent lights did not create an optimum screening environment, it's true, nor did the moans of pain, nor the old lady sitting next to me wearing headphones and singing along about Jesus. But as I sat there, in pain myself and barely able to focus, I realized that this was the future of moviegoing, that this was how most of the world already sees movies. This was reality, not sitting next to the film critic for the *New Yorker* watching *Little Children* at a press screening in Lincoln Center, something I'd done in another life.

April 2008

OSCAR PREVIEW

Michael Clayton

There was a lot of driving in *Michael Clayton*. I like driving in movies but after a while *Michael Clayton* started to seem like a car ad, though it showed how a car ad can be liberal. That's a message for our times.

The Assassination of Jesse James by the Coward Robert Ford

Everyone says that *The Assassination of Jesse James* (I don't have time to say the full title) was derivative of Terrence Malick, but I liked it better than any recent Malick movie. I recommend this film; in fact I recommend it to Terrence Malick. Its pictorialism never interferes with its harsh sadness. And how many Malick films contain a performance as good as Casey Affleck's in this? But you could tell the studio interfered with it.

The Diving Bell and the Butterfly

When I saw *The Diving Bell and the Butterfly* at BAM, in Brooklyn, it was easy to see why it resonated with the local crowd. The subject of this movie is: If only I were paralyzed from head to toe and could only move one eye, then finally I'd be able to finish that book I've been meaning to write.

No one would be able to complain or interrupt me in my work. They'd have to indulge my every whim. My wife would have to be nice to my mistress. If those two couldn't get along, beautiful nurses would tell them to cool it. I wouldn't even have to bathe myself. If I wanted to go to the beach, someone would push me there in a wheelchair. I wouldn't even have to eat!

Which is not to say that I didn't like it. I did like it. For those reasons.

No Country for Old Men

Whenever Javier Bardem took out that pressure hose and put it to someone's head, I kept waiting for his victim to go, "Ouch! Stop it! Why are you doing that? That hurts! Cut it out."

There Will Be Blood

Whenever Daniel Day-Lewis plays an American, he is the scariest person on the planet. And totally convincing. But whenever he plays someone British, which is what he actually is, I don't believe him at all. It's a paradox.

Everyone quotes his line "*I drink your milkshake.*" It's become funny but it's an important lesson. This past year I felt that someone was drinking my milkshake, and it was important for me to see that played out on-screen.

Atonement

There was an interview a while ago with Ian McEwan that Zadie Smith did for the *Believer* in which McEwan said that "cinema is a very inferior, unsophisticated medium." Like many people, I enjoy movies immensely and I don't see why I should pay money to see the adaptation of a book by someone who thinks the cinema is *very* inferior. It was the way McEwan used the word *very* that really bugged me. If he had just said cinema was inferior and unsophisticated, I wouldn't have minded so much.

Everything McEwan writes ends up as a movie. Someday his shopping lists will be filmed. I wonder how he'll feel about the cinema's inferiority and lack of sophistication when he cashes the check for the Untitled Ian McEwan Shopping List Project.

Juno

I can't say anything about *Juno* because I didn't see it. I didn't see it because I hated *Little Miss Sunshine* so much. After I saw *Little Miss Sunshine* I really wished I hadn't. I refuse to make that mistake again. If that's what a feel-good movie is, I can't stand to feel that good. It's physically painful for me to feel that good.

Sweeney Todd

The thing I don't understand about *Sweeney Todd* is why someone made a musical starring two people who can't sing. As far as I know, not only can Depp and Bonham Carter not sing, they also can't dance.

Eastern Promises

Eastern Promises is succinct and well acted by everyone in it, not just Viggo Mortensen. It was like a Hitchcock adaptation of a Conrad novel. To its credit, it had a throwaway quality of making its points and moving on. Of all the films that examined the nature of evil this year, *Eastern Promises* had the most intimate knowledge of evil. And in one sense it was merely a genre film, unlike the super-genre films by the Coens and Paul Thomas Anderson and the guy who made *Jesse James.*

There's an Oscar category for Best Makeup. If they have one for Best Makeup, they should have one for Best Hair. And Viggo Mortensen should win it.

Norbit

Speaking of Best Makeup, the Eddie Murphy fat-suit comedy *Norbit* was nominated in that category, along with only two other films. I really think this movie should be acknowledged by the Academy of Motion Picture Arts and Sciences. They should take full responsibility for that nomination and give *Norbit* an Oscar. Then it should be shown all over the world on double features with *Sweeney Todd.*

Foreign Film Nominations

How does the Academy find five foreign films so obscure that not even film critics have heard of them? The foreign-language nominees are usually bland films from nice places, good (in the moral sense) or nice (meaning innocuous) films no one cares about. This is the view the Academy has of foreign films: they should be nonthreatening.

The best foreign film released in the US last year was *Syndromes and a Century,* a Thai film that was loved by probably everybody who saw it but, even though it was pleasant and from a nice place, wasn't treacly, conventional, or lame. I think the Academy refused to acknowledge *Syndromes and a Century* because they didn't want to embarrass Tom Hanks or whoever the presenter would be by forcing him to try to pronounce "Apichatpong Weerasethakul."

Before the Devil Knows You're Dead

Before the Devil Knows You're Dead was an unharmonious, ugly kind of violent stabbing at the myth of family, a real emanation from the darkness of the second Bush term. I mean it was really ugly, even the film stock it was printed on was soaked in ugliness. It was only made un-ugly when Marisa Tomei took off her clothes, which immediately made everything else in the film look even uglier. There should be an award for cinematography that ugly. It was more coherent and less vague than *No Country for Old Men* and *There Will Be Blood* and probably the best American film of the year. It was made by an 80-year-old director, and the Academy doesn't like to give real Oscars to men that old, only honorary ones. No Oscar for old men. Not even a nomination.

February 2008

WE LOVE TO TORTURE

WHEN PRESIDENT BUSH SOUGHT TO ESTABLISH NEW GUIDELINES ON torture this fall, he claimed that any interrogation technique that shocks the conscience would not be allowed. Hollywood filmmakers, always eager to oppose the President, go the other way in a year-end glut of torture movies that display only techniques designed to shock the conscience.

From mainstream actioners such as *Casino Royale* and *Apocalypto* to horror cut-'em-ups such as *Saw III* and *Turistas* (itself a retread of 2005's breakout torture hit *Hostel*), the kind of entertainment referred to as "torture porn" combines the mise-en-scène of Abu Ghraib with screenwriting evocative of reports from Camp X-Ray.

In reviewing the torture hits, critics take pains to tell readers that these movies are somehow about our collective fears of confinement and mutilation, about confronting some kind of ultimate evil that kicks us in the crotch before it cuts off our head and sends it tumbling down the stairs, punishing us for our desires.

But if we're confronting our fears, we're sure doing it exuberantly. The ingeniously imagineered punishment devices in these movies, along with their chummy torture-chamber repartee and quick recoveries from pain and abuse, aren't so much about the fear of torture as they are about the joy of it—and its necessity. Torture is a duty that filmmakers, like Tom Sawyer painting the fence, have convinced us is a lot of fun.

And like Tom, they've managed to fob the dirty work off on somebody else. In the real world of Guantánamo and secret prisons, the news is about people from other countries being tortured by people from this one. But in the movies it's the other way around.

The victims tend to be first-world dum-dums tortured by third-world thugs, as in the Brazil-set *Turistas*, in which a grab bag of English speakers from the US, Britain, and Australia are tortured by people who speak Portuguese—except when they deliver helpful lectures in English on fair trade.

The new James Bond, we're told, is a secret agent for today, a serious time in which the stakes are high. And, like the kids in *Turistas*, he's tortured by a foreigner. So why does the torture in *Casino Royale* play like one of those frat pranks Rush Limbaugh referred to when he defended Abu Ghraib guards? Reviews of *Casino Royale* shared a certain glee over the phrase *genital torture*; critics couldn't wait to titter over it. And as Bond and Le Chiffre trade quips about itches that need scratching, they might as well be snapping towels at each other in a locker room.

Saw III, on the other hand, functions more like a game show. It's so close to *Deal or No Deal* that Howie Mandel should play its villain, who offers his victims a chance to better themselves even as they're being tortured and killed. The message is explicit: Torture is a form of therapy that's good for its victims, who deserve—even need—it.

It's only Mel Gibson, our official madman, who is held to Amnesty International standards. While the torture in *Casino Royale* is applauded as bravura, Gibson's kitschy "No Fear" version of Mayan history is described by critics as a crime against humanity. That's because for Gibson torture is deeply serious, which is not to say he's against it. While *Apocalypto* comes encoded with a message about the war in Iraq, mostly it exults in the bloodshed of sacrifice and defeat. James Wan and Leigh Whannell, the auteurs behind the *Saw* franchise, throw in phony moralizing as a kind of leavening to the carnival atmosphere of their films. But Gibson proves Samuel Johnson's aphorism that no man is a hypocrite in his pleasures. For Gibson, torture isn't the path to transcendence; it is transcendence.

In the age of Abu Ghraib, the unashamed passion of torture-genre groupies is mainstream and normal. Aintitcool.com commentator "funnyhat," writing about *See No Evil*, a torture entry from last summer, is confused by anti-torture opprobrium. "Why does everyone call it 'torture porn'?" funnyhat asks. "It's entertainment, not a fetish! *See No Evil*, while not the greatest movie, was a great step forward for horror fans who love our torture."

"I like to torture!" Bela Lugosi shouted in a quaint (like the Geneva Convention) 1935 chiller called *The Raven*. "I tear torture out of myself by torturing you," Lugosi added, showing a level of insight denied current films, whose best critic could be Limbaugh. "I'm talking about people having a good time . . . you ever heard of emotional release?" Limbaugh said of the Abu Ghraib pranksters in 2004.

That's a definition of torture to stand next to Bush's. Here's another: Torture is what we watch acted out in front of us as we sit in movie theaters eating nachos. Torture is serial and endless, like entertainment, and comes to us in the guise of fun, as it did at Abu Ghraib. The two are beginning to merge.

December 2006

ALLIED FORCES

IT IS A COMMONPLACE OF AMERICAN MOVIE REVIEWING THAT WHEN A WAR movie comes out that is even a little bit anti-war, the reviewer may refer to the François Truffaut antiwar-movie dictum: Since even a gruesome war movie makes war look exciting, there's really no such thing as an antiwar war movie. *Apocalypse Now* was invented to prove this, *Saving Private Ryan* to bash it into our brains forever.

But a new book by David L. Robb, a Los Angeles–based journalist and former reporter for *Daily Variety* and the *Hollywood Reporter*, makes it clear that the Department of Defense doesn't see it the way Truffaut did. Robb's *Operation Hollywood: How the Pentagon Shapes and Censors the Movies* documents the activities of the Pentagon's film liaison office, which is part of the Office of the Assistant Secretary of Defense for Public Affairs. The liaison office examines and demands changes to movie scripts to ensure the US military is depicted favorably in the Hollywood productions to which the Department of Defense leases hardware or locations.

Robb also shows how film producers, those notoriously demonized liberals, often cave in to Pentagon demands when they need to rent a jet fighter or want to shoot on a military base. To Robb, this is a form of taxpayer-funded censorship. It is also, he claims, unconstitutional. Through this official approval process, he argues, the Pentagon favors and rewards pro-military speech over speech that the Pentagon deems not in the military's interest.

In fact, Robb's book shows, film producers in Southern California have mastered the pre-cave, and often fashion their screenplays with Pentagon approval in mind. ("If this doesn't make every boy in the country want to fly a fighter jet, I'll eat this script," the producer of *Independence Day* wrote to the Pentagon's film office, in a letter quoted by Robb. The movie was denied anyway.) Without military assistance, studios claim, they couldn't afford the kind of realism only an authentic Black Hawk helicopter can deliver.

In the Pentagon, Hollywood has found a partner that understands the art of the deal. In Hollywood, Robb charges, the Pentagon has found something more valuable: a propaganda factory willing to foot the bill for making military recruitment ads in the service of blockbuster entertainment. Though movies that have received help from the Pentagon carry a line in the credits thanking the Department of Defense, few in the audience are aware of the influence the military wields over these productions.

THE MILITARY HAS ASSISTED moviemakers since at least 1927, when *Wings*, the first Oscar winner, was made in cooperation with the Army Air Corps. After World War II the Pentagon decided to codify its guidelines for helping film productions. Then, the communist threat was often the justification for cutting elements the Pentagon didn't like from films that were dependent on military assistance. Such was the case in 1955, Robb writes, when a subplot about a Mexican American's conflict with a racist Texan in his Marine outfit was excised from *Battle Cry*, a Raoul Walsh movie set during World War II.

Today the Pentagon is up-front about what it wants: good PR. Phil Strub, the civilian in charge of the Pentagon's film liaison office, said in a recent interview that what the Pentagon looks for in a film they are asked to assist is "an opportunity to increase the public's awareness of what the military does and as a by-product of that a chance to increase recruitment and retention" of troops. Strub rejects Robb's charge of censorship, saying that the arrangement is a two-way street. "Hollywood wants something from us," he points out. "We negotiate and if they don't like our suggestions, they make the film without us."

(Robb interviewed Strub for his book, along with dozens of other government and industry sources. Only the Marine Corps' film office, which works under the Pentagon's film office, allowed him unrestricted access to their files.)

According to Jonathan Turley, a professor of law at George Washington University and longtime critic of the film office, the relationship is not that simple. Turley, who wrote a foreword to *Operation Hollywood*, says that by refusing assistance to movies that may contain material it doesn't like, the Department of Defense suppresses free speech. "It is not always direct manipulation," says Turley, but it has a "chilling effect" on the kinds of films that get made.

"Our intention in producing *Stripes* is to make a comedy film with patriotic overtones that would hopefully have a positive effect on Army recruiting," the film's producer and co-screenwriter Dan Goldberg wrote to the Pentagon's film office, in a letter quoted by Robb, when he presented the script in a bid for military aid. Micromanaged to within an inch of its funniness, *Stripes* suffered heavy Pentagon interference before it went into production. As Robb details, out went the drugs and the swearing, the sadism of the drill sergeant, the covert operation in Mexico. And into the film's first scene went an actual recruitment ad—not the parody ad envisioned by the filmmakers.

In the dozens of case histories presented by Robb, inaccuracy and a lack of realism are often the reasons the Pentagon gives for the changes it demands. ("Any film that portrays the military as negative is not realistic to us," Robb quotes Strub as saying.) For example, before the Cuban missile crisis drama *Thirteen Days* (2000) could meet Pentagon approval, the portrayal of the hawkish air force general Curtis LeMay as "unintelligent and bellicose" had to be changed, and a mention of the 1962 downing of a U2 reconnaissance plane had to be removed. Producer Peter Almond refused, and the film went on without Pentagon assistance.

Even Clint Eastwood, then the national chairman of the Marine Corps' Toys for Tots program, met with similar trouble over *Heartbreak Ridge,* his 1986 drama about the invasion of Grenada. In exchange for eventual approval, Eastwood was forced to remove a mention of the 1983 terrorist bombing of a Marine barracks in Beirut, had to cut much of his character's swearing, and was pestered on dramatic construction to the point that he felt compelled to call then President Ronald Reagan and lodge a formal complaint.

Ridley Scott was denied assistance for *G.I. Jane* (1997), which starred Demi Moore as a female recruit battling with sexist Navy SEALS. But that didn't stop him and producer Jerry Bruckheimer from going to the Pentagon for help with *Black Hawk Down* (2001) and agreeing to a number of changes.

To Strub, this proves the essential fairness of the approval process. If the film office were censoring filmmakers, why would they come back to work with the Pentagon after past rejections?

Charles Newirth, head of the studio that made *Black Hawk Down,* is sanguine, despite having tangled with the liaison office over *Forrest Gump,* which was denied approval for its (accurate) suggestion that the Vietnam-era army recruited soldiers who would previously have been excluded because of low IQ. "We always try to accommodate the Department of Defense," he told Robb. "Phil Strub is a huge ally of Hollywood."

Thomas Doherty, chair of the film studies program at Brandeis and author of *Projections of War: Hollywood, American Culture, and World War II,* dismisses Robb's charge that the Pentagon is engaging in censorship. "What do you expect?" he said in a recent interview. "When you're going to people for stuff, they're not going to be disinterested. Guys who are in uniform and are allocating their resources should be allowed to sit down and make reasonable demands. . . . Why should the Pentagon be asked to underwrite films that are against it?"

Besides, he says, Hollywood films should be judged on how they use the hardware they lease from the Pentagon, not whether they use it. He sees a big difference between films like *Black Hawk Down*, with its dark portrayal of the Somalia invasion, and rah-rah twaddle like *Pearl Harbor* (2001), even though both received Pentagon assistance.

"Really, there are two kinds of war movies: little boys' war movies and big boys' war movies," says Doherty. "In the big boys' war movies, the most likable characters die." It's up to audiences, not the Pentagon, to determine what is dramatically truthful, he says.

Strub contends that if the Pentagon approval process were as questionable as Robb's book makes it out to be, Congress would do something about it. But, as *Operation Hollywood* shows, the Pentagon system has not gone unchallenged. In 1956, when producer-director Robert Aldrich's script for his war movie *Attack* was rejected by the Pentagon, he told his story to *Daily Variety* and prompted the House Armed Services Committee and the Senate's Judiciary Subcommittee on Constitutional Rights to look into the denial of aid. The matter was soon dropped.

The system was challenged again in 1968, when the Pentagon arranged to have its "Thanks to the Department of Defense" credit cut from John Wayne's pro–Vietnam War movie *The Green Berets*, the only time such a credit has ever been removed.

As Don Baruch, the longtime head of the Pentagon's film office and Strub's predecessor (and a major figure in Robb's book) wrote at the time, he "conferred with Michael Wayne [John Wayne's son and the film's producer] regarding not using DOD credit because (1) 'propaganda value of film' might be affected by the association, (2) might increase letters of inquiry on how film received assistance." Within a year, Benjamin Rosenthal, a congressman from New York, demanded from the General Accounting Office a full disclosure of Pentagon assistance to *The Green Berets*. Little came of his request.

George Washington Law School's Jonathan Turley says that critics of the approval system have little reason to think they would receive much hearing today. "Unless there is a public outcry members of Congress have no interest in this type of reform," he says. "The Armed Services Committee is interested in using its leverage to keep military bases open. The artistic freedom of movies is not exactly an issue burning in their breasts."

J. Hoberman, film critic for the *Village Voice* and a professor at New York University who has taught courses on Hollywood and the military, agrees that the approval system is an affront to the First Amendment. "If the Pentagon wants to go into business of leasing to the movies it should be open to whomever wants to lease and can afford to," he said in an interview. "It's our army. If you can afford the rates you should be able to rent. But if the Department of Defense wants propaganda, they should make it themselves. Films made with Pentagon assistance are the closest things we have to an official art."

July 2004

ATOMIC INDIA

"BOMBAY IS A MINI-AMERICA," SAYS A HOLY MAN IN *WAR AND PEACE*, INDIAN filmmaker Anand Patwardhan's controversial documentary on the nuclear mania that has swept India since 1998. On the Buddha's birthday that year, May 11, the government of Prime Minister Atal Bihari Vajpayee successfully exploded atomic bombs underneath the Pokhran municipality in the Thar Desert, proudly showing Pakistan what for until Pakistan exploded a few of its own.

These "Smiling Buddha" tests revived India's dormant nuclear weapons program. Glorified by the ruling Hindu-nationalist Bharatiya Janata Party (BJP), celebrated in Indian popular culture, and decried by a grassroots protest movement, a newly atomic India reminiscent of America in the decades after Hiroshima has emerged in a flash. "Victory to science" and "Atoms for peace" are its slogans, delivered Bollywood-style in music videos and on looming billboards. The holy man is in the pocket of the BJP; when he compares Bombay to America he does it to flatter. The current rulers of India look forward to a day when their country isn't merely a mini-America but a superpower all its own. In the meantime A. B. Vajpayee is still known throughout the land as Atom Bomb Vajpayee.

War and Peace has won praise at film festivals around the world, including Bombay's, but it is effectively banned in its home country. The censor board continues to demand cuts on a variety of trumped-up charges. "They just don't like it," Patwardhan said at a late September screening of the documentary at the Harvard Film Archive. It seems the BJP doesn't want to be reminded of India's Gandhian tradition of nonviolence and opposition to empire when they're building an atomic empire of their own. In fact, archival footage re-creating Gandhi's assassination is one of the scenes the Indian censors want excised. Although the Indian press has been supportive of Patwardhan, the government isn't budging. Patwardhan senses a whiff of Joe McCarthy and the American Fifties in the air, and not just in India. Last February, the American Museum of Natural History in New York City delayed and relocated a screening of two of Patwardhan's earlier films, after receiving "threats of violence" from activists denouncing them as "anti-Hindu."

In *War and Peace*, an Indian anti-nuclear journalist describes the arms race and its opposition as a struggle for India's soul. The BJP, he says, feels "that there must be some sort of shortcut to India being great, and the version that they are seeking to impose is that of a belligerent and aggressive nationalism." Patwardhan cuts to a billboard showing Indian soldiers posed à la Iwo Jima, planting their country's flag alongside the words SMILE INDIA.

The struggle for America's soul waged in the early atomic era was won handily in our pop culture. Writers and intellectuals fought atomic terror with essays and petitions, but musicians and marketers reacted with a wry humor and a misplaced whimsy that has had a more lasting impact. Bebop musician Slim Gaillard's 1945 song "Atomic Cocktail" set the standard by which future uses of the adjective *atomic* would be measured. Once the word had been attached to booze, using it to ramp up the va-va-voominess of postwar romance wasn't far behind. Hotcha atomic womanhood reached its apotheosis in Wanda Jackson's rockabilly hit "Fujiyama Mama." "I've been to Hiroshima, Nagasaki too / The things I did to them, baby, I can do to you," yelped Jackson, and the bond between sex and atomic devastation was sealed. The ultimate trivialization of the bomb came in a candy wrapper, with the mouth-scorching Atomic FireBall, created in 1954 and with us to this day. The website of the Ferrara Pan Candy Co. tells of a Manhattan Project writ small: "The 'Atomic FireBall' gained worldwide recognition shortly after the product was introduced. The round, spicy, hard candy that was once a dream had become a success." Just like the A-bomb.

After the successful launch of *that* product in July of 1945 at White Sands, NM, physicist J. Robert Oppenheimer told a TV interviewer that lines spoken by the god Krishna in the *Bhagavad Gita* had flashed in his mind: "I am become death, destroyer of worlds." In India in 1998, India's nuclear fathers announced that the Buddha smiled and looked for a suitable cross-cultural response, too. They found it in American-style showbiz. If Oppenheimer searched the sky and saw reflected in the mushroom clouds the sublime myths of an older culture, the fathers of India's nuclear program, though they named the Agni missile for the Hindu god of fire, have adopted the not-so-sublime forms of a newer culture.

The arms race with Pakistan has inspired the entertainment makers of Bollywood and beyond. As a banner at an arms trade show in *War and Peace* reads, to witness this mega event, visibility is the key. Folksy carnivals sponsored by political parties like the Parel Ganesh Festival laud Indian nuclear superiority with a cast of mannequins and colored lights. Baseball caps bearing the symbol of the atom and the slogan NUCLEAR INDIA—global peace power are passed out. Cadbury's 5 Star energy bar sponsors a musical event called "An Evening for Martyrs," which features a Bombay-style Backstreet Boy surrounded by showgirls. Honda pays for a spectacle called "The Fifty-Day War," a combination of Buffalo Bill's Wild West show and a Disneyland ride from the 1950s that ends when a Sergeant York–like hero from the Line of Control dividing Indian- and Pakistani-controlled Kashmir is handed a bouquet and waves.

Patwardhan's film shows Indian science heralded in a way guaranteed to remind American viewers of 1950s science-fiction films, and in Dr. A. P. J. Abdul Kalam, a Muslim nuclear scientist who recently assumed India's largely ceremonial presidency, India seems to have produced a happier Dr. Strangelove. Along with images of deformed children born near nuclear power plants, *War and Peace* presents Indian scientists as lab-coated evangelists for a better tomorrow through radiation. In the United States the all-knowing man of science has become a figure hooted at during screenings of old industrial films. Here, public relations professionals now do the talking for big science. But in India the scientists are still heroes, feted and given a forum. They're living embodiments, we're told, of India's new star power.

The atom bomb has come to India with another American tradition—the curbing of works that seek to expose its dangers. Patwardhan interviews several American historians about a Smithsonian exhibition planned and then retooled in 1995. Designed to feature the *Enola Gay*, the plane that dropped that bomb on Hiroshima, and to catalog atomic destruction in Japan, the exhibit was branded anti-American by veterans' groups and dramatically altered after accusations of treason that echo the charges leveled in India at *War and Peace*. The museum show as realized was as one-sided as a Jerry Bruckheimer epic. Instead of close-ups of the keloid scars of the victims of Hiroshima, it gave the public helicopter shots of a city in ruins—the only photographs of the bombing used in the show.

That kind of political interference hasn't only affected highfalutin presentations like exhibits at national museums and independent film documentaries. In 1950, the Sons of the Pioneers, the western musical group that gave Roy Rogers his start, recorded an ill-fated song called "Old Man Atom." It was penned by a newspaperman named Vern Partlow in 1945, soon after the explosions in Japan. It's something like the Louvin Brothers' "Great Atomic Power," but without references to the Rapture. After the *shhh . . . boom* of a bomb blast, "Old Man Atom" slides into the haunting vocal harmonizing familiar from other Sons of the Pioneers tunes, but in this song the group sings about a different kind of prairie:

Hiroshima, Nagasaki,
Alamogordo, Bikini. . .

Narrated by the atom itself in a basso talking blues, the song relates the story of the new atomic age. A cautionary tale, it explains how:

The science boys from every clime
They all pitched in with overtime
And before they knew it the thing was done
And they'd hitched up the power of the gol-durn sun
And put a harness on ol' Sol
Splittin' atoms while the diplomats was splittin' hairs

Humankind faces a choice, "Old Man Atom" concludes: Get together or disintegrate.

RCA Victor sensed a hit in what was really a novelty song. Before "Old Man Atom" was released, other pop stars of the day, including Bing Crosby, lined up to record it. But when the song came out, organizations like the Joint Committee Against Communism began to protest. RCA Victor pulled the disc from distribution and replaced it with a Pioneers song called "Where Are You." Heard in the context of Hiroshima, "Where Are You" sounds more ominous than "Old Man Atom." ("Then the sun goes to rest / In the arms of the West. / But my own arms caress / Emptiness. / Where are you?") It would've worked as well as Vera Lynn's "We'll Meet Again" as the music at the end of *Dr. Strangelove,* when Slim Pickens rodeo-rides a missile to nuclear oblivion.

Today it seems strange that the premier singing cowboys of their day recorded an atomic song that was suppressed. After all, they also waxed sides with titles like "America Forever" and "What This Country Needs." Yet there had always been a campfire-lit, closing-time-in-the-gardens-of-the-Old-West feel to their music, an apocalyptic melancholy that expresses itself through unearthly hoofbeats heard in the night, raging sunsets and abandoned towns.

A song like "Rollin' Dust," recorded a few months before "Old Man Atom," strikes the same note.

> Oh, the years are long and many since they rode down into town
> It's now just weeds and wormy boards and shacks all tumbled down
> Where once they stood up to the bar and pretty girls discussed
> They now hear ghostly laughter through a veil of heavy dust
> Rollin' dust

If that song, recorded at the dawn of the atomic age, doesn't evoke the nuclear tests in Nevada and New Mexico and the devastation of Hiroshima and Nagasaki, with their dark clouds and houses blown to splinters, what tune from that era does?

Korla Pandit played an eerie organ for the Sons of the Pioneers on that and other tracks. A musical personality from the early days of television who claimed he was a native of New Delhi (though he was probably an African American from Missouri), Pandit forms a coincidental link between the Pioneers' ghost riders in the sky and what an anti-nuclear politician in *War and Peace* calls "the fully armed gods of India." In Hindu belief, the deity Krishna was the adoptive son of the cowherd Nanda. The movement of cows from one place to the next has always been central to both US and Indian culture, and now India gets to play nuclear cowboy, too.

This cowboy lurks at the heart of *War and Peace*. In one scene, at an Indo-American Society convention featuring pamphlets like "Learn Personality Development the Indo-American Way," the camera finds an unsmiling man in a pin-striped suit and black ten-gallon hat. Floating through the crowd silent and alone, he looks like a Hollywood George Raft cast in the role of a western badman. Maybe he has read the pamphlet. By the end of the movie it's clear that the men in charge of India's nuclear future have taken more than a glance at it.

October 2002

ALMOST A PHANTOM

ON F. W. MURNAU

F. W. MURNAU NEVER MADE A TALKING PICTURE (EVEN D. W. GRIFFITH made a couple), yet among the great directors who made only silent films, he continues to fascinate like no other. Whereas we know Fritz Lang and Lubitsch, and Chaplin too, from their sound films as much as from their silents, Murnau is a pure expression of the silent cinema, one who predicted, or invented, the mise-en-scène of sound films, who in a way made sound films without sound. He strikes us as wholly modern in ways his contemporaries among the German Expressionists do not. In part, that's because even his most studio-bound films are suffused with a real feeling for landscape and nature—they breathe, albeit an often pestilent air. And in part it's because he died in a car accident in 1931, after striking out on his own in Tahiti, away from both Hollywood and Berlin. He never had a chance to decline.

Over seven decades, Murnau has followed the trajectory of our culture, sliding from pantheon auteur to posthumous celebrity. Jim Shepard's 1998 fictionalized biography, *Nosferatu: A Novel*, explored Murnau's longings (he was homosexual) as much as his work. And he's been paid a kind of ultimate compliment: John Malkovich played him in 2000's *Shadow of the Vampire*, a loony account of the making of *Nosferatu*. Despite this slightly elevated

E!–ification, Murnau's achievement has never been in question. His best films—*Nosferatu, The Last Laugh, Faust, Sunrise,* and *Tabu*—deserve their reputation as masterpieces. His 1930 *City Girl* should be on that list, despite the studio interference that truncated it. Since interest in Murnau is reaching new levels, the film series "Haunted Visions: The Films of F. W. Murnau," at the Museum of Fine Arts, Boston, and the Harvard Film Archive, comes at a good time, when moviegoers will be open to the unfamiliar works this series brings to light. It's great that those films are all here in new prints. This chance to see all of Murnau's surviving films (nine others are lost) in one series is a first.

Another reason Murnau is unique among directors of his era is the impression he gives of not having a consistent style. He doesn't fall into the trap of style, and yet his films are unmistakably his own. His early exegete Lotte Eisner called her book on German Expressionist cinema *The Haunted Screen,* but it's only Murnau's films that seem truly haunted, haunted from within. This quality emanates from his own consciousness. He never seems to be channeling a Weimar zeitgeist. Other directors of that time and place impose a look, a framework on their films that can prevent us from living inside their emotions today. Murnau's films are not like that.

In his seventh and earliest surviving film, 1921's *Journey into the Night,* the set-bound opening scenes might strike you as trivial. A dancer (Lya de Putti) tries to seduce a doctor (Werner Krauss) away from his work. When the pair relocate to a fishing village, the feeling for landscape Murnau had picked up from the Swedish cinema kicks in and becomes thoroughly mixed with his innate ominousness. And his idea of dramatic construction is already in place. He sets up a situation that at first seems generic or light and then gradually deepens and darkens it. Direction becomes a play of competing forces doomed to defeat each other; tragedy is inescapable. This is also true in 1921's *The Haunted Castle,* a less successful country-house mystery, like Robert Altman's *Gosford Park.* The film is both plot heavy and loaded with characters, which Murnau overcomes, using group compositions in depth and rain-soaked atmosphere. Dream sequences point to his future. One, with the shadow of a clawed hand, brings *Nosferatu* to mind.

If Murnau had made no film other than *Nosferatu*, a "free" adaptation of Bram Stoker's *Dracula*, he would have contributed enough to cinema. There isn't another horror film like it, despite subsequent attempts to re-create its feeling of movement between two worlds—the one we know and one that lies just beneath. The thematic concerns and events consistent from one Murnau film to the next are all present here: movement from city to country; a plague that overtakes the film's world; an evil outsider; a sacrificial woman; compositions uniquely (even painfully) aware of art history; the replacement of intertitles with texts; characters framed in arches and doorways; good people trapped by the mirrors they hold.

Murnau never loses his themes in phantasmagoria—science and economics underpin the film's horror. On some level, *Nosferatu* is a parable about gentrification. A real estate agent (*Dracula*'s Harker, here called Hutter, played by Gustav von Wangenheim) brings the wealthy Count Orlok—Nosferatu (Max Schreck)—into his neighborhood, which Nosferatu devastates. The film's Van Helsing character (John Gottowt) lectures his students in a biology class, and we see microscope views of predatory life forms. "This one . . . clear . . . almost bodiless . . . almost a phantom," intones the professor in the intertitles. The dark world he leads us to is predatory, dreamlike, hidden but real. Murnau created a bridge between the two. (And indeed, bridges appear throughout his work.)

The Grand Duke's Finances, Murnau's one comedy, travels Lubitsch territory in a decidedly Murnavian way. Sunlight streams into this island movie and combines with Murnau's agile use of large-scale city sets and his love of ships and trolleys to set the stage for *Sunrise*. Duke Ramon XII (Harry Liedtke, a Lubitsch actor who's a dead ringer for Bill Clinton), ruler of the Mediterranean kingdom of Abacco, must secure marriage to a Russian countess before his island goes bankrupt and falls to revolution. The film is frenetic and winning. Alfred Abel, the industrialist from *Metropolis*, is a standout in the cast, playing a suave thief named Philipp Collins.

Abel is a desperate poet in 1922's *Phantom*, a melodrama that uses another impressive city set. At one point in the film, this set begins to collapse around Abel and pursue him down a street. Abel's whole life here is a traffic accident; he's struck twice by a carriage like the one in *Nosferatu*. What starts as a glossy, somewhat unfelt tale of pity evolves into a self-aware melodrama in which a sister says to her brother, "We're lost, both of us. We've fallen under the wheels of fate." Family drama is also at the heart of 1922's *The Burning Soil*, which is about grasping for oil rights in a place called the Devil's Field. Here, fire replaces plague, and for once the tinting in silent movies comes off as dramatic rather than nostalgic. Like so much of Murnau, this German film predicts American cinema yet to come. It's a better film than *Giant*.

Murnau was always fortunate in his collaborators. The cinematographers, screenwriters, and set designers he worked with in Germany at UFA and elsewhere were among the best the cinema had in the 1920s. In Emil Jannings he had an actor of real power. Jannings's performance as the doorman in *The Last Laugh* is one of the greatest in movies. Because of its ending, this film's reputation has waned a little. But the ending is shocking, both parodistic and eerie, and Murnau uses his newly mobile camera to show the audience itself, a device he uses again in *Tartuffe*, also with Jannings. *Faust*, featuring Jannings in various incarnations of the Devil, is the culmination of Murnau's German career. It's his most bravura film, overflowing and cosmic.

Sunrise and *City Girl*, the two American films that survive of the three Murnau made, are arguably his best. *Sunrise* is a film encrusted by trivia: it was a huge success when it came out but still lost money because it was the most expensive film Fox had made up to that time; Janet Gaynor won the first Best Actress Oscar for it (and for two other films); the set was enormous; the moving-camera shots were extraordinary. The film still stuns. It's perhaps the best introduction to silent cinema for the uninitiated. It changed the movies in a way that wouldn't happen again until *Citizen Kane*. *City Girl* is the series's revelation. Without these films, John Ford and Terrence Malick would have been impossible, just as Ingmar Bergman could not have existed without Murnau's German films. Malick's *Days of Heaven* is a virtual remake of *City Girl*, but the relevance and beauty of Murnau's films do not depend in any way on movies they influenced. The way the lonely, unassuming Murnau achieved this level of mastery remains a little enigmatic.

Tabu was planned as a collaboration with the documentarist Robert Flaherty, but Murnau and Flaherty parted after shooting began in Tahiti. The film was made using nonactors in natural locations in the South Pacific. More than any novel about the South Seas, it is like a dream, echoing *Nosferatu* at every turn, mythic in a true sense, as if in a myth described by Claude Lévi-Strauss. This tragic exotica made without the support of a studio shows that Murnau could invent anywhere with whatever means he had. At UFA, they used to say that he "had a camera for a head." *Tabu*—the result of two years' effort—seems made inside the director's mind and projected directly onto the screen. Where Murnau would've gone from there is anybody's guess.

October 2004

DAMNING PORTRAITS

ON EMILE DE ANTONIO

THIS COUNTRY HAS RECENTLY SUFFERED THROUGH THE NATIONAL conventions of both parties, so it's worth quoting at length something the playwright Arthur Miller, who was a delegate to the 1968 Democratic National Convention, says in Emile de Antonio's documentary about Eugene McCarthy's bid for the Democratic nomination that year, *America Is Hard to See:* "No human voice could be raised against this successfully. It is a show. It's a piece of theater. It's rehearsed in advance and it takes place in time. There is no place in the convention system for a real discussion of anything. The convention became the farce that it was, namely an elongated stretch of boredom such as I never believed a human being could sustain and still live."

That quote captures much of what de Antonio thought about American politics. For more than a quarter of a century, through ten documentaries, nine of which play starting Friday at the Harvard Film Archive in a series called "Cold War Chronicles: The Films of Emile de Antonio," he worked doggedly to expose the system's lies and the emptiness of its rhetoric. Even his film on the abstract expressionists and the pop artists, *Painters Painting,* does that by providing examples of Americans who lived in the same world as Richard Nixon and J. Edgar Hoover but lived in it as human beings instead of martinets.

In *America Is Hard to See*, de Antonio found one politician, Senator Eugene McCarthy of Minnesota, who wasn't like the others. Initial enthusiasm for McCarthy among the young briefly changed the party. His early success prompted Robert Kennedy to enter the race; Kennedy was assassinated and another Minnesotan, Hubert Humphrey, then the vice president, got the nomination. Humphrey barely lost to Nixon in November.

Since the film also is hard to see (it's rarely screened), one hopes that John Kerry might take time out from his schedule of windsurfing and not defending himself to watch it in his hometown before he becomes the next Hubert Humphrey. De Antonio makes the point that Humphrey was a Forties-style politician in a Sixties world, a radio performer in a TV age, pre-McLuhan all the way. After you see the movie, you realize that Kerry is a Sixties politician trying to win in the 21st century.

Anyone who longs for change in this country, not just John Kerry, should want to see de Antonio's films. It's impossible to dismiss his work the way tonier liberals dismiss Michael Moore. De Antonio made a film about the war in Vietnam while it was raging—*In the Year of the Pig* (1968)—and one about Nixon—*Millhouse: A White Comedy* (1971)—during Nixon's first term, before the Watergate scandal. Dee, as his friends called him, was a kind of cinematic early warning system all his own. His films do without Moore-style stunts and eschew voice-over (which he called "fascistic"). Instead, they put their subjects on trial, using archival footage and the subjects' own words as witnesses for the prosecution. He doesn't hang the subjects of his films; he lets them hang themselves.

De Antonio is not afraid to let scenes run much longer than today's documentarists would. His first film, *Point of Order!* (1964), is a prime example. The public figure is Senator Joseph McCarthy, and it's one of the most damning portraits of a public figure ever put on film. In ninety minutes, without voice-over, *Point of Order!* culls the two hundred hours of network-television footage shot during the 1954 US Army–McCarthy hearings into a chamber play as morbidly fascinating as the Maysles brothers' *Grey Gardens*. In fact, with its decayed black-and-white kinescope look, the film might be called *Gray Ghosts*. Under de Antonio's gaze, McCarthy struts and frets his TV hours until his face becomes a book wherein you can read strange matters. Paranoiac, delusional, McCarthy becomes increasingly macabre. He is defeated by the senators examining him and by Joseph Welch, the Boston lawyer acting as counsel for the US Army, but de Antonio identifies his defeat as the moment in our history when deranged McCarthy-style offensives became part of the Republican Party's DNA.

Mr. Hoover and I (1989), de Antonio's last film and an eloquent summation of his life and work as seen through the file J. Edgar Hoover's FBI kept on him, ends with some words about George H. W. Bush, who was President when the film was made. This message to the future reminds us that de Antonio's films are as relevant today as they were in the 1960s and '70s, and just as needed. Today's Republicans go out of their way to insist that the GOP is the party of Ronald Reagan, but after seeing de Antonio's films, you realize that it's the party of Joe McCarthy, Richard Nixon, and J. Edgar Hoover—de Antonio's obsessions, his main villains. He has located the end of American democracy in these three figures. Sneaks, liars, and hypocrites who would be at home in John Ashcroft's Justice Department, all three were smear specialists. They owed what power they had to their ability to make the population as paranoid as they were, to their ability to instill fear—of pinkos, the Vietnamese, the Russians, "subversives," anyone who didn't see things their way.

In *Millhouse*, de Antonio states explicitly that President Nixon was a wax figure, a stiff. To him, Nixon is a bad actor, someone who owes his success to an incident from a fairy tale, the discovery of microfilm in a pumpkin during the Alger Hiss case. Like Joe McCarthy, Nixon was willing to smear his opponents, even his Republican opponents, by implying that they were communists. Many of Nixon's weird speeches are included in *Millhouse*. "I have never canceled a subscription to a newspaper," he bizarrely tells reporters after his defeat in a California election. "Haven't we got a wonderful candidate for the presidency of the United States," he says about Eisenhower, sucking up to his boss while running for vice president by putting an emphasis on the word *wonderful* that makes the skin crawl. Apropos of God knows what, Nixon says somewhere else, "We must do everything we possibly can to preserve humor." De Antonio includes a Bob Hope tribute to Nixon that includes footage of an uncomfortable President on the receiving end of what amounts to a lap dance from one of Hope's go-go dancers. It's a scene that depicts the awkward, repressed sexuality of the de Antonio villains, a subject never far from his vision of them.

Watching Nixon deliver a heartfelt tribute to bandleader Guy Lombardo makes people's reasons for supporting this kind of politician more understandable. De Antonio's subjects emerge out of a gray murk, a desperate America, like the people in Robert Frank's photographs. It makes sense that de Antonio got his 1958 start in filmmaking as the distributor of Frank's movie *Pull My Daisy*. He'd been an artist's representative for painters in New York before that. Interviewed in *Painters Painting*, Warhol claims that de Antonio got him to abandon commercial illustration and take up painting, and elsewhere Warhol has claimed that de Antonio gave him the idea to make films himself, which he began doing before de Antonio did.

The eyewitnesses to John Kennedy's assassination in *Rush to Judgment* (1967) could be the subjects of either Frank's photos or Warhol's mug-shot paintings. De Antonio films people the way Warhol paints electric chairs and traffic accidents. His style is the arty-meets-pulpy style familiar from Warhol, a kind of *National Enquirer*–on–16mm look that denudes both the medium and its subjects. People in his films are drained of their personalities so that de Antonio can get to the truth of their character. It's a cheap look, and as de Antonio reminds us in *Mr. Hoover*, cheap to artists means freedom.

Sometimes this approach backfires. *In the King of Prussia* (1982) is de Antonio's experimental video about the Plowshares Eight, a group led by Father Daniel Berrigan who broke into a GE plant in Pennsylvania and poured either blood or red paint (it wasn't clear from the film) on nuclear warheads; it comes off more as a criticism of Berrigan than as a testament to his ideas. Stripped by the camera, Berrigan is reduced to Nixon level. De Antonio inadvertently shows him as a guy with a bad haircut, a slight, fey combination of Boris Karloff and Tony Perkins, self-righteous and self-consciously gentle. When he's given a harsh, unjust prison sentence for what he did, it seems more as if the judge (played by Martin Sheen in reenactment) is punishing him for being annoying.

Painters Painting offers up words and images that counter the society of de Antonio movies like *In the Year of the Pig.* If the war in Vietnam was started for reasons as bogus as the excuses that started the war in Iraq, it's because American power no longer has any sense of scale. The painters de Antonio interviews, and whose work he shows leaning against walls in their studios, all testify to the primacy of content and meaning and of things placed in environments. Barnett Newman tells de Antonio that though his paintings may be large, it's scale and not size that counts. The paintings aren't decorations, they have to be encountered the way one encounters people. De Antonio's films are shot through with this idea. He deplores altered photographs introduced as evidence, he hates people who have been "absorbed by the medium." In *Mr. Hoover and I,* which he made a year before his death, he implies that he ("I talk too much, I drink too much, I've been married six times") knows how to live and that J. Edgar Hoover forced a way of life on this country that was akin to death. It's hard to argue with that now.

September 2004

THE BLUEST OF SEAS

ON BORIS BARNET

SOME OF THE CINEMA'S FINEST WORKS WAIT TO BE DISCOVERED BY American moviegoers. Among them: the films of Boris Barnet, a Russian director and actor who, from the 1920s through the 1960s, was forced by the vicissitudes of Soviet filmmaking to move between his true homes—anarchic slapstick and romantic comedy—and the inhospitable gulags of the patriotic war film and kitsch propaganda.

Barnet's films rival those of Eisenstein's or any filmmaker of the Soviet cinema's heroic age. Unlike theirs, his are funny. They are also beautiful, explosive, gliding. Whatever Barnet had to put up with under Stalin, by the late '50s, he'd arrived at a style that transcended considerations of national borders and totalitarian commands. By then, his only rival was Jacques Tati. His 1961 *Alenka,* so poignant and funny and grandly entertaining, is a film by an artist who loved people and loved the movies. Once you've seen it, it's painful to learn that Barnet died by his own hand, in 1965, at age 62. That's tragic, absurd, like finding out that Harpo Marx or Gene Kelly had committed suicide.

The Museum of Fine Arts, Boston, will be screening six of Barnet's films over ten days. The first is 1924's *The Extraordinary Adventures of Mr. West in the Land of the Bolsheviks,* a crazy, politicized comedy in which Barnet plays an American called Cowboy Jeddy. Signed by Lev Kuleshov, the director who discovered Barnet in a Moscow boxing ring, the film bears the mark not only of Barnet's future directing style but also that of Vsevolod Pudovkin, who acts in it as well. Mr. West (Porfiri Podobed), the Harold Lloyd–like president of the YMCA, visits Moscow on a fact-finding mission accompanied by his wrangler bodyguard, Jeddy. West wants to see for himself the Bolshevik savagery he's read about in "New York magazines." Quickly kidnapped by a con-man gang led by Pudovkin, who looks like a low-life Kafka, West learns that even in 1924, salvation in Russia is paid for with American dollars. Barnet's Jeddy is Owen Wilson and Jackie Chan rolled into one; his acrobatics and shooting rampages, with the help of the Moscow police, save the day. Soon West is ready to "burn those New York magazines and hang a portrait of Lenin on the wall," a sentiment still shared on occasion by today's readers of New York magazines.

Remarkable for its successful aping of Keystone comedy and French chase serials, *Mr. West* really comes alive when the actress Aleksandra Khokhlova shows up as a fake countess in Pudovkin's gang. All angles, big eyes, big mouth, and tiny shark teeth, she adds something immeasurable to this pro-America boys' night out, a modernist romp winking at postmodernists yet to be born.

Mr. West shows that Barnet was a comic actor with the good looks of a Randolph Scott and the athletic fearlessness of a Buster Keaton. It says something about his dedication to directing that he gave up acting to make his own films. *The Girl with the Hatbox* proves his choice was right. Made in 1927, this second feature reveals a director perfectly in control of comic timing and characterization. *The House on Trubnaya Square*, Barnet's 1928 follow-up, is generally given the edge for its anarchism and all-out craziness, but *The Girl with the Hatbox* is deeper and more rewarding. It points in the direction of the romantic Barnet who in 1936 would make *By the Bluest of Seas* and, much later, *Alenka*.

Off-the-cuff and hectic in its comic assaults on various Russian social problems of 1928, *The House on Trubnaya Square* follows the steep learning curve of a girl from the country as she comes to political consciousness. Paranya (Vera Maretskaya), the bumpkinette, arrives in Moscow carrying a duck and little else. Barnet moves her through an impressive apartment-building set, where she disrupts the lives of the other residents.

In *The Girl with the Hatbox*, Barnet's heroine, Natasha, is as capable as she is lovable. Maybe that's because she's played by the beautiful Anna Sten, an actress so vivacious that she was subsequently signed to a Hollywood contract by Samuel Goldwyn. Rarely seen in this movie without a hat, scarf, and heavy winter overcoat (Barnet is a poet of winter), Sten, with her cupid's-bow mouth, thick, dark curls, and eyes like beacons, is covered up but sexy. Even knocked unconscious, she radiates star quality. The force of charm is on her side, so much so that Barnet can have her turn the film's final kiss bloody. In this film, however, the violence of his comedy is tempered with an affection for his characters that distinguishes his later work and sets him apart from most other Soviet directors. He explodes his characters out of the monumental Soviet marble. They abandon poses and come to life.

Barnet confirmed his great talent with these two films. He was unparalleled in evoking comedy and romance by the sea or in the snow, in the steppe or in the city, on moving trains or in claustrophobic flats; by the 1930s, it was just a question of whether the ex-boxer would be able to stay in the ring with Stalin. Barnet's version of the class war is that it's petty and to be avoided. His conflicts in both these comedies are between landlords and tenants, not huge political actors, and he believes in the force of love more than in the force of history. His films could take place anywhere people struggle to find a place for themselves free of authority.

As the Stalinist crackdown on the cinema began, Barnet shifted the settings of his movies from Moscow to dream worlds as removed from the Soviet Union as he could get away with making them. After the '20s, romantic longing and a compatible desire to do a job as well as possible under the circumstances take his films from the fast-paced, crazy Moscow of his youth into the hinterlands.

A wayside more than a central work, his 1932 *Okraina* shows us the flip side of the Barnet worldview. Set during World War I, this early sound film unfolds in a war-torn town bereft of compassion or humor. The sound track, like that of Pudovkin's *Deserter* notably eclectic in its use of different kinds of sound sources, helps the director evoke a lonely world. Barnet was a soldier on the front lines of the revolution, and he poured his memories of war into this story about a German POW who goes to work for a shoemaking collective. The town appears blighted, a place that hangs onto existence without the things Barnet loves.

By the Bluest of Seas, which evidently exists in both color and black-and-white versions, is Barnet in his prime. It takes place on an island paradise in the Caspian that, for all its *Tempest*-like isolation, can't escape Soviet bureaucracy. Two fishermen, Alesha (Nikolai Kryuchkov) and Yussuf (Lev Sverdlin), who represent the European Soviet Union and the Central Asian, compete for the love of a pale island blonde, Misha (Yelena Kuzmina), who can't decide between them. The film is never didactic. Its desire is not for Soviet unity but for a kind of perfect union that exists only in tales or dreams. The way Barnet brings this microcosm to life is wholly original and charmed. *By the Bluest of Seas* has been favorably compared with Jean Vigo's *L'Atalante*, but it breathes a salt air all its own. A scene set below deck as the three lovers are tossed by a storm attests that this is one of the essential films of the 1930s, a threesome movie as accomplished as Ernst Lubitsch's *Design for Living*.

The MFA is skipping Barnet's '40s and '50s films and concluding the series with *Alenka*, a film that until we see more by Barnet has to be considered his masterpiece. Named for one of its characters, a little girl who could be a younger version of Misha, the film takes place in 1955, six years before it was made. Surely the most gorgeous Soviet color film of its era, *Alenka* is so vibrant, it has a physical presence. By 1961, Barnet's ability to pop his characters out from vast landscapes was like no one else's. He does the same thing when they occupy train stations, schoolrooms, and ice huts, a rare filmmaker at ease both indoors and out. His special ability with actresses may have something to do with his seven marriages—it's said he remained friends with all his ex-wives. Every woman his camera encounters, from the glamorous to the goofy looking, becomes a model of healthy pulchritude, as if Barnet were a Frank Tashlin with more heart.

Alenka is a journey film in which several characters travel together through the steppe on their way to new homes on the Kazakh frontier. As they progress, they're quizzed by a little girl, and they reveal their life stories to her. The narratives are by turns light and dark, comic and romantic, even instructional. Alenka's own story is about learning math. Barnet's handling of them is both nimble and formal, as if Tati had shot a script meant for Max Ophuls. The comparison is strained because Barnet is so uniquely his own.

It's hard to choose which story is best. One is about a young dentist who longs for her own dentist's chair. Another finds a city girl moving with her love to Siberia because he has the heroic mission of keeping half-built roads clear of snow for the expanding Soviet state. She has to contend not only with cultural isolation and cold but with his bad taste in art as well. Another story, a tragic one about a drowning, is black and somber, the best cinematic evocation of Gogol, surprising and exceptional in a human comedy that's a Russian version of Booth Tarkington, a happy *Magnificent Ambersons* set among Sovcolor wheat fields in Central Asia. Everyone should see this film.

August 2004

ACKNOWLEDGMENTS

Mark Krotov and Dayna Tortorici, publisher and editor at *n+1*, have worked hard to put this book together and have put up with a lot from me over the years. So too has Rachel Ossip, who designed it. Keith Gessen and Mark Greif were the ones who first asked me to write for the magazine. I'm glad they stuck with me. For various other kinds of help at *n+1*, I thank Laura Cremer, Cosme Del Rosario-Bell, Elizabeth Gumport, Chad Harbach, Emily Lyver, Kate Perkins, Nino Rekhviashvili, Nikil Saval, and Jonathon Sturgeon. For their work indexing: Lisa Borst, Jo Constantz, Sarah Gale, Lizzy Harding, and Hannah Kaplan.

Big thanks to my editors at other publications in which pieces in this book first appeared: Thomas Frank and Chris Lehmann at *The Baffler*, Michael Miller at *Bookforum*, Jennifer Schuessler and Alex Star at the *Boston Globe*, Peter Keough at the *Boston Phoenix*, Richard Porton at *Cineaste*, Chris Fujiwara at *FIPRESCI Undercurrent*, Toni D'Angela at *La Furia Umana*, Robert Baird, Christopher Cox, and Giles Harvey at *Harper's*, Tim Cavanaugh at the *Los Angeles Times*, Jonathan Shainin at *The National*, and Thomas Roueché at *TANK*.

For other encouragement, aid, and assignments, I thank Jen Collins, Brittany Gravely, Carol Hayes, Liz Helfgott, Joel Holland, Dave Konopka, Josh Koppel, Irena Kovarova, Lawrence Levi, Whitney Mallett, Amy Ash Nixon, Edward Orloff, Heather Rasmussen, Douglas Pedro Sánchez, Peter Terzian, Pat Wiedenkeller, and the Alameda Free Library in Alameda, California, where I often wrote when I went to Oakland in the summer.

I must single out three friends for their unflagging support. I would not have survived without them. Jennifer Till has provided me with space to write and live in Oakland. Visiting her over the years has kept me sane. Kris Moran and Ryan Webb, who work in the movies, let me write in their house in Asbury Park, New Jersey, at a green metal desk that appeared in *Moonrise Kingdom*. It was there that I finished this book.

The essays in this book originally appeared in *n+1*, with the exception of the following:

The Baffler: "The Nonstop Zombie Buffet" (as "Now Streaming: The Plague Years") (Issue 28, July 2015), "A Cottage for Sale" (Issue 18, December 2009).

Bookforum: "You Say You Want an Evolution" (Summer 2018), "Germanic Episodes" (September/October/November 2017), "Red Badge of Courage" (February/March 2017), "The Interpretation of Screams" (February/March 2016), "Welles Lettres" (September/October/November 2015).

Boston Globe: "Allied Forces" (July 4, 2004), "Atomic India" (October 13, 2002).

Boston Phoenix: "Almost a Phantom" (October 1, 2004), "Damning Portraits" (as "Before Michael Moore") (September 10, 2004), "The Bluest of Seas" (as "Comic Relief") (August 20, 2004).

Cineaste: "Experience Machines" (as "*The Experience Machine* and *Cinema Beyond Territory*") (Fall 2015), "Call to Youth" (as "*Goodbye Cinema, Hello Cinephilia*") (Spring 2011).

FIPRESCI Undercurrent: "Alien Land" (as "*The Grapes of Wrath*") (Issue 5, March 2009), "Insoluble Farber" (Issue 4, October 2008).

Harper's: "*Star Wars* Is Your God" (as "New Movies") (February 2016).

La Furia Umana: "We Need to Confirm that You Know Gregory Arkadin" (Issue 4, April 2010).

Los Angeles Times: "We Love to Torture" (December 18, 2006).

The National: "Oedipal Multiplex" (February 6, 2009).

TANK: "Let's Go to Paris" (Issue 72, Autumn 2017).

INDEX OF TITLES

E

F

G

H

I

INDEX OF NAMES

A

B

E

F

G

H

M

S

X

Y

Z